Cinema and Northern Ireland

Cinema and Northern Ireland

Film, Culture and Politics

John Hill

bfi Publishing

For my father and mother,
Rowan and Isobel Hill

First published in 2006 by the
BRITISH FILM INSTITUTE
21 Stephen Street, London W1T 1LN

The British Film Institute's purpose is to champion moving image culture
in all its richness and diversity across the UK, for the benefit of as wide
an audience as possible, and to create and encourage debate.

Set by Fakenham Photosetting, Fakenham, Norfolk
Printed in the UK by The Cromwell Press, Trowbridge, Wiltshire

Cover design: Clare Skeats
Cover illustration: *Odd Man Out* (Carol Reed, 1947), Two Cities Films

British Library Cataloguing-in-Publication Data
A catalogue record for this book is available from the British Library

ISBN 1–88457–134–3 (pbk)
ISBN 1–88457–133–5 (hbk)

Contents

Acknowledgments

This is a project that has been a long time in the making with the result that I have accumulated extensive debts. Kevin Rockett encouraged me to write such a history in the first place and has been generous with his help. Martin McLoone, engaged in an ongoing exchange of ideas and commented on various chapters. Pamela Church Gibson read the whole manuscript and provided invaluable feedback. Paul Willemen also commented on Chapter 1. I began the book while I was working in the School of Media and Performing Arts in the University of Ulster and completed it after I joined the Department of Media Arts at Royal Holloway, University of London. I am grateful to my colleagues in both places for the supportive environments that they have provided.

The research for the book has involved an extensive trawl of materials held by the Public Record Office (PRO) at Kew, the Public Record Office of Northern Ireland (PRONI) in Belfast, the National Archives Ireland (NAI) in Dublin, the Belfast Newspaper Library, Belfast City Council, the British Film Institute (BFI) Library in London and the BBC Written Archives Centre (BBCWAC) at Caversham. I am grateful to the staff at all these locations (and particularly Trish Hayes at BBCWAC) for the help and guidance that they have provided. I would not have been able to unearth quite so much material without some excellent assistance. Kelly Davidson was involved in the project from an early stage and undertook invaluable work at both PRONI and the Belfast Newspaper Library. Subsequently, Gail Baylis, Andrew Hill and Robert Porter all helped to locate particular materials. I am especially indebted to the University of Ulster, which provided the funding that made the recruitment of this help possible.

I am also immensely grateful to the Faculty of Arts at the University of Ulster for permitting me a period of leave to undertake research for the book as well as to the Arts and Humanities Research Board (AHRB) (now Council), which, both directly and indirectly (through the AHRB Centre for British Film and Television Studies), provided me with the means to move the project towards completion.

A number of other people helped in different ways. The late Mrs Dorothy Hayward generously gave me material relating to her husband, Richard, while her niece, Judith Wilson, also granted me permission to look at material held at the Ulster Folk and Transport Museum (UFTM). Clifford Harkness, Head of Archival Collections at the Museum, was particularly helpful in facilitating access to the Museum's holdings. Mrs Jacqueline McAlister was not only kind enough to talk to me about her father, James Douglas, but also lent me material to which I would not otherwise have had access. The late William MacQuitty also granted me an interview while Trevor Richmond also shared his memories of the making of *Ulster Heritage*. Ian Wilson, Manager of the North Down Heritage Centre, Cahal McLaughlin, Gillian Coward and Stephen Butcher helped me out with tapes; Sunniva O'Flynn arranged viewings for me at the Irish Film Archive in Dublin; and Kathleen Dickson set up screenings for me at the BFI's National Film Archive in London. James Kearney at Film Images in London was particularly helpful in providing me with access to material, while Eugene Finn proved a reliable source of obscure filmographical information. I was also fortunate in being able to draw on Charles Barr and Robert Murphy, and their extensive knowledge of British cinema, for help with historical information. Ruth Barton also helped out with information on recent Irish films while Ciara Chambers provided me with information on newsreels. Both Richard Taylor, formerly Chief Executive of the Northern Ireland Film and Television Commission, and Rod Stoneman, formerly Chief Executive of Bord Scannán na hÉireann/the Irish Film Board, talked to me about the policies of their respective organisations. David Steele of the Research and Statistics Unit at the UK Film Council was also most helpful in responding to my requests for information and furnishing me with relevant material.

I am also grateful to Andrew Lockett, formerly of BFI Publishing, for commissioning the book and to Rebecca Barden, the new Head of Publishing at the BFI, for encouraging me to get on and finish it following a long period of interruption in the writing. Sophia Contento and Tom Cabot were both helpful and efficient in seeing the book through to completion.

In researching and writing this book, I have also been fortunate in being able to draw upon the memories of my own family. It was my father, Rowan Hill, who first alerted me to *The Green Pastures* controversy in Belfast and it is my father and mother, Rowan and Isobel Hill, to whom the book is dedicated.

Introduction

In 2001 I attended a meeting at the UK Film Council in London at which the Head of the New Cinema Fund, Paul Trijbits, showed us the trailer for a film, in which he had invested Lottery funds. The film was *Bloody Sunday* (Paul Greengrass, 2001) and concerned the killing of thirteen unarmed civilians by British paratroopers in Derry in 1972. It was, according to Trijbits, 'a story that deserved to be told', while the trailer itself informed us that the film was about the 'people who were there' rather than 'about politics'. As it turned out, neither of these claims were to go unchallenged. The film was attacked by both Conservative politicians in Britain and Unionist politicians in Northern Ireland for its supposedly 'anti-army' and 'pro-republican' bias. Unionists were particularly incensed by the claims of the local actor James Nesbitt, who plays the civil rights leader Ivan Cooper in the film, that Protestants in Northern Ireland felt a degree of 'collective guilt' over the killings.[1] Such was the animosity (including hate mail) directed at the actor (who is himself from a Protestant background) that he reported his fears for the safety of his parents, who were still living in Northern Ireland.[2] Although the film-makers stood over the accuracy of the film's portrait of events and others queried whether the film actually played down (rather than exaggerated) the extent of the British Army's culpability for the deaths, what the controversy reveals is how difficult it is for any film concerning Northern Ireland to transcend political divisions.[3] Pace the comments of Trijbits, the events of Bloody Sunday were not an unknown story waiting to be told. Rather the events were remembered all too well in Northern Ireland and continued to inform and animate politics in the years that followed (such that the British government was eventually forced into establishing an official enquiry into the day's events some twenty-six years later in 1998). The issue was therefore not whether *the* story of Bloody Sunday should be told so much as which version of the story should be told and with what resonances for the present.

The controversy surrounding *Bloody Sunday* may be read as emblematic of the way in which films made in and about Northern Ireland have nearly always contributed to, and become implicated in, broader political conflicts concerning the region. Established under the Government of Ireland Act of 1920, enacted by the British parliament, the political standing of Northern Ireland has remained contested since its inception. Created in the face of the wish of the majority in Ireland for independence from Britain, the legitimacy of Northern Ireland's political separation from the rest of Ireland has remained an issue not only for the mainly Catholic nationalists within Northern Ireland but also successive Irish governments. In the case of northern unionists (who benefited from one-party rule for nearly fifty years), the partition of Ireland (and the departure of twenty-six counties from the United Kingdom) led to an extreme defensiveness

---

1. 'Unionist politicians angry at Bloody Sunday film', *Financial Times*, 8 January 2002, p. 4.

2. *Belfast Telegraph*, 19 January 2002, p. 9.

3. While welcoming the film's avoidance of naive 'conspiracy theory', Martin McLoone argues that the film's portrait of 'confusion on all sides' actually lets the 'the British authorities and the army off the hook' in his review of the film in *Cinéaste*, vol. xxvii, no. 4, 2002, p. 42. For a more general discussion of the film, and the issues to which it gives rise, see Lance Pettitt, '*Bloody Sunday*: Dramatising Popular History in TV Film', in Rosa Gonzáles (ed.), *The Representation of Ireland/s: Images from Outside and from Within* (Barcelona: PPU, 2003), pp. 45–59.

concerning the constitutional position of the new semi-state that manifested itself in the adoption of authoritarian legal measures, discrimination against the Catholic minority and the domination of the public sphere by Protestantism. It was, however, this very lack of fairness that ultimately proved the Unionist regime's undoing when the failure to accommodate peaceful demands for civil rights led to an escalation of political divisions into armed conflict at the end of the 1960s (and the introduction of direct rule by the British government in 1972). Following a protracted and messy 'war', involving republicans, loyalists and the British Army, during which over 3,000 people were killed, the political situation once again changed following the announcement of the paramilitary ceasefires in 1994. However, despite the reduction in violence that ensued, political life within the North has continued to be dominated by conflicts based upon competing national and religious affiliations and disputes over governance (that have been evident in the problems surrounding the operations of a politically devolved assembly since the late 1990s).

Film history, culture and politics

Given the overwhelming significance of political, religious and ethnic divisions within Northern Ireland, it is to be expected that the cinema, as with most areas of social life, should have been drawn into the political arena. However, while the political history of Northern Ireland is now well known (if not necessarily agreed), the history of film in Northern Ireland is much less so. This is possibly not surprising. For while cinemagoing in Northern Ireland, as elsewhere, was a popular pursuit for most of the twentieth century, Northern Ireland itself, for a variety of economic, political and geographical reasons, did not develop as a significant centre for film production. As a result, most standard histories of British cinema ignore Northern Ireland altogether, while most studies of Irish cinema concentrate overwhelmingly on developments on the rest of the island. However, while film-making in the North of Ireland may have been slight, the few films made in or about Northern Ireland could also be said to have gained an extra significance precisely because of this scarcity. Moreover, due to the excessive symbolism attached to all aspects of social and cultural life within Northern Ireland, few films have escaped the cultural conflicts of the time, characteristically bearing the ideological marks of the society in which they have been made or accruing extra political associations as a result of the ways in which audiences have responded to them. It is considerations such as these that underpin the study that follows. Drawing extensively on primary sources, the book reveals what is, in effect, an unknown history, providing the first account of films made in Northern Ireland and the circumstances in which they were produced and received. However, precisely because of the distinctive characteristics of Northern Irish society, the study also sets out to analyse how films themselves have contributed to, and illuminated what is culturally at stake in, the political conflicts that have characterised the region's history.

These issues inevitably have consequences for the approach that the book adopts. For while the emphasis of the discussion is on actual films, the concern to unravel the political dimensions of the cinema in Northern Ireland leads the study away from straightforward textual analysis. The aim of the book, in this respect, is to combine textual analysis with a discussion of the (political, cultural and industrial) contexts in which films were both produced and received. In this way the analysis is designed to show how political and institutional factors influenced the production of films at particular moments as well as how the interpretations of films were shaped by the cultural and ideological predispositions of the audiences that watched them. However, while the discussion indicates the ways in which patterns of production, representation and reception were interconnected, it also suggests how these did not always neatly coalesce. Thus, the discussion also indicates how, in certain circumstances, the intentions of film-makers and politicians were subverted by the representational conventions that films employed or how audiences 'read' films in ways that defied the meanings that the films themselves seemed to propose. In this respect, the book does not provide one unidirectional history of the cinema and Northern Ireland but rather a number of overlapping accounts of production, state policy, representational conventions and reception that together help to explain the tensions and contests over meaning that have been a recurring feature of films made in and about Northern Ireland.

This also means that many of the films on which the book focuses are unusual. Conventional film histories, particularly those concerned with national cinemas, have been inclined to concentrate on the history of the feature film and the role that it has played in sustaining an industry and elaborating national concerns. In the case of the cinema and Northern Ireland, however, the feature film occupies a much less prominent role due to the lack of obvious economic advantages that have been attached to making films there. As a result, it has been more 'marginal' forms of film production – 'quota quickies', government-sponsored documentaries, information films, travelogues and newsreels – that have, until recently, constituted the main film history of Northern Ireland. However, while these films may have been 'marginal' in terms of the workings of the film industry, this study suggests how they nevertheless assumed an ideological importance at odds with their apparently humble economic status. In devoting space to them, therefore, the book seeks not only to demonstrate the value for film studies of extending analysis beyond the feature film in national and regional film historiography but also to show how even overtly propagandist, or 'univocal', texts may be read productively as sites of representational conflict.

It should also be evident that, while the book's focus is Northern Ireland, the boundaries of the study are nevertheless fluid. For just as Northern Ireland itself cannot be adequately understood without reference to Britain and the rest of Ireland so the cinema in Northern Ireland cannot be discussed separately from developments elsewhere. There is, in this respect, no 'indigenous' Northern Irish cinema as such, given the virtual absence historically of films that could be said to have been exclusively funded by, or made in, Northern Ireland by local personnel. 'Northern Irish' film-making, in this regard, has been heavily dependent historically upon funding, and professional support, from mainly British but also southern Irish sources. As a result, the history of film in Northern Ireland has been interwoven with the histories of British and Irish cinema without fully belonging to either. Indeed, while accounts of 'national' cinemas have traditionally explored the ways in which films may reinforce or subvert established notions of national identity, this is clearly problematic in the case of Northern Ireland, where not only is there no shared sense of national identity among those who live there but the films themselves have participated in a larger cultural struggle related to the politics of partition and the region's identity as 'British' or 'Irish' (or both). Given the increasing complexity of identifying any cinema as 'national', the study of cinema in Northern Ireland therefore affords an illuminating example of a cinema for which the relationship to nationality has always been an issue.

Organisation

The structure of the book itself is as follows. Chapter 1 deals with the beginnings of film production in Northern Ireland in the 1920s and 1930s. It looks at how the Unionist government
identified the propaganda possibilities of film and how unionist ideas fed into productions of the
period. It focuses in particular on the films in which the local actor and singer Richard Hayward was involved. Although these 'quota quickies' have been generally regarded as musical comedies of little consequence, the discussion reveals how the films were informed by a concern to
promote 'Ulster' as a distinct cultural entity. Through an analysis of the films themselves and the
way in which they were received in Britain and the USA, the chapter suggests how the effort
to elaborate a distinctive 'Ulster' imaginary failed due to the strength of already-existing conceptions of 'Irishness'.

While a few 'Ulster' films may have been made in this period, the bulk of films shown in
Northern Ireland cinemas were, of course, mainly from Hollywood or Britain. Chapter 2 looks
at local responses to this influx of films, focusing in particular on the religious and political controversies they generated. While hostility to the supposedly damaging effects of cinema was a
common phenomenon across the USA and Europe, this chapter indicates how censorship campaigns assumed a distinctive character in Northern Ireland due to the unusual correlation
between religion and politics that existed in the region. This led, for example, to the banning of
films in Belfast that had been passed by the British (and Irish) censor, as well as direct involvement in censorship by the Unionist government in the case of films held to be 'subversive'.

Chapter 3 focuses on the role of film during the Second World War. It looks at how the
Unionist regime achieved a degree of favourable wartime propaganda but generally failed to
obtain the level of publicity that it would have liked as a result of the problems involved in mapping Northern Ireland onto the wartime construction of 'British' identity. This theme is pursued
in the following chapter, which examines the attempts by the Unionist government to promote
'Ulster' through informational shorts and travelogues. The discussion identifies the frustrations
faced by the Unionist regime in achieving the kind of 'official' image that it sought, as well as
the emergence of 'unofficial' films that offered a 'reply' to the dominant cinematic constructions
of 'Ulster'. Chapter 5 indicates how the battle between competing sets of images continued into
the 1960s and how, despite the increasing emphasis upon 'modernity' within state-sponsored
films, the continuation of economic and religious divisions within Northern Ireland began to
become manifest. This chapter also indicates how the 'battleground' began to shift towards television following the arrival of TV in Northern Ireland during the 1950s. Although the programmes discussed were not shown in cinemas, they were nevertheless mostly shot on film and
reflect an early blurring of the boundaries between the film and television mediums.

The final two chapters are slightly different in character. Although they preserve a loosely
chronological order, they are more thematic, focusing respectively on the development of film
policy and representations of the 'troubles'. Although much of the book is concerned with the
use of film as an instrument of government propaganda, Chapter 6 focuses specifically on the
development of state policy concerned with the cultural and economic aspects of film and the
consequences that this had for film-making in the region. As this chapter indicates, the emergence of new policy initiatives laid the basis for an upsurge of film production the 1980s and
1990s and many of the films that resulted are considered in Chapter 7. Since the end of the

1960s, the imagery of Northern Ireland has been dominated by the 'troubles' and this chapter assesses the ways in which films have sought to dramatise the most recent phase of the conflict.[4] Given the huge growth in the number of films dealing with the 'troubles' since the 1970s, this discussion is necessarily less comprehensive than that relating to earlier periods. In contrast to the preceding chapters, the discussion is primarily focused on feature films (of which there have been considerably more in this period than any previously) and is also more selective in the films that it subjects to detailed analysis. Whereas there is very little written on the cinema and Northern Ireland prior to the 1970s, the discussion of representations of the 'troubles' has been much more extensive and there now exists a number of good surveys of the topic, as well as detailed assessments of individual films.[5] As a result, I have tried to avoid undue repetition of either my own or others' writing on the topic. Although this means that certain films are dealt with less fully than they might otherwise have been, it is intended that the discussion should do justice to the overall pattern of representations while nevertheless paying attention to some films that have been relatively neglected.

The book's strategy in this regard is to combine an investigation of the forgotten and the unfamiliar with some revisiting of work that is better known. If, by doing so, the book is able not only to add to existing scholarship but also to open up some new avenues of enquiry, then its purpose will have been served.

---

4. As Michael A. Hopkinson observes, the term the 'troubles' (or Troubles) is itself a 'beguiling euphemism' indicative of the problems involved in describing the nature of events in Ireland during 1916–23, as well as in the North since the outbreak of violence in 1969. See 'The Troubles', in Brian Lalor (ed.), *The Encyclopaedia of Ireland* (Dublin: Gill and Macmillan, 2003), p. 1080.

5. My first attempt to think through these issues appeared in Kevin Rockett, Luke Gibbons and John Hill, *Cinema and Ireland* (London: Routledge, 1988), ch. 6. Since this book appeared, there has not only been a lot of new films but also new writing on the subject. Two of the most useful surveys may be found in Martin McLoone, *Irish Film: The Emergence of a Contemporary Cinema* (London: BFI, 2000), ch. 3, and Ruth Barton, *Irish National Cinema* (London: Routledge, 2004), ch. 10. Brian McIlroy offers a more polemical viewpoint in *Shooting to Kill: Filmmaking and the 'Troubles' in Northern Ireland* (Trowbridge: Flicks Books, 1998).

1

'Ulster must be made soft and romantic'

Northern Ireland Film-making in the 1920s and 1930s

The beginnings of local film production in Northern Ireland occurred in the 1930s, when a number of features involving the local actor and singer Richard Hayward were made. The first of these was *The Luck of the Irish*, made in 1935, followed by *The Early Bird* (1936), *Irish and Proud of It* (1936) and *Devil's Rock* (1938). Partly because they have been difficult to see, and partly because they were cheaply and quickly made, these films have commonly been seen as historical oddities unworthy of sustained critical attention.[1] However, while it would be hard to mount a case for these films as 'lost treasures', they do possess considerable historical interest, not only because they were the first feature films to be shot in Northern Ireland but also because of what they reveal about the political and cultural concerns of the period. When they are viewed in context, it is apparent that the films did not emerge out of the blue but grew out of, and contributed to, more general ideological and cultural currents. For, while these films were not 'propaganda', they did enjoy the semi-official support of the state. Moreover, in the way that they sought to represent Northern Ireland on screen, it is also evident that they were influenced by, and overlapped with, other attempts to 'imagine' a distinct Northern Irish – or 'Ulster' – identity during this period.

'A fertile ground for propaganda': film and the promotion of Northern Ireland

Given the turbulence of the early years of the Northern Ireland state, it was unlikely that it would devote much attention to a policy for film production. However, precisely because of the threatened status of the new regime (and the success of unionism during the Home Rule period in exploiting possibilities for propaganda), the Unionist government (elected in May 1921) did appreciate the value of favourable media publicity. Apart from a short period during 1926 and 1927, however, it avoided engaging directly in publicity (at least until 1938 when it opened the Ulster Office in London) and opted to lend support to bodies that were nominally independent. The most important of these, during the early years, was the Ulster Association (For Peace With Honour), which was established in April 1922 to encourage 'a better understanding of Ulster at home and abroad' and to support 'the Prime Minister and Government in the resolute

---

1. The films only became available for viewing again in 1995, when the British Film Institute, in response to requests from the Northern Ireland Film Council, struck new prints for the Centenary of Cinema celebrations.

stand they were making against the attacks on the constitution assured by the Government of Ireland Act'.[2] Although the Association was funded by local businesses, the Unionist Prime Minister, James Craig, was its President and the organisation acted as a semi-official mouthpiece of government. The Association appointed a Director of Publicity, established offices in Belfast and London, and distributed news and information favourable to the new regime across Britain. Thus, by the close of its first year of activities, the organisation claimed to have secured 60,000 columns of information on Northern Ireland in the world's press, and distributed 10,000 'Ulster Publications'.[3] Following the abandonment of the Boundary Commission and subsequent agreement on the border issue in 1925, the Association felt that its propaganda goal had been accomplished and transferred its publicity activities (and London office) to the Ministry of Commerce in 1926. However, given the drain on public expenditure involved in maintaining social services on a par with the rest of the UK, the government came to the conclusion that the cost of sustaining the operation was too high and opted, the following year, to cease its activities in this area and confine its funding to the Ulster Tourist Development Association (UTDA).

This was not as peculiar a decision as it might initially appear. The UTDA was, in fact, the brainchild of the Ulster Association, which had launched the organisation at a conference in January 1924. Robert Baillie, the Chair of the Association's publicity committee, also became the UTDA's first chairman. Although the organisation's purpose was to foster and develop 'tourist traffic in Northern Ireland by advertising the advantages and amenities of the various districts', its close connections with government and the Ulster Association also meant that its promotion of tourism could assume a more directly political character.[4] Thus, an early UTDA pamphlet distributed in America was attacked in the Northern Ireland House of Commons by the Nationalist MP, Patrick O'Neill, as 'nothing more than propaganda for the Presbyterian Church'.[5]

Although the UTDA's ventures into film were primarily concerned with promoting awareness of Northern Ireland as a tourist location, this too could take on a political dimension. As early as 1912, James Craig had recognised the propaganda value of film newsreels by arranging for the recording – 'under the fierce glare of electric light and to the click of a dozen cinematograph machines' – of the signing of the Ulster Covenant by Edward Carson and others on 'Ulster Day'.[6] The Ulster Association had also helped to organise the filming of the opening of the Northern Ireland Parliament in 1921.[7] Given these precedents, the UTDA was also keen to encourage the newsreel companies to visit Northern Ireland and scored a particular publicity success in 1930

2. 'Government Publicity: Short Résumé since 1922', Public Record Office of Northern Ireland (PRONI) CAB9F/123/14.

3. Ibid.

4. Irish News, 31 January 1924, p. 7.

5. Parliament of Northern Ireland, Parliamentary Debates: Official Report, House of Commons (HC), vol. VII, col. 1039, 6 May 1926.

6. Northern Whig, 30 September 1912, p. 5. For a discussion of Craig's role in promoting Unionism at this time, see Alvin Jackson, 'Unionist Myths 1912–1985', Past and Present, no. 136, 1992.

7. The Ulster Association (For Peace With Honour), Annual Report 1922–3 (Belfast, 1923), PRONI CAB6/93.

when several companies (including Gaumont, Pathé and British Movietone) despatched units to cover the newly established Tourist Trophy Motor Car Race on the Ards circuit.[8] The following year, the UTDA also used the occasion of the motor race to arrange the filming of Craig (now Viscount Craigavon) and members of the Cabinet at Parliament Buildings by newsreel cameramen, including representatives from British Movietone News and British Paramount.[9] Craigavon himself was recorded delivering a four-minute speech that emphasised Northern Ireland's 'prosperity' as well as its links with America and safety as a place to visit.[10] However, this seems to have been a relatively unusual occurrence and, while the newsreels did continue to cover Northern Ireland stories, these generally dealt with sporting events rather than overtly political matters.

In addition to the newsreels, the UTDA was also active in encouraging film-makers to include Northern Ireland in various travelogues. In 1927, they helped Sydney Cook of Queensland to complete a film on Northern Ireland that, it was claimed, was destined to be shown in 800 Australian cinemas.[11] In 1928, they also assisted Pathé to film material for the *Pathé Pictorial* series and Gaumont for its cinemagazine, *Gaumont Mirror* (which included footage of the Carrick-a-Rede rope bridge, the glens of Antrim and the mountains of Mourne).[12] In 1932, the Executive Committee of the UTDA also agreed to contribute £100 towards the Northern Ireland section of what later became known as *The Voice of Ireland*, written and directed by Lieutenant-Colonel Victor Haddick.[13] This is commonly taken to be the first indigenous sound feature to be made in Ireland although the shooting of the film was in fact silent, with sound added later in a London studio.[14]

Haddick was himself from the North, born in Donaghdee and educated at Royal Belfast Academical Institution. After a military career in the Leinster Regiment, he was involved in the Everest expedition of 1924, in which Irvine and Mallory both lost their lives. Along with Captain J. B. L. Noel, he made a film record of the expedition, and further filming ventures followed, including *India, Past and Present*, *Romance of Turkey* and *Ireland's Rough-Hewn Destiny*. Somewhat ironically, the contents of this last film had already given rise to controversy due to the small number of scenes relating to the North. For while Haddick himself claimed that the film dealt with 'the agricultural districts of the whole country and not only the Free State', this did not prevent questions being raised in the British House of Commons concerning the involvement of the Empire Marketing Board (which had been established by the British government in 1926 to encourage Empire trade).[15] The Northern Ireland government also felt it was a mistake for

---

8. *The Bioscope*, 27 August 1930, p. 41.

9. Letter from C. W. S. Magill, Secretary and Organiser of the UTDA, to C. H. E. Blackmore, Private Secretary to the Prime Minister, 13 August 1931, PRONI CAB9F/114/1.

10. 'Interview between the Prime Minister and the Cabinet and the Representatives of the Various Film Corporations', PRONI CAB9F/114/1.

11. *The Bioscope*, 15 December 1927, p. 55; *Belfast Telegraph*, 23 February 1928.

12. *Irish News,* 13 March 1928, p. 6; Minutes of UTDA Council of Management, 19 July 1928, PRONI TOUR1/1/1.

13. Minutes of UTDA Executive Committee, 12 May 1932, PRONI TOUR1/1/1.

14. Richard Hayward, 'The First Talkie Made in Ireland', *Ulster Illustrated*, vol. 6, no. 5, July 1958, p. 16.

15. *Belfast Telegraph*, 19 December 1929, p. 7; *Parliamentary Debates* (HC), vol. v, col. 449, 11 December 1929. In response to questioning, the Under-Secretary of State for Dominion Affairs, Mr Lunn, indicated that the EMB had not actually produced the film but only approved it for inclusion in their programme of lectures.

the EMB to have been associated with a film that was mainly devoted to the south.[16] There was, therefore, suspicion of political interference when a screening of the film, and accompanying lecture by Haddick, at the Imperial Institute in London in 1929 was cancelled. According to the papers at the time, the organisers of the event, the Irish Literary Society, had been forced to cancel due to the conditions laid down by the Institute, which included the playing of the British national anthem and a prohibition on Irish pipers and vocalists.[17]

Like *Ireland's Rough-Hewn Destiny*, *The Voice of Ireland* mainly deals with the South. However, as a result of the UTDA's involvement, it does include a substantial section set in the North. According to the *Belfast News-Letter*, about one-third of the picture is devoted to Northern Ireland and each of the six counties is featured.[18] The story of the film is loosely concerned with the return to his native land of an exile, whose travels take him to the four provinces of Ireland, including Ulster. In the scenes set in Northern Ireland, Richard Hayward assumes what he subsequently described as the 'The Voice of Ulster', visiting various locations, performing a number of Ulster songs and providing a spoken commentary.[19] In the few minutes of footage that have survived, this includes stops at various tourist sites (including the Giant's Causeway), a song in 'the sweet town of Coleraine' and short sequences of shots of Belfast ('the Athens of the North') and Bangor ('Belfast's Blackpool').

Although the UTDA had some reservations about the technical standard of the film, it was nevertheless well received when it was premiered in Belfast in November 1932. The *Belfast News-Letter* described the film as 'an unqualified success', while the *Irish News* declared that '[t]he songs, the instrumental music, and the dialogue are undoubtedly a treat'.[20] This encouraged the UTDA to establish a special Film Publicity Committee (chaired by Robert Baillie) the following year. Identifying 'the picture theatres' as 'a fertile ground for propaganda', this committee then resolved to produce its own 'really first-class film' about Northern Ireland.[21] They entered into discussions with G. B. Instructional, a subsidiary of Gaumont British, which proposed a film along the lines of *Contact* (1933), Paul Rotha's famous documentary charting the air journey between London and Cape Town. This was screened in Belfast in early 1934 and was favourably received by UTDA Council members. Unlikely though it may seem in retrospect, the Association was also assured that Rotha – subsequently to become well known for left-wing documentaries such as

---

16. Letter from W. D. Scott, Permanent Secretary to the Ministry of Commerce, to C. H. E. Blackmore, 3 April 1930, PRONI CAB9F/114/1.

17. *Belfast Telegraph*, 19 December 1929, p. 7; *Belfast News-Letter*, 19 December 1929, p. 8. The traditionally unionist daily paper, the *Belfast News-Letter* (founded 1737), has, in recent years, dropped both the hyphen in 'News-Letter' and the name 'Belfast' from its masthead. For the sake of consistency, I have used the hyphenated version of the paper's name throughout the text.

18. *Belfast News-Letter*, 11 November 1932, p. 6.

19. Hayward, 'The First Talkie', p. 16.

20. *Belfast News-Letter*, 11 November 1932, p. 6; *Irish News*, 11 November 1932, p. 3. The nationalist *Irish News*, published in the North, did nevertheless comment that the 'popular use of Derry for Londonderry . . . would have caught the local atmosphere better'.

21. 'Proposed Ulster Film Publicity', 1934, PRONI COM62/1/392.

World of Plenty (1943) – was available if terms could be agreed.[22] However, the Association found the cost (between £1,000 and £2,000) of such a film prohibitive and when it seemed likely that the Belfast-born director Brian Desmond Hurst would shoot part of the feature *The Night Nurse* (subsequently known as *Irish Hearts* in Europe and *Nora O'Neale* in the USA) in Northern Ireland, it was decided to place the plans 'in abeyance'.[23] It was only in 1937, when the UTDA launched a Film Fund, that the proposal for the organisation's own Northern Ireland film was revived. In the intervening period, it continued to encourage film companies to visit Northern Ireland and provided support to the features involving Richard Hayward, which were also assisted by the Ulster Industries Development Association (UIDA).

The origins of this body lay in a speech made by the Prime Minister at the Londonderry Chamber of Commerce in February 1929 urging local tradespeople to sell Ulster-manufactured products, and advocating the slogan 'We Push Ulster Goods'.[24] Subsequently, the Ministry of Commerce sought to give practical effect to the Prime Minister's slogan and agreed to finance a new body, the UIDA, established in June 1929. The body's main aims consisted of attracting 'new industrial undertakings to Northern Ireland' and fostering 'home industries by urging a more extended consumption of home manufactured goods'.[25] The first of these goals proved a difficult one for the organisation (particularly during the trade depression of 1930 and 1931) with the result that the bulk of its energies were devoted to the promotion of 'Ulster goods' through various forms of promotion and 'propaganda'. This included the launch of 'Ulster Shopping Weeks', window-dressing competitions, press advertising and the production of circulars and booklets. The Association was also responsible for the creation of a fictional character 'Andy McDade', a County Antrim farmer who encourages his wife Mary to buy more Ulster produce. A pamphlet, *Andy McDade*, containing a short story about Andy and Mary written in Ulster dialect, a list of local products and a description of the Association's aims was widely distributed in 1929. Articles by 'Andy McDade' also appeared in local papers and, in recognition of the importance of 'the weemin' o' Ulster' to the campaign's success, a second pamphlet, *Andy's Mary*, in which Mary goes shopping for Ulster goods, was published the following year.[26]

The UIDA's interest in film followed on from this. Film not only constituted an industrial activity that was new to Northern Ireland but also provided an effective and 'up-to-date' vehicle for the promotion of 'Ulster goods'.[27] It was on this basis that the UIDA lent its support to the Richard Hayward films and even embarked upon a short film of its own, *The Star of Ulster*

---

22. Ibid. A prestige production for Imperial Airways and the film's funders Shell-Mex, *Contact* was, nevertheless, largely celebratory in character.
23. Minutes of UTDA Executive Committee, 14 June 1934, PRONI TOUR1/1/2. The film was based on a popular novel about hospital life written by J. Johnston Abraham, a surgeon originally from Coleraine. Although part of the film was shot in Dublin, it does not appear as if the proposed filming in the North took place.
24. *Northern Whig*, 1 February 1929, p. 7.
25. 'Ulster Industries Development Association: Note on its Establishment and Functions', 5 April 1932, PRONI CAB9F/108/1.
26. *Belfast News-Letter*, 16 September 1930, p. 5. According to the *Banbridge Chronicle* (6 May 1931), reporting on the UIDA annual lunch, no less than 237,000 copies of the pamphlet were circulated.
27. Ulster Industries Development Association, *Annual Review 1936*, PRONI COM62/1/187.

(1936). The film was designed to promote the organisation's Star Associate scheme, launched in 1935. This scheme encouraged members of the public to 'give first preference to Ulster-made Goods' and to wear the UIDA's Star Emblem, a six-pointed badge intended to represent the six counties of 'Ulster'.[28] Hayward wrote the script and music and also appeared in the film as Andy McDade.[29]

The film itself is set in a village shop in which, according to one contemporary review, 'apparently only Ulster goods are stocked'.[30] The shop is run by a widow, Mrs Milligan (played by Richard Hayward's first wife, Elma Hayward), from whom Andy McDade seeks credit. According to the *Northern Whig*, these 'efforts give opportunity for Ulster vernacular humour' and, as the characters conduct their conversation, 'the camera picks up the many products displayed in the shop'.[31] Andy then inspects some 'Ulster Star' badges and brooches before launching into a song called 'The Star of Ulster'. As he does so, yet more goods are shown. The song also explains the meaning of the star ('It stands for Ulster exports, To Lands across the foam, For Ulster foods and Ulster goods, In ev'ry Ulster home') and encourages members of the audience to wear it ('So please to give this Ulster Star, A place in your lapel, As token of your duty, All Ulster trade to swell'). Once the song is finished, Andy's efforts are rewarded by Mrs Milligan, who provides him with 'one of the wee stars' and a couple of ounces of tobacco. The film was given a special screening in Belfast in January 1937 and was subsequently shown in cinemas across Northern Ireland where it was promoted as 'an Ulster film with Ulster Players for Ulster's Prosperity'.[32]

However, although the UTDA and the UIDA both supported film-making (and, in the case of the Hayward productions, the same films), their aims did not entirely converge. Prior to the establishment of the UIDA, the Ministry of Commerce had sought to encourage the UTDA to take on industrial development functions but the UTDA had considered this undesirable.[33] The Ministry had also encouraged the organisation to consider making a film that might involve the promotion of local industry but this too proved problematic. Following the Belfast screening of *Contact*, the Permanent Secretary to the Ministry of Commerce, W. D. Scott, was impressed with how the film had shown 'machinery in motion, and people at work' and believed that a similar Northern Irish film, containing a similar industrial element, would make 'very striking propaganda'.

---

28. UIDA, *Annual Review 1935*, PRONI COM62/1/187.

29. Although the original Andy McDade pamphlets are uncredited, it seems likely that Hayward also wrote these.

30. *Belfast Telegraph*, 22 January 1937, p. 8.

31. *Northern Whig*, 23 January 1937, p. 9.

32. *Irish Times*, 17 May 1937, p. 2.

33. Memorandum, 'Ulster Industries Development Association: Note on its Establishment and Functions', 5 April 1932, PRONI CAB9F/108/1. It is also worth noting that, although Craigavon was the UIDA's patron and champion, the organisation did not enjoy the unanimous backing of government. In 1937, for example, the Minister of Finance, Hugh Pollock, declared his lack of sympathy for 'this theory that seems to be shouted on all occasions "Use only Ulster Goods"' (*Parliamentary Debates* [HC], vol. xix, col. 635, 18 March 1937). Paul Bew, Peter Gibbon and Henry Patterson explain this divergence of outlook in terms of a division within unionism between the 'minor' capitalist interests – represented by organisations such as the UIDA – and the interests of 'big' capital, such as linen and shipbuilding. See *The State in Northern Ireland 1921–72* (Manchester: Manchester University Press, 1979), p. 85.

Pushing 'Ulster Goods': Richard Hayward as Andy McDade in *The Star of Ulster*

But while he believed 'magnificent things' could be achieved with Northern Irish 'shipyards and linen mills', he found the UTDA reluctant to get 'entangled with industry'.[34] This does, of course, make sense in terms of the UTDA's remit to promote tourism, which typically relies upon discourses of 'escape' from the pressures of modern urban–industrial society. However, it also connects with a particular form of imagining of 'Ulster' prevalent during this period that pulled against this kind of representation of the industrial and urban.

Imagining 'Ulster'

In seeking to encourage visitors to 'Ulster', the UTDA was not only involved in cultivating an attractive image of the region but also negotiating the representation of Northern Ireland's status and identity. There were two significant aspects to this. On the one hand, while Northern Ireland continued to be part of the United Kingdom, the Unionist regime was continually beset by the indifference of the British public and politicians towards it and the problems that this created in being accepted as legitimately 'British'. As a result, the regime was continually con-

---

34. Minute sheet, 8 February 1934, PRONI COM62/1/392. The government did, however, provide some support for this kind of publicity through its support for the Irish Linen Guild, which funded the promotional film *The Wee Blue Blossom*, which was widely shown, in an abbreviated form, in the US.

cerned to establish its 'British' credentials and emphasise, as Craigavon himself put it, that they were not a 'separate people' but 'full-born fellow-citizens of the United Kingdom and immensely proud of it'.[35] At the same time (and interlinked with this desire for 'Britishness'), the regime was also at pains to disavow its 'Irishness' and to assert its cultural distinctiveness from the rest of Ireland. This in turn encouraged an emphasis upon the peculiar cultural character of Ulster.

As Alvin Jackson suggests, the mobilisation of a distinct cultural identity for Ulster gained particular momentum at the time of the third Home Rule Bill in 1912 when the principle of partition was effectively conceded and northern and southern strands of unionism began to diverge. Jackson indicates how at the 1892 Ulster Convention in Belfast, planned to boost Unionist morale, it was still possible for unionism to combine images of 'Celtic revivalism with the iconography of British patriotism' in order to demonstrate how 'a true Irish patriotism was compatible with the imperial connection'.[36] However, after 1912, by which time the maintenance of an all-Ireland Unionist unity had become increasingly fraught (and the idea of 'Irishness' itself had become increasingly associated with cultural nationalism), a distinctive Ulster political and literary culture began to take shape in the form of political tracts, novels and 'Ulster' histories. According to Ian McBride, this was also the period during which 'the invention of "Ulster" as a separate entity' occurred.[37] For McBride, however, this was only a temporary phenomenon and once partition was achieved, he argues, the Unionist government did not attempt to embark upon a 'cultural policy of Ulsterisation'.[38] Whereas Irish nationalism had been fuelled by a cultural vision that legitimated its claim to independent statehood, Ulster Unionism had constructed an ideology of 'Ulster' in order to resist Home Rule rather than to express a positive identity. Once partition was achieved, therefore, the political necessity of 'Ulsterisation' could be said to have passed. However, the unionists had also acquired a semi-state that they had not sought and for which they were, in a sense, culturally under-prepared. Thus, while the preoccupation with the elaboration of an 'Ulster' identity may have lost some of its political urgency in the post-partition period, the idea of Ulster's cultural distinctiveness remained attractive to unionists not only as a means of bolstering Northern Ireland's new political status but also as a response to both the institutionalisation of – Gaelic and Catholic – nationalism in the South and the continuing ambivalence of Northern Ireland's political and cultural relationship to Britain. Thus, in spite of their initial reluctance to accept partition, Unionists soon came, as J. C. Beckett explains, 'to congratulate themselves on their semi-independence' and to develop 'a sort of "Ulster patriotism"'.[39]

One aspect of this was the Unionist regime's preference for referring to Northern Ireland as 'Ulster'. This was, of course, inaccurate: the historical province of Ulster consisted of nine counties (Antrim, Armagh, Cavan, Donegal, Down, Fermanagh, Londonderry, Monaghan and

---

35. 'Foreword', *London Chamber of Commerce Journal*, September 1928, PRONI CAB7F/123/2.

36. Alvin Jackson, 'Irish Unionist Imagery, 1850–1920', in Eve Patten (ed.), *Returning to Ourselves: Second Volume of Papers from the John Hewitt International Summer School* (Belfast: Lagan Press, 1995), p. 353.

37. Ian McBride, 'Ulster and the British Problem', in Richard English and Graham Walker (eds), *Unionism in Modern Ireland: New Perspectives on Politics and Culture* (Basingstoke: Macmillan, 1996), p. 7.

38. Ibid., p. 11.

39. J. C. Beckett, 'Northern Ireland', *Journal of Contemporary History*, vol. 6, no. 1, 1971, p. 130.

Tyrone) whereas the state of Northern Ireland included only six (with Cavan, Donegal and
Monaghan forming part of the newly created Irish Free State). However, precisely because the
term 'Ulster' helped to differentiate the North from the rest of Ireland, unionists were perfectly
happy after partition to use the term to describe only the six counties. According to Oliver Mac-
Donagh, the 'new "Ulster" of the northern Protestants forgot that Donegal, Cavan and Monaghan had ever been part of their province' and, through 'common usage' of the word 'Ulster',
sought to sustain the idea of 'an inviolable territory'.[40] This is apparent, for example, in the semi-
official document *Ulster*, produced by the UTDA, which confidently claims that '[t]o all intents
and purposes . . . the traditional name of "Ulster" and the new political term "Northern Ireland"
are synonymous in the public mind'.[41] This was not, of course, uncontroversial. Recognising
how the recurring use of the term had the effect of reinforcing the North's separation from the
rest of the island, the Dublin government actively sought to counteract the word's 'misuse'.[42]
The British government was also loath to permit the Northern Ireland regime to change the
name of the state to 'Ulster' when this was proposed by Northern Ireland's third Prime Minister, Sir Basil Brooke, in 1948.[43] Nevertheless, the idea of 'Ulster' as a distinct place, separate from
the rest of Ireland, continued to retain its potency for northern unionists.

However, while the term acquired a degree of common currency (reinforced by its embodiment in the titles of organisations such as the UTDA and UIDA), it did not necessarily carry
with it any agreed content beyond the parameters of geographical boundaries. Indeed, for Brian
Graham, the problem historically of unionism has been its failure to create 'an agreed representation – or imagery – of place to legitimate and validate their domicile in the island of Ireland'.[44]
Although he suggests that 'Ulster' is 'a representation of place' that has 'yet to be imagined', this
is not really so. As previously indicated, there have been various attempts from within unionism
to 'imagine' 'Ulster' as a distinctive place. The difficulty for unionism has been that no one version of 'Ulster' identity has achieved hegemony and that any construction of it has had to contend with alternative accounts of the place's identity as 'British' or 'Irish'. As a result, the
'imagining' of 'Ulster' has typically proven not only a highly contentious but also an ideologically problematic enterprise.

---

40. Oliver MacDonagh, *States of Mind: A Study of Anglo-Irish Conflict 1780–1980* (London: George Allen and Unwin,
1983), pp. 26, 22.

41. *Ulster* (Belfast: UTDA, 1937), p. 15.

42. Sean McDougall, 'The Projection of Northern Ireland to Great Britain and Abroad, 1921–39', in Peter Catterrall and
Sean McDougall (eds), *The Northern Ireland Question in British Politics* (Basingstoke: Macmillan, 1996), p. 35. In the
early days, there was also some resistance from diehard unionists who regarded the abandonment of the other three
counties as 'treachery'. It was on this basis that the Earl of Belmore referred to the practice of describing the Six
Counties as Ulster as 'abominable' when objecting to Fermanagh County Council's funding of the UTDA at a
meeting in 1929. See 'Not Ulster', *Northern Whig*, 5 October 1929, p. 7.

43. See Ronan Fanning, 'The Response of the London and Belfast Governments to the Declaration of the Republic of
Ireland, 1948-9', *International Affairs*, vol. 58, no. 1, 1981/2.

44. Brian Graham, 'Ulster: A Representation of Place yet to be Imagined', in Peter Shirlow and Mark McGovern (eds),
Who are 'The People'? Unionism, Protestantism and Loyalism in Northern Ireland (London: Pluto, 1997), p. 34.

Some of the forces at work here may be found in tourist literature of the 1930s, produced by the UTDA at the same time as it was supporting the production of film. Tourism was not only an activity of financial importance for the economically fragile Unionist regime but also helped to reinforce a sense of tangible links between Northern Ireland and Britain. Thus, the Minister of Finance, Hugh Pollock, appealed to the reality of tourist visits from Britain to Northern Ireland as evidence of the increasing ties between Northern Ireland and the rest of the United Kingdom in an article in *The Spectator* in 1930.[45] However, even in a period when most tourism was still primarily domestic, there was an awareness on the part of the UTDA that Northern Ireland was not necessarily perceived by potential British tourists as a part of the UK. As a result, potential visitors from England, Scotland and Wales are assured in tourist literature and promotions that they will not have to contend with customs formalities, passports or motor regulations and that a holiday in Ulster 'offers all the advantages of a trip abroad without the disadvantages' of 'a journey to another country'.[46] However, while the practical realities of Ulster's 'Britishness' may be stressed, the literature is also faced with the problem of convincing its readership of Ulster's Britishness at a more profound level. This is because, as James Loughlin has suggested, the 'dominant image' of Northern Ireland – 'largely industrial and with associations of bigotry, sectarianism and political extremism' – was significantly at odds with the British self-image of 'humour, tolerance, and compromise' and the association of contemporary Britishness with ideas of rural 'organicism'(as found in the speeches and writings of Stanley Baldwin).[47]

The stress on Ulster's rural identity contained in tourist literature therefore served a double purpose: it not only suited the aim of attracting visitors but also distracted from the political turbulence and sectarianism commonly associated with urban-industrial areas (and Belfast, in particular). Thus, from the beginning, the publicity produced by the UTDA was at pains to downplay the industrial character of Northern Ireland in a way that went beyond the requirements of mere tourist promotion. The Belfast-born writer St John Ervine was recruited to write the first travel guide, *Ulster*, for the UTDA in 1926 and, in this, he is eager to stress that Ulster, contrary to popular perception, is 'not mainly an industrial, but . . . an agricultural province'.[48] In 1932, writing in the *Daily Mail*, he was still making substantially the same point:

Another legend almost religiously believed by Englishmen is that Northern Ireland is almost entirely industrialised, a sort of extended Black Country or prolonged Manchester . . . But this legend of

---

45. *The Spectator*, 15 March 1930, p. 417.

46. Viscount Craigavon, 'Foreword', *Ulster* (Belfast: UTDA, 1937), p. 14; *Daily Mail*, 5 July 1932.

47. James Loughlin, *Ulster Unionism and British National Identity since 1885* (London: Pinter, 1995), pp. 98–100. There is a certain oddity here given the advanced industrialisation and urbanisation of Britain and England in particular. However, as Alun Howkins argues, one of the central tensions of English culture has been between 'a recognition of the urban nature of England and English society . . . and a wish to preserve what is essentially a cultural fiction that England retains its "rural" character'. See 'Rurality and English Identity', in David Morley and Kevin Robbins (eds), *British Cultural Studies* (Oxford: Oxford University Press, 2001), p. 146.

48. St John Ervine, *Ulster* (Belfast: UTDA, 1926), p. 5.

an industrial Ulster is peculiarly silly, since Ulster is largely an agricultural community, with . . . some of the loveliest and most diversified scenery that is to be found in the world.[49]

Ervine was a complex character who had initially shown Home Rule sympathies but, following the War of Independence, had become aggressively pro-Union and anti-South.[50] His disavowal of the 'legend of an industrial Ulster', and reclaiming of rural 'Ulster', therefore, amounted to far more than tourist puff but was intimately connected to a broader political and cultural struggle over place and territory. This is particularly evident in his short introduction to Richard Hayward's collection, *Ulster Songs and Ballads of the Town and Country* (1925), in which he records his dismay at English stereotypes of the Ulsterman as 'dour, harsh, humourless, unkindly, and uncouth', 'deeply absorbed in the making of money' and 'almost destitute of culture and charm'. For Ervine, these misplaced perceptions were linked to a reluctance by the English to accept that there are 'beautiful places in the North of Ireland' and not just in the 'south and west'. Linking character with place in this way, he is then led to the conclusion that a 'disbelief in the beauty of Ulster' rests upon 'a political foundation'.[51] For Ervine, therefore, the need to challenge stereotypes of the 'Ulsterman' involved a battle on two fronts: counteracting negative English attitudes towards 'Ulster' on the one hand while reclaiming the South's apparent monopoly on natural beauty (and its associated characteristics) on the other. However, given that the Irish countryside was in a sense already 'spoken for' by both metropolitan discourses of the periphery and cultural nationalism, this was a project that would inevitably prove difficult.

As various writers have noted, there is a long association of Ireland and 'Irishness' with ideas and images of the rural. Luke Gibbons, for example, has identified the importance of European Romanticism in the eighteenth and nineteenth centuries in imagining Ireland as a primitive, if picturesque, contrast to modern urban-industrial society.[52] Martin McLoone, moreover, has indicated how 'this Romantic primitiveness' became 'internalised in Ireland itself'. As he explains, '[t]he combination of a rural utopia, a simple but moral peasantry, and the intimations of the sublime, perfectly suited the religious/political alliance that fuelled Catholic nationalism towards the end of the nineteenth century'.[53] As a result, this identification of Irish nationalism with the rural was des-

---

49. St John Ervine, 'Northern Ireland for the Holidays', *Daily Mail*, 5 July 1932, p. 10. Lord Rothermere, the owner of the *Daily Mail*, was a staunch ally of the Unionist cause who himself contributed an essay ('The Ideal Ten-Days Motor Tour') to the UTDA publication *Ulster for the Motorist* (Belfast, 1936).

50. In addition to his plays and novels, he was the author of a book on the Unionist leader Sir Edward Carson and was given official support in writing a biography of Craigavon. This, however, was later withdrawn due to the extremity of some of his views on the South. For further discussion, see Gillian McIntosh, *The Force of Culture: Unionist Identities in Twentieth-Century Ireland* (Cork: Cork University Press, 1999), ch. 5.

51. St John Ervine, 'Introduction', Richard Hayward, *Ulster Songs and Ballads of the Town and Country* (London: Duckworth, 1925), pp. 7–9.

52. Luke Gibbons, 'Romanticism, Realism and Irish Cinema', in Kevin Rockett, Luke Gibbons and John Hill, *Cinema and Ireland* (London: Routledge, 1988), pp. 194–257.

53. Martin McLoone, 'The Primitive Image', in Eve Patten (ed.), *Returning to Ourselves*, p. 314. See also Maurice Goldring's discussion of 'The Myth of a Rural Civilisation', in *Faith of Our Fathers: The Formation of Irish Nationalist Ideology 1890–1920* (Dublin: Repsol, 1975), pp. 57–73.

tined to become the official ideology of the new Irish state, buttressing its belief in economic self-sufficiency, its leaning towards agriculture and strong suspicion of (urban-industrial) 'Britishness'.

Given this firm association between Irish nationalism and the land, the attempt to construct a distinctive 'Ulster' in terms of the rural proved difficult. Much of the economic basis of partition rested upon the industrial character of the north-east of Ireland and its close economic links with Britain and the British Empire. The modern character of Unionism, and its evolving 'Ulster' character, moreover, derived from the growing strength of industrial and mercantile capital over landed interests.[54] Thus, despite Ervine's claims that 'Ulster' was 'mainly an agricultural province', well over 60 per cent of the Northern Irish population lived either in Belfast or within a thirty-mile radius of the city in 1937.[55] Indeed, according to A. C. Hepburn, the city of Belfast is so much 'the symbol' of the area's 'claim to a distinct identity' that Northern Ireland may usefully be regarded as a 'city-region'.[56] If this is the case, then the attempt to downplay the urban-industrial character of Northern Ireland in favour of 'Ulster' ruralism inevitably exposed unionists to the risk of too close an identification with the forms of rural identity associated with Irish cultural nationalism.

One solution to this problem was an attempt to reconcile the imagery of the rural with the modern. As Martin McLoone has suggested, the acceptance and promotion of 'a romantic, rural sense of Irish identity' by cultural nationalism led to a rejection of not only 'the imperial definition of urban, industrial modernity but also the very notion of modernity itself'.[57] This was less so of the rural identity celebrated by Ulster unionists, however, which is characterised by a much more pronounced concern to divest the rural of the idea of 'primitiveness' and invest it with intimations of the modern. This is apparent, for example, in the poster – 'Come to Ulster, It's Jolly!' – which the UTDA commissioned from William Conor (then best known for his paintings and sketches of Belfast city life). This was intended for display in railway stations across Britain and was shown to the local press in January 1926. According to Conor the idea was:

> to get as far away from the conventional Irish poster of shawled peasant, white-washed, thatched cottage, and brown melancholy bog. The tourist did not come to Ulster to weep over the sorrows of Dark Rosaleen. Besides, Dark Rosaleen in the North had dried her tears long ago, and had a smile on her face, and very often wore silk stockings. Her house, or rather her father's house, was up-to-date. The visitor did not come here to rough it in discomfort.[58]

---

54. For an influential, if not uncontested, statement of this argument, see Peter Gibbon, *The Origins of Ulster Unionism: The Formation of Popular Protestant Politics and Ideology in Nineteenth-Century Ireland* (Manchester: Manchester University Press, 1975).

55. F. S. L. Lyons, *Ireland since the Famine* (London: Fontana, 1973), p. 707. Lyons does note, however, that agriculture remained a significant source of employment.

56. A. C. Hepburn, *A Past Apart: Studies in the History of Catholic Belfast 1850–1950* (Belfast: Ulster Historical Foundation, 1996), p. 142. Significantly, one of the apparent paradoxes that Hepburn is attempting to unpick is how the Catholics of urban Belfast came 'to identify with an all-Ireland nationalism which was distinctively rural, and sometimes positively anti-urban, in its ethos' (ibid., p. 145).

57. Martin McLoone, *Irish Film: The Emergence of a Contemporary Cinema* (London: BFI, 2000), p. 37.

58. *Belfast Telegraph*, 26 January 1926, p. 3. For more on Conor, see John Hewitt, *Art in Ulster 1557–1957* (Belfast: Blackstaff Press, 1977), pp. 86–93.

The poster itself shows modern-looking young girls dancing against a scenic backdrop intended 'to give an impression of life and youth against a typical Ulster background'.[59] The association of youthful femininity (in the form of the 'flapper') with the modernity of Ulster became yet more pronounced in subsequent UTDA posters, even becoming the subject of a debate in 1929, when a local judge called upon the organisation to 'give the girls a rest for a while'.[60]

A similar concern with modernity was also apparent in Richard Hayward's remarks concerning the 'realism' of the films with which he was involved and his desire to show 'Ulster life as it is known to Ulster people'.[61] While it may seem odd that what now look like rather quaint musical comedies should have ever been regarded as realistic, Hayward's claims for them make sense in terms of his concern to avoid the representation of Ulster as backward and primitive. The 'realism' of the films, in this respect, should be understood as intertextual, emerging in relation to pre-existing conventions and stereotypes rather than absolute standards. Thus, during a promotional trip to North America, Hayward sought to differentiate his work from what he regarded as the dominant image of 'the stage Irishman' – 'a clown with a pipestick in his cap' – and attacked Robert Flaherty's *Man of Aran* (1934) for its depiction of 'the Isle of Aran' as 'the last place God made'. 'There could scarcely be the shortage of supplies and the terrible primitiveness which the film showed,' Hayward went on. 'After all, Aran possesses an excellent hotel, fully equipped in the modern manner. There are motor roads and the place is haunted by tourists.'[62] While it has been argued that *Man of Aran*'s bleak vision matched the ideology of frugal self-sufficiency that characterised the Free State at that time, it was much less suited to the North, where, despite the economic problems, it remained important for unionists to demonstrate the economic viability of the state (as well as its economic superiority over the rest of Ireland) if it was to survive. Unlike *Man of Aran*, therefore, Hayward was concerned that *The Luck of the Irish* should not expel the traces of modernity from its representation of rural life. Indeed, during the making of the film, Hayward reported that there had been an argument over the filming of a bus (seen arriving in the village at the start of the film). While studio personnel had apparently wanted 'a decrepit affair with a drunken driver', they were eventually persuaded otherwise by tales of the efficiency of the Northern Ireland Road Transport Board![63]

---

59. *Irish News*, 2 October 1929.

60. Letter to *Belfast News-Letter*, 27 September 1929. In her discussion of the Hollywood actress Colleen Moore, Diane Negra suggests how her image as 'The Modern Girl' in the 1920s connects with the growing assimilation of the Irish into American society. See *Off-White Hollywood: American Culture and Ethnic Female Stardom* (London: Routledge, 2001), ch. 2. Within Ireland itself, however, it was – as the tourist posters indicate – northern unionism, rather than southern nationalism, that was ideologically more likely to promote not only modernity but also its association with changing models of femininity.

61. Richard Hayward quoted in *Irish News*, 5 September 1935, p. 2.

62. *Montreal Gazette*, 30 April 1936.

63. *Irish Independent*, 14 December 1935. Significantly, in the Northern Ireland guide book *Ulster* (1937), the Northern Ireland Road Transport Board encourages visitors to 'see Ulster' in 'comfort supreme' from 'luxuriously equipped' coaches.

Nevertheless, the very fact that there was a struggle over this image suggests how, for all that Hayward may have wished to provide a distinctive representation of 'Ulster', there was no cinematic precedent for this and commercial pressures within the industry were likely to push in the direction of the more familiar cinematic images of the Irish. There is, perhaps, a certain irony here. Luke Gibbons has indicated how, at the time, the bleak imagery of *Man of Aran* was often mistaken for 'realism'. Distinguishing two kinds of romanticism – hard and soft primitivism – he suggests how *Man of Aran* is characterised less by 'realism' than a different kind of romanticism involving the 'hard primitivist ideal at its most powerful, elemental level'.[64] However, if *Man of Aran* sought 'realism' through hard primitivism, the 'realism' of the Hayward films, such as *The Luck of the Irish*, is no less problematic, and mainly consists of a remobilisation of conventions associated with soft primitivism. As a result, the films find it difficult to signal the kind of departure from romantic Irish stereotypes that they seek. Before analysing why this was so, it is worth saying a little more about Hayward himself and how his enthusiasm for 'Ulster' speech and culture also contributed to an imagining of 'Ulster' as pre-eminently rural.

Ulster dialect and song: Richard Hayward

Although Richard Hayward did not direct any of the 1930s features, it seems fair to argue that he was the dominant figure. When the films were made, he was already an established actor, singer and writer and the films clearly bear his stamp. Born in 1892, he published his first collection of poems in 1917 and developed as a writer and actor during the 1920s when he wrote and acted for the Ulster Theatre Players, who performed his first play, *Huge Love*, at the Grand Opera House in Belfast in 1924. He was also a founder member of the Belfast Radio Players, following the opening of the BBC's Belfast station (2BE) in 1924, and his work for radio included a series of comedy sketches in local dialect, 'Double-Sided Records', and the performance of folksongs for *Children's Corner*.[65] In the early 1930s, he broke away from the Ulster Theatre to form the Belfast Repertory Players, along with fellow actor J. R. Mageean and Gerald Morrison (the manager of the Empire Theatre). The group was committed to the production of local plays that included both revivals – such as Lynn Doyle's *Love and Land* (1914) and Dorothea Donn Byrne's *The Land of the Stranger* (1924) – and new work, such as Hugh Quinn's *Mrs McConaghy's Money* (1932) and James Douglas's *The Early Bird* (1936). While many of these, such as *Love and Land* and *The Early Bird*, were rural 'kitchen comedies', organised around the themes of courtship and matchmaking, the group garnered most attention (and critical praise) for its production of the work of a former shipyard worker, Thomas Carnduff. Carnduff's first play, *Workers*, was initially accepted for production by the Ulster Theatre but was

---

64. Gibbons, 'Romanticism, Realism and Irish Cinema', p. 201. Gibbons is drawing on the work of Erwin Panofsky, who (after Lovejoy and Boas) distinguishes 'soft' primitivism – which conceives of 'primitive life' in terms of happiness and plenty ('civilized life purged of its vices') – from 'hard' primitivism – which conceives of it in terms of hardship and suffering ('civilized life stripped of its virtues'). See 'Et In Arcadia Ego: Poussin and the Elegiac Tradition', in *Meaning in the Visual Arts: Papers in and on Art History* (New York: Doubleday Anchor Books, 1955), p. 297.

65. See Rex Cathcart, *The Most Contrary Region: The BBC in Northern Ireland 1924–84* (Belfast: Blackstaff Press, 1984), pp. 27–8, 55.

rejected as unsuitable by the Belfast Opera House. Hayward (who took on the role of a wife-beating shipyard worker) agreed to acquire the play and the Belfast Players performed it with great success in both Belfast (at the Empire) and Dublin (at the Abbey) in 1932. Further Carnduff plays followed: *Machinery* (1933), dealing with workers in a large weaving factory; *Traitors* (1934), set during the 1932 Outdoor Relief Strike; and *Castlereagh* (1935), a historical drama concerned with the 1798 rising.[66] Many of the actors involved in the Belfast Players also appeared in Hayward's film productions. By 1938, however, their activities had largely come to an end, mainly due to the difficulties of finding a permanent home.[67] Although the group dispersed, some of them (including Mageean) went on to found the Ulster Group Theatre in 1939.

A key element of Hayward's work, evident in his work for both the radio and theatre, was his commitment to Ulster songs and speech. Indeed, he was later to write that his 'whole life-work' had been 'bent to an effort to make Ulster better known and better understood and appreciated'.[68] His collection of verse *Love in Ulster* (1922) included a number of poems written in Ulster dialect, while *Ulster Songs and Ballads* collected a range of local material, much of which he went on to record. During the 1930s, he flourished as a singer and, by 1935, he had already recorded 'in the authentic traditional manner' over 150 songs for Columbia and Decca. In his prefatory note to *Ulster Songs and Ballads*, Hayward observes how '[t]he Ballad Singer is fast disappearing from our roads and market towns', the result, he suggests, not only of 'national education and the cheap newspaper' but also 'the kinema'. 'Not so long ago,' he continues, 'every event of national or local importance was put into a ballad, and sung on the streets to a crowd eager alike for musical recreation and the latest titbit of news. Nowadays, the people go to the picture-house for their love story or tale of daring and adventure . . .'.[69] However, if Hayward held the cinema partially responsible for the disappearance of the ballad singer, he also grasped its potential, as with the gramophone record, to keep the ballad tradition alive. The singing of Ulster (and Irish) songs and ballads, therefore, became a major feature of the films in which he was involved. Hayward was also an astute businessman and, whatever his commitment to Ulster culture, he recognised the commercial possibilities that films provided for tie-ins with records (and published sheet music). Thus, in the wake of the release of *The Luck of the Irish*, five songs from the film were heavily promoted by Decca.

Hayward's enthusiasm for folksongs and ballads was matched by his advocacy of Ulster dialect. In the introduction to his first travel book, *In Praise of Ulster*, published in 1938, Hayward declared his pride in having been 'the first person in the world to use the Ulster dialect on radio, on gramophone records, and in talking pictures'.[70] As early as 1922, he began writing poetry in Ulster dialect and subsequently employed it in his work for radio and the theatre. His turn as a farmer and poteen maker, with an enthusiasm for Strabane, in *The Voice of Ireland* was also praised

66. See John Gray (ed.), *Thomas Carnduff: Life and Writings* (Belfast: Lagan Press/Fortnight Educational Press, 1994) for further details.

67. The *Northern Whig* (18 September 1937) reported Hayward's disappointment at his failure to establish a theatre in Belfast that would run plays in the evening and show films, probably 'Continental', in the afternoon.

68. Letter from Richard Hayward to Sir Wilson Hungerford, 26 February 1940, PRONI CAB9F/123/3A.

69. Hayward, *Ulster Songs and Ballads*, pp. 5–6.

70. Richard Hayward, *In Praise of Ulster*, 5th edn (Belfast: William Mullan and Son, 1946), p. 8.

in the local press for its use of 'authentic Ulster dialect'.[71] A revival of enthusiasm for Ulster dialect had contributed to the surge of 'Ulster' literature in the 1910s and survived the following decades. Thus, when the Reverend W. F. Marshall broadcast a series of radio talks on local dialect, *Ulster Speaks*, in 1935, it proved so popular that the talks were subsequently published. Hayward shared Marshall's pride in Ulster speech, arguing that '[t]he proper speech to come out of the mouths of Ulster people is the Ulster speech, and any Ulsterman who is ashamed of it, or who affects a superior air about it, is worse than a fool'.[72] However, as his polemical tone might suggest, the promotion of Ulster dialect as the authentic voice of Ulster was not without its detractors. In his account of Northern Ireland theatre, David Kennedy refers to the 'yelps of protest' from 'offended Ulstermen' concerning 'uncouth Ulster speech and barbarous kitchen comedies'.[73] The BBC's use of Ulster dialect, by Hayward's Radio Players among others, was also criticised in the letters pages of the local newspapers.[74] In 1929, for example, there were complaints of 'misrepresentations of Ulster folk life' in BBC plays and a call to stop the use of 'absurd and ignorant dialects'.[75] While some of this debate was concerned with the accuracy and authenticity of Ulster dialect (as well as the desirability or otherwise of the BBC adopting 'standard English'), it was also indicative of some of the tensions surrounding the expression of local Protestant identity. For while the promotion of Ulster speech could be seen to provide an alternative to 'Irish' identity and culture (which many unionist critics were quick to attack when it found an outlet through the BBC), it could also be seen as too local and insufficiently 'British'. As Cathcart suggests,

[t]he rejection of regional accents, of Ulster dialects and of portraits of rural life revealed in local drama indicated a disposition to deny an Ulster identity and a wish to be aligned with the cultural attitudes and values of the south east of England. 'Malone Road', as correspondents designated the more pretentious middle class, wished to be seen to be metropolitan, not provincial.[76]

It was, indeed, this version of 'Malone Road Britishness' that Hayward opposed.[77] It is clear that he was happy to consider himself an Irishman and he wrote books on the whole of the island not just Ulster. He also did not share an aversion to 'Irish' culture and, through his love of song and music, was led to learn the Irish language and play the Irish harp. However, he was also

71. *Belfast News-Letter*, 11 November 1932, p. 6.

72. Hayward, *In Praise of Ulster*, p. 8. On the same page, Hayward refers his readers to Marshall's booklet.

73. David Kennedy, 'The Drama in Ulster', in Sam Hanna Bell, Nesca A. Robb and John Hewitt (eds), *The Arts in Ulster: A Symposium* (London: George G. Harrap & Co., 1951), p. 51.

74. Cathcart, *The Most Contrary Region*, pp. 41–2, 65–6, 67–70.

75. *Belfast News-Letter*, 16 October 1929, p. 5.

76. Cathcart, *The Most Contrary Region*, p. 46. For further discussion of this controversy, see Martin McLoone, 'The Construction of a Partitionist Mentality: Early Broadcasting in Ireland', in Martin McLoone (ed.), *Broadcasting in a Divided Community: Seventy Years of the BBC in Northern Ireland* (Belfast: Institute of Irish Studies, 1996).

77. The Malone Road is well known as one of the most middle-class areas of Belfast. Subsequently, Hayward was to attack the 'Malone Road accent' as 'artificial' and as having 'arisen entirely through snobbery'. 'The Ulster Dialect: People Should Be Proud of It', *Derry Standard*, 7 October 1953.

a staunch unionist, reported at his Memorial Service in 1964 to have been a member of both the Orange Order and the Standing Committee of the Ulster Unionist Council. Thus, while Hayward saw his work as avoiding politics, it is also clear that his devotion to Ulster dialect, 'scenery and songs' (as *In Praise of Ulster* puts it) contributed to the moulding of a Northern Ireland identity that could be regarded as culturally distinct from the rest of the island. This becomes most evident in his writings, where he increasingly argues for the cultural and historical differences between the two parts of the island. In his 'novel of the Ulster Countryside', *Sugarhouse Entry* (1936), for example, there is an extended exposition on Ulster history and character in which the 'typical Ulsterman' is described as 'fiercely and aggressively Irish' but nonetheless 'a separate kind of Irishman'.[78] In *In Praise of Ulster* this sense of the separateness of Ulster from the rest of Ireland is accounted for in terms of 'a line of demarcation' stretching back to 'the very dawn of really authentic Irish history, about the year A.D. 300' and the identification of 'Ulstermen' with the 'aboriginal pre-Celtic Irish people', the 'Cruithni'.[79] Given the book's emphasis upon the distinctiveness of the 'two peoples' of Ireland, and its insistence upon historical precedent for the border between the North and South, it is perhaps not surprising that it should have achieved a degree of official approval from the Stormont regime, which – because of the book's 'excellent propaganda nature' – sought to secure paper supplies to reprint it both during and after the war.[80]

However, while Hayward's 'Ulster' was to be distinguished from the rest of Ireland, it nevertheless shared much of the 'other' Ireland's rural character. For, just as Ervine had sought to rebut the 'industrial legend' of Ulster, so Hayward's enthusiasm for landscape, folk culture and local dialect inevitably led him to stress the rural, rather than urban-industrial, character of 'Ulster'. Indeed a reviewer for the *Times Literary Supplement* provoked a minor controversy when he complained that Hayward's *Ulster and the City of Belfast* had dwelt unduly on the past and ignored the 'bigotry' of contemporary Northern Ireland. 'Ulster', he observed, 'must be made

---

78. Richard Hayward, *Sugarhouse Entry* (London: Arthur Barker, 1936), p. 32. This same formulation reappears in Hayward's second travel book on Ulster, *Ulster and the City of Belfast* (London: Arthur Barker, 1950) in which he develops his claim that, although '[f]iercely and vitally Irish', the 'Ulster Protestant will yet look with deep suspicion on any Irish movement or tendency' and 'will, for instance, at once detect the hand of Rome in Irish dancing, Irish music, or the Irish language' (p. 35).

79. Hayward, *In Praise of Ulster*, p. 35. For an overview of how 'the myth of the Cruthini' has informed 'Ulster-Scottish cultural identity', see Máiréad Nic Craith, *Plural Identities Singular Narratives: The Case of Northern Ireland* (New York: Berghahn Books, 2002), ch. 5.

80. Government of Northern Ireland Information Services, Report for November 1945, PRONI CAB9F/123/34. See also minutes of UTDA Executive Committee, 14 January 1943, PRONI COM62/1/144. James Loughlin (*Ulster Unionism and British National Identity*, p. 170) provides a somewhat reductionist account of Hayward's travel writing, which he suggests was a response to moments of 'political crisis'. *In Praise of Ulster*, he notes, coincided with the Treaty Ports dispute of 1938, *Ulster and the City of Belfast* with the postwar anti-partition campaign and *Border Foray* (1957) with the IRA's border campaign, begun in 1956. While Loughlin is clearly right to highlight Hayward's unionism, he nevertheless neglects his longstanding interest in 'Ulster' cultural traditions and, thus, over-emphasises the correlation of the books with changing political circumstances (as well as their compatibility with more 'pro-British' forms of Unionism).

soft and romantic.'[81] This could also be said of the Hayward films, all of which employed rural rather than urban settings. Hayward himself argued that the 'working man' did not go to the cinema 'to see the hardships of his existence' but 'to obtain entertainment' and that this was why the Belfast shipyards (featured in Thomas Carnduff's play *Workers*) did not make an appropriate subject for a film.[82] However, while it was certainly the case that the British 'entertainment' film at this time generally avoided working-class subject matter (which was largely confined to the documentary), it is also unlikely that the 'working man' would have been naturally drawn to bucolic comedies of the kind preferred by Hayward. The benefit of the Ulster rural comedy, nevertheless, was that it avoided the very areas of social division and sectarianism to which the dramatisation of the shipyards was liable to lead. However, in choosing to render 'Ulster' 'soft' and 'romantic' in this way, it was also likely – given the pre-existing traditions of representing Ireland – that the project of promoting 'Ulster's' distinctiveness would be subject to strain. As even its title suggests, this is certainly so of the first of the Hayward features, *The Luck of the Irish*.

The Luck of the Irish

Hayward was later to describe how Victor Haddick, with whom he had worked on *The Voice of Ireland*, gave him a copy of the script prior to a trip to London, where he had a chance meeting with Donovan Pedelty.[83] Despite his name, Pedelty was in fact an Englishman who had been working for Paramount as a talent scout and writer and was about to begin his career as a director. He cast Hayward in the role of the Earl of Cameron in his second feature, *Flame in the Heather* (1935), a historical drama set during the Jacobite rebellion of 1745, after which the two men set to work on *The Luck of the Irish*, with funding from the Hollywood studio, Paramount. The involvement of Paramount is explained by the circumstances of the British cinema at this time. Following a dramatic drop in the number of films shown in British cinemas during the 1920s, the British government introduced a quota for British films in the Cinematograph Films Act of 1927. Ironically, this legislation did not apply to Northern Ireland but, according to the trade press, the NI Ministry of Commerce reached a 'verbal agreement' with the British government that the quota would be observed.[84] The effect of the quota was that it immediately stimulated demand for British films, especially among British-based US distributors, which were forced to become involved in either commissioning or producing British films in order to comply with quota requirements. Following some involvement in direct production, Paramount opted to work with British companies such as British and Dominions, which, as Rachael Low indicates, was responsible for churning out around one film per month for the company.[85] Other

81. *Times Literary Supplement*, 23 June 1950.

82. *Dublin Evening Mail*, 8 February 1937.

83. Hayward, 'The First Talkie', pp. 16–17.

84. *Today's Cinema*, 10 August 1937, p. 1. The NI Ministry of Commerce had, in fact, been happy for the Act to apply to Northern Ireland in line with its 'policy of economic solidarity with Great Britain' but was persuaded by local exhibitors that it was unnecessary ('Cinematograph Films Bill: Memorandum by the Minister of Commerce', 23 March 1927, PRONI CAB9F/92/1). Although local exhibitors claimed that they showed more British films than required by the quota, it remained a recurring complaint of the British film trade that Northern Ireland cinemas failed to show sufficient British films.

85. Rachael Low, *Filmmaking in 1930s Britain* (London: George Allen and Unwin, 1985), p. 189.

companies with which Paramount collaborated included Crusade Films, which Pedelty had set up with Victor Greene in order to take advantage of the opportunities that the quota provided. Although Low appears to identify Pedelty as a 'real quota merchant', he saw himself as upgrading the quality of quota production, claiming credit, in the treatment for *The Luck of the Irish*, for 'the first Big Picture "quota film". . . the first costume quota picture and the first full-dress Scottish talkie'. Crusade was responsible for the first three of the Hayward films – *The Luck of the Irish*, *The Early Bird* and *Irish and Proud of It* – all of which received financial backing from Paramount in return for British distribution rights. J. 'Tommy' Hanlon's Irish International Film Agency undertook distribution in Ireland (North and South). All three films took about three weeks to shoot, including about one week of filming on location in Ireland. In the case of *The Luck of the Irish*, filming took place (during September 1935) at the County Antrim village of Glynn and at Upton Castle, Templepatrick, before the rest of the film was completed in the studio at Elstree.

The film's Belfast premiere took place at the Imperial Picture House on 13 December 1935. Just as the screening of Robert Flaherty's *Man of Aran* in Dublin the previous year had, according to Kevin Rockett, assumed the status of a 'national event', so the launch of *The Luck of the Irish* became a semi-official occasion for the North.[86] The event was jointly hosted by the UIDA and their invitations described the film as 'Ulster's First Feature film' with 'authentic Ulster Songs, Ulster Humour, Ulster Scenery, and an all-Ulster Cast'. The screening was attended, as one contemporary observer put it, by '[t]he elite of Ulster' and guests included Lady Craigavon, the Unionist Lord Mayor (Sir Crawford McCullagh) and G. B. Hanna, Parliamentary Secretary to the Ministry of Home Affairs.[87] The film was received enthusiastically and Donovan Pedelty, Victor Haddick and Richard Hayward all made short speeches. During his speech, Victor Haddick gave particular thanks to the UTDA (and to the late Robert Baillie) in acknowledgment of their support for 'films of Ulster' that would 'enhance its prestige and assist its tourist industry'.[88] The UIDA organiser, J. M. Henderson, also played a small part in the film (as Sir Richard O'Donnell) and was subsequently thanked in the press by Pedelty for 'the best "industrial development" ever known in any film'.[89] The film also proved a popular success when it opened in late January 1936 at the Belfast Picture House (in Royal Avenue), where it played four times a day and enjoyed an extended run.

The influence of the film's sponsors – the UIDA and the UTDA – is also apparent in the film itself. In its *Annual Review*, the UIDA reported how 'Ulster manufacturers were enabled to gain elaborate yet subtle publicity' in the film and this is particularly obvious in the scenes involving the Widow Whistler's shop, which proudly displays a 'Buy Ulster Goods' slogan on its

---

86. Rockett, Gibbons and Hill, *Cinema and Ireland*, p. 71.

87. Matt Mulcaghey, *Coleraine Chronicle*, 18 January 1936. Matt Mulcaghey was the pseudonym for Wilson Guy, who was himself a strong advocate of the use of Ulster dialect and a regular broadcaster in the guise of 'the "oul" besom man from Tyrone'.

88. *Belfast News-Letter*, 14 December 1935, p. 5.

89. *Irish News*, 30 September 1935, p.7. Hayward's relationship with the UIDA was obviously close. He is listed in the *Belfast and Ulster Directory for 1936* (Belfast, 1936) as 'manufacturers' representative' for the organisation and occupied offices in the same building in Belfast.

'Ulster's First Feature Film': audiences in Belfast queue to see *The Luck of the Irish*

front door.[90] In the film's first interior scene, the action is delayed (and the establishment of place extended) while the camera slowly tracks across the goods on display inside the shop before the characters Sam Mulhern (Richard Hayward) and the Widow Whistler (Nan Cullen) are brought into shot. The prominence given to the goods inside the shop is reinforced by subsequent compositions and framings. Thus, when Sam and Simon Reid (Harold Griffin) engage in conversation inside the shop, three lemonade bottles clearly occupy the centre of the frame. It is, of course, almost exclusively local products that the film shows, including C&C (Cantrell and Cochrane) lemonade, White's Wafer Oats and copies of the *Belfast Telegraph* (which gratefully acknowledged the free publicity when reporting on the film's production).[91] The film was also accompanied by an advertising campaign in the press by White, Tomkins and Courage (the manufacturers of White's Wafer Oats), which congratulated the film's makers on the beginnings of 'a successful Ulster Film Industry' and drew attention to the impressive display of their goods in the film as 'seen in every grocer's shop in Ulster'.[92] Such was the success of this early form of product placement that it inspired the UIDA, as noted earlier, to embark upon a short film of its own, *The Star of Ulster*, in which a local shop, full of local goods, once again becomes the setting.

The influence of the UTDA is possibly less direct but is undoubtedly evident in the film's enthusiasm for the display of local scenery. The film was praised by *Kine Weekly* for 'the picturesque authenticity of the atmosphere' and there is a clear effort within the film (and those that follow) to 'show off' local 'beauty spots' with the intention of promoting the scenic attractiveness of 'Ulster' and encouraging possible tourists.[93] As with the display of local goods, this results in 'picturesque' shots of local scenery that are only weakly motivated by, or integrated with, the requirements of plot. The film's opening shot of Northern Irish countryside, for example, is held for much longer than normal and is immediately followed by a series of general views of the area. As these provide misleading plot information (implying that a part of Reid's journey from Belfast may have been undertaken by boat) and fail to establish accurate geographical (or spatial)

---

90. UIDA, *Annual Review 1935*, PRONI COM62/1/187.

91. *Belfast Telegraph*, 22 October 1935, p. 5. The prominence given to this newspaper may have contributed to the complaint in the *Irish News* (14 December, 1936, p. 6) that the use of Ulster goods was 'a trifle blatant'.

92. *Belfast News-Letter*, 29 January 1936, p. 13.

93. *Kine Weekly*, 12 December 1935, p. 22.

co-ordinates for the ensuing action, the main purpose of the montage is to offer a display of scenic views. As a result, there is a degree of tension within the film between the forward momentum of the plot and the film's more leisurely presentation of scenery (and musical numbers). Although this kind of tension between narrative and 'pictorial' display is typical of British cinema more generally, it is an especially pronounced feature of the Hayward films, and *Devil's Rock* in particular (a film to which I will return).[94]

The emphasis in *The Luck of the Irish* upon rural scenery lays the basis for the film's portrait of Ulster society more generally. The story is set in the fictional village of Tyr Owen in County Tyrone and primarily concerns the fortunes of the O'Neills. Hoping to win the money that will rescue him from financial difficulties, Sir Brian O'Neill (J. R. Mageean) of Tyr Owen Castle borrows £2,000 to bet on his horse, Knockavoe, winning the Grand National. While Knockavoe does win, it is subsequently disqualified and Sir Brian is faced with the loss of his home. The village factotum, Sam Mulhern, endeavours to help out through the manufacture of fake Celtic vases but his ruse is discovered. Sir Brian looks certain to be evicted but is rescued at the last minute by the arrival of the American, Colonel Peverett, who pays 5,000 guineas for the horse and offers Sir Brian's son the chance to ride it for the Maryland Cup.

According to *Kine Weekly*, the film endeavours to show 'a representative cross-section of Ulster life'.[95] However, it is significant that this supposed 'cross-section' is confined to village life and there is an almost complete avoidance of urban-industrial Northern Ireland. Indeed, the film explicitly counterposes the values of the village community to those of the city. It is the stranger from the city, the bookmaker Simon Reid, who threatens to destabilise existing social relations within the village by reducing the O'Neills (and by implication the village) to penury. The only scene in the film actually set in the city occurs in the office of Reid's boss, Murphy (Harold Goldblatt). This is a deeply unpleasant scene involving Murphy, described in the shooting script as 'a large fat Jew', sat behind his desk, smoking a cigar and congratulating Reid on the deal that he has struck. In the original script, this character is called Stravinsky. Given the change of name, however, it is hard to resist the association not just with Jewishness but also Catholicism. Inevitably, this has consequences for how the imagining of community is staged in the film. For if the city, and its representative Murphy, is the threatening 'other' of village life then so by implication is the Catholicism that is hinted at by the use of Murphy as a name.

However, this reading of the film is complicated by the way that the image of the village contained in the film otherwise converges with traditional views of the (Catholic) rural Irish. For despite Hayward's aspirations to 'realism', the film, as previously suggested, is clearly indebted to a romantic tradition of 'soft primitivism'. For Luke Gibbons, 'the image most in keeping with romantic mythology, and with nostalgia and sentiment, is that which presents nature . . . as a kind of bounteous paradise' in which work becomes 'generally redundant'. The result, he goes on, is 'a dream of social life which revolves around leisure and lawlessness, drink-

---

94. Brian McFarlane and Geoff Mayer, for example, identify a 'dawdling tendency' in British cinema, which they attribute to a 'pictorial rather than dramatic' use of visual techniques in *New Australian Cinema: Sources and Parallels in American and British Film* (Cambridge: Cambridge University Press, 1992), p. 140.

95. *Kine Weekly*, 5 December 1935, p. 6. As this phrase recurs in other publications, it probably derives from a press release.

ing, singing, or when more onerous forms of physical exertion are called for, dancing and various types of sporting activity'.[96] Although Gibbons identifies this tradition with the representation of southern and western (and by extension Catholic) Ireland, it is striking how well his
description fits *The Luck of the Irish*. Although a number of characters have identifiable jobs
(such as shopkeeper, teacher and police sergeant), there is little evidence of actual labour. Even
the Widow Whistler's shop, the supposed hub of local trade and dispenser of Ulster goods,
functions less as the site of business activity than as a communal meeting place (at which Sam,
the sergeant and the teacher gather to listen to the race on the wireless). The well-being of the
villagers appears to depend more upon gambling than productive employment and, when
Knockavoe initially wins the Grand National, the villagers are all free to descend upon the
local pub and celebrate their good fortune in a collective sing-song led by Sam Mulhern. Even
when the horse is later disqualified, and there is talk of financial ruin facing the village, there
is very little to suggest that genuine economic hardship is, in fact, likely to descend upon the
village.

This 'soft' and 'romantic' view of rural life, and its emphasis upon natural bounty, underpins a correspondingly 'natural' and 'harmonious' conception of community. As Gibbons suggests, '[t]he elimination of material concerns brings with it an absence of class or related
economic divisions, so that society is portrayed as a unified non-hierarchical community in
which people have more in common than they have separating each other'.[97] This is also true
of *The Luck of the Irish*, where the threat to the community is entirely external and the village remains fundamentally free of social conflict despite the social distinctions that exist. The
Tyr Owen community is, however, rather more hierarchically structured than Gibbons
describes. The identity of the village is intimately bound up with the fortunes of the local
landed aristocracy, the O'Neills, and the main character of the film, Sam, is defined by his loyalty (and deference) to them (even when his loyalty is not reciprocated and Sir Brian seeks to
expel him from the county).[98] The distinctive element of *The Luck of the Irish* is not its denial
of social division (which is common enough in romantic images of Ireland) but the way it
then mobilises an image of 'organic' community for Northern Protestants rather than
Southern Catholics. However, in doing so, it succeeds not only in eliminating the traces of
urban-industrial 'Ulster' but also the industrial classes that had given Ulster Unionism so

---

96. Luke Gibbons, 'The Romantic Image: Some Themes and Variations', *The Green on the Screen* (Dublin: Irish Film
    Institute, 1984), p. 35.

97. Ibid., p. 36.

98. This tends to confirm how Hayward's concern to present the modernity of Ulster is subverted by the film's use
    of romantic conventions that continue to rely upon premodern ideologies of status. As Paul Willemen suggests,
    'a cultural text's commitment to individual subjectivity as against the requirements of submission to status
    (caste, class, gender and so on) identities' provides a 'yardstick' against which to measure that text's commitment
    to 'modernisation'. See 'Questions of Modernisation and Indian Cinema', in Ria Lavrijsen (ed.), *Global
    Encounters in the World of Art: Collisions of Tradition and Modernity* (Amsterdam: Royal Tropical Institute, 1998),
    p. 105.

A traditional view of rural Ireland: Sam Mulhern (Richard Hayward) leads a communal sing-song in *The Luck of the Irish*

much of its contemporary character.[99] Moreover, given that the rural imagery that the film employs brought with it (from novels, plays and other films) pre-existing connotations of 'Irishness', it was also likely to prove an ideologically fraught strategy given the absence of guarantees that the film's 'Ulster' dimensions would be apparent to all of the film's spectators.

This seems to be confirmed by an assessment of the competing influences at work in the film's production, promotion and reception. In the case of the film's production, for example, it is evident that economic pressures led to a degree of ideological ambivalence (and even confusion) on the part of the final film. One aspect of this issue is suggested by a report on the film in the Northern Ireland-friendly *Daily Express*, written by Alexander Boath. While Boath wel-

99. Perry Anderson has famously argued that the English revolution of the seventeenth century was the 'least pure bourgeois revolution of any major European country' insofar as it failed to achieve a complete hegemony over the old social order. Thus, while economically subordinate, the aristocracy retained its political and cultural power and the culture of the dominant class remained cast in 'a normatively agrarian mould'. (See 'The Origins of the Present Crisis', *New Left Review*, no. 23, January–February 1964, pp. 26–53.) Similarly, it could be argued that the industrial and mercantile classes that came economically to dominate Unionism arrived at a similar 'compromise' with the local landed aristocracy, which continued to exert a disproportionate political and ideological influence. The continued imagining of 'Ulster' in terms of a quasi-feudal social order, therefore, connects with a corresponding absence of a fully elaborated 'modern' unionist ideology.

comed the film for its portrayal of 'the real Ulster', he went on to complain about the film's title. 'The film is about Ulster, for Ulster, by Ulster,' he observes, 'but its title is "The Luck of the Irish". I wonder why.'[100] Although Boath's question is rhetorical, he clearly recognises that, whatever the circumstances surrounding the film's production, *The Luck of the Irish* was more likely to travel and win audiences, in both Britain and the US, as an 'Irish' rather than an 'Ulster' film. Indeed, when the film finally reached the United States in 1937, *Variety* suggested it would be advisable to 'soft pedal' on 'the fact that the cast and story are both indigenous to Northern Ireland' if the film was to appeal to 'the sons of Erin'.[101] As this would suggest, Irish–American identity was predominantly Catholic and nationalist in orientation and Irish–American audiences were therefore unlikely to respond positively to an overtly 'unionist', or Protestant, film from Ireland.[102] Donovan Pedelty, who had worked in the US, was undoubtedly conscious of this and, as both scenarist and director, sought to play down some of the film's 'Ulster' dimensions as well as play up some of its more stereotypically 'Irish' elements.[103] Thus, the explicit reference to Sam as 'a Protestant' in the film's shooting script is omitted from the final film, while the radio commentator's remark that 'Ulster will be proud of Knockavoe tonight' is changed to 'Ireland will be proud'.[104] The film's ending, involving the rescue of the O'Neills by the American Colonel, is also changed from the original treatment in which Sam and the schoolteacher, Gavin (R. H. McCandless), discover the Earl of Tyrone's treasure. The introduction of an American character (and his wealth) as a solution to the O'Neills' problems appears, therefore, to have been a fairly transparent attempt to curry favour with the Irish–American audience to which it was hoped the film would appeal.

Given these changes, it also became much easier to promote the film as straightforwardly 'Irish', with the result that the film was marketed differently to audiences inside and outside of Northern Ireland. Thus, while the film was launched in Belfast as 'Ulster's First Feature film' containing 'authentic Ulster Songs, Ulster Humour, Ulster Scenery, and an all-Ulster Cast', the invitations to the press show in Dublin (in January 1936) described the film as 'a delightful Irish comedy filmed in Ireland'.[105] Given the film's potential attractiveness to the predominantly Catholic Irish migrant community in Britain, the British publicity materials also stressed the

---

100. *Daily Express*, 3 September 1935.

101. *Variety*, 20 January 1937.

102. The cultivation by unionists of a 'Scotch-Irish' lineage as a counterweight to the nationalist sentiments of Irish-American culture is discussed in Chapter 5.

103. During the making of the film, Pedelty told the *Irish News* (11 September 1935, p. 3) that 'an Irish picture has an audience ready made for it all over the world' and that he expected the film to be a 'big success' because there are 'more Irishmen living outside Ireland than live in Ireland'.

104. In *The Early Bird*, a poster for the *Irish Independent*, advertising a convention on the 'Progress of the Gaelic Revival', is clearly visible in the newspaper office. Given the context this seems anachronistic but probably derives from a similar impulse to make the proceedings more obviously 'Irish' (and nationalist).

105. This dual approach to promotion continued with subsequent films. Thus, while the film's distributor in Ireland promoted *Devil's Rock* in Belfast as 'the first full-length feature ever photographed and recorded entirely in Ulster', it was described as '[p]hotographed and recorded entirely in Ireland' when premiered in Dublin a week later (in December 1937).

'Irish' angle but, no doubt conscious of some of the sensitivities involved (and the religious complexion of different British cities), provided accompanying feature material headed both 'Story
of Ulster Life' and 'Romantic Comedy of Irish Life'. Given these factors – the film's title, the
way in which the film was promoted and the film's own use of romantic conventions derived
from popular theatre and the 'old country' film – it is hardly surprising that the reviews of the
film outside Northern Ireland played down (or simply ignored) its 'Ulster' characteristics.[106] In
Britain, the distinctiveness of the Ulster dialect used in the film completely failed to register,
while the characters themselves were interpreted as typically 'Irish'. *Kine Weekly*, for example,
referred to the Ulster dialect as 'Irish brogue', while the *Daily Film Renter* not only praised the
film for the quality of its 'character studies of Irish village life' but considered the film's dialogue
to have been 'spoken with the ease and fluency one would expect of Erin's country-folk'.[107]
Similar sentiments were expressed when the film reached North America. In Canada, the film's
'simple story, scenes, actors, songs, dialogue, [and] dialect' were held to be 'as Irish as Con-
nemara', while the New York *Film Daily* dubbed it 'an authentic Irish film'.[108] Even in the south
of Ireland, there was no difficulty in accepting the film's Irish credentials. The *Dublin Herald*
claimed it was 'the most typically Irish film yet seen in Dublin', while the nationalist *Irish Press*
went so far as to suggest, in a phrase subsequently employed in British publicity, that it was 'the
first real Irish film'.[109] The attractiveness of the film within Ireland was further reinforced by its
avoidance of sexual suggestiveness. The establishment of the Legion of Decency in the US in
1934, in order to ensure implementation of the Hays Code, had encouraged campaigns in Ireland against the 'immoral' character of American and British films. Thus, it became common for
priests at Sunday Mass to urge their congregations to boycott cinemas, unless they operated a
'clean film' policy.[110] It was therefore hardly coincidental that, the day after *The Luck of the Irish*
was shown to the press, the nationalist *Irish News* spoke approvingly of the prospects for an Irish
film industry that could capitalise on the 'present tendency towards clean films'.[111]

---

106. Dennis Clark and William J. Lynch refer to 'the "Old Country" film' in their survey of popular 'Irish' film genres in
'Hollywood and Hibernia: The Irish in the Movies', in Randall M. Miller (ed.), *The Kaleidoscopic Lens: How
Hollywood Views Ethnic Groups* (Englewood, NJ: Jerome S. Ozer, 1980), p. 106.

107. *Kine Weekly*, 10 October 1935; *Daily Film Renter*, 11 December 1935.

108. *Toronto Star*, 8 May 1936; *Film Daily*, 6 February 1936.

109. *Dublin Herald*, 3 January 1936; *Irish Press*, 7 January 1936. An earlier review in the same paper (23 December 1935)
also reclaimed the film for a vaguely nationalist reading, given Hugh O'Neill's historic resistance to English rule in
Ulster. As Stephen Howe notes, such were the shifts in 'political, religious and cultural allegiances among both
Irish-Gaelic and "Old English" elites' during the sixteenth century that this has led, within writing on Irish history,
to 'the transmutation of Hugh O'Neill, English (and Protestant) raised and educated, soldier in Elizabeth's army,
holder of an English earldom, apostle of cultural Anglicisation, into The O'Neill, self-proclaimed prince of an
independent Catholic, Gaelic Ireland'. See *Ireland and Empire: Colonial Legacies in Irish History and Culture* (Oxford:
Oxford University Press, 2000), p. 27.

110. *Northern Whig*, 15 March 1935, p. 7. The campaign against 'immoral' films in the North during the 1930s is
discussed in the following chapter.

111. *Irish News*, 14 December 1935, p. 4. For a discussion of the 'clean screen' campaign and Ireland, see Kevin Rockett,
Irish Film Censorship: A Cultural Journey from Silent Cinema to Internet Pornography (co-ed. Emer Rockett) (Dublin:
Four Courts Press, 2004), pp. 97–104.

The Early Bird

The initial response to *The Luck of the Irish* encouraged both Pedelty and Hayward to expand their activities. At the film's launch in Dublin in January 1936, Pedelty sent a telegram announcing the 'inauguration' of 'a continuously active Irish film industry embracing every aspect of the island'.[112] The following month Hayward established his own company, Richard Hayward Film Productions Ltd, with the backing of local businessmen (including Wilson Boyd of Bushmills Distillery, whose whiskey received the appropriate promotion in the subsequent films). Reporting his plans to the press, Hayward announced a programme of three films for 1936, after which he predicted that the establishment of local studios could become a 'distinct possibility'.[113] The first production was to be *The Early Bird*. This was a film version of James Douglas's play that the Belfast Repertory Players had performed at the Empire Theatre just a week prior to the screening of *The Luck of the Irish* in the city. Filming began in June 1936 at Glenarm, followed by studio work at the newly opened Highbury Studios. The UIDA once again sponsored the Belfast premiere of the film, which opened at the Picture House in November. It proved so successful that it was also chosen to open the new Broadway Cinema in the Falls Road in December. This was the latest in the chain of luxury suburban cinemas belonging to Curran Theatres and had a capacity of 1,500. The opening of the cinema was attended by cast members, including Richard Hayward, who made a short speech and sang some ballads.[114]

The Early Bird itself was described by Hayward as 'a very well-constructed comedy on robust country lines' that made use of the matchmaking theme already popular from plays such as Lynn Doyle's *Love and Land*.[115] The play's author, James Douglas, was from Coleraine and had served in the 10th Battalion Royal Inniskilling Fusiliers (Ulster Division), with whom he fought at the Battle of the Somme. He studied art in both Dublin and Belfast and was a painter as well as writer. Prior to *The Early Bird*, his best-known work was *The Wrang McMunn*, which was performed at the Abbey Theatre. Like Hayward, he had an interest in local songs and dialect and provided the cover design for the collection of North Antrim songs and poems edited by his friend Sam Henry, *Rowlock Rhymes and Songs of Exile* (1933). Indeed, so strong was his use of local dialect that Hayward himself wrote to Douglas expressing his doubts that audiences would understand it and indicating that he would have 'to water it down to a more or less standard County Down speech', which he claimed now seemed to be 'the accepted language of Ulster drama'.

Although Douglas was hired to write the screenplay (and also provided sketches for the sets), the play was significantly reworked by Pedelty for the film version. This not only involved a further toning down and elimination of much of the play's dialogue but also major changes to the plot.

---

112. *Dublin Herald*, 3 January 1936.

113. *Irish News*, 13 March 1935. The third of the three films announced by Hayward was Victor Haddick's 'Power', set against a background of the Shannon hydro-electric power station at Ardnacrusha (opened in 1929). This seems to confirm the enthusiasm of Hayward and Haddick for more modern images of Ireland. However, the fact that it was the only one of the three that did not get made would also suggest how the film industry of the time failed to find such subjects congenial.

114. *Irish News*, 14 December 1936, p. 6.

115. *Coleraine Chronicle*, 18 January 1936, p. 4.

Charlie Simpson (Jimmy Mageean) attempts unsuccessfully to woo widow Rose Madill (Nan Cullen) in *The Early Bird*

Douglas's play is largely concerned with the rivalry between a small farmer Daniel Duff (Richard Hayward) and the local vet Charlie Simpson (Jimmy Mageean) for the hand of an attractive widow, Rose Madill (Nan Cullen). While this survives in the final film, it is considerably embellished through the addition of extra characters and plot-lines. As the original play is set in just two locations (the Duffs' farmhouse kitchen and Rose Madill's parlour), this necessarily involves a degree of opening out of the action. Thus, the 'swarry' (or soirée), which is only mentioned in the play, becomes a major set-piece (involving a speech, a game of blind man's buff and a song). As with *The Luck of the Irish*, a number of musical interludes are also added in order to showcase both Hayward's singing and the local scenery. These include scenes of Dan singing the 'Comber Ballad' against the Antrim coastline and picking flowers in the Glens, to the accompaniment of 'The Muttonburn Stream' ('that wee river in Ulster'). The most striking changes from the play, however, relate to the character of Mrs Gordon (Charlotte Tedlie). In the play, she is a minister's wife whose preoccupation with 'the immodest behaviour of girls of today' is the source of gentle amusement. In the film, this character becomes the proprietor of the local newspaper and President of the 'Ballytober Uplift League', and her obsessive preoccupation with the moral propriety of the villagers becomes a major plank of the film.

This has its interesting aspects. Like *The Luck of the Irish*, the film provides a fundamentally benign vision of community in which, whatever the courtship rivalries, all remain relatively united. However, unlike *The Luck of the Irish*, there is a much sharper sense of social division as a result of the malign role played by Mrs Gordon. She is not only the newspaper proprietor but is also the local landlord and owner of 'half the land and houses' in the district. This then leads to a striking scene at the start of the film when the McBains are seen to ride through the village on a farm cart, having been evicted by Mrs Gordon. A hand-written placard attached to the cart reads, 'Evicted by bigotry'. Although the McBains' 'offence' is 'indecent behaviour' (it appears that they were not married), the image of eviction and suggestion of bigotry inevitably hints at other factors, particularly given the pre-existing associations of such imagery in an Irish context (and in early films sympathetic to nationalism, such as Kalem's *The Lad from Old Ireland* [1910]). Moreover, even in its own terms, the film's unflattering portrait of moral puritanism is significant given the prevalence of similar zealotry (including hostility towards the cinema) within Northern Irish society. In this respect, there is an interesting subversion of Ervine's stereotype of the 'dour' and 'humourless' Ulsterman, given the determination of the villagers, under the leadership of Daniel, to circumvent Mrs Gordon's strictures and indulge in social pleasures (as when they conspire to get rid of her from the soirée and engage in singing and dancing). Indeed, despite the welcome that *The Luck of the Irish* had received within Ireland as an example of a 'clean film', the Irish censor regarded this follow-up film as 'crude and vulgar' and required cuts before its release in the South. 'The amount given to men in their shirts is disgusting,' he observed, and '[i]t is no credit to Ireland to release such stuff'.[116]

However, although the film begins to hint at genuine tensions within Northern Irish society, in the end these are mostly side-stepped. This is because of the way in which the economic and moral conflicts surrounding Mrs Gordon are largely displaced onto questions of gender. The 'problem' posed, in the end, by Mrs Gordon is not her economic privilege or her moral zeal but rather her occupation of an 'unnatural' masculine role. Hence, the solution to the community's problems, and the resolution of the plot, involves her comeuppance and subsequent acceptance of a 'proper' female role. First, this involves Daniel's refusal to accept eviction and threat to sue her for libel unless she hands over ownership of the newspaper to her husband (and provides her tenants with twenty-year leases). This is then followed by the stirring of her hen-pecked husband, Harold (Charles Fagan), who, when encouraged by Daniel to give her 'two black eyes', looks as though he intends to strangle his wife before forcibly removing her false teeth. Thus, by the end of the film Mrs Gordon has been removed from the workplace (the newspaper office) and, dressed in a more 'feminine' fashion than before, is seen sitting contentedly beside Rose and her new-born baby. This, in turn, has a parallel in the 'taming' of Daniel's man-hating niece Susan (Elma Hayward), who declares that she has 'as much use for men as a cow has for a concertina' and whose scheming (including the throwing away of Daniel's trousers) has been responsible for much of the film's comic action. Inspired by the events around him, the slow-witted

---

116. Censor's Decision Reserve Books, Film Censors Office 3, National Archives Ireland (NAI) 98/28/13, p. 3730, no. 11061.

Archie (Terence Grainger) kisses Susan and insists they should be married, while Daniel proudly declares him to be 'a man'.

The exception to this general drift is the treatment of Daniel himself. Unlike the original play, in which he appears to be a reasonably staid farmer, Daniel is something of a dreamer who wanders the countryside leaving his niece and farmhand, Jamie (Charles Owens), to do the work. Thus, while marriage to Rose marks something of a belated entry to adulthood, it is also a kind of 'emasculation'. At the film's end, Susan warns that it won't be him who'll be wearing 'the breeks' and, in the concluding scene, we see him washing the baby's nappies while Rose and Mrs Gordon look on. This is of interest because it is the only one of the films in which the Hayward character actually gets married. Indeed, in *The Luck of the Irish* the character of Sam Mulhern is consciously striving to avoid marriage to the Widow Whistler by encouraging the sergeant to wed her instead. In *The Star of Ulster*, which takes its cue from the shop scenes in *The Luck of the Irish*, the rather sedate – and contentedly married – Andy McDade of the original pamphlet has now become a bachelor. In *Devil's Rock*, in which Hayward resumes the role of Sam Mulhern, the character has no wish to settle down (and confesses his contentment that the local widow should have married someone else). While connected to the popular stereotype of the 'Ulster bachelor' contained in the 'Ulster kitchen comedy' (and itself rooted in patterns of farm ownership), Hayward's persona also reflects an ambivalence towards social responsibility that partly derives from the films' reliance upon the conventions of romanticism. Robert B. Ray, for example, has suggested the way in which Hollywood films (such as the Western) are often structured around an opposition between 'official' and 'outlaw' values. Thus, while we are encouraged to admire the characters who uphold the official values of the community (marriage, law and order, trade) it is often the characters who resist settling down who exert the main dramatic or emotional hold upon us.[117] Adopting a similar perspective, it may be seen how the characters played by Hayward assist the community (by helping the young lovers to get married in both *The Luck of the Irish* and *The Early Bird*, by supporting Sir Brian and Mr Gordon in the same films) but also remain partly detached from it or reluctant to participate fully in it. Thus, at the end of *The Luck of the Irish*, the young couple drive off, while the camera holds on Sam, left on his own looking down the road after them. Even more strikingly, Sam turns down the offer of a well-paid job at the end of *Devil's Rock*, preferring instead to take to the road with his dog.

In this way, the films' dependence upon romantic conventions that downplay the need for work helps to undermine the efforts of the films to imbue their vision of Ulster rural life with Protestant industriousness. Two aspects of this are worth emphasising. As has already been noted, the aesthetic of the films is partly governed by the touristic desire to display local scenery and landscape. The 'tourist gaze', in this respect, necessarily involves a break from routine in which the places that are gazed upon provide, as John Urry puts it, 'contrasts with work'.[118] Therefore, in seeking to render Ulster scenery attractive to potential visitors, these films inevitably gravitate towards a way of looking at the land

---

117. Robert B. Ray, *A Certain Tendency of the Hollywood Cinema, 1930–1980* (Princeton: Princeton University Press, 1985), pp. 58–9.

118. John Urry, *The Tourist Gaze*, 2nd edn (London: Sage, 2002), p. 3.

Ambivalence towards the
community: Sam Mulhern
(Richard Hayward) on his
own at the end of *The Luck of
the Irish*

derived from tourism and romanticism that associates it with leisure (singing, courtship) rather than
work and ownership. This also holds consequences for the films' project of generating a distinctive
'Ulster' (and Protestant) rural imagery. John Wilson Foster, for example, suggests how certain northern Protestant writers (such as the novelist Shan Bullock) have drawn a contrast between the 'wildness' of the land associated with the Catholic Irish and the cultivated, or 'Protestantised', land upon
which human labour has imposed order.[119] Whatever the actual merits of this distinction, it is
nonetheless a route that is unavailable to the Hayward films given their (tourist) emphasis upon the
picturesque aspects of landscape and resulting lack of interest in physical labour and cultivation.[120]

---

119. John Wilson Foster, *Forces and Themes in Ulster Fiction* (Dublin: Gill and Macmillan, 1974), p. 34. The historical roots
     of this distinction may be traced back to what Stephen Howe refers to as an 'early English legitimisation' of
     'colonial enterprise' in terms of a 'post-reformation . . . doctrine of entitlement through industry' whereby 'only by
     mixing his labour with the soil could a man justly claim rights to ownership of that soil' (*Ireland and Empire*, p. 24).

120. This emphasis upon the picturesque aspects of landscape may also be associated with the nostalgic address of other
     films of this period. *Wings of the Morning* (1937), for example, uses a song by John McCormack as the pretext for a
     short montage of shots of Irish scenery intended, presumably, for Irish audiences in Britain and the US. Ruth
     Barton notes a similar sequence in *My Irish Molly* (1938) in her discussion of British films partly aimed at the Irish
     immigrant audience in Britain. See *Irish National Cinema* (London: Routledge, 2004), pp. 56–8.

These points also connect to the representation of shops and small businesses contained in the films. For while the image of the shop, with its associated virtues of trade and self-reliant enterprise, carries a resonance across Britain (and beyond), it has nevertheless held a particular appeal for literary portraits of Protestant 'Ulster'. David Kennedy, for example, notes the 'glorification of the wee shop' contained in St John Ervine's play *Boyd's Shop* (1936) and the special appeal that it has held for 'Presbyterian Ulster'.[121] In this play, the shop not only symbolises the virtues of trade but also a sense of family tradition and moral integrity that even the church is seen to lack. However, as Foster's discussion of Ervine's novels suggests, this image of the 'wee shop' is also tinged with ambivalence. As he points out, the 'sense of place' and tradition attached to the shop is 'both a good (suggesting security and ancestral pride) and an evil (suggesting staid provincialism and unadventurousness)'.[122] In a sense, it is this same tension that films such as *The Luck of the Irish* and *Devil's Rock* suggest when they also draw upon this image of the shop. For while the films may appear to uphold the sober virtues of Protestant Ulster (trade, service to the community, matrimony), they also celebrate, by virtue of their resort to traditional romantic conventions, a certain playfulness and distance from the work ethic (in the form of song and dance, wanderlust and a refusal of responsibility and respectability). It is probably significant, therefore, that when Sam walks off at the end of *Devil's Rock*, he is accompanied by a musician playing the uillean pipes. The character has not appeared previously in the film and is played by R. L. O'Mealy, a traditional Irish musician who had taken part in the BBC radio programme *Irish Nights*. His introduction, and association with Sam's wandering, therefore, seems to dramatise, almost self-consciously, a certain tension between the romantic lure of Catholic nationalist 'Irishness', on the one hand, and the comparative stolidity of 'Protestant Ulster', on the other.

Irish and Proud of It

As previously suggested, because of the need to sell the Hayward/Pedelty films abroad, there were increasing commercial pressures upon them to conform to certain pre-given images of Ireland as 'unspoiled' and 'primitive'. Thus, in comparison to *The Luck of the Irish*, in which one of Sam Mulhern's many jobs is as a chauffeur, there is a complete absence of modern transport in *The Early Bird*. Most of the characters ride bikes, while the wealthiest woman in the village, Mrs Gordon, appears to go everywhere on foot. This elimination of the modern is further extended in *Irish and Proud of It*. Given that it was shot at Clogher Head in County Louth, this film is the least Northern Irish of the three Crusade productions and is also the most eccentric. Richard Hayward abandons his persona of the simple rustic in favour of a dapper, if jaded, London-Irish businessman, Donagh O'Connor, who is dropped in his birthplace by some aviator friends weary of his nostalgic speechifying about Ireland and his irksome claim that they lack 'the guts to go home'. Despatched to the village of Ballyvoraine in this way, he then wanders through the film in full evening dress rather than the soft hat, waistcoat and collarless shirt familiar from pre-

---

121.   Kennedy, 'The Drama in Ulster', p. 62. A song actually entitled 'The Wee Shop' is sung in both *The Luck of the Irish* and *Devil's Rock* in addition to making an appearance in Hayward's novel, *Sugarhouse Entry*.

122.   Foster, *Forces and Themes*, pp. 130–1. Interestingly enough, for all his attachment to place, Hayward also describes himself as 'a confirmed wanderer and extreme individualist' in *Ulster and the City of Belfast*, p. 18.

The cast of *Irish and Proud of It*, including Richard Hayward in evening dress

vious roles. As for the village itself, he finds it is in the grip of a gang of illicit still operators, under the unlikely leadership of a Chicago gangster, Mike Finnegan (George Pembroke), who suspects him of being a government agent sent from Dublin to investigate their activities.

While in some ways the most technically well executed of the films, it is also the crudest ideologically in terms of its portrait of contemporary Ireland. Whereas the previous two films focused primarily on the internal dynamics of the local community, the narrative of *Irish and Proud of It* is mainly concerned with the impact of two 'outsiders' – O'Connor and Finnegan – on the life of the village. While the men's relationships with the villagers – one benign, the other malign – are clearly opposed, the men nevertheless share a background of urban-industrial modernity that contrasts with the experience of traditional village life. O'Connor is a successful businessman who has made his fortune through the manufacture of modern, scientifically based food concentrates. His sentimental desire to return to the village where he was born is therefore based upon a clear opposition between the enervating demands of modern (urban-industrial) living and the assumed simplicities of rural life. This is emphasised in the way that the village is portrayed. When O'Connor arrives in Ballyvoraine, he discovers a place where, apart from the arrival of gangsters, time has largely stood still. The village is apparently devoid of modern forms of communication and transport and O'Connor is unable to locate either a telephone or a taxi. Most of the villagers travel on foot and follow O'Connor around as though he were some form of exotic species. As with *The Luck of the Irish*, there is little evidence of work and the main social activities appear to consist of drinking, singing and fighting. However, in comparison to the earlier films, there is also an increased sense of the austerity (and indeed poverty) of village life, as well as a greater emphasis upon the 'wildness' of the surrounding landscape.

Significantly, this landscape is associated with the daughter of a small farmer, Moira Flaherty (Dinah Sheridan), who discovers O'Connor while walking the fields. Described as a 'bonny colleen' in the British trade press, Moira's innocence and simplicity proves immediately attractive to O'Connor and appears to vindicate his wish to return.[123] As with many subsequent films involving Ireland, the returning exile is, in this way, involved in an encounter with a beautiful woman whose closeness to the land and nature appears to embody the 'authentic' spirit of Ireland. There is, in this respect, some anticipation of one of the best known of Irish-theme films, *The Quiet Man* (1952), in which John Wayne's Irish-American exile Sean returns to his place of birth and meets Maureen O'Hara's Mary Kate. However, whereas in *The Quiet Man*, Mary Kate mediates Sean's entry into the community (through his submission to its long-established courtship rituals), O'Connor remains an outsider in *Irish and Proud of It*. As with other characters played by Hayward, he helps to solve the community's problems – by ridding the village of the bootleggers and reuniting Moira with her sweetheart Sean (Liam Gaffney) – but then has to depart. In this respect, the film follows *The Luck of the Irish* in making a deliberate pitch to the American audience. O'Connor is recruited by an Irish-American business magnate to travel (albeit reluctantly) to America where his singing is destined to make him a radio star.

Despite the film's own confidence in Hayward's appeal to American audiences, the response to the film in the United States was poor. *The New York Times* thought it '[n]aive and sentimental' and too heavily reliant upon 'the staples of Irish films'.[124] Others were actively offended. The *Irish Echo* described the film as 'a disgrace to the Irish race' and called for a Board of Censors selected from New York Irish societies to take action against its 'defamation' of the Irish character.[125] The *Gaelic American* was equally outraged, claiming that:

> Irish producers seem to subscribe to the quaint theory that Irish romance can best be portrayed on the screen by a series of drunken brawls . . . They picture lovely Irish girls frequenting the lowest dives and drinking almost as heavily as the men . . . to convey to American audiences the idea that Ireland is a land of poverty, dirts and drunks.[126]

---

123. *Daily Film Renter*, 31 October 1936, p. 4.

124. *The New York Times*, 3 November 1938.

125. 'Not So Proud', *Irish Echo*, 12 November 1938.

126. *Irish News*, 26 November 1938, p. 3. The New York *Gaelic American* had been centrally involved in the campaign against the Hollywood film, *The Callahans and the Murphys* (1927), which, according to Frank Walsh, had first revealed the power of 'united action' by 'Irish and Catholic organizations' within the US. (See *Sin and Censorship: The Catholic Church and the Motion Picture Industry* [New Haven: Yale University Press, 1996], pp. 36–45.) Partly due to the improving economic position of the Irish-American middle class, the portrait of the Irish in Hollywood as 'backward' continued to be a matter of some sensitivity. The criticisms of *Irish and Proud of It* therefore follow closely those directed against John Ford's *The Informer* (1935), which Gregory Black reports was attacked for its scenes of 'drinking', 'poverty' and 'violence', as well as its insult to 'Celtic womanhood', in *Hollywood Censored: Morality Codes, Catholics, and the Movies* (Cambridge: Cambridge University Press, 1994), p. 298.

Dinah Sheridan as the 'bonny colleen' Moira in *Irish and Proud of It*

Hayward himself was sanguine about such criticisms, claiming they were the work of 'sentimental Americans' who sought images of 'a fantastic Ireland that does not exist'.[127] However, while it is certainly possible to detect a nostalgic desire for more idealised images of Ireland, and especially Irish womanhood, in these attacks, it is significant that they also carry echoes of Hayward's own criticisms of the 'stage Irishman'. It will be recalled that Hayward had previously decried the 'false impressions' that the cinema had given of 'modern Ireland' and explained how he had sought to avoid stereotypes of the Irish drunk.[128] The publicity material for *The Early Bird* had also promised that 'those who hoped to see promiscuous brawling, fighting and other alleged Irish mannerisms' would be 'disappointed'. However, this could hardly be said of *Irish and Proud of It*, which, in an ambivalent advertisement for Bushmills whiskey, features Jimmy Mageean in a prominent role as Moira's alcoholic father and concludes with a brawl in a public house. As in *The Quiet Man*, this violence may be regarded as a form of community ritual that helps dissolve social conflicts (and permits O'Connor to express urges denied him in 'civilised'

127. *Irish News*, 26 November 1938, p. 3.

128. *Montreal Gazette*, 30 April 1936.

society). However, lacking the later film's self-consciousness, *Irish and Proud of It* displays a much greater willingness to embrace the conventional tropes of Irish 'backwardness' and marks a significant retreat from Hayward's earlier ambitions. Indeed, Hayward appears to have admitted as much when he later told the press that a 'certain non-Irish element and a preference for the stage Irishman, introducing drunken men and pigs' in his films had been the result of interference from Paramount.[129]

As it turned out, *Irish and Proud of It* was to be the last collaboration between Hayward and Crusade. It is not entirely clear why this was so. The negative reaction to *Irish and Proud of It* among the very audience to which it was supposed to appeal may have been a factor. Pedelty may also have felt that, after three films, the seam of Irish rural comedy was exhausted and it was time to move on to other kinds of film (which included two more with his 'discovery', Dinah Sheridan).[130] The industrial climate was also changing and the Cinematograph Films Act of 1938 was set to introduce a cost test for quota films (intended to eliminate the 'quota quickie'). As a result, Hayward was now left to find alternative backing and his rate of production, of necessity, slowed. His first project was the UIDA-backed *The Star of Ulster*, made at Wembley in December 1936. This, however, was only a ten-minute short and his ambition remained the making of features. Despite his Ulster allegiances, he sought the support of the Free State government, declaring, in February 1937, his willingness 'to set up a Film Industry in the Free State' if backing was forthcoming.[131] This idea, however, came to nought and it was not until August 1937 that he was once again ready to go into production with *Devil's Rock*.

Devil's Rock

At a press lunch in November, Hayward indicated the film's novelty. It was, he indicated, 'a personal, private enterprise' and had been 'made entirely in Northern Ireland'. This, he suggested, was partly in response to criticisms of his earlier films 'that they did not show enough of Ulster'. 'I have tried to meet this criticism', he continued, 'by making this picture entirely here.' However, as there were no film studios in Northern Ireland, this had consequences for how the film could be shot. He commissioned his old friend Victor Haddick to write 'a scenario with a minimum of interior work' and shot virtually the whole film 'in the open'. He also acquired a new kind of microphone that would permit the recording of natural sound.[132]

The film itself was shot in the Cushendun area along the north Antrim coast and mainly involved local personnel. The original intention appears to have been that Hayward should both produce and direct but, in the end, Germain, or 'Jimmy', Burger, the cameraman on Hayward's previous two films, took on the task of directing. The plot involves the exploits of Sam Mulhern (Richard Hayward), a local sheep-drover, who has the idea of organising a concert so that Mrs Huggins (Nancy Cullen), a local widow who manages the beach huts, can open a tea-shop. As in *The Luck of the Irish*, there is also a romantic subplot involving a visiting businessman, John

---

129. *Irish News*, 30 November 1937, p. 7.

130. His former colleague, Victor Greene, did proceed, however, to produce *The Londonderry Air* (1938) for 20th
        Century-Fox, which included both Jimmy Mageean and Liam Gaffney from *Irish and Proud of It* in the cast.

131. 'Hayward Wants Government Aid', *Kine Weekly*, 18 February 1937, p. 22.

132. *Irish News*, 30 November 1937, p. 7.

Browne (Terence Grainger), and a local woman Geraldine Lamour (Geraldine Mitchell), who is holidaying with her younger sister, Veronica (Gloria Grainger). The film's title is taken from the rock on which Veronica becomes stranded near the film's end, before she is rescued by Sam and the rest of the villagers. Inevitably, given the constraints under which the film was shot, the film displays some unusual characteristics. As Hayward indicates, there are virtually no indoor scenes (apart from the concert) and most of the action – including a scene at the local school – occurs outside. Given the staging of virtually all of the action in the open, this inevitably reinforces the sense of a simple rural community that is at one with nature. As in previous representations, the 'naturalness' of this community (and its corresponding absence of social division) is reinforced not only by the easy intermingling of different social strata but also by the scenes of the villagers coming together near the end of the film to help Veronica (and engage in what the publicity at the time referred to as 'community shouting'). As such the film possesses clear affinities with traditional portraits of Ireland as a simple rural paradise and the film itself goes so far as to describe the village of Craigadown, in which the action is set, as 'a little bit of heaven on the coast of Ireland' in an opening title.

This portrait is, however, complicated by the film's ending, which signals a decisive retreat from the heightened 'primitivism' of the previous film. Browne, it transpires, has been involved in a survey of the Irish coastline in order to identify a suitable location for a luxury hotel. Following Veronica's rescue, he announces his decision to make Craigadown a tourist centre and a montage of modern tourist amenities – including a new swimming pool (described as 'the finest' in Ireland) and golf course – then follows. To a contemporary observer, this looks very much like commercial despoliation of the very landscape and coastline celebrated in the earlier parts of the film. Viewed in context, however, it is clear that it is intended to celebrate not only contemporary Ulster's prosperity (and business enterprise) but also its combination of natural scenic beauty with modern – rather than primitive – facilities. As with Conor (and his poster for the UTDA) discussed earlier, it is assumed that while visitors to Ulster may wish to see the 'beauty spots' of Ulster, they do not necessarily expect 'to rough it in discomfort'!

However, the most striking feature of the film is the extent to which it pursues its twin aims of showcasing music and scenery. As previously noted, the earlier films had tended to deviate from 'classical' conventions of narrative and style in the way that they emphasised the display of scenery and musical performance at the expense of the forward movement of the plot. In *Devil's Rock*, however, this tendency becomes so magnified that it assumes the characteristics of what Tom Gunning has described, with reference to early American cinema, as a 'cinema of attractions'. 'Rather than narrative development based on active characters within detailed fictional environments, the cinema of attractions', he suggests, 'presented a series of curious or novel views to a spectator' consisting, *inter alia*, of 'non-fictional actualities' (including 'natural wonders'), 'vaudeville acts' and 'trick films'.[133] Although Gunning associates the 'cinema of attractions' with a specific period (pre-1908), he is also at pains to identify the survival of 'attractions' within 'classical' narrative cinema. 'The desire to display may interact with the

---

133. Tom Gunning, 'Early American Cinema', in John Hill and Pamela Church Gibson (eds), *The Oxford Guide to Film Studies* (Oxford: Oxford University Press, 1998), p. 258.

Richard Hayward returns to the role of the simple rustic in the first feature film to be shot entirely in Northern Ireland, *Devil's Rock*

desire to tell a story', he argues, and the 'subordination' of 'attractions' to 'narrative integration' will vary from film to film.[134] In the case of *Devil's Rock*, however, the relationship character-istic of 'classical' cinema is virtually reversed and it is the narrative that is subordinated to, or provides a bare pretext for, the display of 'attractions'. Thus, while the film does, of course, pro-vide a coherent fictional world and a set of recognisable characters, it possesses only the barest of plots and pays little attention to narrative development (as in Sam's organisation of the con-cert or the capture of the thieves). Even the film's narrative climax – the rescue of Veronica – is itself a kind of sensational 'attraction', given the way it is suddenly introduced into the film without adequate narrative preparation. The predominant logic of the film, therefore, is less a carefully plotted unfolding of the action than the presentation, or showing, of precisely the kind of 'attractions' identified by Gunning: local scenery (Northern Ireland's very own 'natural won-ders'), musical numbers (including not only Sam's ballads but also a string of actual 'vaudeville

---

134. Tom Gunning '"Now You See It, Now You Don't": The Temporality of the Cinema of Attractions', *The Velvet Light Trap*, no. 32, Autumn 1993, p. 4. He also notes that, in certain genres, such as the musical, the attractions 'threaten to mutiny' (ibid.).

acts' during the concert) and optical 'tricks' (obtrusive optical transitions and wipes involving diamonds and rectangles).

Two main drives are at work here. As previously noted, the first is fundamentally touristic in outlook, motivating the display of Northern Ireland's scenic attractions. The second may be described as 'balladeering' in character, involving 'performances' of songs and ballads that 'promote' local culture and speech. These are, however, interlinked. A good example is provided by the sequence that follows the first encounter between Sam and the police sergeant (Charles Fagan), when John and Geraldine are shown walking, arm in arm, along the shore. There is a subsequent shot of the couple from inside a cave that initially provides a decorative 'frame within a frame'. However, the camera then loses its interest in the couple and, as they depart the frame, it pans across the inside of the cave. A montage of eleven shots, consisting of various unrelated views of countryside, picturesque buildings and ruins, then follows. While this occurs, Hayward is heard singing 'The Rose of Tralee' on the soundtrack. Although the song is loosely inspired by Sam's apparent sighting of the couple, they are not seen from his point of view but from a visually pleasing perspective that does not correspond to any character's look. So, while, as in *The Luck of the Irish*, the film makes use of a romantic couple (a staple of classical cinema), the film is largely unconcerned with private desire (or, indeed, psychologised narrative). Its interests – and attention – reside much more in scenery and song, which, in effect, become detached from the plot. This leads, in turn, to an aesthetic of display in which close-ups, point-of-view shots and reverse-field cutting (that would 'psychologise' space) are, by and large, missing and the address to the spectator is much less mediated by plot and character.

In his discussion of the use of the zoom, Paul Willemen suggests how certain kinds of stylistic obtrusiveness may signal 'a nostalgia for pre-modern types of public narratorial performance'.[135] In the same way, it is certainly possible to argue that the aesthetic adopted by *Devil's Rock* involves an attempt to reconcile contemporary narrative conventions with the traditions of public performance associated with the ballad singer so admired by Hayward. However, while this may be the case, the film – along with its predecessors – was mainly regarded as falling short of Hollywood-style classicism and criticised for being 'primitive' and slow.[136] *Kine Weekly* complained that the film consisted of 'a naive story . . . naively put over', while the *Monthly Film Bulletin* criticised the production as 'halting and uncertain', arguing that there was an 'incompleteness in all the incidents and a tiresome dragging in of "local colour"'.[137] Even loyal supporters expressed their doubts. Alexander Boath, of the *Daily Express*, reported his disappointment with the film, which he considered unlikely to achieve commercial success. 'The story was poor, the continuity slipshod and the whole atmosphere unreal,' he went on.[138] While

---

135. Paul Willemen, 'The Zoom in Popular Cinema: A Question of Performance', *New Cinemas: The Journal of Contemporary Film*, vol. 1, no. 1, 2002, p. 13.

136. Thus, in the US, there had already been criticism of *The Luck of the Irish* for its 'old-fashioned treatment, slow tempo and general lack of modernism' in *Film Daily*, 6 February 1936.

137. *Kine Weekly*, 10 March 1938, p. 26; *Monthly Film Bulletin*, 31 March 1938, p. 69.

138. *Daily Express*, 4 December 1937. As in the case of *The Luck of the Irish*, he was also concerned about the integrity of the film's 'Ulster' identity. 'It was an "all-Ulster production",' he continued, 'but the title was in Irish, with the English translation bracketed beneath', a feature he attributed to the film's attempt to appeal to audiences in the south of Ireland.

the response in Northern Ireland was rather more sympathetic, the *Belfast Telegraph* still felt obliged to report that the film's story was 'unsophisticated in the extreme'.[139]

Given this largely unfavourable reaction to the film, and the lack of a distributor outside Ireland, it was perhaps to be expected that this was the last of the Hayward features. While, in September 1937, the *Northern Whig* had observed that it was 'pleasing to see that in one direction at least Ulster are loyal to local "products"' and that 'the Ulster film industry can produce pictures to compete in the open market', this was hardly the case.[140] The 'Ulster' audience, no matter how 'loyal', was of insufficient size to sustain a profitable film industry, while the films' low budgets and lack of stars made their appeal to audiences elsewhere extremely limited. Following the release of *Devil's Rock*, there was talk in the press of a possible merger of Hayward's company with Tom Cooper's Hibernia Company (responsible for *The Dawn* [1936]) and Jimmy O'Dea's O'D Productions (responsible for *Blarney* [1938]).[141] These plans, however, came to nothing.

Although *Devil's Rock* was Hayward's last Northern Ireland feature, it was not his last film and he continued, for the next few years, to engage in the production of travelogues and documentaries. The first of these was *In the Footsteps of St Patrick*, a short film dealing with places associated with the life of St Patrick, which was trade shown in Dublin in March 1939 and then in Belfast in July. Although it includes scenes from both sides of the border, the film was mainly devoted to the North and reflected Hayward's continuing enthusiasm for Ulster scenery and songs.[142] According to the *Belfast News-Letter*, the film successfully captured 'the spirit of our exquisitely simple countryside' and was likely to do much 'to strengthen the consciousness of Ulster'.[143] However, since partition, St Patrick, and the celebration of St Patrick's Day, had become increasingly associated with Irish nationalism and Catholicism. Thus, despite Hayward's unionism, and concern to reclaim St Patrick for 'Ulster', the film still acquired a reputation for being 'a bit "rebel"' when it was shown in Belfast at the Classic.[144]

The film was photographed by Louis Morrison, who had acted as stills cameraman on *Devil's Rock*. Morrison had been involved in film in Northern Ireland for a number of years. In the 1920s, he was involved in plans for a local film company, Associated Irish Films, which planned to work with local drama groups, such as the Ulster Players and Northern Drama League, on film versions of plays by local writers, including Lynn Doyle, St John Ervine and Richard Rowley.[145] The coming of sound appears to have put paid to these ideas and Morrison sub-

139. *Belfast Telegraph*, 30 November 1937.

140. *Northern Whig*, 1 September 1937, p. 10.

141. *Kine Weekly*, 30 December 1937, p. 17.

142. The *Irish Press* (11 March 1939) reported that the film contained 'over a dozen Ulster folk songs', while the *Northern Whig Weekly* (29 July 1939) praised the film's many '"shots" of the lovely Ulster countryside'.

143. *Belfast News-Letter*, 26 July 1939.

144. The phrase belongs to the Belfast projectionist, George Shanahan, in an interview with Liam O'Leary, 11 November 1980 (PRONI T.P.27). The film was also praised by the nationalist critic Liam MacGabhann as the best of 'all the previous Irish travel films by a long way'. Writing in the *Irish Press* (14 March 1939), he declared 'Richard Hayward, poet, songster, actor, producer, novelist, is a man out of Orange Ulster. And God bless this more than Irish Ulsterman, say I, for showing us how things are done.'

145. *The Bioscope*, 19 September 1928, p. 64.

sequently became the secretary of an amateur film guild, the Provincial Film Society of Northern Ireland, involving the local playwright C. K. Ayre (Charles Kerr) and photographer Charles Haig. Formed with the purpose of 'producing Film Plays of Ulster, Irish and general interest' utilising 'local talent and ability', the group shot some documentary material, including footage of the Tourist Trophy Motor Race, and embarked upon a professional production entitled 'Kitty of Coleraine'.[146] Although the Society undertook 'experimental "shoots"', and launched a search for 'young women with pretty faces', this project does not appear to have come to fruition.[147] Subsequently, Morrison became the moving spirit behind the establishment of the cinemagazine, *Ulster Movie Sound News*. The first public screening of this took place in Belfast in May 1937 and dealt with events in Northern Ireland during Coronation week. A second (showing the Trooping of the Colour at Ballykinler, RUC sports at Balmoral and the motor race at Ballyclare) and a third (dealing with the Royal visit by the newly crowned King George VI) followed.[148] Morrison planned a monthly 'Ulster Movie News Journal' and sought assistance from the Ministry of Commerce under new legislation designed to attract new industries to Northern Ireland (the New Industries Act of 1937). The Ministry was sceptical whether film fell within the scope of this measure and recommended Morrison to contact both the UIDA and UTDA, for whom Morrison offered to make a tourist film free of cost.[149] Morrison also had ambitions to produce 'full length and short films', beginning with the St Patrick film (which he developed in association with the writer Harry S. Gibson).[150] The film that resulted, *In the Footsteps of St Patrick*, lay the basis for further collaboration between Morrison and Hayward and, in August 1939, the two men, accompanied by Germain Burger (the director of *Devil's Rock*), set off on a journey down the River Shannon as part of their project, *Where the Shannon Flows Down to the Sea*. This resulted in both a short film, released in 1940, as well as an accompanying book, *Where the River Shannon Flows* (written by Hayward with illustrations by Morrison). Over the next few years other travelogue films and books followed, including *Lough Corrib* (1942) and *In the Kingdom of Kerry* (1945), focused mainly on Killarney.

Conclusion

This chapter has discussed the first 'indigenous' film production in Northern Ireland and the way that this was linked to a concern to promote the distinctive character of 'Ulster'. However, partly because of the films' links with tourism, partly because of the commercial pressures at work (and the expectations of audiences in Britain and the US) and partly because of the films' employment of romantic conventions more commonly associated with the representation of the

---

146. *Northern Whig*, 7 January 1929, p. 5; *The Bioscope*, 9 January 1929, p. 71.

147. *Irish News*, 4 October 1929, p. 8.

148. *Daily Express*, 22 May 1937; PRONI COM62/1/615.

149. W. D. Scott, Permanent Secretary at the Ministry of Commerce, who met Morrison, also harboured doubts regarding Morrison's technical competence. In a hand-written note, he records that he saw the third *Ulster Movie Sound News*, showing the Royal visit, at the Tonic, Bangor. 'The photography was atrocious,' he records, 'and the sound effects so bad and so obviously faked that they moved a large audience to laughter at certain points' (PRONI COM62/1/615).

150. *Today's Cinema*, 18 August 1937, p. 41.

southern (and by implication Catholic and nationalist) Irish, it has been argued that this proved a problematic enterprise. Thus, while the films were welcomed in Northern Ireland as manifestations of 'Ulster' film, they were widely regarded as straightforwardly (southern) 'Irish' elsewhere. In this way, the films also reveal some of the difficulties faced by northern unionists in accommodating prevailing conceptions of both 'Britishness' and 'Irishness', neither of which appeared to offer a cultural identity to which they were ideologically suited. This may be one reason why the use of predominantly rural images in the 1930s films did not always pass without criticism within Northern Ireland. In a letter to the *Irish News*, a correspondent complained that 'we have seen the Ulster-Irish filmed *ad nauseam* in comedy and satire, exaggerating "quaint" and "picturesque" features of a bygone age'. The film 'that could portray industrial and cultural Ulster', he continued, 'still remains unmade'.[151] With the onset of the Second World War, however, a cinematic image of 'industrial Ulster' did begin to emerge. Why this occurred, and with what ideological consequences, will be discussed in Chapter 3.

---

151. John M. Davidson, 'Unknown Ulster', *Irish News*, 31 May 1938, p. 2.

2

'Ulster will fight again'

Cinema and Censorship in the 1930s

While film production in Northern Ireland began in the 1920s and 1930s, and displayed a concern to elaborate an 'Ulster' identity, a more general interest in film and its impact upon local society was also evident during this period. As in the rest of the United Kingdom, the 1930s witnessed a substantial growth in cinema audiences and cinema-building following the coming of sound. The Picture House in Royal Avenue hosted the first commercial screening of a 'talkie' (Al Jolson's *The Singing Fool*) in April 1929 and also became Belfast's first 'super-cinema' when it was acquired by Paramount in 1930 and was redesigned to accommodate 3,000 (compared with 800 before).[1] New builds in both the centre of Belfast and across the suburbs followed, reaching a peak in December 1936, when no less than three new cinemas – the Curzon, the Park and the Broadway – all opened on the same day.[2] This was paralleled by the spread of new cinemas across Northern Ireland and included the opening in 1936 of the Tonic in Bangor (the cinema that was subsequently to feature in Richard Hayward's *Devil's Rock*). As a result of these developments, there were over one hundred permanent cinemas in Northern Ireland by the end of 1936.[3] Although this meant that there were actually fewer cinemas per head of population than the UK average, there can be little doubt that cinemagoing in Northern Ireland (and Belfast in particular) was increasing and that it constituted a major leisure activity for much of the population (and the Belfast working class in particular). S. Rowson indicates that the figures for cinema admissions in Britain averaged twenty-two visits per year in 1934 and, although no equivalent figures for Northern Ireland appear to exist, it is likely that average attendances in Northern Ireland were not far behind.[4] Given these circumstances, it was hardly surprising that both the content and possible effects of the films shown in these cinemas were destined to become the source of political and moral controversy during the 1930s. Thus, while Alexander Walker optimistically claims that the cinema in Northern Ireland was 'amazingly free of opposition or cant from church or

---

1. *Northern Whig*, 3 December 1930, p. 11.

2. Michael Open, *Fading Lights, Silver Screens: A History of Belfast Cinemas* (Antrim: Greystone Books, 1985), p. 8.

3. Parliament of Northern Ireland, *Parliamentary Debates: Official Report*, House of Commons (HC), vol. xix, col. 113, 26 November 1936.

4. S. Rowson, 'A Statistical Survey of the Cinema Industry in Great Britain in 1934', *Journal of the Royal Statistical Society*, vol. 99, 1936, p. 70.

chapel' and permitted 'common fantasy' to overcome 'daily schisms', this was clearly not the case.[5]

Defending Ulster: the campaign for cinema censorship

In the early years of the Northern Ireland state, cinema exhibition mainly attracted political interest on the occasion of the annual budget. Under the Government of Ireland Act, the United Kingdom government retained control of the bulk of taxation (as well as most aspects of trade). However, the Northern Ireland government was permitted to set and collect a small range of taxes, including entertainment duties, which, as a result, were typically higher in Northern Ireland than in Britain.[6] This, in turn, led to regular appeals in the Northern Ireland House of Commons for reductions. Although such appeals were mainly made on behalf of the cinema proprietors, whom it was contended were faced with financial hardships, opponents of the tax also spoke up on behalf of the cinemagoer. In 1927, for example, the nationalist MP Joseph Devlin made a particularly impassioned plea on behalf of those 'who work in the mills and factories' and, for whom, the cinema provided 'some glimmer of brightness and cheer in the grimness of their daily toil'.[7] Significantly, while Hugh Pollock, the Unionist Minister of Finance, expressed some sympathy for the owners (whom he had met earlier in the year), he was much less moved by the plight of factory workers. Permitting the defence of his economic policies to stray into moralism, he argued (with reference to a proposal to exempt outdoor sports from the tax) that:

> it must be in the interest of the Government to encourage anything that will help to develop the physical strength of the people, rather than to encourage those who go to a heated atmosphere to watch an exhibition of pictures that is not always . . . desirable for a great number of the young people who attend.[8]

Suspicion of the 'undesirable' effects of cinema was not, of course, uncommon in either Britain or Ireland. However, given the rapid spread of cinema in Northern Ireland during the 1930s, it was inevitable that arguments about the 'desirability' of cinema in general and of individual films

---

5. Michael Open, 'Foreword', *Fading Lights, Silver Screens*, p. vii. Walker's comments may be contrasted with those of a visitor to Belfast during the Second World War. '[O]ne finds that the human business of entertainment of the people is governed', he reports, 'by religious politics. The Presbyterians don't like that film. Black-garbed, shock-faced ministers tell the manager to take it off . . . The Catholics . . .? Not much of it from them. Only the remnants of what is politely known as "an illegal Organisation" make trouble' (Melchior A. A. Sinkins, *Kine Weekly*, 13 January 1944, p. 80).

6. For more detail on Northern Ireland taxation policy, see Patrick Buckland, *The Factory of Grievances: Devolved Government in Northern Ireland 1921–39* (Dublin: Gill and Macmillan, 1970), pp. 81–3.

7. *Parliamentary Debates* (HC), vol. 8, col. 1612, 19 May 1927. Devlin's comments may well have been born of a recognition that Catholic men and women (many of whom worked in the linen industry) earned on average less than their Protestant counterparts. See A. C. Hepburn, *A Past Apart: Studies in the History of Catholic Belfast 1850-1950* (Belfast: Ulster Historical Foundation, 1996), ch. 6.

8. *Parliamentary Debates* (HC), vol. 8, col. 1624, 19 May 1927.

in particular should acquire an extra urgency. As one local Protestant minister was to complain in 1935, 'Belfast has gone kinema mad . . . and craving for this thing is like the craving for alcohol'.[9]

Moreover, while the controversies surrounding film partly echoed similar disputes in Britain and the rest of Ireland, they also acquired a particular intensity in the case of Northern Ireland. In her history of British cinema in the 1930s, for example, Rachael Low notes how opponents of the cinema could be 'moved to hysterical incoherence by imaginary horrors'.[10] What she does not point out, however, is that her example – deliberately chosen for its extremity – is taken from an address by a Northern Ireland cleric (Canon D. H. Hall) to the Church of Ireland General Synod in Belfast in 1932.[11] Outbursts such as these were not, of course, unusual in Northern Ireland and acquired a particular potency as a result of the intimate relationship that existed between religion, cultural identity and politics in the region. For while, as Linda Colley has indicated, Protestantism (and opposition to Catholic Europe) was central to the 'invention' of 'Britishness' in the eighteenth century, the decline of religious observance and rise of secularism in the late nineteenth century had reduced the ideological and political significance of Protestantism for Britain (and England, in particular).[12] This was hardly the case in the north of Ireland, however, where Ulster unionism's defence of its 'British' identity retained its strongly Protestant – and anti-Catholic – dimensions. As Alan Megahey points out, Ireland in the late nineteenth century was the only part of the United Kingdom in which Catholics were in a majority and in which, following the disestablishment of the Church of Ireland in 1871, there was no established Church.[13] As a result, the growing political confidence of Irish nationalism during the nineteenth century helped to unite the (Episcopalian and Presbyterian) Protestant churches in opposition to the campaign for Home Rule, which was widely regarded by them as a threat to Protestant traditions – and, of course, property – by an alien Catholicism. The subsequent partition of Ireland and close identification of the southern state with the Catholic church also ensured the strongly sectarian character of the new political arrangements in the North. As the first Northern Ireland Prime Minister, James Craig, was notoriously to comment in 1934, 'we are a Protestant Parliament and a Protestant State' (just as, he claimed, southern Ireland was proud to declare itself 'a Catholic State').[14]

Given the centrality of religion to Unionism's sense of political identity, the strength of fundamentalist forms of Protestantism and the relative smallness of Northern Irish society, the

---

9. Rev. Hunter, of the Irish Evangelical Church, quoted in *Kine Weekly*, 7 February 1935, p. 27. During this period it was common to link both drink and the cinema not only with harmful social and moral effects but also with a decline in church attendance.

10. Rachael Low, *Filmmaking in 1930s Britain* (London: George Allen and Unwin, 1985), p. 55.

11. *Northern Whig*, 12 May 1932, p. 8.

12. Linda Colley, *Britons: Forging the Nation 1707–1837* (London: Pimlico, 1992), pp. 367–9. On the nineteenth century, see James Loughlin, *Ulster Unionism and British National Identity since 1885* (London: Pinter, 1995), ch. 1.

13. Alan Megahey, '"God will defend the right": The Protestant Churches and Opposition to Home Rule', in D. George Boyce and Alan O'Day (eds), *Defenders of the Union: A Survey of British and Irish Unionism since 1801* (London: Routledge, 2001), p. 160.

14. Quoted in Patrick Buckland, *James Craig* (Dublin: Gill and Macmillan, 1980), p. 109.

Protestant churches were in a position to exercise much greater influence over politicians than was the case in Britain.[15] The power of the churches, in this regard, was demonstrated during the 1920s when the United Education Committee of the Protestant Churches successfully campaigned for clerical involvement in the appointment of school teachers and the preservation of bible teaching.[16] The crossover between religion and politics was also apparent in the activities of independent unionist organisations, which, through a combination of religious fundamentalism and social radicalism, were able to win support among the Protestant working class and, in doing so, threaten the cross-class unity upon which Ulster Unionism depended. The Local Option Party, led by the Rev. A. Wylie Blue, for example, stood temperance candidates against official Unionists at the 1929 Northern Ireland parliamentary elections on a platform that linked the 'moral' issues of drinking and gambling with the 'social' issues of poverty and unemployment.

Given this strong connection between religion and politics in Northern Ireland, it is not surprising that the religious and moral campaigns directed against the cinema should have acquired a distinctive character. For although virtually all the films entering Northern Ireland had been passed and certificated by the British Board of Film Censors (BBFC), there was still a strong feeling that many films regarded as suitable for showing in Britain should not be seen in Northern Ireland. Just as Catholicism in the South could be seen to be demanding the censorship of films in order to preserve the moral purity of the Irish nation, so popular Protestantism in the North fought for increased regulation of the cinema and censorship in order to preserve what it regarded as the special moral and political character of the northern state. There was, in this respect, a degree of pride that the very forces of rationalism and secularisation that were undermining religious faith in Britain were being successfully held at bay in 'Ulster' due to the dedication of the Protestant churches and the vigour of their activities. As John D. Brewer and Gareth I. Higgins indicate, 'Bible Protestants' characteristically regard themselves as 'the faithful few', or 'holy remnant', in 'an unrighteous, sinful and secular world'.[17] For this group, therefore, the maintenance of a 'Protestant state' not only involved the defence of Northern Ireland's constitutional position against political attack but also the protection of Ulster 'virtue' against the encroachments of a 'sinful and secular world'. It is unlikely to be a coincidence, therefore, that the Unionist government was involved in the production of a film in 1930 entitled *Ulster, the Garden of Eden* in which, according to one critic, 'Ulster' is shown as 'a place where nothing stronger than curds and whey was ever sold in hotel bars on Sunday, where the youth of the

---

15. Patrick Buckland, for example, notes how Unionist politicians lacked 'mystique' and remained vulnerable to sharp reminders of 'the claims and narrow horizons of their supporters' in 'A Protestant State: Unionists in Government, 1921–39', in Boyce and O'Day (eds), *Defenders of the Union*, pp. 218–19.

16. See Donald Harman Akenson, *Education and Enmity: The Control of Schooling in Northern Ireland 1920–50* (Newton Abbot: David & Charles, 1973), chs. 4, 5. An indication of the mood at this time is provided by a review of the year in the *Belfast News-Letter* (28 February 1928, p. 11) reporting the claims of the Rev. W. Corkey (a leader of the United Education Committee) that 'secularism in the education system' – and the threat of 'Bolshevism and anarchy' it represented – was 'the greatest foe' then facing Ulster.

17. John D. Brewer and Gareth I. Higgins, 'Understanding Anti-Catholicism in Northern Ireland', *Sociology*, vol. 33, no. 2, 1999, p. 245.

country motored miles for simple Bible instruction at Antrim, and where turf sportsmen and Sunday golfers tumbled over each other in a mad scramble for being early and often at church'.[18]

The special place enjoyed by the 'Ulster Sunday' in the unionist imaginary meant that the issue of the Sunday opening of cinemas (and, indeed, all amusements) struck a particularly sensitive chord. The question of Sunday opening became an issue in Britain when, in response to the confusion surrounding the matter, the government passed the Sunday Entertainment Act in 1932, permitting the licensing of cinemas for Sunday openings by local authorities. While this led to a number of local battles in England, the general trend was towards a lessening of restrictions. Thus, by 1934, S. Rowson estimates that nearly a quarter of cinemas in England and Wales had already obtained permission to open on Sundays.[19] Even in those areas that held out against Sunday opening, such as Nottingham, opposition to Sunday opening waned during the Second World War, when cinemas were permitted to provide entertainment for the armed services.[20] In Northern Ireland, however, the hostility to Sunday opening was both more virulent and more enduring. Although the Sunday Entertainment Act did not, in fact, extend to Northern Ireland, this did not prevent religious groups from taking advantage of the controversy surrounding the issue to call on the Northern Ireland government to introduce legislation to ban all Sunday amusements and to apply pressure upon any local authority that might consider allowing Sunday opening, even if only for the purposes of charity. Such was the implacable hostility of religious groups to Sunday opening that they maintained their campaign during (and, indeed, long after) the war. Thus, in 1940, the Belfast Corporation Police Committee refused the military permission to open just one cinema in Belfast for uniformed members of the armed forces quartered in the Belfast area.[21] Faced with 'huge deputations from the churches and religious organisations', a full meeting of Belfast Council also voted against Sunday opening later the same year.[22] The matter was also discussed by the Northern Ireland Cabinet, which felt some sympathy towards the military but decided the issue was too 'controversial' for them to intervene with

---

18. *Belfast News-Letter*, 3 December 1930, p. 7. Although the report indicates that the film was partly written by George B. Hanna, Parliamentary Secretary to the Ministry of Home Affairs, I have been unable to establish the exact circumstances in which this film was made. The fact that the film was attacked for its idealised image of Ulster by a stalwart of the temperance movement, Rev. T. M. Johnstone, also indicates how Unionist politicians could themselves fall victim to allegations of 'sinfulness' should their actions be perceived as falling short of those demanded by the religious lobby. That the Unionist government took such complaints as these seriously is evidenced by Hanna's decision to respond to Johnstone's earlier attack on the government for the 'sinful management' of Northern Ireland affairs (*Northern Whig*, 29 November 1930, p. 5).

19. S. Rowson, 'A Statistical Survey of the Cinema Industry', p. 92. Jeffrey Richards also describes how the battle for Sunday opening in Birmingham had been effectively won by the end of 1933 in 'The Cinema and Cinema-going in Birmingham in the 1930s', in John K. Walton and James Walvin (eds), *Leisure in Britain 1780–1939* (Manchester: Manchester University Press, 1983), pp. 41–3.

20. See Mark Jancovich and Lucy Faire with Sarah Stubbings, *The Place of the Audience: Cultural Geographies of Film Consumption* (London: BFI, 2003), pp. 124–5.

21. Minutes of the Police Committee, 2 May 1940.

22. *Kine Weekly*, 19 December 1940, p. 10.

local authorities.[23] Such became the frustration of the army at the obstructiveness of local politicians (and their apparent insensitivity to the larger demands of the war effort) that they eventually took the matter out of the politicians' hands and employed powers under the Army Act (which the local authority could not revoke) to open four cinemas in Belfast in 1942.[24]

The hostility of Protestant groups in Northern Ireland to Sunday opening was almost matched by their distaste for 'the fleshly and lustful products' to be found in local cinemas during the rest of the week.[25] Thus, while the BBFC had extensive rules governing the moral aspects of films that included the prohibition of 'nude figures', 'indecorous dancing', 'excessively passionate love scenes', 'scenes suggestive of immorality', 'illicit sexual relations' and 'situations accentuating delicate marital relations', these were deemed to be insufficient by local campaigners.[26] At the Church of Ireland General Synod in 1932, a report from the United Council of Churches complained that 'the amount of control over the pictures exhibited in cinemas was inadequate and unsatisfactory' and that the 'meshes of the net of the British Board of Film Censors were wide enough to allow many films of a morally undesirable character to reach the general public, such as those which contained stories of marital infidelity and of a fast life, bedroom scenes, gangster crimes,&c'.[27] In order to stem this flow of 'morally undesirable' films into Northern Ireland, religious campaigners called upon both the government and the local authorities in the region to exercise additional controls. One of the few features of the Irish Free State admired by Protestant activists, in this respect, was its adoption (under the guidance of the Catholic church) of a system of state censorship that generally permitted only one – universal – classification category. Thus, at the 1932 Church of Ireland Synod, one delegate was moved to declare his admiration for the Free State's possession of 'a real and effective' system of film censorship and advocated the introduction of a similar system in the North.[28] In the absence of such an arrangement, the campaigners also applied pressure upon local authorities in the area to take firmer action against the cinema. For while, in 1923, the British Home Office had recommended that local authorities should only issue licences to those cinemas that accepted the BBFC classification of films, the BBFC was a voluntary rather than a state body. As a result, local authorities retained the legal right to accept or ignore the Board's decisions. Although some local

23. Letter from A. Robinson, Secretary to the Cabinet, to the General Officer Commanding the Northern Ireland District, 9 May 1940, PRONI HA8/642.

24. Minutes of the Police Committee, 1 October 1942; 'Army to open Belfast Halls', Kine Weekly, 24 September 1942, p. 1.

25. Rev. T. M. Johnstone quoted in the Belfast Telegraph, 11 January 1932, p. 11.

26. These were included in the forty-three rules identified by the organisation's second President, T. P. O'Connor, in the first official statement of the Board's policy in 1917. See National Council of Public Morals, The Cinema: Its Present Position and Future Possibilities (orig. 1917) (New York: Arno Press, 1970), pp. 254–5.

27. Northern Whig, 12 May 1932, p. 8. Such sentiments were given added momentum by the BBFC's own Annual Report for 1931, which highlighted the apparent growth of 'sex' films containing 'various phases of immorality, and incidents which tend to bring the Institution of Marriage into contempt'. See British Board of Film Censors, Report, Year Ended December 31st, 1931 (London), p. 9.

28. The Northern Ireland Minister of Commerce, J. Milne Barbour, who was in attendance, is reported to have smiled at this point (Northern Whig, 12 May 1932, p. 8).

authorities (especially those in and around London) were prepared to extend greater tolerance towards certain films than the BBFC, other authorities, often under pressure from local campaigners, applied even tougher standards than the Board, banning or reclassifying films that it had already approved. It was certainly this possibility that churches and religious groups in Northern Ireland were keen to exploit and lay behind the formation of the Film Committee of the Churches in Northern Ireland in 1930 with the purpose of preventing the exhibition in Northern Ireland of 'all immoral and objectionable films'.[29]

'The evil effects of undesirable pictures': the Film Committee of the Churches in Northern Ireland

Although the Committee was reported as representing all the churches in Northern Ireland, it was, in effect, a Protestant group. This was not, however, the result of any real differences between the churches on the matter of film censorship. The Catholic church had played a key role in shaping film censorship in the South and Catholic clergy and nationalist politicians in the North were no less outspoken than their Protestant and unionist counterparts in denouncing the evils of cinema. In 1930, the nationalist senator (and former editor of the *Irish News*), Thomas Campbell, had called for 'strong steps . . . to meet the menace to public morality' that films were deemed to represent.[30] The Nationalist MP Joseph Connellan also demanded 'a more stringent censorship of cinematograph productions' in the same year.[31] However, despite the shared enthusiasm of Protestants and Catholics for tougher film censorship, the situation in Northern Ireland was hardly congenial to the making of common cause. Not only were a high proportion of Protestant clerics and activists bitterly anti-Catholic, but the overwhelmingly Protestant ethos of the government, its sectarian character and willingness to discriminate against Catholics had led to an increasing alienation of Catholics from public life, which culminated in the collective withdrawal of Nationalist MPs from the Northern Ireland parliament in May 1932 (initially for eighteen months but, in effect, until the end of the Second World War). Given these circumstances, it was therefore the Protestant churches that were at the head of the pro-censorship campaign and that were responsible for investing it with a distinctive 'Ulster' flavour.

Established with the purpose of protecting 'children and young people visiting cinemas from the evil effects of undesirable pictures', the Churches Film Committee initially sought the implementation, by local authorities or government, of four regulations relating to film exhibition.[32]

---

29. *Northern Whig*, 18 September 1930.

30. *Parliamentary Debates* (The Senate), vol. xii, col. 167, 21 May 1930. Marianne Elliott associates Campbell with a 'deeply conservative, middle class and clerically driven' strand of nationalist politics in *The Catholics of Ulster* (New York: Basic Books, 2001), p. 397.

31. *Parliamentary Debates* (HC), vol. xii, col. 2192, 29 October 1930. Although there was agreement among the churches over the need for stronger film censorship, the case of Sunday opening did not provoke the same kind of opposition among Catholics as it did Protestants, with the result that the denial of Sunday amusements within Northern Ireland came to acquire an increasingly sectarian character. The divisiveness of this issue was still evident some thirty years later when the supposedly non-sectarian Northern Ireland Labour Party found itself split in 1964 over the closure on Sundays of children's playgrounds in Belfast.

32. Minutes of the Police Committee, 19 March 1931.

The two most controversial of these were the banning of all children under the age of sixteen from films that had not been passed for universal exhibition and the demand that all cinemas should submit the details of their programme to the local authority one week in advance. The first issue was a complicated one and had already led to controversy in Britain. The BBFC, at this time, certified films as either 'U', or suitable for universal exhibition, or as 'A', suitable for exhibition to adults or to children under sixteen when accompanied by an adult. There was, however, a degree of confusion surrounding the 'A' certificate, which many regarded as implying the film was unsuitable for children. As a result, a number of local authorities in England (including Liverpool and Sheffield) decided to ban under-sixteens from films with 'A' certificates.[33] The Northern Ireland Minister of Home Affairs, Sir Dawson Bates, also appeared to take the view that an 'A' certificate implied that a film was suitable for 'adult audiences only' when he defended the role of the BBFC in the Northern Ireland House of Commons in 1930.[34]

It was certainly this position that the Film Committee adopted in its lobbying of the Northern Ireland Home Office, which subsequently issued a circular letter in March 1931 containing 'model conditions' for cinema licences.[35] This followed consultation with the BBFC, which noted that it had been the practice in Northern Ireland 'for "A" and "U" films to be shown indiscriminately'.[36] However, while these 'model conditions' were partly based on the Committee's proposals, they did not require the exclusion of under-sixteens from 'A'-certificate films but merely called for a more prominent display of a film's certificate (and its definition). The Film Committee also met with the Belfast Corporation's Police Committee, which established a sub-committee that subsequently agreed to recommend the adoption of an amended version of the Film Committee's proposals.[37] The sub-committee, however, had reckoned without the opposition of the exhibitors in Belfast, who expressed their indignation that 'any concession should have been made'.[38] The cinema owners argued that the 'A' certificate did not necessarily mean that a film was unsuitable for children, emphasised the practical difficulties involved in determining the ages of young people and stressed the potential financial costs to their business.[39] They also objected to the proposal that they submit lists of films to the local authority on the grounds that films were booked well in advance and could not be substituted at short notice.[40]

The Police Committee was clearly divided on how to balance the competing interests of the trade and the religious lobby and asked the subcommittee to investigate the matter further.

33. For a discussion of the controversy surrounding the 'A' certificate in England, see Rachael Low, *Filmmaking in 1930s Britain*, ch. 4.

34. *Parliamentary Debates* (HC), vol. xii, col. 2192, 29 October 1930.

35. 'Cinematograph Licences – Model Conditions', Ministry of Home Affairs, 26 March 1931, PRONI HA8/639.

36. British Board of Film Censors, *Report*, Year Ended December 31st, 1931 (London), p.12.

37. Minutes of the Police Sub-Committee, 10 April 1931.

38. *Kine Weekly*, 16 April 1931, p. 52.

39. Dorothy Knowles indicates how the losses to the trade in Britain as a result of a ban on children attending 'A'-certificated films eventually led to an ending of the practice. See *The Censor, The Drama and the Film, 1900–1934* (London: George Allen and Unwin, 1934), p. 183.

40. Minutes of the Police Committee, 16 April 1931.

In the interim, the churches stepped up their campaign, calling for the establishment of a committee to censor all films at the beginning of 1932.[41] Despite the mounting pressure, the sub-committee eventually chose to overturn its original decision and reject the Film Committee's demands. However, some concessions to the churches were made. With the agreement of the exhibitors, members of the Film Committee were to be allowed free entry to Belfast cinemas and, if any film was judged to be unsuitable for exhibition to children, the Police Committee would arrange to view the film and take action as appropriate.[42] While the Film Committee complained that their full demands had not been met (and resorted to improbable claims that local exhibitors were reinserting scenes into films cut by the BBFC), the invitation to the group to draw films to the attention of the Police Committee was obviously a highly tempting one and it did not take long for the Committee to begin to target specific films. The first of these was *Frankenstein* (1931), which, as a result of the intervention of the Churches Film Committee, was banned in Belfast by the Police Committee in April 1932.

'Blasphemous and unedifying': the banning of *Frankenstein*

James Whale's *Frankenstein*, the second of Universal's cycle of 1930s horror films, had already provoked controversy in both the US and Britain. In the case of Britain, the BBFC insisted upon 300 feet of cuts (of around seven minutes) before passing the film with an 'A' certificate.[43] However, this was insufficient for some groups – such as 'The Order of the Child' – which claimed that the film was entirely unsuitable for children and argued for the introduction of a third certificate (a demand to which the BBFC eventually acceded in 1933 when it introduced the 'H' certificate).[44] Given the stance of the local Churches Film Committee on 'A' certificates, it was poised for action when the film reached Belfast, lodging a complaint with the Police Committee on the very day the film opened at the Classic on 19 April 1932.[45] The Police Committee arranged a special screening of the film for the following day before deciding to ban the film on the grounds that it was both 'blasphemous and unedifying'.[46] However, while in England a major concern was the heavily cut scene between the monster and the young girl Maria that concludes with her drowning, the focus of attention in Northern Ireland was much more upon the apparent blasphemy involved in the film's portrait of a scientist regarded as emulating God in his creation of human life.

---

41. *Kine Weekly*, 21 January 1932. The paper also reports that local clergy were delivering sermons attacking the attitude of the Police Committee.

42. Minutes of the Police Committee, 11 February 1932.

43. *Kine Weekly*, 18 February 1932, p. 39. Despite the Protestant clerics' admiration for the stringency of censorship in the South, the film was also passed on appeal by the Irish Film Censorship Board despite the reservations of the Official Film Censor, James Montgomery, concerning the film's possible effects upon children. See Kevin Rockett, *Irish Film Censorship: A Cultural Journey from Silent Cinema to Internet Pornography* (co-ed. Emer Rockett) (Dublin: Four Courts Press, 2004), p. 160.

44. *Kine Weekly*, 28 January 1932.

45. Minutes of Special Meeting of Police Committee, 20 April 1932.

46. *Northern Whig*, 21 April 1932, p. 7.

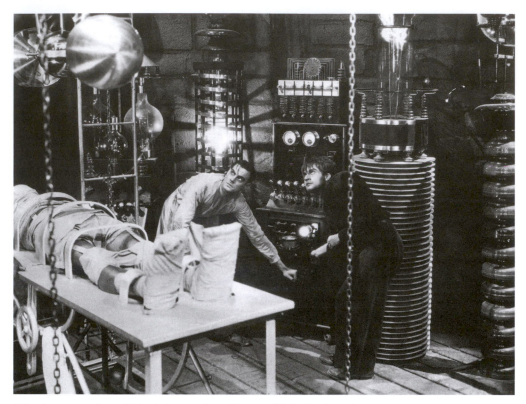

'Blasphemous and unedifying': the creation of human life in *Frankenstein*

However, just five members of the Police Committee had attended the special screening and only three had voted in favour of a ban. This led Universal Pictures to call upon the Police Committee to review its decision, arguing that it had been taken with 'undue haste' and that it did not 'represent a mandate from the Police Committee, the Corporation, or the citizens'.[47] There was also considerable criticism of the decision in the press, with the *Northern Whig* reporting a 'chorus of protest' following the banning of the film.[48] This was manifest in the number of letters that appeared in all of the local newspapers. Some correspondents queried whether the film was, in fact, blasphemous, while others derided the Police Committee for conniving to make Belfast 'one of the dreariest cities in the British Isles'. Another correspondent also poured scorn on the 'voluntary martyrdom' of 'our local Film Committee' whose 'zeal for the moral welfare of our people' led them to seek out 'even the slightest impropriety'.[49] Although the Police Committee initially claimed that it was impossible to re-open the matter, it later agreed to a second private screening of the film to which it invited not only members of Belfast City

47. *Belfast News-Letter*, 23 April 1932, p. 7.

48. *Northern Whig*, 22 April 1932, p. 7.

49. *Belfast Telegraph*, 23 April 1932, p. 10.

Council but also members of the Northern Ireland House of Commons and Senate. A discussion of the film at a lively meeting of the full Council then followed.

The Northern Ireland Labour Party councillor and Stormont MP Harry Midgley led the argument for overthrowing the ban. Midgley's case took a number of forms. Following on from a letter to the press in which he had described the Churches Film Committee as 'self-appointed custodians of ethics and morality', he argued that the group had exerted undue influence upon the Police Committee and had overridden the rights of the majority.[50] He also expressed concern for the effects that such a decision might have upon the Belfast film trade and the employment that it provided. Finally, he reiterated his view that the case against the film was fundamentally mistaken. Far from being blasphemous, Midgley suggested, the film's warning that man could not 'usurp the functions of God' invested it with 'a high moral purpose' that paid 'Christian ethics a compliment'.[51] In this he was supported by Alderman Pierce, who also argued that the film provided 'proof of the futility of man trying to abrogate the Divine right of creating life'.[52] Such views as these, however, failed to prevail. Alderman Nixon, a longstanding member of the Police Committee who had voted in favour of the ban, reiterated his conviction that the film was blasphemous, objecting to its 'central idea of vitalising a corpse'.[53] Others, such as Alderman Williamson, lay stress on the film's psychological effects, claiming that 'the black art' involved in the film's creation of the monster would make an 'evil' impression upon the 'immature brain'. '[I]n the interests of the nation and of the people', he concluded, 'these things should not be allowed.'[54] After an hour and a half's discussion, observed by a packed gallery, the Council eventually ratified the Police Committee's decision by a small majority. Midgley continued to fight for a lifting of the ban and subsequently asked the Police Committee to suggest cuts that might make the screening of the film acceptable. However, this too was rejected.[55] Indeed, the Committee was to remain resolute on this matter for years to come. In 1939, General Film Distributors sought to have the ban overturned on the occasion of the film's re-issue. Although a private viewing of the film was organised, the Committee opted to re-affirm its decision of 1932.[56]

While the banning of *Frankenstein* was an undoubted victory for the Churches Film Committee, it was also one that was contradictory in its effects. As Annette Kuhn has argued (drawing on the work of Michel Foucault), censorship is rarely simply 'repressive' but also 'productive' in the way that it gives rise to other discourses surrounding the act of censorship.[57] In this respect, the ban on *Frankenstein* not only led to considerable criticism of the churches' role in

---

50. Ibid.

51. *Northern Whig*, 3 May 1932, p. 7; *Belfast Telegraph*, 23 April 1932, p. 10.

52. *Northern Whig*, 3 May 1932, p. 7.

53. Ibid.

54. Ibid. Even more extravagantly, Williamson argued that the viewing of such a film by pregnant mothers would lead to 'mentally defective and otherwise abnormal children' and that recent incidents of arson in Ballywalter provided evidence of the harmful effects wrought by cinemagoing.

55. Minutes of the Police Committee, 26 May 1932.

56. Minutes of a Special Meeting of the Police Committee, 23 January 1939.

57. Annette Kuhn, *Cinema, Censorship and Sexuality, 1909–1925* (London: Routledge, 1988), pp. 2–4.

the press but also stimulated interest in the film, including a huge demand for Mary Shelley's novel on which it was based.[58] The film also continued to be shown in other parts of Northern Ireland and this encouraged travel out of the city to those places where the film could be seen. The Picture House in nearby Lisburn, for example, ran three screenings of the film a day, while the British trade press took pleasure in reporting that the film was 'breaking records' wherever it was being shown.[59] The ban also became the object of ridicule during Queens University's annual Student Rag Week, when a replica of Frankenstein's monster was paraded through Belfast and subsequently dropped from a quayside crane into the River Lagan to the accompaniment of the 'sounds of mourning' from 'the "Pro Tanto Quid Banned"' playing the 'Dead March'.[60]

Despite the element of farce surrounding the *Frankenstein* ban, the Churches Film Committee doggedly maintained its stance, pressing other local councils to follow Belfast's example and lobbying the Northern Ireland government for a system of state censorship that would prevent inconsistencies in local authority decision-making.[61] Emboldened by the success of the protest, the campaigners also extended their activities to other areas and both Sunday opening and the location of new cinemas in Belfast became matters of controversy. The issue of the siting of cinemas in Belfast gained particular momentum at the beginning of 1935 when the churches organised 'a huge deputation' to the City Council to demand a ban on the opening of cinemas close to places of worship (particularly in residential areas).[62] A 'monster protest meeting' was also called to protest against plans to build a new cinema on the Lisburn Road, close to the Ulsterville Presbyterian Church.[63] As a consequence, Belfast Corporation refused planning permission to a number of cinemas before imposing a blanket ban on all new developments within 120 yards of any church.[64] While this represented a major victory for the churches, and led to fears in the trade that cinema-building in Belfast would now grind to a halt, it also proved short-lived. For when the matter was referred to the Northern Ireland Home Office, it was discovered that the Corporation had exceeded its authority under the Planning Act and that the distance ban could not be sustained.[65] The churches then pressed for the introduction of new legislation on the issue by drawing attention to the problems posed by 'unruly' cinema queues for midweek religious services.[66] However, although the Belfast Corporation Police Committee met to consider the matter, it decided that the Corporation already possessed sufficient legal

---

58. *Northern Whig*, 22 April 1932, p. 7.

59. *Belfast News-Letter*, 19 May 1932, p. 1; *Kine Weekly*, 19 May 1932, p. 15.

60. *Northern Whig*, 4 May 1932, p. 7.

61. At a meeting with the Minister of Home Affairs in November 1932, a deputation from the Churches Film Committee indicated their approval of 'cowboy pictures' and Charlie Chaplin but expressed their objections to 'undesirable . . . sex and gangster stuff'. 'Deputation Regarding Censorship of Films', 22 November 1932, PRONI HA8/639.

62. *Kine Weekly*, 21 February 1935, p. 13.

63. *Kine Weekly*, 28 February 1935, p. 19. The reference to a 'monster meeting' self-consciously appropriated the language of the movement for Catholic Emancipation led by Daniel O'Connell in the nineteenth century.

64. *Kine Weekly*, 7 November 1935, p. 35.

65. *Kine Weekly*, 2 April 1936, p. 19.

66. *Daily Film Renter*, 4 May 1936, p. 7.

powers under the Belfast Improvement Act to deal with any 'nuisance' for which cinema queues might be held responsible.[67] Despite these setbacks, it was not long before a new issue – the proposal to show the film *The Green Pastures* in Northern Ireland – inspired religious groups to new levels of campaigning zeal.

'Profoundly offensive to the religious views of the people of Northern Ireland': the banning of *The Green Pastures*

The Green Pastures (1936) was an adaptation of Marc Connelly's all–black musical of the same name that had run successfully in theatres in the United States. Intended, as the opening title explains, to show how 'negroes in the Deep South visualize God and Heaven in terms of people and things they know in their everyday life', the film depicts stories taken from the Old Testament, as told to a group of young children by an elderly black Sunday school teacher in contemporary Louisiana. The original stage play had, in fact, been banned by the Lord Chamberlain in Britain so the certification of the film by the BBFC became a matter of some anxiety for the organisation. Since its inception, the BBFC had maintained that 'the materialised figure of Christ' constituted a basis for the cutting or banning of a film. However, although the film gives physical embodiment to God (credited in the film as 'De Lawd'), the film only alludes to the crucifixion of Christ, which takes place off-screen towards the film's close. Following consultation with 'leading Ecclesiastical authorities', the Board reached the conclusion that neither 'subject matter' nor 'treatment' were 'blasphemous' and, following some cuts, the film was passed with a 'U' certificate in November 1936.[68] Anthony Aldgate and James Robertson report that the BBFC anticipated that criticism of the film would 'vanish' following the film's general release and suggest that the organisation's prediction 'proved to be accurate'.[69] However, while the controversy may have died down in England, this was certainly not the case in Northern Ireland.

For, while at this stage no cinema in the area had announced its intention to book the film, the BBFC's decision to award the film a certificate immediately prompted a campaign to stop the film from being shown in the North. A few days prior to the film's opening in London, a letter appeared in the *Northern Whig* calling on 'the people of Northern Ireland' to 'see to it' that 'no film is shown in this part of the United Kingdom which would in any way bring disrespect to the religion which our forefathers upheld in the face of many difficulties'.[70] The following month the Churches Film Committee also declared that 'any representation of Almighty God shown on the cinema screen would be repugnant to the religious convictions of the majority of our people' and called on the Minister of Home Affairs and the Belfast Corporation Police Committee 'to prohibit the exhibition of any such film in the cinemas of Belfast and Northern Ireland'.[71] This was followed a couple of weeks later by a call for a ban from the Ruling Elders'

---

67. Minutes of the Police Committee, 21 May 1936.

68. Rt Hon. Lord Tyrrell of Avon, '*Review of Censorship paper read at the Summer Conference of the Cinematograph Exhibitors' Association of Great Britain and Ireland*, 23 June 1937, p. 5.

69. Anthony Aldgate and James Robertson, *Censorship in Theatre and Cinema* (Edinburgh: Edinburgh University Press, 2005), p. 161.

70. 'Everyman', *Northern Whig*, 26 November 1936, p. 9.

71. 'Belfast Film Protest', *Irish News*, 5 December 1936, p. 2.

Union of the Presbyterian Church in Ireland on the grounds that the film was 'profoundly offensive to the religious views of the people of Northern Ireland'.[72]

Matters then came to a head when it emerged that the film might, indeed, be shown in Belfast. The film was due to begin a run at the Classic and, in March 1937, a special screening for the Police Committee was organised to which various local clergymen as well as members of Belfast Corporation and the Northern Ireland Cabinet, were invited. To the astonishment of the religious groups that had canvassed for a ban, the Committee then resolved, on the basis of a majority vote, to permit the film to be shown.[73] The Committee's decision was, however, subject to the approval of the full Council, which conducted a stormy special meeting, attended by over a hundred people representing the Ruling Elders' Union, the following week. A spokesman for the deputation, K. M. Alexander, called on the meeting to take a stand against 'the immoral inrush' and 'materialistic anti-God tendency of the times in which they lived'. The film, he claimed, was 'impious and false and an insult to the Christian religion' that would only lead to 'tears of indignation, shame and sorrow' should it be shown in the city.[74] As in the case of *Frankenstein*, Harry Midgley sought to defend the film on the grounds that it was neither irreverent nor blasphemous but portrayed 'the greatness, power, love and mercy of God' in a manner that 'many people in Belfast' might 'emulate with improvement to themselves'.[75] Despite his protests that a council that often sneered at parts of Ireland 'for being priest-ridden' was now in danger of becoming 'clerical-ridden', the Council voted decisively (by thirty-one votes to twelve) in favour of a ban.[76] In this they were soon to be followed by other councils, including those in Bangor, Coleraine, Derry and Newry.

While religious groups in Britain had also protested against *The Green Pastures*, the success of the religious lobby in Northern Ireland in securing the banning of the film appeared to demonstrate the distinctive ideological circumstances prevailing there. When the issue first loomed on the horizon, the British trade paper *Today's Cinema* ran the headline 'Ulster Will Fight Again – But This Time Against *Green Pastures*', hinting at how the protests directed against the film possessed a political dimension that was absent elsewhere.[77] This sense of Ulster's

---

72. *Northern Whig*, 19 December 1936, p. 3.

73. Minutes of a Special Meeting of the Police Committee, 20 March 1937. The meeting's decision partly confirmed the BBFC's belief that opposition to the film was less among those who had actually seen the film and certain of the clerics who attended the screening were reported to be well disposed towards it. However, for others, the very conception of the film was such an abomination that not to see it became a matter of pride. It was certainly in this spirit that the Rev. T. M. Johnstone was able to declare that it was unnecessary 'to enter a public-house to know the evils of alcohol or a bookmaker's den to know the enormity of the tragedy of gambling' (*Northern Whig*, 22 March 1937, p. 12).

74. *Northern Whig*, 26 March 1937, p. 7.

75. Ibid.

76. *Irish News*, 26 March 1937, p. 6.

77. *Today's Cinema*, 8 December 1936, p. 4. The phrase 'Ulster will fight' derives, of course, from the slogan employed by Ulster Unionists in opposition to Home Rule: 'Ulster will fight and Ulster will be right'. The phrase was first coined by Lord Randolph Churchill at a rally in Belfast in 1886. See Tim Pat Coogan, *Ireland in the Twentieth Century* (London: Arrow Books, 2004), p. 1.

destiny being at stake was also manifest in the correspondence that followed. Writing in the *Belfast Telegraph*, 'True Blue' called on the 'men and women of Ulster' not to allow themselves to become 'the generation that permitted the Sabbath to be desecrated, the morals of the country to fall below that of beasts, the drink evil to flourish, and . . . God to be depicted on the screen in an irreverent way'.[78] Another correspondent enquired whether 'the Orangemen of Ulster' were prepared 'to stand idly by and allow the God of their fathers . . . for which they fought and died, to be caricatured', while a representative of the Ulster Evangelical Protestant Society suggested that condoning the film would constitute the 'first step on the road' to making 'loyal, God-fearing Ulster another Soviet Russia'.[79]

However, while the acolytes of 'God-fearing Ulster' were undoubtedly vexed by the film's breach of the Second Commandment (forbidding 'any likeness of any thing that is in heaven above'), it was also clear that it was the representation of God as a black man that provoked the most indignation.[80] It is worth noting, in this regard, that while Cecil B. DeMille's story of the life of Christ, *King of Kings* (1927), did not possess a BBFC certificate due to its breach of the regulation governing the materialisation of Christ, it had nevertheless been shown without apparent incident at Belfast's Picture House in 1929.[81] The fact that *The Green Pastures* caused so much upset in comparison appeared to stem from the film's interpretation of the Old Testament from a supposedly black perspective and corresponding representation of 'De Lawd' (Rex Ingram) in 'the form of a negro dressed in a frock coat and top hat'.[82] Accordingly, objections to the representation of God were quickly translated into a racial discourse by the film's opponents. An early correspondent on the matter queried the benefit for the 'advanced and . . . civilized' Christian of going to see 'a film purporting to show the negro's (a so-called semi-civilized man) idea of God', while the indefatigable Rev. T. M. Johnstone delivered a sermon comparing the degradation of musical taste and culture by 'negro conceptions of rhythm' to the debasement of religion resulting from 'negro conceptions of Biblical truth'.[83] Similar sentiments were expressed by the deputation to the

---

78. *Belfast Telegraph*, 2 January 1937, p. 9.

79. *Northern Whig*, 25 March 1937, p. 9; *Northern Whig*, 23 March 1937, p. 11.

80. This was also the case in the South where the Irish censor, James Montgomery, was startled by 'the conception of God made to the images and likeness of a nigger who is the centre man in a Christy minstrel musical comedy'. His decision to ban the film also suggests how Protestantism and Catholicism in Ireland were united in their disdain for the film's use of black actors in this particular context (Record of Films Censored, Film Censors Office 2, NAI 98/27/14, 11 February 1937, p. 11524).

81. *Northern Whig*, 8 January 1929, p. 10. Due to the BBFC's strict ban on the materialisation of Christ, the film was not, in fact, submitted to the Board but was passed for exhibition by various local authorities.

82. The Ruling Elders' Union of the Presbyterian Church in Ireland quoted in *Northern Whig*, 19 December 1936, p. 3. The extent to which the film constituted a 'genuine' expression of US 'black culture' is, of course, problematic insofar as the original play and film screenplay were written by a white man. As a result, the film has been criticised for what Daniel J. Leab refers to as its 'condescendingly sentimentalized white view of blacks and . . . resulting stereotypes' in *From Sambo to Superspade: The Black Experience in Motion Pictures* (Boston, MA: Houghton Mifflin, 1975), p. 96. However, while the film may depend on ideologically problematic racial stereotypes, the subversive aspects of the film's portrayal of God and, by extension, all humanity as black may have been underestimated by retrospective accounts of the film.

83. *Belfast Telegraph*, 2 January 1937, p. 4; *Northern Whig*, 22 March 1937, p. 12.

A threat to 'loyal God-fearing Ulster'?: Rex Ingram as 'De Lawd' in *The Green Pastures*

meeting of the Belfast City Council, one of whose number suggested that the Council should be seeking to 'raise the negroes themselves up to our moral and cultural standards' rather than lowering the 'moral thinking of our people' to the level of 'people in the bush and the jungle'.[84] The strongly racialised character of the discourse surrounding the film was not, of course, exclusive to Northern Ireland but it did assume a particularly potent form there. This was not, perhaps, surprising. The political identity of unionism partly rested upon Northern Ireland's membership of, and fierce identification with, the British empire and the sense of intellectual and religious superiority over its colonised peoples that this endowed. Moreover, as Steve Bruce observes, the Calvinist belief, informing popular Protestantism in Northern Ireland, that some had been 'chosen for salvation' led to a 'form of racism' in the way that it was characteristically assumed that 'people of other races' would be unlikely to constitute a 'part of the elect'.[85] Thus, while the emphasis upon the Old Testament's 'God of Wrath', and God's disappointment with the sinfulness of the world, suggests the film's own indebtedness to a fundamentalist sensibility, the representation of God, and

---

84. *Belfast Telegraph*, 26 March 1937, p. 3.

85. Steve Bruce, *God Save Ulster: The Religion and Politics of Paisleyism* (Oxford: Oxford University Press, 1989), p. 10.

God's 'chosen people', as 'uncivilised' blacks must nevertheless have seemed particularly blasphemous (and politically abhorrent) for the Protestant fundamentalists of Ulster.

'Subversive of law and order': film and the threat of communism

Although the religious activists in Northern Ireland achieved a number of censorship successes, they nevertheless failed in their object of a system of state censorship. Thus, despite various calls for it to introduce such a system, the Unionist government continued to maintain that it was unnecessary. In March 1936, for example, the Northern Ireland Home Secretary, Sir Dawson Bates, rejected the call for a Northern Ireland film censor on the grounds that local authorities already possessed 'adequate powers' and that he could 'see no reason for any change in the existing arrangements'.[86] However, despite the Minister's apparent willingness to leave film censorship to the BBFC and local authorities, he was not opposed to state censorship in principle. The BBFC and the local authorities, in this respect, were assumed to be responsible for the regulation of moral rather than political matters. If films were seen to pose a threat to public order, however, then the role of the government was held to be different.

As numerous commentators have observed, the history of the Unionist regime in Northern Ireland was characterised by extreme constitutional defensiveness. Born out of, and confronted with, political violence, its immediate concern was to defend and consolidate its political position. This led the new government to create an armed Special Constabulary that was exclusively Protestant (and partly drawn from the paramilitary Ulster Volunteer Force, established to oppose Home Rule). The permanent police force that followed, the Royal Ulster Constabulary (RUC), formed in 1922, was also armed, mainly Protestant and, in the minds of most Catholics, closely identified with the Unionists. Police activities were reinforced by legislation such as the Civil Authorities (Special Powers) Act of 1922, which gave sweeping powers to the Minister of Home Affairs, including the authority to intern and arrest without trial, interrogate, execute, flog, ban meetings and proscribe organisations. Despite the subsequent decline of IRA activities and agreement on the boundary issue in 1925, the Unionist government remained reluctant to relax its grip on security. The Ulster Special Constabulary B men – or B Specials – were maintained as a part-time back-up for the RUC, while the Special Powers Act was repeatedly renewed before becoming permanent in 1933 (until its eventual repeal forty years later). Although these measures were justified by reference to the need to maintain law and order and uphold the constitution, the practical effect was the sacrifice of Catholic rights and liberties. As Jennifer Todd argues,

> [t]he practical moral community, in whose interests and for whose benefit the Union was maintained and partition imposed, was a Protestant one . . . Northern Ireland, in this sense, was founded on an exclusivist legitimating principle, which was impervious to more generalized and universalistic pleas for justice and democracy if these were to conflict with unionists' basic interest in the survival of the state and the union.[87]

---

86. *Parliamentary Debates* (HC), vol. xviii, col. 628, 24 March 1936.
87. Jennifer Todd, 'Unionist Political Thought, 1920–72', in D. George Boyce, Robert Eccleshall and Vincent Geoghagan (eds), *Political Thought in Ireland since the Seventeenth Century* (London: Routledge, 1993), p. 197.

It was certainly in this spirit that the Unionist government gerrymandered electoral boundaries, abolished proportional representation for both local and parliamentary elections, openly discriminated against Catholics in public employment and housing and exercised political censorship. Under the Special Powers legislation, the state's powers of censorship were substantial and even extended to private mail. Thus, as late as 1930, the Northern Ireland Home Secretary was more than happy to report to the Northern Ireland House of Commons that '[c]orrespondence for delivery to, or emanating from, persons in Northern Ireland suspected of being engaged in seditious activities' remained 'subjected to censorship'.[88] Bans on republican newspapers such as *An Phoblacht* and *The Nation* were also in place. However, despite the strong authoritarian bent of the Unionist regime, it was only when the importation of Soviet films into Northern Ireland became a possibility that state censorship of films was contemplated.

Although the BBFC was not a state body, as in the Irish Free State, and was perceived to be primarily concerned with questions of morality, it did, nevertheless, play a political role. Indeed, for Ivor Montagu, the Board's appearance of formal independence actually meant that the British government was able to operate a 'more effective' form of political censorship insofar as it could not be held responsible for 'its acts in the Houses of Parliament'.[89] Thus, while the majority of the BBFC's rules did concern moral issues, a significant number were also political in character, dealing with 'relations of capital and labour', 'British prestige in the Empire', 'references to controversial politics' and 'subjects calculated or possibly intended to foment social unrest or discontent'.[90]

These rules governing film content were certainly sufficient to ensure the banning by the BBFC of such Soviet films as Sergei Eisenstein's *Battleship Potemkin* in 1926 and Vladimir Pudovkin's *Mother* in 1928. However, the arrival of *Potemkin* in Britain also aroused the interest of the Special Branch at New Scotland Yard. Convinced that a flood of propaganda films was about to follow, they persuaded the Home Office in Britain to allow (as was already possible in the case of 'obscene' materials) the seizure of films at ports. The first warrant authorising the seizure of a film (Wolkonski's *Black Sunday*) was issued in January 1927 and, over the next three years, a number of other warrants followed.[91] New Scotland Yard forwarded the details of these warrants to the Inspector General of the RUC, beginning in May 1927 with a letter concerning *Storm over Gothland* (a film based on Erwin Piscator's play about a proto-communist community in fourteenth-century Gothland).[92] This letter was then forwarded to the Northern Ireland Ministry of Home Affairs, which responded by issuing instructions that the RUC should seize the film if found in Northern Ireland. Over the following two years, Scotland Yard con-

---

88. *Parliamentary Debates* (HC), vol. xii, col. 1143, 13 May 1930.

89. Ivor Montagu, *The Political Censorship of Films* (London: Victor Gollancz, 1929), p. 14.

90. See Nicholas Pronay, 'The Political Censorship of Films in Britain between the Wars', in Nicholas Pronay and D. W. Spring (eds), *Propaganda, Politics and Film, 1918–45* (Basingstoke: Macmillan, 1982), pp. 98–125. Pronay also notes that the general rule about 'controversial politics' was extended to 'offensive political propaganda' in 1931.

91. For a discussion of the background, see Temple Willcox, 'Soviet Films, Censorship and the British Government: A Matter of the Public Interest', *Historical Journal of Film, Radio and Television*, vol. 10, no. 3, 1990, pp. 275–92.

92. Letter from Assistant Commissioner, New Scotland Yard, to the Inspector General, Royal Ulster Constabulary, 2 May 1927, PRONI HA32/1/518.

tinued to contact the RUC about films and gramophone records – mainly Soviet works such as *Mother* (1926), *Ten Days That Shook the World* (1928), *The Fall of the Romanoff Dynasty* (1927) and *Storm over Asia* (1928) and, in the case of records, speeches of Soviet leaders – for which warrants had been issued. The RUC, in turn, followed suit by issuing warrants for Northern Ireland. There appears, however, to have been little evidence of a desire to show these films in Northern Ireland until the RUC (alerted by a police informer) warned the Ministry of Home Affairs of the launch of a Workers' Film Guild (WFG) in Belfast.[93]

The object of the WFG was 'to present to its members film productions of a definitely working class character, which, because of their nature are not accessible to the general public'. An inaugural meeting was held on 13 December 1929 when there was a screening of *Two Days* (a 1927 Ukrainian film directed by Georgi Stabovoi, concerning the Russian Civil War, which had been shown by the London Workers' Film Society the previous month) and speeches by William McMullen (the former Labour MP for West Belfast) and Thomas Geehan (secretary of the local branch of the Labour Defence League) about a recent trip to Russia.[94] Plans to show both Eisenstein's *Battleship Potemkin* and *Ten Days That Shook the World* (aka *October*) were also announced. Both of these films had been named in the Scotland Yard warrants that had been forwarded to the RUC (and Ivor Montagu reports that Scotland Yard officers had visited the offices of *Potemkin*'s British distributor in February 1929 when ways of circumventing the BBFC's banning of the film were being sought).[95] As a result, the Northern Ireland Home Office indicated its approval for the seizure of the films should they reach Northern Ireland. Up until this point, the Northern Ireland Home Office had simply assumed that warrants issued by the British Home Secretary could be automatically extended to Northern Ireland. However, once the exhibition of Soviet films in Northern Ireland became an actual possibility, the question of their validity was examined more closely. The warrants, in fact, only referred to 'importation into England' and the Home Office in London confirmed that the requests from Scotland Yard had been based upon a 'misapprehension' and that the British Home Secretary did not, in fact, have powers to deal with the exhibition of films in Northern Ireland.[96] The Northern Ireland Ministry of Home Affairs responded quickly and wrote to the Home Office in London indicating its intention to make an order under the Special Powers Act that would prevent the exhibition of 'such undesirable films'.[97] Under Regulation 26 of the Act, the Northern Ireland authorities already had powers to ban newspapers and these were now to be extended to include the prohibition of films and records under a new regulation (26A). Although the civil servants in London sounded a note of caution, the Ministry was not to be deterred. As has been seen, atheistic communism held a particular fear for Ulster unionism, threatening both the cross-class

93. Letter from Inspector General, Royal Ulster Constabulary, to the Secretary, Ministry of Home Affairs, 17 December 1929, PRONI HA32/1/569.

94. Tommy Geehan was subsequently a member of the Workers' Revolutionary Party (a forerunner of the Communist Party of Ireland) and was one of the leaders of the Outdoor Relief strike in 1932. See Ronnie Munck and Bill Rolston, *Belfast in the Thirties: An Oral History* (Belfast: Blackstaff Press, 1987), ch. 1.

95. Montagu, *The Political Censorship of Films*, p. 12.

96. Letter from C. M. Martin-Jones to W. A. Magill, 29 March 1930, PRONI HA32/1/569.

97. Letter from G. A. Harris to Martin-Jones, 2 April 1930, PRONI HA32/1/569.

unity and sense of a shared religious identity upon which it relied. As a result, the government showed no hesitation in implementing an order which it argued would 'prevent the introduction into this country of any films or gramophone records that would be subversive of law and order or that would interfere with religion or morality'.[98]

In doing so, however, the Home Secretary and the police in Northern Ireland obtained much more extensive powers than their counterparts in Britain. As the civil servants in London pointed out, the Scotland Yard warrants could not be used 'to detain a film indefinitely'. Moreover, there was only one occasion when films had actually been detained. These were the ones found in Irish labour leader James Larkin's luggage on his entry into England in March 1928 and even these had been returned to him following examination.[99] Moreover, since the election of a new Labour government in 1929 there had been a marked improvement in Anglo-Soviet relations. As a result, the British government was on the verge of rescinding the original warrants and proceeded to do so barely a month after the introduction of the Northern Ireland Regulation.

Given the reputation of the Special Powers Act, there was also understandable apprehension within Northern Ireland regarding the purpose of the government's new order. The nationalist *Irish News* published the details of the regulation under the headline 'Mysterious Home Office Order' and ran an editorial – 'Another Dawson Bates Scandal' – that attacked the Northern Ireland Home Secretary's action.[100] Given the existing powers of the BBFC (which included, as has been noted, a prohibition against subjects 'calculated . . . to foment social unrest'), the paper argued that the order was unnecessary and, not unreasonably, assumed that it would be directed against expressions of nationalist culture. Given that the order referred to both films and gramophone records, the paper speculated that:

> Perhaps we are to have the spectacle of the unfortunate constable with ears cocked for the sound of 'The Soldier's Song' or 'The Boys of the County Cork'. When the first bars of such seditious music reach his beat, he must, perforce, shake off his ordinary limitations as an officer of the law and invade the home of a citizen armed with the authority of this extraordinary Order.[101]

In the event, the fears of the paper were not as wide of the mark as knowledge of the background to the case might suggest. For despite the haste with which the order was introduced, it was several years before it was actually employed. This was so even when one of the films named

---

98.   George B. Hanna, Parliamentary Secretary of the Ministry of Home Affairs, *Parliamentary Debates* (HC), vol. xii, col. 1630, 29 May 1930.

99.   Letter from Home Office to G. A. Harris, 12 April 1930, PRONI HA32/1/569. Temple Willcox indicates that these were recordings of the tenth anniversary celebrations of the 1917 Russian revolution and that the incident led to a protest by the Irish High Commission and a question in Parliament ('Soviet Films, Censorship and the British Government', p. 277).

100.   *Irish News*, 24 May 1930, pp. 4–5. Bates was an especially unpopular figure with the Catholic community because of the stridency of his anti-Catholicism, which included a refusal to employ any Catholics in the Ministry of Home Affairs.

101.   Ibid., p. 4.

in the original warrants – *Mother* – reached Northern Ireland a few months later in October 1930. Following a request by the Atlas Film Company (the distribution arm of the Federation of Workers' Film Societies) to show the film in Belfast, the Police Committee organised a special screening. Claiming that the film (which was still banned by the BBFC) would be 'subversive to discipline', the Committee then agreed unanimously to ban it (and in doing so, presumably, saved the RUC the bother of seizing it).[102]

Given the effectiveness, therefore, of both the BBFC and Belfast Corporation in preventing the public exhibition of 'communist propaganda', there was very little need for the new powers and, in October 1935, the Home Secretary confirmed that he had yet to issue an order under the Regulation. However, he also informed the Northern Ireland House of Commons that he regarded as 'valuable' the 'power to make such order' and refused to consider revoking it.[103] What this 'value' might be was demonstrated the following year when the Special Powers Act was used to ban, not a 'subversive' Soviet film, but rather a British film about the Irish War of Independence, *Ourselves Alone* (1936). The film itself was directed by Brian Desmond Hurst and based on the play *The Trouble* by Dudley Sturrock and Noel Scott. The film begins with the rescue of two captured members of the IRA, Connolly (Clifford Evans) and Maloney (Tony Quinn), by a flying column under the command of the mysterious 'Mick O'Dea'. 'O'Dea' is subsequently revealed to be Terence Elliott (Niall MacGinnis), whose sister Maureen (Antoinette Cellier) is engaged to the RIC County Inspector, Hannay (John Lodge). Following a raid by the police on an IRA hide-out, Terence is killed by the English Intelligence Officer Wiltshire (John Loder). Hannay realises, however, that it is Wiltshire whom Maureen really loves and asks to be released from their engagement by claiming that he was responsible for the death of her brother.

'Purely Sinn Fein propaganda': the banning of *Ourselves Alone*

As in the case of the bannings of both *Frankenstein* and *The Green Pastures* by Belfast City Council, *Ourselves Alone* (*River of Unrest* in the US) had already been passed for public exhibition by the BBFC. This was itself significant, for the BBFC was not known for its leniency towards films concerning recent Irish history. As early as 1926, the Board banned outright Isaac Eppel's *Irish Destiny*, the first fictional film to deal with the Irish War of Independence.[104] During the 1930s, a number of other films dealing with the Irish 'troubles' were also rigorously vetted at script stage and, in some cases, subject to cuts. Partly as a response to the growing number of calls for tougher censorship at the start of the 1930s, the BBFC had introduced a voluntary system of vetting scenarios and scripts prior to shooting. The vetting was handled by the Vice-president of the BBFC, Colonel J. C. Hanna (who had seen military action in Ireland), and, from April

---

102. *Belfast News-Letter*, 14 October 1930, p. 6. It appears to have been another seven years before the film was eventually seen in Belfast as part of a film show arranged by the Northern Ireland Socialist Party.

103. *Parliamentary Debates* (HC), vol. xvii, col. 2635, 17 October 1935.

104. A shorter, re-edited version of the film appears to have been submitted to the censor the following year under the title of *An Irish Mother*. This was eventually passed with cuts. Although the precise contents of this version of the film are unknown, Kevin Rockett suggests it probably excluded the more controversial material dealing with the engagements between the British Army and the IRA in *The Irish Filmography* (Dublin: Red Mountain, 1996), p. 11.

The mysterious IRA man, 'Mick O'Dea' (Niall MacGinnis) reveals his true identity to the RIC Inspector Hannay (John Lodge) in *Ourselves Alone*

1934, the daughter of the then President, Miss N. Shortt (later Mrs Crouzet). Like Hanna, Edward Shortt, the BBFC's President from 1929 to 1936, also had personal connections with Ireland, having earned a reputation for 'counter-subversion techniques' and 'wholesale arrests' following his appointment to the post of Chief Secretary of Ireland in 1918.[105] Given this situation, it was hardly surprising that the BBFC was keen to discourage the making of films about the circumstances in Ireland and sought to eliminate material that might be regarded as 'controversial'.[106] The system was supported by the Motion Picture Producers and Distributors of America (MPPDA), which, fearful of jeopardising overseas revenues, collaborated with the BBFC on such matters.[107] Thus, in the case of a number of 'troubles' films – including *The*

105. Pronay, 'The Political Censorship of Films', p. 112.

106. For a summary of the BBFC reports on scenarios and scripts dealing with Ireland, see James C. Robertson, *The British Board of Film Censors: Film Censorship in Britain, 1896–1950* (London: Croom Helm, 1985), pp. 86–9.

107. For a discussion of the BBFC's relationship with the MPPDA, see Louisa Burns-Bisogno, *Censoring Irish Nationalism: The British, Irish and American Suppression of Republican Images in Film and Television, 1909–1995* (Jefferson, NC: McFarland & Co., 1997), chs 4, 5.

Informer (1935), *The Plough and the Stars* (1936) and *Beloved Enemy* (1936) – the BBFC engaged in protracted correspondence with Joseph Breen, the administrator of the MPPDA's Production Code, regarding the precise contents of each film. Even then cuts were still possible, as proved to be the case with *The Informer*, which was cut by over four minutes when it eventually came before the Board in June 1935. As a result, the likelihood of a film about Ireland containing either strong anti-British or pro-republican attitudes and being passed as suitable for exhibition was virtually nil. Nevertheless, the actions of the BBFC still proved insufficient to prevent further demands for the censorship of 'troubles' films once they arrived in Northern Ireland.

In the case of *Ourselves Alone* the origin of the controversy surrounding the film may be traced to the intervention of the Unionist MP (and subsequent Minister of Labour) William Grant in the Northern Ireland House of Commons on 25 November 1936. Speaking of the need for the maintenance of 'law and order' in Northern Ireland, he reported that he had attended a private screening of *Ourselves Alone* that morning. He continued:

> I do not wish to be taken as an alarmist or anything of that kind, but I am of the opinion that if that picture is shown in Belfast next week it may tend to create trouble in the city . . . I know that the Belfast Corporation is the local authority responsible for dealing with the matter but, at the same time, I think some steps should be taken by the Ministry of Home Affairs in conjunction with the local authority. They should attend a private view of this picture before it is exhibited to the public next week. If they are satisfied that the picture would not tend to create a disturbance in the city of Belfast, I am perfectly satisfied. I do not want to suggest for a moment there is anything wrong, but I do feel that this picture is purely Sinn Fein propaganda, and that some action should be taken.[108]

In response, Dawson Bates, the Northern Ireland Minister of Home Affairs, declared that, while he was not 'a picture fan', he would not have 'the slightest hesitation' in seeing that the picture was banned in Belfast should it prove to be 'what is alleged'.[109]

As a consequence of Grant's intervention, a special screening of the film was arranged for the following day. This was attended by Bates, along with his Parliamentary Secretary, G. B. Hanna, the Inspector General of the RUC, Sir Charles Wickham, the Belfast City Commissioner and officials from the Northern Ireland Home Office. No statement was issued and it was generally assumed that the matter would be left to the Belfast Police Committee, which looked at the film the following day and decided 'not to take exception' to its public exhibition.[110] While the newspapers generally assumed that this was the end of the matter, this

---

108. *Parliamentary Debates* (HC), vol. xix, col. 62, 25 November 1936. Grant was a 'Labour' Unionist MP who belonged to the Ulster Unionist Labour Association (UULA) formed in 1918 by Edward Carson to secure the loyalty of working-class unionists. The organisation was, however, virulently anti-socialist and anti-communist in character and, according to Michael Farrell, distinguished from the Unionist Party only by its 'even more extreme sectarian and Loyalist position'. See *Northern Ireland: The Orange State*, 2nd edn (London: Pluto Press, 1980), p. 367.

109. *Parliamentary Debates* (HC), vol. xix, col. 63, 25 November 1936.

110. Minutes of a Special Meeting of the Police Committee, 27 November 1936.

turned out not to be so. For, on the very same day that the Police Committee met to consider the film, a Prohibition order preventing the exhibition of the film anywhere in Northern Ireland was prepared for signature by the Home Secretary. When this was publicly announced, the news was greeted with both surprise and alarm. The *Irish News* was particularly incensed and denounced the Minister for capitulating to 'strong partisan views'. It also held the ban to be 'stupid', not only for overturning the Police Committee's decision but for giving rise to the 'absurd' suspicion that the staunchly unionist committee might possess 'strong Sinn Fein sympathies'.[111]

Members of Belfast Corporation also lamented the fact that the police had failed to inform the Police Committee of the impending ban and felt the authority of the Corporation had been undermined. In the Committee's defence, Councillor Harcourt, the Committee's chairman, argued that it had approved the film from 'a moral and spiritual aspect' but had not reached a conclusion regarding its 'political aspect'.[112] Dawson Bates himself was reluctant to be drawn into making public comment on his action, but some insight into his position is provided by the response of the Northern Ireland Home Office to a letter from John Maxwell, the chairman and managing director of Associated British Picture Corporation (ABPC) which distributed the film. In the wake of the ban, Maxwell wrote to Bates to complain that it was likely to cost his company 'several thousands of pounds'. He went on:

> The picture was produced in good faith and during production particular care was taken to avoid taking sides on the political issues between the North and South. It was with that object in mind that a Northerner was engaged to direct the film. That we have succeeded in being impartial is, I submit, proven . . . by the fact that it has been shown in thousands of cinemas in the UK without any complaint, even in towns like Liverpool and Glasgow.

> . . . It was our intention to show this picture at our own theatre in Belfast, the Hippodrome, and if I had any thought that *Ourselves Alone* would provoke a disturbance I would certainly not have risked doing such damage to the goodwill of our property. It is just my conviction that this is definitely the type of picture that is good entertainment and should be shown . . .

The letter then concludes with an offer to remove 'any particular incidents which you consider are provocative or would offend'.[113] The matter was dealt with by Walter Magill, Permanent Secretary to the Ministry of Home Affairs, who drafted a response claiming that the showing of the film would 'give rise to disorder' and that cuts were 'impracticable' given that the decision to ban the film was not based on an 'objection to particular incidents' but 'the effect which would be produced by the picture as a whole'.[114] The final version of the letter was sent to

---

111. *Irish News*, 30 November 1936, p. 4. As was the case in The Northern Ireland Parliament, Belfast Corporation was dominated by the Unionist Party, particularly since the abolition of PR for local elections in 1922 and the withdrawal from full participation in the political system by nationalists during the 1930s.

112. *Belfast Telegraph*, 2 January 1937, p. 4.

113. Letter from John Maxwell to Sir Dawson Bates, 9 December 1936, PRONI HA32/1/640.

114. Memo from Magill to Dawson Bates, 11 December 1936, PRONI HA32/1/640.

Maxwell on 15 December, signed by Magill on behalf of the Minister. In it, he regrets the ban but argues that it was necessary for the following reasons:

> You will readily understand that a film exhibited in Great Britain with reference to events in Northern Ireland might afford excellent entertainment to an audience without arousing any strong personal feelings among its members, while the exhibition of a similar film here – where the bitter memories engendered by the conditions which form the theme of the film are still fresh and where, in fact, many of the participants in the troubles are still alive – might easily produce a different result.

> . . . [T]he minister feels sure that you will on consideration appreciate the serious danger of disorder which would have been incurred if the picture had been shown here at the present time.[115]

'We're the ones really alone': the meanings of *Ourselves Alone*

As befits a film that had been passed by the BBFC, *Ourselves Alone* initially appears to be conspicuously lacking in 'subversive' qualities. Certainly, the film's director, Brian Desmond Hurst, who was himself a Northern Ireland Protestant, took the view that the film was 'definitely pro-British'.[116] The film is structured around, and invites our identification with, the characters on the 'British' side, Hannay and Wiltshire, who are also played by the film's main 'stars'. The film places emphasis upon the constant risks to the safety of the British Army and even goes so far as to reclaim the meaning of the film's title for them. As Wiltshire complains bitterly in one scene: 'Sinn Fein. Do you know what that means? Ourselves alone. They're all watching you, whispering and spying, murdering and informing. Sinn Fein. That ought to be our motto, not theirs. We're the ones really alone.' The film ends, moreover, with a victory for the British side in which an IRA flying column is captured, the IRA leader, Mick O'Dea, is killed and the English officer Wiltshire is rescued from execution. In line with the conventions of classical narrative cinema (and the preferences of the BBFC), the film also foregrounds romantic intrigue at the expense of social and political factors. Accordingly, romance is not only central to the unfolding and eventual resolution of the plot but also underpins the film's humanist faith in the capacity of the romantic feeling of individuals (in this case an English officer and an Anglo-Irish woman whose brother is an IRA leader) to triumph over otherwise intractable political divisions.

However, while the film may be seen to privilege a broadly 'British' perspective, there are also a number of subordinate strands within the film that subject this dominant discourse to strain. For, if the narrative organisation of the film favours the British characters, it is still sufficiently loose to permit time for events that run counter to the film's main line. Unusually for classical narrative cinema, the appearance of the film's main leads is delayed for over fifteen minutes,

---

115. Letter from W. Magill to John Maxwell, 15 December 1936, PRONI HA32/1/640.
116. *Belfast Telegraph*, 19 December 1936, p. 10. Hurst also pointed to the involvement of Dudley Sturrock, a former British Army major who had served in Ireland. Sturrock not only co-wrote the play on which the film was based but also acted as the film's 'technical adviser'.

during which time the introductory scenes establish a substantially different tone from that which follows. The film begins with an ambush on a RIC lorry that is largely presented from the perspective of the ambushers, the IRA flying column. This no doubt contributed to the perception, encouraged by the film's publicists and repeated by a number of commentators, that the film was generally fair to both sides. This opening sequence is then followed by a striking display of community solidarity – reinforced by a 360-degree pan – when the police auxiliaries, the Black and Tans, aggressively search the local public house. Despite the inevitable presence of an informer, this sequence also lends credence to Wiltshire's claim that the police and the army are, indeed, 'alone' and lacking in popular support.[117] The script also includes strong expressions of anti-British sentiment ('Hell itself could be no worse than Ireland under English rule,' declares the IRA commandant Connolly), as well as some comments commending the courage of the IRA (Hannay shakes Connolly's hand, exclaiming 'You're a dirty Sinner but by God you've got guts'). Connolly, along with Hogan (Paul Farrell), also evades capture at the film's end and this (along with a knowledge of history) inevitably qualifies the sense of British accomplishment that the film otherwise strives to communicate. Moreover, the casting of an Anglo-Irish (and presumably Protestant) aristocrat as an IRA leader (and brother of the female lead) also contributes to a blurring of the moral and political distinctions that the film draws.

As a result, the film is much more ideologically ambivalent than Hurst acknowledges, encouraging a degree of bleakness and fatalism that ultimately works against the optimism of its romantic ending. Thus, there is some justification for the Unionist politicians' view that it is not just individual incidents but the overall atmosphere of the film that, from their point of view, is 'suspect'. However, even if the politicians did detect an unsympathetic undercurrent to the film, this is hardly likely to constitute a full explanation of their decision to ban the film. For, as Magill had implied in his letter to Maxwell, the political meaning of the film was heavily dependent upon context and the conditions shaping responses to the film in Northern Ireland were different from those elsewhere. In England, the film attracted little controversy and its publicists were concerned that audiences would lack the knowledge necessary to appreciate fully the film's story and title. As a result, a campaign to explain the meaning of the name 'Sinn Fein' to British audiences was undertaken.[118] In the South of Ireland, the Irish censor, James Montgomery, passed the film but complained that it favoured the British and might 'lead to protests'.[119] While the film enjoyed commercial success (and ran for five weeks in Dublin), it was also heavily criticised for its 'inaccuracies', 'unreal' roles and events that 'could never have happened' by the

---

117. As Kevin Rockett points out, the presence of an informer in an Irish historical film usually serves as 'a means of showing communal cohesiveness and unity' insofar as the informer's 'difference' helps to define 'the community's solidarity in opposition to the British presence'. See 'The Silent Period', in Kevin Rockett, Luke Gibbons and John Hill, *Cinema and Ireland* (London: Routledge, 1988), p. 11.

118. A fuller discussion of the film's publicity campaign, and critical reception, may be found in John Hill, '"Purely Sinn Fein Propaganda": The Banning of *Ourselves Alone* (1936)', *Historical Journal of Film, Radio and Television*, vol. 20, no. 3, August 2000, pp. 317–33.

119. Record of Films Censored, Film Censors Office 2, NAI 98/27/13, 5 May 1936, p. 10380. Montgomery was particularly upset by the portrait of the main antagonists, describing Hannay as 'a Bayard of the RIC' and Terence O'Neill – the IRA leader – as 'an Oxford man from the big house'.

nationalist *Irish Press* (founded by Eamon de Valera).[120] The irony of this was not lost on the *Northern Whig*, which commented that the film's banning in the North was particularly intriguing given that 'the Nationalist Press' in the South had 'condemned' it as 'pro-British' while 'the I.R.A. element' had 'urged a boycott against it'.[121]

Given the variety of responses to the film, it is evident that it was the political conditions under which the film was viewed, as much as the film itself, that were responsible for the way in which it was perceived. In the case of Northern Ireland, the sensitivity towards films dealing with the conflict was particularly acute. Belfast was a city with a history of civil disturbances and there was especially severe rioting (leading to several deaths) in the summer of 1935 when the Home Secretary, Dawson Bates, lifted a ban on all marches as a result of opposition from the Orange Order. These riots had in turn led to a curfew and caused some cinemas temporarily to close.[122] Given these circumstances, unionist claims that the exhibition of controversial films might lead to social disorder were not entirely without foundation. On the other hand, it is also evident that the decision to ban *Ourselves Alone* was not based solely on a concern for 'law and order' but also involved a degree of distaste for the public manifestation of what could be interpreted as anti-unionist or pro-nationalist sentiments. As Jennifer Todd argues, it was

> [t]he unspoken assumption . . . that unionists would organize the public sphere, that a unionist, British and Protestant ethos should predominate in public, and that Catholic social organization should not intrude into public space. When it did, informal sectarian and formal state means of repression were used to reaffirm the unionist and British nature of Northern Ireland.[123]

However, this fundamentally political concern to maintain the unionist ethos of the public sphere – particularly in the shared public spaces of the city centre – also endowed the actions of the government and its supporters with a double-edged quality. For while the banning of *Ourselves Alone* may have been justified on the basis of a perceived threat to public disorder, it was also the case, as the *Irish News* pointed out, that it was the labelling of *Ourselves Alone* as Sinn Fein 'propaganda' by unionists that largely created the situation in which the film would be liable to provoke disturbance.[124] Thus, just as Unionist politicians had been criticised for inflaming the situation during the 1935 riots, so the demagoguery of politicians such as Grant may be seen to have contained an element of indirect incitement to working-class loyalists to employ 'informal sectarian' means against 'undesirable' films should the authorities fail to take the appropriate action.[125] In

---

120. *Irish Press*, 14 July 1936, p. 5.

121. *Northern Whig*, 30 November 1936, p. 7.

122. 'Riots force Belfast halls to close', *Kine Weekly*, 25 July 1935, p. 19.

123. Todd, 'Unionist Political Thought', p. 201.

124. *Irish News*, 30 November 1936, p. 4.

125. Grant was, in fact, a leading contributor to the parliamentary debate that followed the first phase of the 1935 riots when he attacked the Inspector-General of the RUC ('an Englishman' with 'queer ideas about Northern Ireland') for encouraging the Home Secretary to place a ban on Orange marches and blamed the disturbances on the attitudes of Catholics towards a recent Royal visit (*Parliamentary Debates* [HC], vol. xvii, cols 2431, 2425, 10 July 1935).

this respect, for all its subscription to the rhetoric of 'law and order', popular unionism was also happy to take advantage of mob violence as and when necessary.

The Plough and the Stars

This fine line between maintaining and undermining public order was certainly evident in the ensuing controversy surrounding *The Plough and the Stars*. As a result of the *Ourselves Alone* ban, all films with a 'troubles' element now appeared to have the capacity to attract controversy. There was speculation in the trade press that John Ford's *The Informer* (1935) would also be banned in Belfast but the Police Committee denied that it had been asked to view it.[126] Nevertheless, the Police Committee had clearly been stung by the action of the Home Secretary in overturning its decision regarding *Ourselves Alone* and was now increasingly alert to the political character of films due to be shown in Belfast. Thus, when John Ford's film version of *The Plough and the Stars* was scheduled to open in the city in April 1937, it decided to flex its muscles and refused the film permission to be shown. As the play had been publicly performed in Belfast as recently as November 1935, this decision undoubtedly reflected a double standard, typical of much censorship, regarding the social composition of the audience for films as opposed to plays.[127] However, given the film's greater sympathy for Irish nationalism than the original play, it is also apparent that the ban went beyond a familiar middle-class concern to regulate the potential unruliness of (the young, working-class, male) cinema audience and manifest a more directly political concern to maintain unionist hegemony within the public sphere.[128] Thus, while there has been discussion of how, at particular historical moments, the cinema could provide an alternative, and even oppositional, public sphere for the subordinate social groups frequenting the cinema, the possibility of cinema providing alternative forms of political identification for nationalists in Belfast was held firmly in check.[129]

Certainly the effect of the ban, and the politicising of the climate around it, was to fuel protests (and 'informal' forms of 'regulation') in those areas where the film was allowed to be shown.[130] In Strabane, a man of 'certain political opinions' was responsible for throwing a stone

---

126. *Kine Weekly*, 10 December 1936, p. 39. However, the film (which had been passed with cuts by the BBFC in June 1935) does not appear to have been shown in Belfast until November 1938, by which time the atmosphere concerning 'political' films had cooled considerably.

127. The same double standard was also evident in the case of *Frankenstein*, given that this had enjoyed a run in Belfast as a play prior to its banning as a film. The main exception to this general rule was, of course, *The Green Pastures*, which, at least in England, could be seen on film but not on the stage.

128. For a discussion of some of the changes between play and film, see my 'Images of Violence', in Rockett, Gibbons and Hill, *Cinema and Ireland*, pp. 156–7.

129. For a discussion, with reference to early American film, of the cinema as an alternative public sphere', see Miriam Hansen, *Babel and Babylon: Spectatorship in American Silent Film* (Cambridge, MA: Harvard University Press, 1991), ch. 3.

130. Disturbances in cinemas were not, of course, uncommon in Ireland and *The Bioscope* (3 December 1930, p. 44) reports that Alfred Hitchcock's *Juno and the Paycock* was met with protests when it was screened in the city of Derry. This followed similar disturbances in the South, including in Limerick, where the film was burned. Such incidents were, of course, nationalist in orientation and stemmed from similar protests against Sean O'Casey's plays at the Abbey Theatre in Dublin. The novelty of events in the North was that the disturbances primarily involved unionists.

Banned in Belfast: John Ford's *The Plough and the Stars*

through the screen during the showing of the film, while, in Omagh, unionist youths exploded stink bombs inside the cinema, subsequently gathering in a threatening manner outside the cinema manager's home.[131] While the Strabane man received a two-month prison sentence as a result of the damage he caused to property, the *Irish News* noted, in the case of the incident in the cinema in Omagh, that while 'a few R.U.C. men were present' they failed to intervene. In opting not to do so, they also demonstrated something of the apparent ambivalence of the 'forces of law and order' when confronted with disorderly acts on the part of loyalists.[132]

Certainly the police were more likely to intervene in situations in which the actions of loyalists were challenged, as the example of *Beloved Enemy*, a Hollywood film loosely based on the life of Michael Collins, demonstrates. The Belfast Police Committee was sufficiently anxious about the film to arrange a special screening of it but decided, in the end, not to object to its

---

131. *Belfast Telegraph*, 26 November 1937, p. 3; *Irish News*, 6 October 1937, p. 5. Although no cinema seemed prepared to risk showing it in Belfast, Tom Cooper's amateur film, *The Dawn* (1936), an openly nationalist drama set during the Irish War of Independence, was shown elsewhere in Northern Ireland, where it too attracted protests. Audiences prevented the completion of a screening in Omagh while, in Enniskillen, there were fears that the film would be stolen. As a result, the Northern Ireland Home Secretary was faced with a question on the matter in the Northern Ireland House of Commons (*Parliamentary Debates* [HC], vol. xix, col. 1049, 27 April 1937).

132. *Irish News*, 6 October 1937, p. 5.

exhibition.[133] However, by this time, the climate surrounding 'troubles' movies had become so heated that almost any image of recent Irish history, no matter how apparently innocuous, was liable to generate a partisan response. Thus, when the film was shown in the Hippodrome in Belfast, 'a section of the crowd became unruly'. As the *Irish News* reports:

> The film is based on the Anglo-Irish war, and when a scene showing Dublin children writing 'Up the Rebels' on the back of a British official's car appeared on the screen a section of the crowd in the gallery became noisy, sang 'Dolly's Brae', and shouted party remarks.

> Another section in the gallery retaliated by shouting 'Up the Rebels' and also singing party songs.

> Members of the audience stood up and sang 'God Save the King' while the others remained seated and sang the 'The Soldier's Song'.

> The situation looked ugly, and a number of people rose from their seats and left the theatre. The lights were switched on and the police summoned.[134]

As a result of such disturbances, there were reports in the press that the Northern Ireland government was contemplating a total ban on all films 'dealing with the Anglo-Irish troubles'.[135] The *Northern Whig* also indicated that plans were afoot for the BBFC to 'seek Ulster's views' before 'passing any film dealing with Ireland'.[136] These arrangements would have invested the Northern Ireland government with considerable powers not just over British films but those from Hollywood as well. However, no formal agreement appears to have been reached and the Unionist regime did not press the matter. As previously noted, the British government successfully maintained an arm's-length relationship with the BBFC that allowed it to maintain a discreet distance from controversial censorship decisions (and sustain the convenient fiction that there was no political censorship in Britain). In contrast, the Northern Ireland Home Secretary's use of Special Powers legislation not only implicated him directly in acts of censorship but also rendered the Unionist government liable to criticism, at home and in Britain, for departing from conventional British standards of tolerance and for undermining British economic interests. In this respect, the Unionist regime must have sensed some of the political dangers involved in deviating too overtly from established practice in Britain (at least until the onset of war transformed the situation there).

---

133. The Committee also viewed *Parnell* in December 1937 and allowed it to be shown.

134. *Irish News*, 25 September 1937, p. 5. As with *Ourselves Alone*, the meanings extracted from *Beloved Enemy* also changed according to context. Thus, while it was capable of soliciting nationalist approval in the heightened political atmosphere of Belfast, it was described as 'an insult to the men who fought for Irish freedom' by the two men responsible for stealing the film in Dundalk on the other side of the border (*Northern Whig*, 23 June 1938, p. 10).

135. *Kine Weekly*, 7 October 1937, p. 16.

136. *Northern Whig*, 1 January 1938, p. 12.

Conclusion

While Ulster unionism may have achieved unity through opposition to Home Rule, it also consisted of a sometimes uneasy alliance of disparate economic, political and religious interests. Jennifer Todd distinguishes two main strands of 'unionist political culture', which she refers to as the 'Ulster British' and 'Ulster Loyalist' traditions.[137] Although Todd sees these as relatively distinct strands, they also represent, as she acknowledges, 'ideological poles' of the same tradition. Thus, while unionism was certainly less fractured during its period of political dominance than was subsequently the case (following the proliferation of different unionist parties from the 1960s onwards), there is also evidence of a clear tension, historically varying according to the political circumstances and social actors involved, between the apparent loyalty of unionists to Britain, and 'Britishness', on the one hand, and their loyalty to 'Ulster', and local interests, on the other.[138]

Accordingly, just as the first Northern Ireland films may be seen to have cultivated a distinctive 'Ulster' identity, so many of the conflicts surrounding censorship and Sunday opening in Northern Ireland involved a defence of what were perceived to be distinctively 'Ulster' religious values and political interests. As a result, the departure from 'British' norms and practices that followed threw into relief the ambivalent relationship of unionism to the very 'Britishness' with which unionist politicians and religious campaigners were otherwise identified. Similarly, the struggles over cinema also exposed some of the tensions within unionism between ('Ulster Loyalist') ideological and ('Ulster British') economic interests. Thus, while the demands for greater prohibitions upon the cinema stemmed from the 'populist' wing of unionism, they also clashed with both local and 'British' business interests. Capital investment in cinemas represented a significant contribution to the local economy, and the cinema trade in Northern Ireland also possessed close ties to London-based distributors and, in some case, exhibitors.[139] However, while exhibitors were able to exercise some degree of check on the demands of the religious campaigners and local politicians, it was also a tribute to the relative political strength of 'Ulster Loyalism' (and its ally fundamentalist Protestantism) that the trade in Northern Ireland was less successful than in Britain in resisting the attacks upon it.

---

137. Jennifer Todd, 'Two Traditions in Unionist Political Culture', *Irish Political Studies*, no. 2, 1987, p. 3. This distinction partly overlaps with Paul Bew, Peter Gibbon and Henry Patterson's identification of two forces – the 'populists' and the *via Britannica* group – within unionism during the interwar period. See *The State in Northern Ireland, 1921–72* (Manchester: Manchester University Press, 1979), ch. 3.

138. David Miller has sought to explain this tension in terms of a theory of 'contractarianism' whereby the loyalty of northern Protestants to the British crown is conditional upon the fulfilment of the sovereign's obligations to them. See *Queen's Rebels: Ulster Loyalism in Historical Perspective* (Dublin: Gill and Macmillan, 1978).

139. *Kine Weekly*, 15 July 1937, p. 14. Virtually all the cinemas in Northern Ireland depended upon London-based British and US distributors for a supply of films. Although, at this time, the majority of cinemas in Northern Ireland were locally owned, a growing number were linked to British cinema chains (such as ABPC, which was involved in the *Ourselves Alone* affair).

3

'Ulster at Arms'

Film and the Second World War

The Second World War is often identified as a turning-point for Northern Ireland and the Unionist regime. During the 1930s, the Northern Ireland economy had performed poorly. Agriculture had achieved some growth in productivity but output per capita remained well below the British average (only 52 per cent in 1939).[1] Linen and shipbuilding – the other two staples of the local economy – had experienced a severe downturn in demand and now faced long-term decline. Despite the government's introduction of New Industries legislation (in 1932 and 1937), the incentives proved insufficient to attract the kind of new industries (such as chemicals, electrical goods and motor vehicles) that had bolstered the English economy (although Short and Harland did open an aircraft factory in Belfast in 1937). As a result of these economic difficulties, there was an average rate of unemployment in Northern Ireland of 27 per cent between 1931 and 1939, while living standards were at least one-third less than in the rest of the UK.[2]

To this extent, the Second World War provided a temporary respite for the economy, boosting demand and employment. Due to the increased activity in engineering, shipbuilding and aircraft production, employment rose dramatically. According to Roy Foster, 'the numbers in the shipyards trebled . . . engineering workers, doubled [and] those employed in aircraft production increased threefold'.[3] Shirt-making and the clothing industry also expanded while new industrial activities, such as the production of dried milk, were launched. Farming was also boosted by the payment of uniform prices throughout the United Kingdom and central government measures (including the encouragement of mechanisation) to ensure the supply of essential foods.[4]

However, while this economic contribution to the war effort played a significant role in strengthening relations between the Northern Irish and British governments, it was not the

1. D. S. Johnson, 'The Northern Ireland Economy, 1914–39', in Liam Kennedy and Philip Ollerenshaw (eds), *An Economic History of Ulster, 1820–1940* (Manchester: Manchester University Press, 1985), p. 198.
2. Ibid., pp. 191, 221.
3. R. F. Foster, *Modern Ireland 1600–1972* (London: Penguin, 1989), p. 558. Foster goes on to indicate that, during the war, 'Northern Ireland produced 140 warships, 10 per cent of the entire merchant shipping of the UK, 1,500 heavy bombers and innumerable quantities of guns, tanks and ammunition'.
4. See K. S. Isles, 'Northern Ireland: An Economic Survey', in T. W. Moody and J. C. Beckett (eds), *Ulster since 1800: A Political and Economic Survey* (London: BBC, 1955), pp. 117–18.

most significant factor. Indeed, particularly at the beginning of the war, there was a degree of irritation in Britain at the persistence of higher rates of unemployment within Northern Ireland than in Britain and the recurrence of strikes and industrial action (which led Churchill to express his 'shock' at what was happening in October 1942).[5] The perception of Northern Ireland's difference from the rest of Britain was also reinforced by the British government's decision – against the wishes of the Unionist government – not to introduce conscription in Northern Ireland due to the hostility (given Northern Ireland's political situation) of the Roman Catholic church, nationalist politicians and the Irish government towards it.

Given these circumstances, it was the important strategic role played by Northern Ireland during the war that proved the decisive factor in reinforcing Northern Ireland's position within the UK. As part of the Anglo-Eire agreement of 1938 (which ended the 'economic war' between Britain and Ireland), the British government agreed to return to the Irish government what became known as the 'Treaty Ports' of Cobh, Berehaven and Lough Swilly. These had all been used by the Royal Navy during the First World War but were now generally regarded as inadequate for a modern naval fleet. However, they acquired a renewed significance when Ireland declared itself neutral during the war and refused Britain permission to make use of the ports. Initially, Irish neutrality looked as if it might threaten Northern Ireland Unionists when, in June 1940, Churchill appeared prepared to declare in favour of Irish unity in return for Ireland abandoning its neutrality. However, when the Irish Taoiseach, Eamon de Valera, rejected the offer, Northern Ireland assumed a crucial strategic role for Britain and the Allied Forces. As Brian Barton explains, Northern Ireland's 'ports, anchorages and airfields became bases for anti-submarine escorts, maritime reconnaissance and coastal command' and played a key role 'in keeping the sea lanes open during the Battle of the Atlantic'.[6] This was certainly the view of Churchill himself who, in his victory speech of 13 May 1945, paid the following tribute to Northern Ireland's contribution to the war effort:

> The sense of envelopment, which might at any moment turn to strangulation, lay heavy upon us. We had only the North-Western Approach between Ulster and Scotland through which to bring in the means of life and to send out the forces to war. Owing to the actions of the Dublin government . . . the approaches which the Southern Irish ports and airfields could so easily have guarded were closed by the hostile aircraft and U-boats. This was indeed a deadly moment in our life, and if it had not been for the loyalty and friendship of Northern Ireland we should have been forced to come to close quarters [with Mr de Valera] or perish from the face of the earth.[7]

As this suggests, Northern Ireland's military and economic contribution to the war (as well as its sacrifice during the blitz of Belfast in 1941) ultimately earned for the Unionists the gratitude of the British government. Despite the landslide victory of the Labour Party in the General

---

5. Brian Barton, *Northern Ireland in the Second World War* (Belfast: Ulster Historical Foundation, 1995), p. 57.

6. Ibid., p. 88.

7. Winston S. Churchill, *The Second World War, vol. vi, Triumph and Tragedy* (London: Cassell, 1954), p. 667. Significantly, this reprinting of the speech omits the controversial reference to de Valera.

Election of July 1945 and Unionist fears of the consequences of this for Northern Ireland's constitutional (and economic) status, a new postwar settlement in fact strengthened the hand of the Unionist regime. Through agreements signed in 1946 and 1949, the new Labour government recognised Northern Ireland's right to the same level of social services as the rest of the United Kingdom, which, in contrast to previous British governments, it was also prepared to underwrite financially. Even more significantly, Labour passed the Ireland Bill in 1949 in response to Ireland's decision to leave the Commonwealth and declare itself a fully independent republic. Partly out of pique at the Irish government's actions during and after the war, and partly as a reward for Northern Ireland's contribution to the war effort, the British government included a 'declaratory clause', which recognised that Northern Ireland would remain within the United Kingdom so long as the Parliament of Northern Ireland wished it.

However, although these developments provided the Unionists of Northern Ireland with increased constitutional security and lay the basis for the relative economic well-being of the postwar years, this outcome was by no means inevitable. In 1937, the Irish Free State had adopted a new constitution, retitling itself 'Eire' and laying territorial claim to the six counties of the North, that had revivified Irish nationalist ambitions. During the early stages of the war, the Unionist government won few friends in Britain as a result of Northern Ireland's lack of preparedness for war, poor industrial performance and relatively low levels of voluntary recruitment. It also experienced the shock of the British Cabinet's apparent willingness to abandon Northern Ireland in the interests of the greater good of winning the war. This sense of insecurity and fear of the future also led to upheavals within the Northern Ireland government itself. This included a backbench revolt that led to the resignation of Craigavon's successor as Prime Minister, John Andrews, after only three years in office and his replacement by Sir Basil Brooke in 1943. Given these circumstances, the Unionist government was unable to feel confident of its position and felt under continuing pressure to assert its full-hearted support for the war effort, its loyalty to the Crown and integral status as part of the United Kingdom.

One manifestation of this attitude may be detected in the government's concern to continue to generate good publicity for Northern Ireland and exploit propaganda possibilities. In 1939, it appointed its first Belfast-based Press Officer, the former editor of the *Northern Whig*, Frank Adams, whose responsibilities included the distribution of news concerning Northern Ireland and liaison with the Ministry of Information and the Ulster Office in London.[8] The Office of the Agent for Northern Ireland in London had been established in 1938 in order to promote Northern Ireland and encourage trade (with the UIDA's J. M. Henderson taking up the post of trade officer). Following the outbreak of war, and the change in Northern Ireland's economic circumstances, the Office increasingly devoted itself to publicity, a trend that was accelerated once Basil Brooke became Prime Minister in January 1943. A Cabinet Publicity committee ('to supervise and control publicity') was established and, in recognition of its reduced responsibility

---

8. Adams also acted as Regional Liaison Officer for the Ministry of Information between 1940 and 1944. Significantly, Adams' appointment followed a recommendation from Sir Roland Nugent, who argued that 'latent sympathy for Ulster' in Britain was fading and called for an increased co-ordination of the government's publicity activities (Memorandum, 7 October 1938, PRONI FIN18/18/497).

for trade matters, the London office was placed under the aegis of the Cabinet Office, rather than the Ministry of Commerce. Sir Ernest Cooper, formerly of the Ministry of Commerce in Belfast, was appointed Director of Information Services with a specific remit to secure 'increased publicity for Northern Ireland'.[9] As a part of their activities, both Adams in Belfast and Cooper in London (assisted by his Press Officer E. P. Northwood) sought to encourage the use of film as a vehicle for the promotion of Northern Ireland (and its role in the war). Although the Northern Ireland government itself was prepared to commit small amounts to projects, it looked mainly to newsreel companies and British Ministries (particularly the Ministry of Information, which had been established in 1939) to undertake such work. As will be seen these efforts to encourage films dealing with Northern Ireland met with mixed results. The project closest to the government's heart – a film about the strategic importance of Northern Ireland – did not proceed but a few others did. These were mainly short films and included *Ulster* (1941), made for the British Council; *Simple Silage* (1942), made for the Northern Ireland Ministry of Agriculture; *A Letter from Ulster* (1943), made by the Ministry of Information's Crown Film Unit; *Ulster at Arms* (1944), made for the Ministry of Supply; and *The Story of the Ulster Home Guard* (1945), made by the Army Kinema Service for the War Office.[10] While conventional histories of wartime British cinema have paid these films little attention (or, more commonly, ignored them altogether), they are nevertheless significant works in the context of Northern Ireland and help to illuminate many of the issues at stake in representing the region at this time.

From travelogue to wartime propaganda: *Ulster*

The first of these – *Ulster* – was not in fact conceived as a wartime film and only became so after the first material had been shot. As early as 20 December 1933, C. W. S. Magill, Secretary and Organiser of the UTDA, wrote to W. D. Scott, Permanent Secretary at the Ministry of Commerce, enclosing the minutes of the first meeting of the UTDA's Film Publicity Committee. He drew attention to the Committee's resolution to make a publicity film about Ulster but noted that 'the main obstacle to be overcome is finance'.[11] Ultimately, this proved to be a much greater problem than even he could have anticipated. As indicated in Chapter 1, the original plan was put into abeyance until 1937 when the Association revived the idea and launched a special appeal. Magill wrote to potential sponsors:

'It is proposed that the Picture be of the type known as 'Documentary'. This implies that it will not advertise Ulster in a direct manner to audiences but will, in an indirect, but nevertheless

9. 'Government Publicity: Short Résumé since 1922', PRONI CAB9F/123/313.

10. A silent 16mm short entitled *Things Seen in Northern Ireland* (1940) was also made for use in the classroom. The film remained in circulation during the postwar period, when Adams reported no less than ninety borrowings from the Central Film Library in three months during 1946 ('Films on Ulster Themes', 6 May 1946, PRONI CAB9F/123/81). However, the film was later withdrawn from distribution after Northwood of the Ulster Office used it to illustrate a lecture to the Travel Association. Northwood described the film as a 'dreadful production', commenting that 'most of the scenes in it, especially those depicting donkeys, urchins, thatched cottages, etc, are much more a sad reflection on Northern Ireland than a boost' (Letter from Northwood to Adams, 30 July 1947, PRONI CAB9F/123/81).

11. Letter from C. W. S. Magill to W. D. Scott, 20 December 1933, PRONI COM62/1/392.

effective way, carry a message throughout the world that Ulster is a place which is well worth while visiting.[12]

The film was expected to secure theatrical exhibition and was likely to cost a minimum of £1,500. Although the UTDA embarked upon discussions with potential production companies, the response to the appeal was poor and the Belfast Corporation's General Purposes Committee caused some controversy when it refused an award of £100.[13] Thus, by the end of October 1937, the fund had reached a mere £109.[14]

Once again, the Association came close to abandoning the project but was rescued by the Ministry of Commerce, which agreed to provide a one-off grant of £1,000 in May 1938.[15] However, in accordance with the wishes of the Prime Minister (Craigavon), they did so on the understanding that the film would be in Technicolor.[16] This created further difficulties for the UTDA, which pointed out that a Technicolor film would cost at least three times as much as a black-and-white film and would be unsuitable for reduction to 16mm.[17] The Association, however, persevered with the idea of making the film in colour and, in 1939, they renewed their appeal for contributions to the film fund. In the interim, they also helped with another – colour – project involving James Fitzpatrick, the globe-trotting writer-producer responsible for *Traveltalks*, a series of ten-minute travelogues made for MGM. Fitzpatrick arrived in Northern Ireland in June 1938, when he was given the full support of the UTDA, which also covered his travelling and living expenses.[18] However, due to bad weather, filming was suspended and it appears that the film was never completed (although Fitzpatrick did eventually return to Northern Ireland in 1945 when he made *Over the Seas to Belfast* [1946] and *Roaming through Northern Ireland* [1949]).

Nearly six years after its initial conception, filming eventually began – in 1939 – on the UTDA's own project. It had become apparent that the money for a colour film would not be raised and the Prime Minister reluctantly conceded that a black-and-white film was 'the only feasible proposition'.[19] The UTDA entrusted final negotiations concerning choice of a production company to the Film Department of the Travel and Industrial Development Association of Great Britain and Northern Ireland, which awarded the contract to the Strand Film Company, a commercial documentary outfit formed by Ralph Keene, Donald Taylor and Paul Rotha in

---

12. Letter from Magill to J. Milne Barbour, 20 January 1937, PRONI COM62/1/392.

13. *Belfast News-Letter*, 13 April 1937, p. 11.

14. Minutes of the UTDA Film and Broadcasting Sub-Committee, 27 October 1937, PRONI TOUR1/1/4.

15. Letter from the Permanent Secretary, Ministry of Commerce, to Magill, 23 May 1938, PRONI TOUR1/3/4.

16. Letter from Robert Gransden, Secretary to the Cabinet, to Scott, Permanent Secretary to the Ministry of Commerce, 23 June 1938, PRONI CAB9F/114/1.

17. Letter from Magill to Scott, 29 June 1938, PRONI TOUR1/3/4.

18. Minutes of the UTDA Council of Management, 21 July 1938, PRONI COM62/1/92.

19. Hand-written memo, 3 June 1939, PRONI CAB9F/114/1.

1935.[20] Ralph Keene arrived in August 1939 to undertake the shooting and he explained to the press the ideas behind the production:

> It would commence with the approach to Ulster on a cross-Channel vessel laden with holiday-makers, and then would follow scenes in the Ulster capital, including industries, people, and important buildings, the University and Stormont. The next stage would be the country with farmers and fishermen. 'Shots' would be taken of such local industries as salmon and eel fishing, flax-growing and turf-cutting. The historical sequence would deal with St Patrick, St Columba, and Derry, and towards the end there would be pictures of Ulster's fine motor-roads along which visitors could enjoy themselves . . . There would be no actors except the ordinary workers at their daily tasks.[21]

Filming was expected to occupy four to six weeks. War, however, was declared on 3 September and, due to the 'difficulties of the situation', filming was suspended.[22] Both Donald Taylor of Strand and A. F. Primrose of the British Travel Association recommended that the UTDA complete the film but with a new focus on 'How Ulster is Facing the Problems of War'.[23] The UTDA Council of Management, however, rejected this idea, preferring to resume production once hostilities ceased (which they presumably believed would occur rather sooner than it did). However, despite the UTDA's reluctance to proceed with the film, the British Council (which assumed responsibility for the British Travel Association in 1939) decided that Strand should nevertheless go ahead and finish it. As funds did not stretch to reshooting the entire film, the new version – under the provisional title of 'Ulster in Peace and Wartime' – was planned to combine previously shot material with new footage of aeroplane manufacture, shipbuilding, linen production, agriculture and the Services.[24] Keene, along with his cameraman George Noble, then returned to Northern Ireland in August 1940, where he was assisted by both the UTDA and Northern Ireland government officials.

In line with this revised conception, the final version of the film employs a before-and-after structure. The film's opening shots convey life in Northern Ireland prior to the outbreak of war, followed by a short survey of the – economic and military – contribution of Northern Ireland afterwards. What is noticeable, however, is how this is also presented in terms of a broad shift from a mainly rural to a predominantly urban-industrial society. Thus, while the film begins – in line with Keene's original plans – with shots of a ship arriving in Belfast, attention is quickly diverted to rural Ulster. The narration, written by the Unionist government's staunch ally of old St John Ervine, comments that 'Ulster is not only an industrial area' but possesses 'a wonderful

---

20. The Travel Association of Great Britain and Northern Ireland was founded in 1928 and, through the production of overseas publicity, sought to increase the number of overseas visitors to the UK, stimulate demand for British goods and services and promote international understanding. See Philip M. Taylor, *The Projection of Britain: British Overseas Publicity and Propaganda 1919–1939* (Cambridge: Cambridge University Press, 1981), pp. 93–9.

21. *Belfast News-Letter*, 9 August 1939, p. 10.

22. Minutes of UTDA Finance Committee, 29 September 1939, PRONI COM62/1/144.

23. Minutes of UTDA Council of Management, 7 December 1939, PRONI COM62/1/144.

24. Minutes of the UTDA Film and Broadcasting Sub-Committee, 8 August 1940, PRONI COM62/1/44.

variety of scenery'.[25] Shots of the Northern Irish countryside, farming and fishing then follow. As with earlier representations of rural 'Ulster', this sequence is redolent of Celtic romanticism. This is apparent in both the film's choice of imagery (a young girl and goat outside a simple cottage, for example) and its visual style, involving the careful framing and composition of figures against picturesque backdrops (a farmer making hay beneath a mountain, two men walking through a field with the coastline stretching out before them). The mood that these images evoke is reinforced by the heavily marked use of musical accompaniment. This consists of both ethereal choral music (by Richard Addinsell) and a rendition of the Scots song 'I Know Where I'm Going' (subsequently to feature in film director Michael Powell's paean to Celtic mysticism of the same name).[26] The effect of this is that, while the film does go on to register key industrial aspects of Ulster identity, it does so in a way that suggests a virtual fall from prelapsarian rural grace ('These quiet fields were typical of the serenity of Ulster until 1939', is how the commentary chooses to put it).

Nevertheless, what is most striking (and original), in the context of film representations of Northern Ireland, is the emphasis that the film places upon imagery of industrial labour – shipbuilding, munitions manufacture, the production of nets, parachutes and cigarettes. The film, in this regard, reveals its debt to British documentary film-making of the 1930s and its concern to extend the range of social representation through the showing of 'ordinary' people at work and at leisure. In contrast to previous images of Northern Ireland in terms of farmers and shopkeepers, the film, under pressure of wartime conditions, now locates industrial workers (including women workers) as the bedrock of the imagined community of 'Ulster'.[27] The consequences of this, however, are of interest.

It has been common to note how documentary film in the 1930s tended to furnish a depoliticised view of the working class, in which labour is detached from its specific relations of economic production and presented as emblematic of general humanist values.[28] It was also noted in Chapter 1, how difficult it was to find an imagery of urban-industrial Northern Ireland that could successfully avoid the connotations of political conflict and sectarianism that so often attached to the city of Belfast. In one sense, the film does this by imbuing industrialism with the same romanticism as its scenes of rural life. Although the dominant impulse of British documentary film-making in the 1930s was its enthusiasm for social documentation and public

25. St John Ervine was suggested to Strand by the Chairman of the UTDA, Fred Storey. However, it is an interesting indicator of the changing cultural climate that a member of the UTDA Council of Management felt that the commentary should be written by an industrialist (Minutes of the UTDA Council of Management, 12 September 1940, PRONI COM62/1/144).

26. The Weekly Edition of *The Times* apparently reported, in 1941, that '[t]hose who have been content to think of Ulster as a hard political or industrial entity will learn from this film of the loveliness of the six Counties, and their appealing melodic associations'. Quoted in the minutes of the UTDA Council of Management, 14 August 1941, PRONI COM62/1/92.

27. As in the rest of the UK, the employment of women in Northern Ireland rose sharply during the war, rising to a total of 118,600 in 1943. See Barton, *Northern Ireland in the Second World War*, p. 82.

28. See, for example, Stuart Hood, 'John Grierson and the Documentary Film Movement', in James Curran and Vincent Porter (eds), *British Cinema History* (London: Weidenfeld and Nicolson, 1983).

communication, this sociological concern was also tempered by an aesthetic interest in the creative possibilities of the film medium. As John Corner indicates, many of the documentaries of this period reveal an awareness of how 'aesthetic design, including pleasingness of rhythm and beauty of composition' could enhance 'viewers' awareness of . . . working processes'.[29] Andrew Higson links this strand of creative experiment to a discourse of 'poetic realism', which, he argues, encouraged the romanticisation of 'the object of documentation into a thing of aesthetic beauty'.[30] Although *Ulster* lacks the fully developed 'poetic' qualities of films such as *Coal Face* (1935) or *Night Mail* (1936), it is nevertheless clearly influenced by their example. Workers, who are seen but not heard, are presented in a series of aesthetically pleasing shots that emphasise the 'dignity' (and, in some cases, physical beauty) of their labour. This is paralleled by a similar aestheticisation of industrial machinery and objects. The reintroduction of Addinsell's music (initially over shots of women workers making nets) also invests the industrial imagery with some of the same ethereal connotations as the rural scenes. As a consequence, the imagery of the workforce loses much of its specific content and connotations, assuming the status of abstract, or generalised, 'heroic' labour.

However, while this kind of celebration of the 'people's war', through the romanticisation of labour, would have been unremarkable in an English context, inevitably it is more problematic in a Northern Irish one. This is most clearly seen in the film's final montage sequence. As Higson indicates, montage in documentary film has 'the ability to deal with the multiple, to establish connections and relations, and make visible systems of interdependence across a broad social fabric'.[31] In this respect, the use of montage in wartime documentaries (such as *Listen to Britain* [1942]) was a key element in stressing social interconnectedness and realising a vision of the 'national community'. The film *Ulster* also makes use of montage in order to celebrate the way in which 'ordinary' people are bound together in the 'national' project of winning the war. However, while this involves shots of saluting soldiers as well as various agricultural and industrial workers (some of whom have been seen earlier in the film), they are superimposed over an overhead shot of the Parliamentary Buildings at Stormont.[32] The accompanying voice-over also declares:

> The Northern Ireland Parliament made this declaration at the outbreak of war. The people of loyal Ulster will share the burden of their kith and kin in every part of the Empire to the uttermost extent of their resources. Britain's difficulty is Northern Ireland's opportunity to place all

---

29. John Corner, *The Art of Record: A Critical Introduction to Documentary* (Manchester: Manchester University Press, 1996), p. 63.
30. Andrew Higson, *Waving the Flag: Constructing a National Cinema in Britain* (Oxford: Clarendon Press, 1995), p. 192.
31. Ibid., p. 195.
32. The Parliament Buildings at Stormont were opened, by the Prince of Wales, in 1932. Designed along classical lines, the building was described by the *Belfast News-Letter* (16 November 1932, p. 6) as embodying 'solidity, strength and dignity'. Featuring a statue of Britannia atop the building, and an allegorical carving of Ulster handing the torch of loyalty to Britain, the building was intended to celebrate not only the grandeur of the new regime but also the strength of its ties to Britain. As a result, the image of the building came to assume an iconic status for the Northern Ireland government, repeatedly employed in official publications and publicity material.

her possessions, human and material, at the service of our King. The people of Ulster have long loved and have defended liberty. They will not fail to defend it now.

In this way, the film appropriates the vocabulary or wartime populist documentary to project not only Northern Ireland's oneness with Britain (reversing the old nationalist epithet concerning Britain's 'difficulties') but also its own – apparently consensual – 'national' community. This is, of course, a selective, and implicitly partisan, imagining of 'the people of Ulster' that suppresses the problematic relationship of the Northern Ireland Parliament to the whole of its 'people', as well as the social and religious divisions that characterise the Northern Irish 'community' (and which made the introduction of conscription in Northern Ireland impossible). Nevertheless, from the point of view of the Unionist regime, keen to assert Northern Ireland's 'British' credentials and loyalty to Empire, the film was clearly a success and a major propaganda boost for it. The UTDA was certainly pleased with the result and arranged a premiere in Belfast, which was attended by members of the Cabinet, including the Prime Minister, J. M. Andrews, who described it as 'a wonderful film'.[33] Subsequently the film was distributed in UK cinemas by General Film Distributors (a subsidiary of Rank) and shown (on 16mm) by Ministry of Information mobile units. In the light of this, the UTDA Council of Management, in a formulation that suggests how readily its tourist role assumed a political complexion, expressed its satisfaction that the film had 'helped to bring the claims of Northern Ireland before the people of Great Britain'.[34]

Simple Silage

Ulster would not, of course, have been completed had it not been for the intervention of the British Council. Although the Northern Ireland government was keen to encourage film propaganda, it was much less enthusiastic about paying for it and the Ministry of Finance was generally reluctant to commit more than small amounts. As early as February 1940, Richard Hayward identified the benefits of 'a propaganda picture for Northern Ireland'. He met with Sir Wilson Hungerford, Stormont MP and secretary of the Ulster Unionist Council, and subsequently wrote to him, explaining his conception:

> We need a picture on the lines of 'THE LIONS HAS WINGS' – and we *MUST HAVE* such a picture. Through such a vehicle we could tell – *directly and vividly* – the story of the birth of this country, the story of our unity with the Empire, the story of our industrial history and worth, the story of the part played by Ulstermen in the great places of the world, the story of Ulster and the

---

33. *Belfast Telegraph*, 25 April 1941, p. 7.

34. Minutes of UTDA Council of Management, 14 August 1941, PRONI COM62/1/92. Given the highly flattering manner in which the film presents the importance of Northern Ireland's wartime role, the organisation initially feared that the film's release outside of the UK might encourage further bombing of Belfast (which had begun in April 1941). The British Council, however, brushed aside such anxieties, responding that they found it 'difficult to see how the film could do anything but good'. (Letter from Neville Kearney, British Council, to Fred Storey, Chairman of the UTDA, 25 June 1941, PRONI CAB9F/114/1.)

United States of America, and above all the story of Ulster in the present fight against the vile things for which Hitler, and his merry band of murderers, stands.[35]

Hungerford subsequently wrote to R. Gransden, of the Cabinet Secretariat, expressing his sympathy for the idea and seeking possible government support. 'There is no doubt the time is very opportune to put Ulster's story over without bringing in the political aspect,' he wrote. However, 'to put on a film on the lines suggested', he continued, 'would require a lot of money, and could only be fathered by the Government, as the British Government fathered the others'.[36] Hungerford's letter went to Craigavon who agreed that Hayward's proposal had 'many merits'. However, he considered that 'it would be quite out of the question for the Government to consider putting up the substantial sum of money which would be required' and 'that references to Ulster on news reels from time to time might be quite as effective as the showing of a special Ulster film'.[37]

Although such an ambitious undertaking as Hayward's was beyond the means of the Stormont regime, it did contemplate smaller, more directly functional, projects, such as the informational short *Simple Silage*, which was produced for the Ministry of Agriculture. According to William MacQuitty, the film's origins reside in a Ministry of Agriculture demonstration held at his farm in 1941. MacQuitty was born in Belfast in 1905 and had acquired a small farm (located only three miles from Stormont) on his return from China (where he had worked as a banker) in 1939. Due to the cost and shortage of imported foodstuffs, the Ministry of Agriculture was involved in the promotion of silage (i.e. young grass fermented in a pit or silo) and brought a group of farmers to MacQuitty's farm to observe his approach. The visit prompted MacQuitty to suggest the production of a film, which, in the face of initial indifference, he offered to make himself.[38] Given his lack of film experience, he then recruited Richard Hayward and Louis Morrison to act as director and cameraman respectively. Hayward was also responsible for negotiating terms. Still keen to be of service to the government, and anticipating further work, he agreed to shoot the film for the Ministry at a reduced rate. 'I am anxious that a Northern Ireland Government production should be in the hands of a Northern Ireland unit,' he declared, before assuring the Ministry of 'a worth-while piece of national propaganda'.[39]

The film that resulted was a straightforward piece of informational exposition, demonstrating the various methods for preparing silage and alerting farmers to the assistance available from the Ministry of Agriculture. The Ministry had initially anticipated that the film would involve a small element of dramatisation in order to bring out the 'human element'.[40] For these scenes

35. Letter from Richard Hayward to Sir Wilson Hungerford, 26 February 1940, PRONI CAB9F/123/3A.
36. Letter from Sir Wilson Hungerford to R. Gransden (Cabinet Secretariat), 29 February 1940, PRONI CAB9F/123/3A.
37. Letter from L. G. P. Freer to Sir Wilson Hungerford, 1 March 1940, PRONI CAB9F/123/3A.
38. William MacQuitty, *A Life to Remember* (London: Quartet Books, 1991), p. 269.
39. Letter from Richard Hayward to W. A. V. Sanderson, Ministry of Agriculture, 15 August 1941, Ulster Folk and Transport Museum (UFTM). This correspondence between Hayward and the Ministry seems not to tally with MacQuitty's claim that the film was made without the Ministry's agreement.
40. Letter from Sanderson to MacQuitty, 13 August 1941, UFTM.

Hayward revived his old character of Sam Mulhern in the form of a farmer who is converted to the benefits of silage. Although material along these lines was shot, it was omitted from the final version of the film. Hayward did, however, deliver the narration and also employed instrumental versions of some local songs on the soundtrack. As such, the film maintains some of the concerns with rural life and local culture evident in Hayward's films of the 1930s but with a new emphasis – given the context – on labour and modern approaches to agriculture. Thus, a key sequence occurs in the Ministry of Agriculture laboratories, where research staff are engaged in evaluating the quality and feeding value of silage.

The film's premiere took place at the Classic Cinema in Belfast in February 1942. This was attended by the Minister of Agriculture, Lord Glentoran (who made a speech declaring the importance of increasing milk supplies), as well as other members of the Cabinet (including Sir Basil Brooke, then Minister of Commerce), the Lord Mayor of Belfast (Sir Crawford McCullagh), various Stormont MPs and members of the Ulster Farmers' Union Executive. Local cinemas were given the film for free and special screenings at farmers' meetings were still taking place over two years later. However, while the film was well received and letters to the local press looked forward to further locally produced films, this was to be the only film produced for (and funded by) the Northern Ireland government during the war.[41] It did, however, provide a degree of assistance to three other productions financed by Ministries in Britain.

A Letter from Ulster

The first of these was *A Letter from Ulster*, which William MacQuitty also claims the credit for inspiring. Following the production of *Simple Silage*, MacQuitty had been asked to go to London, where he met Jack Beddington and Lord Arthur Elton of the Ministry of Information (MOI) Films Division. Asked about ideas for a further film, he suggested one dealing with 'the American troops flooding into Ulster and how they're settling in their training camps'.[42] The following year he got a call from Ian Dalrymple of the Crown Film Unit, who asked him to work as assistant director on such a project. This was, perhaps, the most prestigious production concerning Northern Ireland made during the war. The Crown Film Unit (formerly the GPO Film Unit) had become the main production arm of the MOI. Ian Dalrymple had become Head of the Unit in 1940 and had written one of the first wartime propaganda films to appear in cinemas, *The Lion Has Wings* (1939). Although the Crown Film Unit undertook a relatively small number of projects, compared with the large numbers of information films produced by other production outfits (such as Realist and Strand), they were generally budgeted at a higher level and were intended for theatrical release. The Unit was particularly associated with the

---

41. Two letters appeared in the *Belfast News-Letter* and *Belfast Telegraph*, by 'Ulster First' and 'Agricola' respectively, on 5 February 1942, praising the excellence of the film. Their tone and sentiments, however, suggest that they may well have been written by Hayward himself. The letter in the *News-Letter*, for example, points out that the film 'is purely local and Ulster should be proud of a first-class job done by Ulster producers in our own province'. 'There are numerous other subjects which could be dealt with in a similar fashion', the letter continues, 'so here's looking forward to many more films of the calibre of "Simple Silage" and to the firm establishment of documentary film production in Ulster!'.

42. MacQuitty, *A Life to Remember*, p. 272.

wartime development of the 'story documentary'. These films built on the experiments of prewar films, such as Harry Watt's *North Sea* (1938), and included *Target for Tonight* (1941), *Coastal Command* (1942) and *Fires Were Started* (1943). Anticipating the development of the 'drama-documentary', these films were inspired by actual events, made use of 'real' people (rather than professional actors) and adopted a semi-observational style. Described in the local press as a 'documentary with a difference', *A Letter from Ulster* was to draw on many of the same features.[43]

Although the film does employ a small number of actors (including Charles Fagan from the Belfast Players), most of the cast are non-professionals, including the two soldiers – Sergeant Donald Prill and Private Walter Newffield – in the leading roles. According to a MOI press release, the selection process involved 'parading the men and talking to them' with the intention of finding two 'who were typical'.[44] The film was also shot almost entirely on location, mainly at Tynan Abbey (the estate of Norman Stronge, the Speaker of the Northern Ireland Parliament).[45] However, while the film uses actual locations and real soldiers, its characters and story (written by Shaun Terence Young) are fictional. Two brothers – Don and Wally Carver – are told by their Colonel to write a ten-page letter home when he discovers that they are not receiving mail. The brothers' letter (and their discussion over its composition) then becomes the source of the film's voice-over, in which they describe and comment on their experiences since arriving in Northern Ireland. This involves recalling their arrival at the camp (and the friendliness of a Cockney private, Stines, who has stayed on to help them), teaching baseball to local children, military manoeuvres, an assault course and a forty-eight-hour period of leave.

For K. R. M. Short, the film was one of the first concerned with the general 'problem of Americans on British soil'.[46] However, because of the film's Irish setting, other factors were necessarily brought into play. Indeed, the publicity for the film consistently referred to it as showing how 'the American troops are settling down in Ireland' and rarely mentioned either Britain or, indeed, Ulster.[47] This was undoubtedly related to the fact that, although the film was distributed in Britain by MGM, it was primarily intended for audiences in the USA where, according to MacQuitty, the film was shown in 10,000 cinemas.[48] This, in turn, necessitated a degree of circumspection in the way that the situation in Ireland was presented.

American troops had first arrived in Northern Ireland in January 1942, reaching a peak of over 120,000 (about one-tenth of the local population) in June 1944. During these years,

---

43. *Belfast Telegraph*, 17 July 1942, p. 4.

44. Public Record Office (PRO) INF/6/347.

45. In a dark historical twist, Stronge, aged eighty-six, and his son were murdered, and Tynan Abbey burned down, in 1981 by the Provisional IRA as a reprisal for an Ulster Defence Association gun attack on Bernadette McAliskey (formerly Devlin).

46. K. R. M. Short, 'Cinematic Support for the Anglo-American Détente, 1939–43', in Philip M. Taylor (ed.), *Britain and the Cinema in the Second World War* (Basingstoke: Macmillan, 1988), p. 134. He notes how the film was followed by the Strand production *Welcome to Britain* (1943), which provided advice to visiting American troops (on pub manners, currency and prostitutes).

47. PRO INF6/347. The film itself was actually made under the working title of *A Letter Home* and 'Ulster' was only a late addition, probably to avoid confusion with the earlier Carol Reed short, *A Letter from Home* (1941).

48. Letter from MacQuitty to Sir Basil Brooke, 19 April 1943, PRONI COM61/661.

Northern Ireland offered an important base for American naval and air operations as well as providing a holding area and training ground for successive groups of soldiers.[49] However, the presence of American troops on Irish soil was not, as in the rest of the United Kingdom, uncontroversial. De Valera regarded the arrival of American troops as a breach of Irish sovereignty (and neutrality) and declared that 'no matter what troops occupy the Six Counties, the Irish people's claim for the union of the whole national territory and for supreme jurisdiction over it, will remain unabated'.[50] De Valera's protests also encouraged the IRA's northern command to launch a fresh campaign in March 1942 intended to 'sabotage . . . war industries and enemy military objectives'.[51] This animosity towards the presence of American troops was shared by the leadership of the Catholic church in Northern Ireland as well as many within the Catholic population. In his 1942 survey, conducted for Mass Observation, Tom Harrisson reported that many Northern Ireland Catholics regarded the presence of American troops as 'an insult' and suspected that they were 'really there to ensure partition and possibly even to invade the south'.[52] Matters were not helped by the shooting of a bus driver by a GI near Derry, which Hurst indicates occurred shortly before his arrival to make a 'goodwill documentary'.[53] Given these circumstances, and the need to appeal to an American (and Irish-American) audience, it is probably unsurprising that the film, in addition to highlighting various connections between Northern Ireland and the USA, should seek to avoid the overt unionism of Ulster. Instead, it plays lightly with the issue of the border, provides an image of 'Ulster' that represents Catholics (and not just Protestants) and draws upon readily recognisable signifiers of 'Irish' (rather than 'British') culture.

The film's address to an American audience is most apparent in the scenes during the men's leave when the two brothers visit Carrickfergus Castle and the town of Strabane. In terms of geography (and documentary verisimilitude), this constitutes a somewhat unlikely outing but nevertheless permits the film to highlight the links between the North of Ireland and the USA. In Strabane, for example, the men go to Gray's Printing Shop, where they see the press on which, we are told, 'they trained the men who were later to print the Declaration of Independence'. The film's awareness of its intended American audience also has consequences for the film's treatment of 'Ulster' more generally. In its report on the making of the film, the Belfast Telegraph had claimed that it would not be 'confined to troops' and would feature 'Ulster people,

49. Barton, Northern Ireland in the Second World War, p. 98.

50. Quoted in Robert Fiske, In Time of War: Ireland, Ulster and the Price of Neutrality 1939–45 (Dublin: Gill and Macmillan, 1983), p. 529.

51. Quoted in Jonathan Bardon, A History of Ulster (Belfast: Blackstaff Press, 1992), p. 582. J. Bowyer Bell reports that the Americans were aware of the problem of the IRA and, through an intermediary, sought to avoid trouble. Although there were reports of assaults on Americans in nationalist areas, the IRA campaign itself was directed against RUC men rather than troops. See J. Bowyer Bell, The Secret Army: A History of the I.R.A. 1916–1970 (London: Sphere, 1970), p. 261.

52. Quoted in Barton, Northern Ireland in the Second World War, p. 124.

53. Brian Desmond Hurst, Autobiography, unpublished, undated, p. 123, BFI Library, London. Hurst also claims that 'the Germans at the Embassy in Dublin were spreading rumours that the Americans who were stationed in Ulster, were behaving like an army of occupation and beating up the people of the North'.

Ulster scenery, ways of speech and Ulster music'.[54] However, while the film did employ local people, its representation of the locality was also much less definite than this suggests. In the case of music, for example, it is noticeable how the songs used in the film possess a general connection with Ireland rather than any particular association with Ulster (or Britain). Thus, at the concert for the US troops, a local man, Denis Martin, sings 'The Rose of Tralee' (the same song sung by Cavan O'Connor to a rapt audience of nationalist villagers in a bar in *Ourselves Alone*). Later, when the two brothers visit the Red Cross Centre in Derry (the name actually used in the film in preference to Londonderry), they hear a rendition of 'When Irish Eyes are Smiling'.[55] In this way, the film evokes a more general sense of 'Irishness' than the use of 'Ulster' in the film's title might suggest. This is largely true of the film as a whole.

For, just as the Hayward films in the 1930s were unable to escape the romantic conventions traditionally associated with the representation of Ireland, so *A Letter from Ulster* depends heavily upon those images of Ireland likely to be most familiar to an American audience. While the American GIs may be 'ordinary guys' (rather than jaded businessmen or returning exiles), their arrival in Ireland is nevertheless premised upon an implied contrast between their experiences in Northern Ireland and their prior life in the US. This was certainly the view of the *Motion Picture Herald* (a US trade paper), which noted how Hurst had successfully created 'a grand backcloth of sweeping mountains and sleepy villages' that stood in 'odd contrast to the highpowered efficiency of many of the towns' from which the men had come.[56] This contrast is evident in the scenes involving the men's encounters with the locals, as when their tanks are seen parked outside a cottage in order to enjoy some fresh milk. Later in the film, Don and Wally stop at a thatched cottage for water for their 'peep' (a troop-carrying jeep), when they are invited in for tea and end up helping to gather the hay. While such scenes as these are intended to show the friendliness of the welcome that the American troops are receiving in Northern Ireland, they also reverberate with associations of Ireland as a simpler, slower and more traditional kind of society. In doing so, they also blur the distinctions between the different parts of the island by invoking a relatively undifferentiated notion of rural 'Irishness'.

This may also be seen in an earlier scene involving the men driving through the local countryside. During this trip, they succeed in getting lost and discover from a farmer that they are in the 'Free State'. Although American troops were under instructions not to cross the border (given de Valera's objections to their presence on Irish territory), the matter is made light of and the men subsequently joke with a local RUC man that 'there don't seem to be any boundaries around here'. The apparent ease with which visitors get lost in the Irish countryside is a recurring narrative trope within films set in Ireland, typically confirming a sense of either the 'primitiveness' or 'other-worldliness' of Irish life. In this context, it also dilutes the very distinctions between North and South that the Unionist government was attempting so

---

54. *Belfast Telegraph*, 17 July 1942, p. 4. The article also indicates that Richard Hayward had 'placed his vast store of Ulster lore at the service of the production'.

55. Given that Tom Harrisson of Mass Observation had noted that, in the city of Derry, 'Catholics tend to dislike or despise' the American troops, the choice of Derry as a location was clearly of propaganda significance. See Barton, *Northern Ireland in the Second World War*, p. 124.

56. *Motion Picture Herald*, 2 January 1943, p. 1094.

'When Irish Eyes are Smiling': the two brothers visit the Red Cross Centre in Derry in *A Letter from Ulster*

assiduously to reinforce. For, despite the efforts of the Unionists during this period to emphasise the separateness of 'Ulster' from 'Eire' and to avoid reference to the border issue, this jokey
acknowledgment of the permeability of the Irish border gently subverts their efforts to maintain a rigid sense of 'partition'.

Intriguingly, the only scene shot in a city – at the Roman Catholic St Mary's Church in Belfast
– was a late addition to the film and carries no association with the urban-industrial. In their descrip-
tions of the film's production, both Hurst and MacQuitty tell of the need to include a scene that
would act as a counterweight to the open-air service at the army camp (in which the men recite the
Lord's Prayer).[57] This was probably felt necessary given the reservations concerning the presence of
troops among Northern Ireland Catholics and the pre-eminence of Catholicism among Irish-
Americans. It also conformed to the more general British government policy of encouraging Christian co-operation, which manifested itself in two Ministry of Information films, *The Sword of the Spirit*
(1943), on the contribution of English Catholics to the war effort, and *Catholics in Britain* (1945).[58]

---

57. MacQuitty, *A Life to Remember*, p. 276.

58. The title of *The Sword of the Spirit* refers to the initiative launched by Cardinal Hinsley, the Roman Catholic
    Archbishop of Westminster, to bring the churches together 'in a crusade of prayer, study, and action for the
    restoration of a Christian order of justice and peace'. For further information, see Angus Calder, *The People's War:
    Britain 1939–1945* (London: Panther, 1971), p. 556.

'There don't seem to be any boundaries around here': American GI Wally (Walter Newffield) asks the RUC for directions in *A Letter from Ulster*

It is probably no coincidence, therefore, that a MOI memo concerning *A Letter from Ulster* was written on the back of a press release entitled 'Dutch Catholics and Protestants in fight against Hitlerism'.[59]

As a result of these factors, the film is unusual in attempting to offer a more inclusive 'imagining' of 'Ulster' than that found in earlier films, as well as an element of 'balance' between the representation of Protestants and Catholics. Indeed, Hurst appears to have forgotten that the film's two main characters are, in fact, brothers and writes that one of them was Catholic and the other Protestant.[60] What is also noticeable, however, is that a scene that was initially introduced to rectify an imbalance comes close to overwhelming what comes before it. The scene is shot inside the church and involves two extended tracking shots along the faces of the congregation. Compared with the rather perfunctory mid-shot of the men at camp preceding it, this is a technically accomplished scene involving the film's most elaborate camera movements (including a tilt down the altar), striking chiaroscuro effects and affecting choral music. The scene is reminiscent of John Ford, with whom Hurst worked, and is suffused with a sense of the religiosity to

59. PRO INF5/87.

60. Hurst, *Autobiography*, p. 123.

be found in such Ford films as *The Informer* and *Mary of Scotland* (1936). While the scene does, of course, draw upon its own stock of conventional imagery (concerning devout, Catholic Ireland), its appearance in this context is nevertheless significant and provided a rare acknowledgment within wartime films of the Catholic presence within Northern Ireland. This did not, of course, prevent the Unionist government from using the film to its own advantage. A special screening in Belfast was arranged and attended by the Prime Minister, J. M. Andrews, whose speech emphasised the bond between Ulster and the United States as well as Ulster's contribution to 'the fight for world freedom'. 'Depicting as it does the unity of two great democracies,' he declared, 'I have no doubt that this film will meet with enthusiastic appreciation both in the United Kingdom and the United States.'[61] A press release, incorporating Andrews' speech, was then sent to the MOI in an effort to influence the way in which the film was promoted (particularly in the US).[62]

Ulster at Arms

The next film to be made in Northern Ireland – *Ulster at Arms* – began filming later that year (in October 1943). Its history, however, went back two years. In October 1941, Ernest Cooper, then at the Ministry of Commerce, had visited the Ministry of Supply Films Division in London where he had seen a film supervised by Frank Green (he does not specify a title). This prompted him to propose a film on the war industries in Northern Ireland into which 'several points on propaganda that would be pertinent to our own situation' could be worked.[63] His idea was backed by the then Minister of Commerce, Sir Basil Brooke, whose office sought approval for expenditure on a film designed to stimulate 'workers in factories to pull out their maximum effort in connection with war production'.[64] Brooke also wrote to Brendan Bracken, the Minister for Information, requesting MOI support for such a project.[65] When this was not forthcoming, the Ministry looked set to proceed with a local exhibitor, George Lodge of Ulster Cinematograph Theatres, who had already provided a synopsis under the title of 'Ulster at War'. However, although the Ministry of Finance sanctioned expenditure of £2,000 (double the cost of *Simple Silage*), the film did not proceed. Elements of the idea, however, resurfaced with the making of *Ulster at Arms*.

The British Ministry of Supply was responsible for organising a film service in factories, which it extended to Northern Ireland in April 1943. This involved two projection units visiting about twenty-four factories every fortnight. After a financial agreement had been reached with the Northern Ireland government, a third unit was added at the end of the year. A major component of the Ministry's film programme was the news magazine, *Warwork News*, which it launched in spring 1942. It was also as part of this series that the Ministry commissioned British Paramount News to make *Ulster at Arms*, 'a brief survey', as the film's commentary puts it, 'of

61. *Belfast Telegraph*, 12 January 1943, p. 4.

62. Letter from E. P. Northwood to E. Hudson, 15 January 1943, PRO INF5/87.

63. Letter from E. H. Cooper to A. J. Whitehead, Ministry of Supply, 22 October 1941, PRONI COM61/661.

64. Letter from D. A. E. Harkness, Ministry of Commerce, to Capt. G. H. Petherick, Ministry of Finance, 25 October 1941, PRONI FIN 18/21/318.

65. Letter from Sir Basil Brooke to Brendan Bracken, 18 November 1941, PRONI COM61/661.

Ulster's war effort'. Although it does not appear as though the Northern Ireland government was directly involved in the film's preparation, it was consulted about it at the editing stage. Northwood viewed the film with Frank Green and – presumably because of its suggestion of 'primitiveness' – objected to a shot of 'an ass and a cart', which Green agreed to remove.[66] The script was also vetted in Belfast, although not all of the Northern Ireland government's recommendations were accepted.[67]

Like *Ulster*, the film consists mainly of footage of agricultural and industrial production. However, compared to the earlier film, its style is more direct and functional and avoids its 'poetic' elements. The Irish accent of the earlier film is also abandoned in favour of a middle-class English voice-over delivered in the breezy style typical of the newsreel genre of this period.[68] Like *Ulster*, the film places considerable emphasis upon 'ordinary' workers (particularly women factory workers) but, once again, we do not hear the voices of the workers themselves, who are effectively 'spoken for' by the narration. This superficial populism is also, as in *Ulster*, entwined with a pro-Unionist discourse. The film opens with a low-angle shot of the statue at Stormont of Edward Carson, the leader of the Ulster Unionists in their opposition to Irish nationalism and Home Rule, unveiled in 1933. A second shot of the statue and one of the Parliament Buildings then follow. Over these the narration comments, 'Yielding place to no one as a loyal member of the British Commonwealth, Northern Ireland, still cherishing the memory of Lord Carson, demonstrates that loyalty in the most practical manner possible.' Later in the film, similar sentiments are expressed over shots of shipbuilding: 'Loyalty to the British Commonwealth nowhere burns more fiercely than in Ulster. To that loyalty Northern Ireland gives practical expression.'

Given the film's strong support for the Unionist position in Northern Ireland (and over-looking of the divided loyalties of the people living there), it is not surprising that the Unionist

---

66. Letter from Northwood to Adams, 1 December 1943, PRONI CAB9F/123/81.

67. The officials at Stormont, for example, did not like the description of Northern Ireland as the 'Denmark of the United Kingdom', presumably because Denmark was then under German occupation. The phrase, however, remained. See letter from W. Irwin, Works Relation Officer, to W. D. Scott, 16 December 1943, PRONI COM61/661.

68. The issue of voice in British wartime documentary has been the subject of some discussion and assumes a particular significance in the context of Northern Ireland. As John Ellis has argued, the employment of 'classless' and/or regional accents in voice-overs played a crucial role in sustaining the populism of wartime cinema ('Victory of the Voice?', *Screen*, vol. 22, no. 2, 1981). In this respect, the use of an Irish accent in *Ulster* represented a shift away from 'stage standard English' but, given its relative unfamiliarity to a British audience, ran the risk of reinforcing a sense of Northern Ireland's 'otherness'. The use of a recognisably English accent in *Ulster at Arms*, on the other hand, did not guarantee Northern Ireland's place within the British 'national community' either. As Annette Kuhn suggests, in relation to the wartime documentary *Desert Victory* (1943), the discursive use of 'we' employed in the film is central to its construction of a 'collective mode of address' ('*Desert Victory* and the People's War', *Screen*, vol. 22, no. 2, 1981). However, it is noticeable that the voice-over of *Ulster at Arms* remains impersonal and avoids the first-person plural. In this respect, the film does not employ a rhetoric that incorporates Ulster into a British 'we' but rather, through the use of phrases such as 'exported to Britain', indicates Northern Ireland's separation from Britain.

government was delighted with the film and sought to ensure its widespread distribution.[69] The film was originally shown as part of *Warwork News* No. 39 and only lasted around seven minutes. However, about three times that material was shot and Ernest Cooper, in particular, was keen to show a longer, twenty-minute version in cinemas on the grounds that it provided important 'ammunition' with which 'to fight the Ulster battle'.[70] His initial plan was that it should be shown in cinemas in Britain but this idea was scotched by the Ministry of Information, which considered it would be taking up time that they wanted for 'more important' films.[71] At Cooper's behest, the Northern Ireland government nevertheless went ahead and purchased the film from the Ministry of Supply for distribution in Northern Ireland and overseas. The Ministry of Finance arranged a distribution deal with Egan Film Service, which, to the irritation of some local exhibitors, was a Dublin-based company. However, as *Warwork News* had already been shown in virtually every war factory in Northern Ireland, the company had great difficulty in securing bookings for the film (particularly in first-run cinemas) and the returns to the government were disappointing.[72] It was, nevertheless, able to take consolation from the fact that the film had been shown by the Ministry of Supply to an estimated total of 145,000 workers in 720 factories across the UK.[73]

The Story of the Ulster Home Guard

The final film to deal with Northern Ireland in wartime was *The Story of the Ulster Home Guard*. As early as 1941, the Northern Ireland Ministry of Public Security had come up with the idea of making a film to stimulate recruitment to the Ulster Home Guard (given the fall in numbers since the end of 1940). This, however, was shelved on the grounds of expense and a 'Russian atrocity film' was instead re-edited for local use.[74] Given the stand-down of the Home Guard in December 1944, *The Story of the Ulster Home Guard* was inevitably conceived rather differently and involved a retrospective look at the force's history. The film was made by the Army Kinema Service for the War Office under the supervision of Major J. H. A. Davis, Army Staff Officer to the Inspector General of the RUC. It mainly consisted of material shot by AKS cameramen, although the film concludes with material of the stand-down parade filmed in London by Paramount News. On the grounds that the film would be 'valuable for Ulster publicity purposes', the Northern Ireland Ministry of Finance also contributed around £200 for the addition of music and technical refinements to the film's soundtrack.[75]

   This was possibly the most problematic of the Northern Ireland wartime films, given the local history of the Home Guard in Northern Ireland. Following the German advances in

69. The *Belfast News-Letter* (1 February 1944, p. 3) was particularly enthused by the film following a special screening in Belfast. 'Even in its ten minutes', the paper reported, 'it moved one spectator to an enthusiastic, "Up Ulster"!'.

70. Letter from Cooper to R. Gransden, Cabinet Secretariat, 13 April 1944, PRONI CAB9F123/81.

71. Letter from Cooper to Gransden, 23 March 1944, PRONI CAB9F/123/3B.

72. Letter from Egan Film Service to Ministry of Finance, 12 September 1944, PRONI FIN18/24/159.

73. F. M. Adams, 'Films on Ulster Themes', 6 May 1946, PRONI CAB9F/123/81.

74. Letter from Ministry of Home Affairs to Capt. G. H. Petherick, Ministry of Finance, 19 November 1942, PRONI FIN18/21/321.

75. Minutes of the Cabinet Publicity Committee, 3 May 1945, PRONI CAB9F/123/81.

France and fears of a possible invasion, the British Secretary of War, Sir Anthony Eden, announced, in May 1940, the formation of a new force known as Local Defence Volunteers (subsequently to become the Home Guard). The Northern Ireland government was permitted to follow suit but it did so on a different basis from the rest of the United Kingdom. At Craig's suggestion, it was decided that the Ulster Special Constabulary – or B Specials – would form the nucleus of the new force. The force, moreover, was not to be under military command, as in the rest of the UK, but under the direction of the Inspector-General of the RUC. This provoked considerable criticism both within Northern Ireland and Britain.[76] The B Specials had originally been an auxiliary paramilitary force mobilised by the British in 1920 during the Irish War of Independence. It was an exclusively Protestant force, originally recruited from the old Ulster Volunteer Force and Orange Order, and continued to support the RUC (until its eventual disbandment, due to the manner of its handling of civil rights marchers, in 1970). Craig's decision to attach the Ulster Local Defence Volunteers (later Ulster Home Guard) to the B Specials, therefore, invested the body with a strongly sectarian character that meant that Catholics were reluctant to join (or, if they did, that they quickly left).

This effective exclusion of Catholics from the local Home Guard may be related to what Maurice Goldring describes as the Unionist regime's 'two wars'. While the first of these was against 'fascism', the second was conducted against 'local "disloyal" elements', which, for unionists, often simply meant the whole Catholic community.[77] As Brian Barton suggests, the Unionist government 'tended to think of northern Nationalists as a sort of fifth column – pro-German and anti-British by instinct and tradition, ever willing to aid and abet the enemy'.[78] As a result, it did not believe that it could take the risk of arms falling into the hands of the IRA, preferring that the Home Guard should become, in effect, an extension of the supremely 'loyal' B Specials. The price of this, as the Northern Ireland government's official historian John Blake acknowledges, was that many northern nationalists 'suspected that the Government might utilise the L.D.V.s for purposes other than the defence of the homeland against enemy raids or enemy attack'.[79] Although, as Blake argues, these fears were 'unfounded', the sectarian character of the Home Guard remained a bone of contention within Northern Ireland and led to a degree of inter-communal friction. One of the Guard's responsibilities included the manning of roadblocks and checking of identity cards and, as various commentators have noted, this often provided the occasion for the harassment of local Catholics.[80]

---

76. See Fiske, *In Time of War*, pp. 266–71.

77. Maurice Goldring, *Belfast: From Loyalty to Rebellion* (London: Lawrence and Wishart, 1991), p. 95.

78. Barton, *Northern Ireland in the Second World War*, pp. 126–7. Contrary to this perception, however, northern Catholics did join the British forces. Moreover, as Barton (p. 54) also indicates, between September 1941 and May 1945, there were more volunteers for military service (18,600) from southern Ireland than from Northern Ireland (11,500).

79. John W. Blake, *Northern Ireland in the Second World War* (Belfast: HMSO, 1956), p. 182. The context of the production of this official history is discussed by Gillian McIntosh, *The Force of Culture: Unionist Identities in Twentieth-Century Ireland* (Cork: Cork University Press, 1999), ch. 5.

80. See, for example, David Harkness, *Northern Ireland since 1920* (Dublin: Helicon, 1983), pp. 103–4.

Needless to say, *The Story of the Ulster Home Guard*, made with the full co-operation of the RUC, ignores this controversial history and offers a straightforward celebration of the force's activities. The result is, however, somewhat awkward. The rationale for the Home Guard's existence had been the threat of an invasion that did not, in the end, materialise. Thus, just as the reputation of the Home Guard in Britain suffered as a result of its lack of military action, so Michael Farrell claims that the Ulster Home Guard also became 'something of a white elephant'.[81] This is a problem that the film cannot quite overcome. Although the film does identify the Home Guard's role in manning anti-aircraft batteries and defending public utilities, the largest proportion of the film is devoted to the force's various training exercises. Insofar as the film was shot after the stand-down of the Guard, much of this appears to consist of – often less than convincing – reconstructions. Moreover, these are reconstructions of what were only rehearsals for military action that did not prove necessary. As a result, the film lacks an appropriate climax and this is reflected in the film's sudden transition from ambush exercises to the announcement of the stand-down. Thus, despite the commentary's insistence on the value of these manoeuvres, they assume a somewhat artificial character and fail to endow the activities of the Ulster Home Guard with a genuine sense of achievement.

As a result, the film is probably less successful in identifying the Ulster Home Guard's actual accomplishments than in endorsing its loyalty to Britain and contribution to the British war effort. The film begins with an extended sequence explaining Northern Ireland's military importance and implicitly criticising the stand of the Irish government. Over a lengthy pan of the Northern Irish countryside, the commentary informs us that 'by 1940, Northern Ireland had become the strategic base which guarded the last remaining lifeline from Great Britain to the outside world'. The possession of this base 'by enemy or neutral', it continues, 'would have spelt defeat'. This is then followed by three shots of Churchill's letter to J. M. Andrews, following his resignation as Northern Ireland Prime Minister in 1943, in which Churchill had declared that '[b]ut for the loyalty of Northern Ireland . . . we should have been confronted with slavery and death'. The commentary then continues with an account of how German victories in northern France had meant that 'only these islands stood between them and world domination'. At this point, the film employs three shots of the sea breaking against the Giant's Causeway. Although intended as a metaphor for the coming military 'storm', the shots also invest Northern Ireland's contribution to the war effort with a mythic status based upon the use of natural imagery.[82] It

---

81. Michael Farrell, *Northern Ireland: The Orange State*, 2nd edn (London: Pluto Press, 1980), p. 157. For an assessment of the British Home Guard's wartime role, see Calder, *The People's War*, pp. 140–7.

82. In this respect, it anticipates the use, in George Morrison's *Mise Éire* (1959) and *Saoirse?* (1960) of shots of 'waves and sea hitting a rocky shore', which Kevin Rockett interprets as evoking 'the eternality of nature and Ireland', in Kevin Rockett, Luke Gibbons and John Hill, *Cinema and Ireland* (London: Routledge, 1988), p. 87. *The Story of the Ulster Home Guard* uses similar images to much the same end but in the service of 'Ulster' rather than Ireland. The special place of the Giant's Causeway for Northern Ireland film may be noted in this regard. Although the recurrence of images of the Causeway in travelogue films from the 1920s onwards is undoubtedly due to its importance as a tourist site (stretching back to the eighteenth century), it also possesses an added symbolic significance for the ideological construction of Ulster as 'British'. For, given its sharing of geological features with the Scottish island of Staffa, the Causeway has, according to legend, bridged the sea between Ulster and Scotland.

is only following this extended opening that the film introduces the origins of the Home Guard. While the film employs headlines from local newspapers (and makes a brief – and ambiguous – allusion to the Ulster Special Constabulary), this is primarily presented as a response to Eden's call for volunteers and the voice-over deliberately blurs the distinction between recruitment in Northern Ireland and the rest of Britain. In this way, the film seeks to stress the Ulster Home Guard's shared participation in the British war effort. This is also evident at the end of the film, showing the stand-down parade in London at which, the commentary tells us, the Ulster volunteers 'took their place among Home Guard contingents from all over Great Britain'. Intercut with shots of members of the Royal Family, the British credentials of the Ulster Home Guard are clearly registered even if its actual history had involved a clear departure from British standards.

Once again, the Northern Ireland government was pleased with the result and sought to ensure a wide circulation for the film. It purchased six 35mm copies for showing in Northern Ireland, where it provided the film to cinemas free of charge.[83] It also financed a further fifty copies for distribution in Britain where it was shown on the ABC circuit.[84] The Ulster Office subsequently noted that '[p]eople who saw it shown in London suburban cinemas report that it was interesting and well received by audiences'.[85]

In search of an Ulster film

Although this and preceding films (especially *Ulster* and *Ulster at Arms*) represented genuine propaganda victories for the Unionist government in Northern Ireland, they also experienced some setbacks. In 1944, for example, they were vexed by a *March of Time* newsreel 'The Irish Question', dealing with Irish neutrality. The *March of Time* series was American in origin (founded by *Time* in 1935) and had pioneered a new kind of pictorial journalism that was characteristically more discursive and ideas-driven than its British contemporaries. The Northern Ireland government had benefited from an earlier edition of the series – 'Ulster versus Eire' – that had been made with its support in 1938.[86] This dealt with the news that de Valera intended to raise the question of partition at talks between British and Irish ministers (that subsequently led to the agreement ending the 'Economic War' between Britain and Ireland and the return of the southern naval ports). The film briefly reviews arguments for and against partition before turning to Craigavon's decision to hold a snap election in response (in January 1938).[87]

83. Government of Northern Ireland Information Services report for August 1945, PRONI CAB9F/123/34.

84. Report of Northern Ireland Government Press Office, July 1945, PRONI CAB9F/123/34.

85. Government of Northern Ireland Information Services report for December 1945, PRONI CAB9F/123/34.

86. The Northern Irish government appears to have actively cultivated *March of Time* following the production of an edition dealing with the South, 'Irish Republic – 1937' (released in May). A representative of *March of Time* was encouraged to visit Northern Ireland in July 1937, when he was assured of 'every assistance' by the Ministry of Commerce (Minute Sheet, 31 July 1937, PRONI COM62/1/614).

87. David Harkness argues, however, that while the reports of de Valera's intentions may have dictated 'the precise timing' of the election, Craig was more concerned 'to ditch' a challenge from the newly formed Progressive Unionists 'representing a growing impatience with unchanging and inactive leadership' (*Northern Ireland since 1920*, p. 63).

Although the film does acknowledge the high rate of unemployment in Northern Ireland, it is entirely uncritical of the electoral system in the North, presenting the election result as a straightforward vindication of Craig's strategy and commenting, without any hint of irony, that 'Ulstermen still bristle at the thought of becoming a helpless political and religious minority in the new republic'. The position of the 'political and religious minority' within 'Protestant Ulster' (as the film describes Northern Ireland) is simply ignored. A special screening of the film in Belfast was organised with various members of the government as guests. These included Craigavon himself, who commented that the film had dealt with the subject 'in a very fair manner'.[88]

The response to 'The Irish Question', however, was rather different. Unlike the earlier film, this had been made with the sanction of the Irish government and filming was restricted to approved scenes and subjects.[89] Although the film deals with criticisms of Ireland's neutrality (and US calls for Ireland to dismiss Axis diplomats from Irish soil), it also seeks to put across Ireland's case with 'tolerant understanding and humour' (as the publicity for the film put it). To this end, an Irish narrator is employed to argue 'Ireland's cause' with 'fine eloquence and vigour' before giving way to a more conventional American voiceover. It was the Irish commentary to which the Unionists mainly objected, particularly its claim that 'no Irishman will feel his people are truly free until Northern Ireland, still under the British Crown, is restored to Eire and all Ireland is one'.

Before he had even seen the film, Ernest Cooper wrote to Brendan Bracken, the Minister for Information, requesting that the newsreel's distribution within the United Kingdom be discontinued on the grounds that its 'political import' ran counter to 'the wishes of the Prime Minister and the Government of Great Britain'.[90] Bracken promised to look into the matter but claimed – somewhat disingenuously – that there was 'no censorship of the political contents of films shown in this country' and that his Ministry had 'no authority over *March of Time*'.[91]

---

88. *Kine Weekly*, 30 June 1938, p. 26. When the film was first shown in London, the secretary of the Ulster Unionist Council, Sir Wilson Hungerford (who appears in the film), reported to Craigavon that the film was 'exceedingly pro Ulster' and that it was likely that 'our opponents will not like it' (Letter from Hungerford to Craigavon, 27 April 1938, PRONI CAB9F/123/3A).

89. See Donal Ó Drisceoil, *Censorship in Ireland, 1939–45: Neutrality, Politics and Society* (Cork: Cork University Press, 1996), pp. 43–5. Under Emergency Powers legislation, there were very strict rules governing newsreel coverage of the war, which meant that most British and American newsreels were banned or cut by the Irish censor. There were also some expressions of hostility towards British newsreels in the North and the cinema owner James Curran (whose businesses included the Broadway in the Catholic Falls Road) reported that he was unable to show 'British propaganda films' in at least three of his theatres (*Kine Weekly*, 13 January 1944, p. 82).

90. Letter from Sir Ernest Cooper to Brendan Bracken, 14 June 1944, PRONI CAB9F/123/81. Rather ominously, Cooper also comments that if the film were to be shown in Northern Ireland, he felt that 'the public would deal with it adequately'.

91. Bracken to Cooper, 16 June 1944, CAB9F/123/81. Bracken's point appears to be that newsreels were only censored on 'security' and not 'political' grounds. However, as Nicholas Pronay and Jeremy Croft indicate, this was really no more than a convenient fiction and the MOI Press and Censorship Division exerted quite considerable control over the content of newsreels ('British Film Censorship and Propaganda Policy during the Second World War', in Curran and Porter (eds), *British Cinema History*, pp. 148–9). This would suggest that the film's contents had not, in fact, proved a problem for the Ministry.

Although Cooper was disappointed, and continued to regard the film as 'preeminently a propaganda film for Eire', he advised against further action by the Northern Ireland government on the grounds that the film actually said relatively little about partition and that the film's 'closing few words' – concerning the lack of 'logic in the Irish point of view' – damned 'the whole political argument'.[92]

While the *March of Time*'s relatively sympathetic treatment of Eire (and its allusions to Irish unity) in 'The Irish Question' constituted a minor irritation for the representatives of the Unionist government, it was the failure to convince the MOI to make a film dealing with the strategic military importance of Northern Ireland to the war effort that proved the biggest disappointment. This idea was particularly identified with Northern Ireland's third wartime Prime Minister, Sir Basil Brooke. As Minister of Commerce, he had supported the idea for a war industries film and, when he became Prime Minister in January 1943, he continued to be alert to the propaganda possibilities of film. He encouraged the Linen Industry Post War Planning Committee to consider making a film along the lines of the British Council's film on the Lancashire cotton industry, *Queen Cotton* (1941). He also developed the idea of a war effort film, recruiting the interest of William MacQuitty (who had by then moved to London to join Sydney Box's company Verity Films), who provided him with a synopsis for a film entitled 'Ulster Goes To It' in April 1943.[93] A few months later, he also wrote to the British Home Secretary, Herbert Morrison, to enquire about the possibility of 'an Ulster film' being made 'under official auspices'. Suggesting three possible themes – the general contribution of Northern Ireland to the war effort, the impact of war on Northern Ireland life, and the specific story of linen – he argued that this would 'show others what we are doing in Northern Ireland, and . . . demonstrate our unity of purpose with Great Britain and the Allied Nations in the present struggle'.[94] Morrison responded that he was 'most interested' in the idea but suggested that Brooke contact the Ministry of Information.[95] Bracken was, however, no more enthusiastic than he had been when Brooke had contacted him two years previously. While the film was one 'which we should always be glad to make', he responded, the 'heavy production programme' of the films division prevented him from making any commitment to proceed with it.[96] This could well have been the end of the matter. However, mainly due to the perseverance of Northern Ireland government personnel, especially in the London office, the idea of an 'Ulster film' was pursued until practically the end of the war.

92. Letter from Cooper to Sir Roland Nugent, 21 June 1944, PRONI CAB9F/123/81. Cooper's views mellowed somewhat once he had actually seen the film. His remarks regarding the film's ending refer to the closing commentary, spoken by the American narrator, that 'those who seek the answer to the Irish question of today or to the Irish question of tomorrow must look not to logic but to the poetry of the Irish'.

93. Letter from William MacQuitty to Sir Basil Brooke, 19 April 1943, PRONI COM61/661.

94. Letter from Brooke to Herbert Morrison, 31 August 1943, PRONI CAB9F/123/81.

95. Letter from Morrison to Brooke, 22 September 1943, PRONI CAB9F/123/81. Although a Labour politician, initially hostile to Ulster Unionism, Morrison moved towards support for the Unionist regime as a result of his wartime experiences.

96. Letter from Bracken to Brooke, 2 November 1943, PRONI CAB9F/123/81.

The idea appears to have received new momentum following a meeting between Ernest Cooper, of the London Office, and Jack Beddington, Head of the MOI's Films Division, in March 1944. Incensed by Beddington's attitude that he did not see 'why so much time should be given up to . . . a community about the size of Birmingham', Cooper described his response as follows:

> I . . . proceeded to ask him . . . if he knew anything about the strategic position of Ulster, and whether or not he knew that the Province of Ulster had given protection to every Canadian and American soldier that had entered this country. I proceeded to tell him about the defences of Ulster and what they meant to the protection of the Mersey and Clyde and how from Ulster we gave Atlantic cover that could not have been provided from the shores of England or Scotland. I then produced from my pocket the editorial from the ECONOMIST of last week in which this strategical position was emphasised. That did it, because I did not realise when I produced it that the ECONOMIST is Brendan Bracken's paper. Beddington immediately changed his tune and brought in his producer and they collaborated as to whether or not they could produce a good film showing the strategic position of Ulster.[97]

Beddington advised Cooper to seek the approval of Bracken and, following a meeting in April, Cooper reported that a film on the 'strategic position of Ulster' had now been agreed.[98] However, while various treatments were prepared (and a production company identified) no real progress was made.

As a result, Jack Beddington wrote to Cooper at the beginning of 1945 suggesting that the project should be abandoned. He argued that, at such a late stage in the war, it was now 'too late' for the film 'to serve a useful purpose' and that the prospects for commercial distribution were slight.[99] The Northern Ireland government was, however, reluctant to drop the project. 'The film, if produced,' Adams wrote after consultation with the Chairman of the Cabinet Publicity Committee, 'will have a high publicity value for Ulster, and for this reason we should do all we can to ensure that the Ministry of Information proceeds with its production.'[100] A meeting at the MOI in London was arranged with Adams, Northwood and A. J. Kelly, Liaison Officer in the Home Office, all in attendance. They were dismayed, however, to discover that Beddington had sent his apologies and was represented by his Deputy, R. Nunn–May, and a colleague, Nicolas Bentley. Despite a lively argument concerning the pros and cons of the production, there was no agreement and Adams subsequently reported that the MOI representatives appeared 'superciliously indifferent to the whole matter'.[101] Adams then

---

97.   Letter from Cooper to Gransden, 23 March 1944, PRONI CAB9F/123/3B. Despite his obvious frustration with Beddington, Cooper had, in fact, described him as 'a great friend' on his arrival at the MOI in a letter to G. Lodge, 19 November 1941, PRONI COM61/661.

98.   Letter from Cooper to Gransden, 5 April 1944, PRONI CAB9F/123/81.

99.   Letter from Beddington to Cooper, 6 January 1945, PRONI CAB9F/123/81.

100. Letter from Adams to Northwood, 9 January 1945, PRONI CAB9F/123/81.

101. 'Proposed M.O.I. Film on Ulster's War Activities and Strategic Importance. Memorandum by Government Press Officer on Interview at M.O.I. Headquarters', 30 January 1945. Kelly also wrote to Gransden on the 31 January. 'My impression is that they are obviously "stone-walling"', he reports, 'and do not want to do the film' (PRONI CAB9F/123/81).

wrote to Beddington, outlining the substance of the Northern Ireland position and pressing him to send a scriptwriter to Northern Ireland forthwith. While Beddington agreed to do so, the writer would only be an 'investigator' who would 'make a report' on what could be done. On the basis of this report, the MOI would then 'consider once more the possibilities'.[102] Further delay occurred before a journalist, Ian Bevan, arrived in Northern Ireland in March, when he visited various locations and met with relevant personnel, including the Prime Minister. Although Adams believed that Bevan was 'impressed with the possibility of making a successful film' and that a film cameraman would be despatched to Northern Ireland shortly thereafter, this turned out not to be so.[103]

Bevan visited the London Office and gave Northwood a preview of his report. In a letter to Adams, Northwood recorded his shocked reaction:

> To my astonishment, the first part of the report deals with politics as between Eire and Northern Ireland. Here is a typical extract: 'Certain political factors must be taken into consideration in considering any film on Ulster and the War Strategy. The most vital political issue in Eire today is partition and every effort will be made after the war to induce England to end the present scheme whereby, in Eire's view, the six counties of the North are cut off from the rest of Ireland . . . Any film which makes out a strong case for Ulster's strategical importance is also, by implication, an argument for the maintenance of the Union between Great Britain and Northern Ireland! . . .'

> The whole lengthy introduction to the report runs along these lines and is so brazenly designed to kill enthusiasm for the film that one wonders whether Bevan was well primed in the enemy camp before he left England or whether he was the victim of a violent and complete conversion to Eire propaganda during his brief visit to Dublin! He even goes so far as to mention Eire's contribution to the War Effort, and the numbers of young Ulstermen standing at street corners!

Northwood attempted to put a brave face on the matter, claiming that 'on the merits of the material available' the MOI could scarcely avoid proceeding with the project but admitting that it looked 'as if political factors will weigh the scales against it'.[104] Sure enough, a few weeks later Beddington wrote to Adams declaring that it would be 'impracticable' to make the film at this stage. Bevan's report, he argued, had confirmed his 'apprehensions about the difficulty of making a film on Ulster's part in the war strategy' and that it would now be 'impossible' to get suitable visual material for the film without reconstruction.[105] At this stage the Northern Ireland government finally threw in the towel and the Cabinet Publicity Committee decided, in the light of Beddington's letter, that 'no further action could profitably be undertaken'.[106]

102. Letter from Adams to Beddington, 5 February 1945; letter from Beddington to Adams, 14 February 1945, PRONI CAB9F/123/81.

103. 'Proposed Ulster Strategic Film. Visit of Mr Ian Bevan (Representing Films Division, M.O.I., London)', PRONI CAB9F/123/81.

104. Letter from Northwood to Adams, 4 April 1945, PRONI CAB9F/123/81.

105. Letter from Beddington to Adams, 19 April 1945, PRONI CAB9F/123/81.

106. Minutes of the Cabinet Publicity Committee, 3 May 1945, PRONI CAB9F/123/81.

Wartime cinema and Northern Ireland

It is difficult to be certain about the reasons for the failure of the project. A substantial number of films were abandoned by the MOI in the later years of the war and this has been accounted for in terms of the changing circumstances of the war, organisational changes following Ian Dalrymple's departure from the Crown Film Unit in 1943 and unofficial censorship.[107] However, reviewing the correspondence, it is also clear that there was never genuine enthusiasm within the MOI Films Division for the idea. While this may be partly attributed to reservations about the costs of such a production as well as its timing, other factors were surely at play. These may have been, as Northwood suspected, partly 'political'. Although Beddington (who had been Director of Publicity and Advertising at Shell-Mex and British Petroleum) was hardly a political radical, many of those involved in wartime documentary production were of a left-of-centre persuasion and there may well have been little appetite within the Films Division for a project in support of the Northern Ireland regime. Despite the Minister Brendan Bracken's known hostility to Irish neutrality, it was also the policy of the MOI, at least in the early years, to cultivate good relations with the Irish government in the hope that it might be persuaded to enter the war.[108] In pursuit of these objectives, the MOI issued a directive to the BBC in 1940 that it should avoid 'controversy or propaganda about the Partition of Ireland'. If the news from Ireland made a reference to the issue necessary, the directive continued, 'the point to be consistently made is that Partition is a problem for the Irish themselves to solve: the British government would be ready to accept any agreement reached by the different sections of the Irish people'.[109] Such attitudes, of course, diverged radically from those of the Northern Ireland government and, as Rex Cathcart has indicated, inevitably led to friction over broadcasting policy and related matters.[110]

While the MOI's interest in courting Ireland began to decline from 1943 onwards (once Britain's wartime fortunes had begun to turn), it did not lead to any significant increase in enthusiasm for the Northern Irish regime. Maurice Goldring links this to a perception that Northern Ireland was not fully pulling its weight. For all the efforts of the Unionist regime 'to appear deeply committed to the defence of democracy and the war against fascism', he argues, there was still a degree of 'resentment in British circles at what was seen as Ulster's lack of commitment'.[111] Thus, despite the military importance of Northern Ireland to Britain, the low levels of military recruitment in Northern Ireland, the relatively low productivity (and high rate of industrial action) of the workforce and the continuing failure of the Unionist government to

107. See James Chapman, *The British at War: Cinema, State and Propaganda, 1939–45* (London: I. B. Tauris, 1998), pp. 135–6, and Pronay and Croft, 'British Film Censorship and Propaganda Policy', pp. 154–5.

108. Bracken was, in fact, born in Ireland but is described by his biographer as '[o]utChurchilling Churchill in his denunciation of Irish neutrality'. See Andrew Boyle, *Poor, Dear Brendan: The Quest for Brendan Bracken* (London: Hutchinson, 1974), p. 262.

109. Directive from the MOI Empire Division, cited in BBC internal memo, 13 May 1940, BBC Written Archives Centre (WAC) R34/347/1.

110. Rex Cathcart, *The Most Contrary Region: The BBC in Northern Ireland 1924–84* (Belfast: Blackstaff Press, 1984), pp. 108–28.

111. Goldring, *Belfast*, p. 89.

conform to British standards of democracy in its dealings with the minority Catholic population meant that the Northern Ireland government could not depend upon a sympathetic hearing within British government. Thus, when the Northern Ireland government was contemplating the production of a pamphlet celebrating Ulster's contribution to the war effort in 1943 (not long before its actions in support of the war effort film), the head of the Northern Ireland Civil Service, Sir Wilfred Spender, felt it appropriate to sound a note of caution. 'It might not be very judicious for the Government to boast of Ulster's part [in the war],' he suggested, 'when, in official circles, there is a good deal of criticism of what our workers are doing and also criticism of the lack of response of our young men in joining the fighting forces.'[112]

Whatever the specific reasons for them, the problems that the Northern Ireland government faced in securing the co-operation of the MOI for a war effort film were symptomatic of a larger trend. According to Frances Thorpe and Nicholas Pronay, some '1,887 films were officially "presented" to people in Britain and overseas by propaganda agencies of the British government' during the Second World War. In addition they estimate that some 380 feature films and 3,200 newsreels were approved by the Ministry of Information.[113] Even allowing for the small percentage of the overall United Kingdom population that Northern Ireland represents, the number of 'official' and 'semi-official' films made about Northern Ireland during this period seems small (and certainly out of step with the claims made for its economic and military importance). The Northern Ireland government certainly felt that it was being given a raw deal by the MOI. In his letter to Brooke in 1941, Bracken had claimed that 'making films with a special regional appeal' would be at the expense of the MOI's 'national programme'.[114] However, the representatives of the Northern Ireland government were all too aware of the MOI films being made in Scotland and, in a hand-written minute, a frustrated official observed that, at a time when it was apparently too busy to make a Northern Ireland film, the MOI had supported five Scottish films – including *Power for the Highlands* (1943), *Clydebuilt* (1944) and *Highland Doctor* (1944) – in an eighteen-month period.[115] At their meeting at the MOI in January 1945, Adams and Northwood also complained about the MOI's treatment of Northern Ireland in comparison to Scotland. '[O]ne of the functions of the M.O.I. Films Division', they argued, 'is to illustrate and interpret . . . the war effort of the United Kingdom *as a whole*' (my italics).[116]

However, the problem faced by the Ulster Unionists was that, at an ideological level, Northern Ireland – unlike Scotland – did not seem to constitute a 'natural' part of the 'whole'. For, despite the Unionist government's desperate wish to be seen as truly 'British', the contemporary 'imaginings' of 'British' national identity – as revealed, for example, in wartime films – rendered this problematic. There were two aspects to this: the privileged position that 'Englishness'

---

112. Sir Wilfred Spender, Memo, 18 February 1943, PRONI FIN18/23/319.

113. Frances Thorpe and Nicholas Pronay with Clive Coultass, *British Official Films in the Second World War* (Oxford: Clio Press, 1980), p. ix.

114. Letter from Brendan Bracken to Sir Basil Brooke, 26 November 1941, PRONI COM61/661.

115. Hand-written minute, Ministry of Commerce, 8 June 1944, PRONI COM61/661. The author does not note, however, that many of these films also had official support – and presumably funding – from the Scottish Office.

116. 'Proposed M.O.I. Film on Ulster's War Activities and Strategic Importance. Memorandum by Government Press Officer on Interview at M.O.I. Headquarters', 30 January 1945, PRONI CAB9F/123/81.

occupied within prevailing conceptions of 'British' national identity, on the one hand, and the apparent inability of the Northern Irish to register as fully, or authentically, 'British', on the other.

While it was certainly the case that films about Scotland and Wales were made during the Second World War, and that Scottish and Welsh actors appeared in British feature films, it was still a predominantly *English* sense of identity that prevailed. As Jeffrey Richards puts it:

> despite the almost obligatory presence of Gordon Jackson or John Laurie as the token Scotsman in films which depicted the national effort in microcosm (*The Foreman Went to France* (1942); *Millions Like Us* (1943); *The Way Ahead* (1944)) and despite the occasional nods in the direction of Wales (*The Proud Valley* (1940); *The Silent Village* (1942)), the national identity derived almost entirely from England, which was often used interchangeably with Britain to describe the nation.[117]

This interchangeability may be seen in one of the first wartime features to appear in cinemas, *The Lion Has Wings*. Ian Dalrymple, the Head of the Crown Film Unit from 1940 to 1943 and the film's writer, explained how he had wanted to open the film with 'the suggestion that there was a British ideology, arising from our national character; that it was valuable to the world; and that it should not be lost'.[118] However, in realisation, this sense of 'British ideology' is almost exclusively associated with England. Thus, when the film's commentary tells us that 'This is Britain where we believe in freedom', the images that follow are of typically English rural scenes and historical monuments. There is a subsequent reference to Scotland but the narrator's jocular comments concerning 'throwing heavy things about in a way only Scotsmen can understand' simply serves to underline the film's Anglocentric conception of 'Britishness'. If the ideology of 'Britishness' evident in *The Lion Has Wings* marginalises Scotland, however, it excludes Northern Ireland altogether. It will, of course, be recalled that this was the very film that inspired Richard Hayward to agitate for a similar propaganda feature for 'Ulster'. The fact that he regarded such a film as necessary therefore highlights how a film dealing with the British 'national character' did not feel under any obligation to refer to Northern Ireland in the first place.

However, while the expression of 'British' identity in British wartime cinema undoubtedly privileged 'Englishness', it would be wrong to dismiss altogether the attempts of British films to provide a more wide-ranging view of Britain. As Charles Barr argues, in relation to Ealing war films, the use of 'characters and actors from Scotland, Wales and identified English regions' reveals a genuine attempt 'to create inclusive images of *Britain*'.[119] However, it is also significant that these 'inclusive images of Britain' rarely extended to Northern Ireland. There was no Northern Irish equivalent of Gordon Jackson or Mervyn Johns and the Ulsterman, unlike the Scotsman or Welshman, did not find a place among the many groups of servicemen and workers repre-

---

117. Jeffrey Richards, 'National Identity in British Wartime Films', in Taylor (ed.), *Britain and the Cinema in the Second World War*, p. 44.

118. *The Cine-Technician*, February–March 1940, p. 11.

119. Charles Barr, *Ealing Studios* (London: Cameron and Tayleur in association with David & Charles, 1977), p. 37.

No recognisable Northern Irish traits: Niall MacGinnis as the Irish sailor, Mick Corrigan, in *We Dive at Dawn*

senting 'the national effort in microcosm'.[120] An Irishman, Mick Corrigan, does appear among the sailors in Gainsborough's *We Dive at Dawn* (Anthony Asquith, 1943) but he is played by the southern Irish actor Niall MacGinnis and displays no recognisable Northern Irish traits. Significantly, the character is also involved in a subplot involving doubts regarding his forthcoming marriage (to an English woman). Insofar as the character opts for 'commitment' by the end of the film, this may also be read allegorically as an encouragement to neutral Ireland to follow suit and to make its own commitment to the Allied war effort (a theme also to be found in Ealing's *The Halfway House* [1944]).

A part of the problem here is suggested by a letter to the Northern Ireland government, written in 1944, identifying the continuing influence of 'false conceptions' of the Ulsterman and the 'Black North' upon the British public. 'There is no doubt that for a very long time the Ulsterman has been represented', the author writes, 'as a dour bigot, with no regard for manners,

120. Both Jackson and Johns appear in a postwar Ealing film, *The Captive Heart* (1946), set in a prisoner-of-war camp, alongside the Northern Ireland actor Sam Kydd. However, while Jackson and Johns are clearly Scottish and Welsh, Kydd plays an Englishman!

culture or law or order'.[121] If this was so, then it would have been difficult for British film-makers to draw upon popular stereotypes of the Ulsterman (alongside those of the Scots and the Welsh), given their generally unsympathetic associations. The absence of Northern Irish characters from British wartime films, therefore, seems to indicate how the perceived attributes of the Ulsterman failed to correspond to many of the British characteristics celebrated in wartime films (such as democratic sentiment, sympathy for the underdog, camaraderie) and, as a result, how Northern Ireland itself did not appear fully to belong to the British 'national community' that these films were engaged in constructing.

Conclusion

There is, perhaps, a certain paradox in evidence here. In terms of film, the Northern Ireland government found great difficulty in achieving any significant degree of visibility in official and semi-official productions. Although a few films were made, they were insufficient in number to play any significant role in affecting popular attitudes in Britain. In this respect, films (such as *Ulster at Arms* and *The Story of the Ulster Home Guard*) may have played a more important role in consolidating attitudes among unionists within Northern Ireland than in convincing audiences elsewhere. This is particularly so given the evidence of the scepticism that audiences could often bring towards propaganda films.[122]

Nevertheless, in the period following the war, the Unionist government emerged stronger and more secure than ever before. What this suggests is that, while the Unionist regime may not have won its own particular 'propaganda war', it was still able to capitalise on the distaste of the British government for Irish neutrality and 'cash in' the political debt it felt it was owed. This does not seem to have involved, however, any deep-seated ideological commitment to, or identification with, the region on the part of the British government or, indeed, the British people for whom Northern Ireland remained largely unknown and 'other'. Therefore, while the political issue of the border appeared to be temporarily settled, the political and ideological battle for Northern Ireland's 'Britishness' continued to be waged by unionism and to be challenged by its opponents. How this representational battle over the political status and cultural identity of Northern Ireland carried over into the postwar period is discussed in the following chapter.

---

121. Letter from Rural Development Council of Northern Ireland to Ministry of Commerce, 4 September 1944, PRONI CAB9F/123/32.

122. For an attempt to assess the political effectiveness of wartime shorts, see Chapman, *The British at War*, ch. 4.

4

'What ideas and beliefs concerning Ulster'?

The Struggle Over Film Images in the Postwar Period

As early as 1938, Sir Roland Nugent, the first Chair of the Northern Ireland Cabinet Publicity Committee and the Minister of Commerce from 1945 to 1949, stressed the necessity of the Unionist government in Northern Ireland agreeing 'what ideas and beliefs concerning Ulster' it wished 'to implant in the British consciousness' and of bending publicity to that purpose.[1] Although the government often claimed that its publicity was non-political, in the sense that it was not employed in support of any particular political party (i.e. the Ulster Unionist Party), there is no doubt that it was 'political' in the broader sense of cultivating a particular view of Northern Ireland, and its political status, for circulation in Britain and abroad. Thus, in 1947, the former Unionist Prime Minister J. M. Andrews was happy to inform the Northern Ireland House of Commons that while 'party propaganda at the public expense' could not be defended, 'propaganda for the purpose of maintaining our constitutional position within the United Kingdom' was 'perfectly justified'.[2] Despite the benefits that had accrued to the regime as a result of Northern Ireland's strategic importance during the war, the Unionists remained convinced of the need for continuing vigilance regarding its political position, particularly given the claims of the southern Irish government, under de Valera's 1937 constitution, to jurisdiction over the whole of the island. However, while there was an accepted need for film publicity favourable to Northern Ireland, there was also a reluctance to pay for it. As an official of the Ministry of Commerce commented drily in 1946, '[t]he cost of film production is very high, and the NI Government has so far ventured very little money in this sphere of public relations'. 'When such films are shown,' he continued, 'everyone agrees that they are a good thing, but no one seems willing to put cash down for production.'[3]

The situation governing film funding was, in a number of respects, a mirror of the Northern Ireland government's economic position more generally. As Arthur Aughey suggests, a major priority for Unionism in power was the maintenance of economic and social parity with Britain in order to demonstrate not only that Northern Ireland was 'properly' British but also to differentiate

---

1. 'Publicity', Memorandum by Sir R. Nugent, 7 October 1938, PRONI FIN18/18/497.
2. Parliament of Northern Ireland, *Parliamentary Debates: Official Report*, House of Commons (HC), vol. xxx, col. 4532, 27 February 1947.
3. Memo, A. A. K. Arnold, Ministry of Commerce, 11 June 1946, PRONI COM62/1/991.

it, in terms of living standards, from the South.[4] Thus, while the Unionist government benefited from the willingness of the new Labour government to underwrite the costs of the same level of social services as in Britain, it also increased the economic dependence of Northern Ireland upon the British state. With respect to film (and publicity more generally), the Northern Ireland regime also maintained that state-supported film production should be on a par with other parts of the United Kingdom. However, as was more generally the case, the maintenance of parity was only possible as the result of an economic subvention on the part of the British government. This then put the Unionist government in the position of having to rely upon organisations in Britain – such as the Central Office of Information and the Travel Association of Great Britain and Northern Ireland – to make films for Northern Ireland, which led, in turn, to disputes concerning not only Northern Ireland's entitlement to support but also, in some cases, the images of 'Ulster' that were to be produced.

During the postwar period, therefore, the Unionist government was not only engaged in a battle to secure funding for the films to which it felt it was entitled but also to exercise control over the film images that government-funded bodies in Britain were producing. It was particularly concerned that these films should not blur what it perceived to be the separate characteristics of the North and the South and vigilantly scrutinised scripts for hints of nationalist culture or suggestions of economic backwardness or 'primitiveness'. That it was not always successful in achieving its objectives also suggests how a lack of economic control over productions inevitably restricted its exercise of editorial power. Moreover, despite the political advantages that the Second World War bestowed upon the Unionists, the election of a Labour government in Britain and the rising tide of republican sentiment in the South also contributed to renewed levels of opposition to partition. Partly due to the activities of the Anti-Partition League and the Irish Ministry of External Affairs, the Northern Ireland government was faced in the postwar period with a small number of films that openly promoted 'ideas and beliefs' that challenged the legitimacy of the unionist position. The purpose of the discussion that follows, therefore, is to assess the 'struggle' over ideas and images in which films about Northern Ireland were – implicitly and explicitly – engaged in the 1940s and 1950s. The chapter begins with an examination of the 'official' government films that were made after the war and a consideration of how these were involved in the construction of a particular conception of 'Ulster'. This is then followed by an examination of the various 'unofficial' films that departed from the Unionist regime's preferred image of itself and an assessment of how unionists responded to these.

'Ulster films should be made by Ulster people': *Back Home in Ireland*

The first film-maker to seek government support in the postwar period was, perhaps not surprisingly, Richard Hayward. Hayward had joined forces with his former colleagues Louis Morrison, Donovan Pedelty and Harry Bailey to produce a film inspired by the presence of US troops in Northern Ireland. Concentrating on the historical ties between the USA and Northern Ireland, the resulting film, *Back Home in Ireland* (1946), was described by Hayward as neither

---

4. Arthur Aughey, 'Unionism', in Arthur Aughey and Duncan Morrow (eds), *Northern Ireland Politics* (London: Longman, 1996), pp. 32–4.

a 'documentary nor a travelogue' but rather 'an experiment in screen journalism' that had evolved as the production proceeded.[5] While this makes it sound more formally adventurous than it actually is, the film does, nevertheless, follow in the path of the wartime 'story documentary' in combining elements of documentary and drama. The film is jointly narrated by a fictional American sergeant stationed in Northern Ireland during the war and by Hayward himself, who, in a shameless piece of self-promotion, is introduced as the author of *In Praise of Ulster*. The book is shown to occupy pride of place in the window display of a Belfast bookshop from which Hayward emerges to lead the American on a tour of Northern Ireland locations with a US connection, including Boneybefore (the birthplace of future US President Andrew Jackson), Broughshane (the homeplace of the ancestors of Sam Houston, the first President of the Republic of Texas) and Strabane (the home of the grandparents of President Woodrow Wilson). This material is interwoven with documentary footage of General Eisenhower's official visit to Northern Ireland (including his inspection of the monument, outside Belfast City Hall, commemorating the landing of US troops) in August 1945 and of the Northern Ireland Prime Minister, Sir Basil Brooke, arriving at the Belfast Red Cross Club to make a farewell speech to the US forces stationed in Northern Ireland.[6] There are also a number of extended musical interludes in which Hayward, appearing in the rural costume familiar from his earlier films, performs on the harp or engages in singing. These sequences, in turn, provide the occasion for short montages of scenic display or, in one instance, suggestive comedy when an unmarried couple sing 'The Yellow Rose of Texas' while hanging out their underwear. The film then ends with a staged 'reconstruction' of GIs departing Belfast, while dancers from the Empire Theatre, egged on by Hayward's fictional alter ego ('the old guy in the fisherman's hat'), engage in an unusual amalgam of Irish figure dancing and chorus-line hoofing.

Although Hayward regarded the film as precisely 'the kind of picture which Ulster should make and go on making', it also illustrates some of the financial and ideological problems involved in this kind of locally-based project.[7] It appears, for example, that the men embarked upon production at their own expense and would only see a return if they secured a distribution deal. The film, however, failed to arouse much enthusiasm in Britain, where it was regarded as possessing 'very little commercial value'.[8] Hayward's former distribution company, Paramount, eventually acquired the British and Irish rights to the film but for a sum much less than Hayward had anticipated. Despite Hayward's protests, the distributor was entirely unsentimental. '[I]t is a rather too common type of documentary', a representative from Paramount observed, 'that would hardly see daylight except for the fact that it ranks . . . as exhibitor

5. '*Back Home in Ireland*', PRONI CAB9F/123/81.

6. Brooke had, in fact, agreed to Hayward filming him repeat part of the speech in return for an editorial veto over the finished film by the Cabinet. However, due to the problems of recording synchronised sound in Belfast, the filming never took place. Letter from Richard Hayward to the Secretary to the Cabinet, 22 November 1945, PRONI CAB9F/123/81.

7. '*Back Home in Ireland*', PRONI CAB9F/123/81.

8. Letter from S. F. Ditcham, Joint Managing Director of General Film Distributors, to Richard Hayward, 5 February 1946, UFTM.

quota.'[9] Hayward, nevertheless, remained adamant that the film would 'reap . . . the equivalent of a feature' in Northern Ireland and urged Paramount to organise a proper premiere for the film in Belfast.[10] This took place in April and was attended by the Northern Ireland Prime Minister, Basil Brooke, who expressed the hope that the film would be widely shown in the US in order 'to allow the parents of the boys Ulster people welcomed to see something of the Ulster countryside and of Ulster folk'.[11]

Given this encouragement, Hayward almost immediately sought the help of the government to distribute the film in the US.[12] Despite Brooke's remarks, however, the government was unwilling to do more than help ease 'official restrictions'.[13] This reluctance to do more undoubtedly rested on a belief that the film's value as propaganda would prove limited. When the film was in production (and Hayward had sought permission to film the Prime Minister), the Government Press Officer, Frank Adams, had asked for the film's title to be changed to 'Back Home in Ulster' on the grounds that the use of the word 'Ireland' obliterated the distinction between 'Ulster' and 'Eire'.[14] It was also evident that, while Hayward regarded the film as showing 'what Ulster is' and 'what Ulster stands for', the film's overwhelming emphasis upon rural imagery and use of Irish dancing and 'old Irish songs' confused its pro-Ulster message given the nationalist associations that had now become attached to these.[15] Thus, much as Adams had feared when calling for a change to the film's title, reviewers of the film in Britain were much more impressed by the film's 'Irish' than its 'Ulster' credentials. The British trade paper *Today's Cinema*, for example, not only called attention to how many of America's 'most famous Irish sons' had sprung from 'the land of the shamrock' but singled out for praise the film's inclusion of 'Irish ditty', dancing by 'Irish lassies' and 'lovely Irish backgrounds'.[16]

---

9. Letter from F. E. Hutchinson, Paramount, to Richard Hayward, 20 February 1946, UFTM. Following pressure from the documentary movement, the government had, in 1938, introduced (through the Cinematograph Films Act) a quota for short films as well as for features. This was changed to quotas for 'first feature' and 'supporting programme' in 1948.

10. Letter from Hayward to Hutchinson, 22 February 1946, UFTM.

11. *Northern Whig*, 4 April 1946, p. 4.

12. Letter from Hayward to Gransden, 12 April 1946, PRONI CAB9F/123/81.

13. Letter from Gransden to Hayward, 16 April 1946, PRONI CAB9F/123/81.

14. Letter from Adams to E. P. Northwood, 19 November 1945, PRONI CAB9F/123/81. Although the Irish word 'Eire' (adopted by the Irish government as the name for the southern state in 1937) refers to all of Ireland (and could be taken to imply a territorial claim over the North), the Unionist government nevertheless felt that the use of the term helped to reinforce the differences between the two parts of the island, particularly if Northern Ireland was consistently referred to as 'Ulster'. This view was expressed clearly in a letter from Northwood, the Press Officer in the London Ulster Office, to Adams in Belfast in the wake of Winston Churchill's victory broadcast in 1945. 'The more the word Eire is repeated,' observes Northwood, 'the more it is driven home that Northern Ireland is part of the United Kingdom, or at the very least, an entity separate from Eire, and that immensely helps to get rid of a certain sub-conscious feeling in English minds that Eire and Northern Ireland ought to be one' (Report on the Work of the Government Publicity Office during May 1945, PRONI CAB9F/123/34).

15. The Gaelic League, formed in 1893, had been particularly concerned to mobilise music and dancing in the service of cultural nationalism. For a discussion of the nationalist 'invention' of an Irish dancing tradition, see R.V. Comerford, *Ireland* (London: Hodder Arnold, 2003), ch. 6.

16. *Today's Cinema*, 15 March 1946.

Too 'Irish' for the Unionist government in Northern Ireland: Richard Hayward plays the harp while the villagers dance in *Back Home in Ireland*

Hayward had, in fact, opted not to use the word 'Ulster' in the film's title on the grounds that it 'would not have the same drawing power in the U.S.A.'.[17] He also considered the film's inclusion of Irish dancing to be 'essential "sugar-coating"' that would add to the film's appeal in 'non Irish markets'.[18] However, while these elements may have resulted in the film appearing to be too 'Irish' for the Northern Ireland government, they still proved insufficient to win over American distributors for whom, unlike British reviewers, the film appeared to be 'too Ulster'. As Hayward's New York business associate explained, '[t]he great resistance seems to be that it is Ulster and American-Irish audiences would be largely antagonistic'.[19] As a result the film achieved only limited distribution and was unable to recoup its costs, leaving Hayward and his colleagues out of pocket. Given these harsh economic realities, it was to be expected that Hayward should now attempt to place his activities on a firmer financial footing.

He did so by proposing the establishment of a Northern Ireland Film Unit that would be backed by the Northern Ireland government. Hayward argued that 'Ulster films should be made by Ulster people' who alone could provide 'a feeling for the Ulster countryside' and a 'really sympathetic understanding of the genius of Ulster'. He therefore suggested that the unit should begin with 'a film survey of the Six Counties' in the form of six films covering 'the history, scenery, industry, agriculture, sport, education and special crafts of each County'. 'If, as a working artist, I have any qualities of value to the Government,' he concluded, 'I place these qualities at your service.'[20] The government, however, was not persuaded of the merits of Hayward's idea nor, indeed, of the quality of his work. Thus, notwithstanding his remarks at the film's Belfast premiere, Brooke

---

17. Hand-written note, 22 November 1945, PRONI CAB9F/123/81.

18. Letter from Richard Hayward to R. Gransden, 9 April 1946, PRONI CAB9F/123/81.

19. Letter from Edward L. Kingsley to Hayward, 12 February 1947, UFTM. Kingsley also described the film as 'too Ulster' in a subsequent letter.

20. Letter from Hayward to Gransden, 9 April 1946, PRONI CAB9F/123/81.

took the view that *Back Home in Ireland* 'did not strike him as a very promising example of the type of work which Mr. Hayward's organisation might be expected to turn out'.[21] The production of six films was also regarded as too ambitious and there was a reluctance to grant Hayward a monopoly of government-funded production in Northern Ireland. As a result, the Cabinet Publicity Committee agreed it was better to work with the newly established Central Office of Information (COI) and, in doing so, avail themselves of 'the best British producers' (and not just local talent).[22]

'A raw deal': the Central Office of Information, Northern Ireland film and *Ulster*

However, collaboration with the COI was destined to bring problems of its own. The Central Office of Information had been established in 1946 to carry on some of the publicity functions previously undertaken by the Ministry of Information. As a part of this reorganisation, the MOI Films Division was merged with the Films Division of the British Council and became a part of the COI. In Northern Ireland, this meant the closure of the MOI Regional Office (which at this time was mainly concerned with the operation of the mobile film units). Although the COI was establishing Regional Offices in England and Wales, the Northern Ireland government was reluctant to follow suit. After the election of the Labour government in Britain, the Unionist regime had seriously contemplated demanding increased devolution, or even dominion status, for Northern Ireland before a recognition of the harsh economic consequences of doing so dented its enthusiasm.[23] A similar fear of Labour policies was also manifest in response to the COI proposals. According to the Cabinet Secretary, Robert Gransden, 'serious difficulties' were likely to arise if 'a regional organisation in Northern Ireland [is] controlled from London and charged with the responsibility of propagating, even objectively, policies of [a] Labour administration which may not be in accordance with the views of our own Government'.[24] As a result, the Unionist government successfully argued against the establishment of a regional COI office in Northern Ireland and, in addition to assuming responsibility for the MOI film units (which continued a full service until February 1952), undertook to provide an agency service on behalf of the COI with regard to general publicity.[25] The arrangement was formally announced in the Northern Ireland House of Commons in early 1947 and began on 1 April.[26] Although this was, in effect, a continuation of the existing MOI service, its transfer to the Northern Ireland government heightened concerns about the government's intentions concerning the use of film for propaganda purposes. The following day, for example, the nationalist *Irish News* complained about a lack of information on the service and offered ironic suggestions for possible film pro-

---

21. Minutes of the Cabinet Publicity Committee, 6 May 1946, PRONI CAB9F/123/37.

22. Ibid.

23. See David Harkness, *Northern Ireland since 1920* (Dublin: Helicon, 1983), pp. 106–8.

24. 'Ministry of Information Services: Future Organisation in Northern Ireland', Cabinet Publicity Committee, 22 February 1946, PRONI CAB9F/123/32.

25. After February 1952, film shows continued with one operator. In a typical month (January 1947), the two mobile film units were responsible for seventy-three shows, involving over 9,000 people, at locations such as schools and factories (Report for the Cabinet Publicity Committee, PRONI CAB9F/123/42).

26. *Parliamentary Debates* (HC), vol. xxx, col. 4523, 27 February 1947.

ductions: 'Forty Thousand Odd Men Out' on unemployment, 'Red Tape Over Orange Lily' on government bureaucracy and 'The Border Bogey' on 'the wicked ogre who haunted the Border' but turns out to be 'a kindly old gentleman'.[27]

However, if the Unionist government sought and obtained a degree of organisational auto-nomy in relation to publicity, it still expected the COI to foot the bill and disputes over fund-ing, particularly of film, were destined to follow. The initial view of the British Treasury was that when Northern Ireland was 'the sole or predominant subject' of a film made for overseas pub-licity, the cost should be borne by the Northern Ireland government.[28] The Northern Ireland government, however, took the view that 'overseas publicity' constituted an 'Imperial', rather than a 'transferred', service and argued that the costs, in these cases, should be met by the British government.[29] The Treasury eventually conceded this point and agreed that, if the Northern Ire-land government paid for publicity matter intended purely for local circulation, the COI would pay for material for circulation in the UK and overseas.[30] There was, however, an element of pyrrhic victory about this. For just as the absence of a regional COI office meant that less was spent on Northern Ireland publicity than would have been otherwise the case, so the fact that both the British Treasury and the COI initially sought to avoid the financial burden of making films for Northern Ireland meant that the Unionist regime was – almost inevitably – destined to receive less than what it regarded as its 'fair share'.[31]

This was not for want of trying on the part of the Northern Ireland Government Press Officer, Frank Adams, who set up an inter-departmental Films Consultative Committee to ensure that 'Northern Ireland obtained the maximum benefit from the production activities of C.O.I. Films Division'.[32] He also wasted no time in visiting the Division's Director, R. E. Trit-ton, following the latter's appointment in May 1946. At their first meeting, he rehearsed the Unionist government's sense of grievance regarding the Ministry of Information, which he claimed had given Northern Ireland 'a very "raw deal"' during the war and urged the COI to embark immediately upon a Northern Ireland production.[33] In particular, he pressed the COI to take over a film project (subsequently to become *Ulster* [1948]) that the British Council had begun in 1944 but not completed. At that time, Ronald Riley of Technique Film Productions had visited Northern Ireland and prepared a script entitled 'The Six Counties'. Despite the calls later for the film's completion, the Unionist government was not initially well disposed towards

---

27. 'Funds, and Ideas, for Films', *Irish News*, 28 February 1947, p. 2.

28. Letter from W. H. Fisher, Treasury, to W. G. Crossley, COI, 1 August 1946, PRO INF12/576.

29. Letter from Crossley to S. Lees, Treasury, 9 September 1946, PRO INF12/576.

30. Letter from R. Gransden to J. I. Cook, 5 July 1946, PRONI COM62/1/991; letter from Lees to Crossley, 18 September 1946, PRO INF12/576.

31. While the Unionist government had resisted the establishment of a COI regional office, it was still lamenting some fifteen years later the perceived inequities to which this led. Thus, in a letter to the COI Director-General in October 1961, the Northern Ireland Government Director of Information complained that the lack of a regional office in Northern Ireland meant that Northern Ireland was 'virtually ignored in regard to the daily collection and despatch by C.O.I. of news and feature material (press, radio, TV and pictorial)', PRONI CAB9F/123/73.

32. Minutes of the Films Consultative Committee, 10 May 1946, PRONI CAB9F/123/37.

33. 'Production of Northern Ireland Films', Cabinet Publicity Committee, 3 June 1946, PRONI CAB9F/123/37.

this. While it was felt that the focus of the film on a local farming family was 'attractive and suitable', objections to the script were also raised. These indicate not only the close scrutiny to which film projects such as this were subjected by senior politicians and their officials but also the degree of paranoia with which even mild expressions of minority nationalist identity could be met. Thus, the use of the phrase 'the six counties' in the film's title and commentary was vigorously opposed on the grounds that it was an expression used 'by opponents of Ulster's constitutional position as a term of belittlement'.[34] The Northern Ireland Prime Minister, Basil Brooke, also expressed his views on the matter and took exception to the family's name – the McQuades – which he deemed to be insufficiently 'representative' (i.e. 'Protestant'). Searching for a suitable alternative, Adams revealed the semiological complexities involved in selecting a name fit for a fictional 'Ulster' family. 'Common names in Northern Ireland such as Russell, Johnston, Scott, Gillespie' do not 'give the same local colour to the family as a "Mac" name', he observed. 'McKeown would probably be ruled out on the same grounds as McQuade', while 'the O'anybodies would automatically disappear', he went on. 'McConnell, McCracken or McLure' emerged as the most suitable candidates and, sure enough, the family was rechristened the McConnells in the final version of the film (which, unsurprisingly, also went under a different title).[35] After some more setbacks, a revised script was delivered to the British Council in March 1946 but, given the restructuring of the organisation's film operations, the project ground to a halt for a second time. The Northern Ireland government contemplated going ahead with the film on its own but held the cost to be too high and it was at this point that the COI's support was enlisted.

The COI agreed to take on the project but commissioned yet more script changes. This led to further problems for the representatives of the Unionist government, who, clearly fearful of connotations of Irish nationalist culture, sought to eliminate an episode involving a 'Ceilhe Band' – along with shots of a donkey and cart – on the grounds that these were not 'representative of the Ulster which we wish to "put across"'.[36] The title of the film also proved a continuing source of concern and various possibilities were contemplated, including 'The Hand of Ulster', 'This is Ulster' (which subsequently become the title of an official government publication in 1954 as well as a COI film in 1959), 'Ulster Today', 'Ulster Panorama' and 'Ulster Mirror' (which became the title of BBC Northern Ireland's first television magazine programme in 1954). Eventually 'The Voice of Ulster' was settled upon but even this proved a problem and was rejected by the film's theatrical distributor, MGM, which thought it contained 'an undesirable touch of propaganda' (partly due to the fact that the Ulster Unionist Party had recently distributed a magazine bearing the same

---

34. 'Note on outline treatment prepared by Technique Film Productions for Ulster Technicolour Film', 9 November 1944, PRONI CAB9F/123/32. However, while reference to 'the six counties' may involve a reluctance to recognise Northern Ireland's official designation, the rhetoric of 'the six counties' had, of course, derived from the Unionists' own campaign, under James Craig, for partition involving six rather than the nine counties of Ulster.

35. 'Some further comments on the outline for the British Council's "Ulster" film', 17 November 1944, PRONI CAB9F/123/32.

36. Letter from Adams to Northwood, 23 July 1947, PRONI CAB9F/123/81.

name).[37] After consideration of various other proposals ('Window on Ulster', 'Ulster Progress', 'Modern Ulster'), the plain title of *Ulster* was finally agreed upon and, some five years after its initial conception, the film was eventually released in the UK in 1949 (where by the end of November, it was reported to have received 300 showings).[38] In one of the few contemporary reviews of the film, the English trade paper *Today's Cinema* described its portrait of 'life and scenery in Ulster' as 'very good'.[39]

The film itself departs significantly from the original drafts of the script and consists of a loose mix of disparate elements, including Northern Ireland's scenic attractions, historical monuments, agricultural and industrial activities and plans for postwar reconstruction. Like *Ulster* (1941) before it, the film reveals a debt to the poetic-realist strand of documentary film-making, combining features of the conventional expositional mode of documentary films with more expressive and associative elements. Unusually the film employs four narrators. These consist of an unnamed Englishman as well as three local speakers, intended to represent the voices of a local farmer and shipyard worker, as well as a female designer employed at a linen factory. Although the English speaker remains the most 'objective' and authoritative voice (particularly in comparison to the more 'emotional' tenor of the woman's comments), the film nevertheless departs from the standard format of expositional voice-over in order to create an interplay of voices that mark out the different facets of Northern Ireland life (and, to some extent, express the 'unity-in-difference' of the imagined community of 'Ulster'). This expressive interest in aural montage also extends to the visuals. This is particularly evident during the sequence in which the female narrator describes her work as a linen designer. This begins with a straightforward illustrative shot of women at work but, taking its cue from the female narrator's claim that her work reflects the 'colour and charm' of the Ulster countryside, proceeds to a series of close-ups of the designs intercut with visually similar shots of birds, a waterfall, the seashore and a farmer scything hay.

Like the earlier *Ulster*, this mix of informational and aesthetic strategies also reflects a tension within the film between a 'realist' interest in day-to-day life and work in Northern Ireland and a 'romantic' impulse towards the aestheticisation of landscape and labour (both agricultural and industrial). This in turn corresponds to an element of tension within the film concerning the kind of image of 'Ulster' it is projecting. As previously noted, the Northern Ireland government was keen to remove from the film an episode involving Irish dancing as well as a shot of a donkey and cart. Significantly, both of these survive in the finished film, which, for all of its enthusiasm for the hard work and enterprise of the 'Ulster' people, remains wedded to a romantic view of the 'Celtic' Irish periphery (as seen from the metropolitan, English centre). Thus, while the film does contain shots of Northern Ireland's industries (such as linen and shipbuild-

---

37. Report of Government of Northern Ireland Press Officer for August 1948, CAB/9F/123/43. Earlier in the year, Brooke had cautioned against indiscriminate circulation of the magazine *The Voice of Ulster* on the grounds that it was likely to cause affront to 'Roman Catholics and Socialists' (Minutes of the Cabinet Publicity Committee, 11 May 1948, CAB9F/123/41).

38. Report of the Government Press Officer for November 1949, PRONI CAB9F/123/44. Although the film was released, and certificated by the British Board of Film Censors, under the title *Ulster*, the surviving print retains the original title, *The Voice of Ulster*.

39. *Today's Cinema*, 29 September 1948, p. 16.

ing), it does so in terms of an aesthetic framework that emphasises the beauty of the landscape (and, indeed, work), the closeness of the people to the land and the 'natural' rhythms of everyday life (which, as has been seen, even extends to the portrait of linen production). The film's concluding shots are eloquent in this regard. The final piece of commentary, spoken by the English narrator, declares that 'the youth of Ulster can look forward to living in a land that is . . . a land of enterprise, a land of prosperity'. Although this speech is accompanied by shots of men at a construction site and a group of women leaving work, the sequence then dissolves (on the word 'prosperity') to shots of sheep, flying birds and the Northern Ireland coastline. In a sense the image of postwar reconstruction and industrial endeavour that the ending of the film is attempting to promote is subverted by the film's continuing investment in a romantic image of 'Ulster' as an enduring haven of rural tranquillity and scenic splendour. As a result, the film is torn between an image of 'Ulster' as a modern, industrial economy wedded to Britain and a rural image of Ulster as a part of an Ireland apparently at odds with the modernity characteristic of Britain.

Despite its lengthy gestation, and delayed distribution, *Ulster* remained the most significant COI project for several years. During 1948, the Northern Ireland government pressed for the production of another COI film entitled 'Ulster, A Modern Democracy' but were informed that this was 'impracticable'.[40] In the same year, Adams and Northwood also met with John Grierson, the new Controller of the COI Films Division, who reportedly assured them that 'there should be no difficulty in making four films a year on Northern Ireland themes'.[41] However, the planned film 'I Came from Belfast', which was due to form part of a series of COI films entitled 'Where Do You Come From?', was abandoned in the face of obstacles from the British Treasury (which expected films to relate directly to exports to dollar countries).[42] Proposals for films on shipbuilding and linen were also rejected on the grounds that the Irish Linen Guild's film *Irish Symphony* had already lent support to the linen industry, while an earlier COI film on shipbuilding *Down to the Sea* (1948) had included some scenes of Belfast.[43] Under pressure, the COI eventually agreed to include Northern Ireland in plans for the Festival of Britain (celebrating Britain's artistic, industrial and scientific achievements) in 1951. However, given that this

40. 'Note by the Government Press and Publicity Officer on C.O.I. Production Programme', Films Consultative Committee, 13 July 1948, PRONI COM62/1/991.

41. 'C.O.I. Film Production Programme: Northern Ireland Subjects', 13 December 1948, PRONI CAB9F/123/41.

42. The COI had initially proposed that Londonderry (or Derry) – Northern Ireland's second city with a Catholic majority and poor record of employment – should be the focus of the 'I Came from . . .' film but, no doubt fearful that this would not necessarily lead to good publicity, the idea had been scotched by the Northern Ireland government who claimed that the city was 'quite an exception to the general run of Ulster towns' (Letter to Northwood, 17 August 1948, PRONI CAB9F/123/81).

43. 'Addendum', Report of the Press Officer for July 1949, PRONI CAB9F/123/44. The Irish Linen Guild film referred to here appears to have been distributed under the title *Irish Interlude* (1948). Involving members of the Ulster Group Theatre (including Joseph Tomelty) and directed by David Villiers (the director of 1948's *Ulster*), the film was designed to encourage girls leaving school to enter the linen industry. A later film entitled *Irish Symphony*, also directed by David Villiers, was released in 1952 and focused on selected areas of work, including the manufacture of linen.

was not regarded as overseas publicity, the Northern Ireland government ended up bearing the full cost of the film that followed. As a result, Adams expressed growing frustration at the COI's reluctance to undertake work at its own expense. 'It is becoming increasingly apparent that Northern Ireland will not get an adequate supply of films, which are so sorely needed for show-ing in Great Britain and overseas, particularly in the United States,' he argued, 'unless it has its own Government production unit or unless the Government commissions films direct from a production company and bears the cost . . . on the Northern Ireland Budget.'[44] Partly on the advice of Adams, the government had, of course, already rejected Hayward's proposal for a gov-ernment film unit. It now considered the matter of directly funding film again but approached the matter with caution. A deputation from the Ulster Unionist Council had already met the Cabinet Publicity Committee in June 1949 and called for an increase in the scale of its publicity operations, including the production of more 'Ulster films' (on topics such as 'the Life of Carson and the Twelfth of July demonstrations').[45] However, while the Committee was eager to get more films made, it worried whether the 'publicity results' that films yielded were 'commensu-rate with the amount of money' spent on them and decided against any new initiative for the time being.[46]

The one exception to this policy was, of course, the Festival of Britain film entitled *Land of Ulster* (1951), which the Northern Ireland Ministry of Agriculture had agreed to sponsor. Northern Ireland's contribution to the UK-wide Festival was mainly concentrated on the Farm and Factory Exhibition at Castlereagh, intended to showcase Northern Ireland's industrial and agricultural achievements. In line with plans for the Exhibition, *Land of Ulster* was designed to 'tell the story of the development, organisation and characteristics of farming in Northern Ire-land' and stress the contribution of the Northern Ireland government in encouraging and sus-taining agricultural activity.[47] The Farm and Factory Exhibition itself ran from 1 June until 31 August 1951, when the film was shown as part of a regular daily programme of films provided by the Government Film Service in a special 120-seater cinema. Other films shown included *Ulster* (under the title *The Voice of Ulster*) and Humphrey Jennings' Festival of Britain film, *Family Portrait* (1950), an Anglocentric look at the British 'family', which makes only a fleeting refer-ence to Belfast.[48] Over the course of the Exhibition, there were a reported 663 film shows with a daily average attendance of 660.[49] The popularity of these film shows appears to have rekin-dled Adams' enthusiasm for the publicity value of Northern Ireland films and, at the end of 1951, he proposed making a 16mm magazine film aimed mainly for non-theatrical distribution. The film, he suggested, would deal with 'the constitutional position, agriculture (briefly), old and

44. Report of the Press Officer for August 1949, PRONI CAB9F/123/44.

45. Minutes of the Cabinet Publicity Committee, 1 June 1949, PRONI CAB9F/123/44.

46. Minutes of the Cabinet Publicity Committee, 22 June 1949, PRONI CAB9F/123/44; Minutes of the Cabinet Publicity Committee, 25 October 1949, PRONI CAB9F/123/81.

47. Letter from A. A. K. Arnold, Secretary of the Festival of Britain Official Committee for Northern Ireland, to the Ministry of Finance, 6 December 1949, PRONI FIN18/29/174. As the only surviving print of the film that I have been able to locate lacks a soundtrack, it is difficult to evaluate the extent to which these goals were achieved.

48. *Belfast News-Letter*, 6 June 1951, p. 6.

49. Report of the Press Officer for September 1951, PRONI CAB9F/123/48.

new industries, and holiday and sporting events . . . as well as glimpses of typical Ulster scenery'.[50] The Northern Ireland Ministry of Finance was persuaded to back the project and the London company, Random Films, undertook filming in 1952. The film itself was distributed in 1953 under the title of *Ulster Magazine* and was described by a contemporary review as an 'unpretentious but likeable review from which much can be learned by school classes and (probably) most adult audiences'.[51]

'The light entertainment of not over-critical audiences':
Ulster Story and *Call of the Land*

Given the lack of significant Central Office of Information funding, the other main source of support available to Northern Ireland at this time was the British Travel Association of Great Britain and Northern Ireland. The film activities of this organisation had been transferred to the British Council during the war but it had resumed its support for film once the war ended. This included the sponsorship of James Fitzpatrick, who returned to Northern Ireland in 1945 as part of a tour of the UK and shot material – in colour – for two *Traveltalks*: *Over the Seas to Belfast* (1946) and *Roaming through Northern Ireland* (1949). Both the UTDA and the Northern Ireland Government Press Office assisted Fitzpatrick during his visit and were generally happy with his work.[52] The British Travel Association also embarked upon a series of films entitled 'What the Boys Saw' intended 'to interest people in other countries in the attractions of Britain' and to show Britain as seen by visiting servicemen. These were not planned to be studies of 'Britain at War' but rather portraits of 'the lasting scenic and historic beauties of the country, its sports and industries and traditional customs, its familiar institutions, and above all the spirit of the British nation itself'.[53] The Association proposed to include one film – subsequently to become known as *Ulster Story* (1947) – on Northern Ireland and recruited the support of the UTDA (which paid a subscription to the Travel Association). However, although the film dutifully presents many of Northern Ireland's 'scenic and historic beauties' (such as the Giant's Causeway and the cathedrals at Armagh), its evocation of the 'spirit' of the 'nation' proved highly contentious when the film was finally shown in Belfast in 1948.

This was partly to do with a number of factual inaccuracies contained within the film but was mainly the result of the film's suggestion of economic backwardness and hardship within Northern Ireland. At one point in the film the rather supercilious commentary (spoken in an English accent) declares that little has changed over 'the passing centuries' and that 'the life' of most of the people is 'rustic and simple'. The accompanying shot shows boys in a cart pulled by a donkey. Images such as these proved too much for the local press, such as the *Belfast News-Letter*, which complained of the film's 'strange emphasis on "stage Irish-

50. 'Suggested Production of a Magazine Film of Northern Ireland', 8 November 1951, PRONI CAB9F/123/48.

51. *Film User*, June 1953, p. 319.

52. In his report to the Cabinet Publicity Committee for March 1946, Adams records that he and Fred Storey, of the UTDA, were editing and correcting one of Fitzpatrick's scripts in which, he claims, 'the story of Ulster is extremely well told' (PRONI CAB9F/123/37).

53. Report to the Cabinet Publicity Committee for February 1946, PRONI CAB9F/123/37.

ness"'.[54] 'Not a single horse or tractor is shown in the rural scenes', the paper went on, 'but there are at least three donkeys – one of which might interest the N.S.P.C.A.'. Continuing in the same vein, the report concluded that it was 'something of a mystery how the cameraman travelled so far through the province and saw so many hovels and not a good-sized, prosperous farmhouse'.[55] The government had, in fact, been aware of the film from its inception but, embarrassed by the local response to the film, sought to distance itself from it. 'The Government here was not consulted when the film was under preparation nor have they any responsibility for it,' wrote the Cabinet Parliamentary Secretary (on behalf of the Prime Minister), somewhat misleadingly, the day after the *News-Letter*'s criticisms appeared.[56] Given problems of this kind, Unionist government officials hoped that they would be able to exercise more control over the next Travel Association project to deal with Northern Ireland. However, this too was to prove a major disappointment to them.

The idea for *Call of the Land* came from Richard Fisher, the co-producer and co-writer of *Ulster Story* and also Films Adviser to the Travel Association. Unlike *Ulster Story*, the film was to be shot in colour and, in order to increase its commercial value as a second feature, also incorporated a fictional element. This ultimately led to a scenario in which a young Canadian of Irish extraction arrives in Northern Ireland to dispose of a smallholding bequeathed to him by his grandfather. He is, however, waylaid by the daughter of a neighbour, who takes him on a tour of Northern Ireland. As a result, he decides not only to remain in Northern Ireland but also to marry his local 'guide'.[57] The Travel Association was prepared to cover half the costs and Adams persuaded the Ministry of Finance to pay for the other half. He did so on the grounds that the government would 'secure virtually a determining role in what the film should contain and how

---

54. *Belfast News-Letter*, 10 February 1948, p. 4. Although the review does not explicitly make the point, it seems likely that the film was also perceived as failing to maintain a sufficiently clear distinction between 'Ulster' and the rest of Ireland. The actuality of partition is not introduced until the very end of the film and, even then, the narrator makes light of the matter through facetious references to 'the little green Emerald Isle' and the ability of 'fairies' to cross the border 'without much interference'.

55. These criticisms had been anticipated by the Ulster Office in London, which, in its report to the Cabinet Publicity Committee for February 1948, noted complaints concerning 'mistakes in detail' and 'the inclusion of matter, which, it is felt, should have been omitted'. It was, however, the view in London that the film 'taken as a whole' and looked at 'from the point of view of its general effect on the minds of, say, an English audience' still constituted 'good propaganda' (PRONI CAB9F/123/42).

56. Letter from R. Gransden to H.A. Humphreys, 11 February 1948, PRONI CAB9F/123/81.

57. Both Harvey O'Brien and Stephanie Rains have identified the importance of the 'returning' American in Irish tourist films of the late 1950s, particularly following the success of *The Quiet Man*. *Call of the Land* anticipates this development but seeks to deploy the 'homecoming' narrative in the interests of 'Ulster' rather than Ireland more generally. However, as neither print nor script of the film appears to have survived, it is impossible to assess the ideological differences that result (although the choice of a Canadian, rather than an American, as the lead character is itself significant, given the strength of Protestantism among Irish-Canadians compared to Irish-Americans). On the Irish travelogue, see Harvey O'Brien, 'Culture, Commodity and Céad Míle Fáilte: U.S. and Irish Tourist Films as a Vision of Ireland', *Éire-Ireland*, vol. xxxvii, nos 1–2, 2002; and Stephanie Rains, 'Home from Home: Diasporic Images of Ireland in Film and Tourism', in Michael Cronin and Barbara O'Connor (eds), *Irish Tourism: Image, Culture and Identity* (Clevedon: Channel View Publications, 2003).

the material (apart from the shots of primarily travel interest) should be treated'. '[T]he "Ulster Story"', he argued, 'must be "put over" in a way that would justify Government participation' and 'Mr. Fisher entirely agrees with this'.[58] Agreement on the production was reached prior to the Belfast screening of *Ulster Story* so, without knowing the reaction this film would provoke, Adams was impressed by claims that it had been shown in 1,600 cinemas in the UK and accepted for distribution by Universal in the USA and Rank in Australia, Canada, New Zealand and South Africa.[59]

Although the project was given the go-ahead, its passage to eventual completion and exhibition proved even more troubled than those of its predecessors. The film began shooting in 1948 but production was nearly halted following the establishment of the Northern Ireland Tourist Board (NITB) the same year. Under the Development of Tourist Traffic Act (1948), the NITB was a statutory body funded by the Ministry of Commerce, which also appointed members of the Board. While the UTDA continued as a voluntary body, the establishment of the new organisation involved a degree of merger and the Advertising Committee of the UTDA was placed in charge of the NITB's publicity programme. However, despite this element of continuity, the new Board was involved in taking stock of its publicity policy and proposed to reduce its subscription to the British Travel Association by three-quarters. It did so on the grounds that the kind of publicity in which the Travel Association was engaged was mainly oriented towards overseas visitors, who were unlikely to visit Northern Ireland. 'We have no London, no Chester, no Stratford-on-Avon,' explained the Ministry of Commerce. 'No matter what money is spent, we would not hope to attract the Swedes, or the French, or the Dutch, or the Belgians to Northern Ireland.'[60] Although the UTDA had not directly contributed to the cost of *Call of the Land*, the Travel Association took the view that its involvement in the film had been premised upon the UTDA subscription remaining at its existing level and threatened to pull the plug on the project. The government (which regarded the film as more than simply tourist promotion) then applied pressure to the NITB, which had little option but to restore its contribution to the original level.[61]

The results, however, were not inspiring. Northwood of the Ulster Office saw a rough cut of the film in London but was not prepared to give it his approval. While he thought the film

58. 'Proposed Colour Film of Ulster by Baze Film Productions: Memorandum by the Government Publicity Officer', 16 December 1947, PRONI CAB9F/123/82.

59. Adams, 'Supplementary Note on Proposed Ulster Film in Colour by Baze Productions Ltd.', 17 December 1947, PRONI FIN18/28.

60. Letter from G. H. E. Parr to General W. Brooke Purdon, 10 September 1948, PRONI CAB9F/123/82. The basic soundness of the NITB position is confirmed by the *Second Annual Report of the Northern Ireland Tourist Board* (1 April 1949–31 March 1950), Cmd. 292 (Belfast: HMSO, 1950, p. 4), which indicates that 90 per cent of holiday traffic to Northern Ireland arose from Scotland, the North of England and the rest of Ireland.

61. NITB policy did, nevertheless, shift towards more modest 16mm projects intended for non-theatrical distribution. The first NITB film, *Northern Ireland Coast*, dealing with the Northern Ireland coastline from Londonderry to Warrenpoint, was produced by George Middleton (who also worked as an ITN cameraman) and narrated by the local writer Sam Hanna Bell. A companion-piece, *Letter from Northern Ireland* (1955), dealing mainly with inland holiday attractions, followed.

contained some 'excellent views' of 'places of historic and tourist interest' (such as the Giant's Causeway, the Mourne Mountains and the Protestant cathedral in Armagh), he was less impressed by the 'so-called story' and expressed 'serious doubts' about the film's 'effectiveness as a vehicle of Ulster publicity'.[62] The Secretary of the Festival of Britain Official Committee for Northern Ireland, A. A. K. Arnold, also saw the film and was even more critical. Arnold had been seeking government approval for the production of what became the Festival of Britain film, *Land of Ulster*. However, as *Call of the Land* remained unfinished, the Ministry of Finance was reluctant to commit to a new project and suggested to Arnold that the Travel Association film might feature in the Festival instead. Arnold was, however, vehemently opposed to this. *Call of the Land*, he declared, was no more than a 'run-of-the-mill tourist propaganda film designed for the light entertainment of not over-critical audiences', which could 'by no stretch of the imagination' be regarded as 'a definitive film on Northern Ireland, or a serious study of any aspect of local life'. In what must have made uncomfortable reading for the government officials at whom his remarks were directed, he concluded that if the production was intended as 'a "prestige" film', then 'it would reflect a complete lack of a considered film propaganda policy on the part of its sponsors'.[63] Given such negative reactions, it is not surprising that further editing of the film followed. However, this does not appear to have substantially altered the quality of the finished product, which struggled to achieve commercial distribution, even as a quota picture. The trade paper *Kine Weekly* was particularly hard on the film, describing it as 'a tedious affair . . . ruined by indifferent direction, acting and colour work'.[64] Thus, when the film eventually appeared at the end of 1952, it obtained only a limited distribution in a few small-town cinemas. Given the original promises of worldwide distribution (and dubbing into French and Spanish), Adams could not disguise his disappointment. Reviewing a list of the film's screenings, he wrote to Northwood: 'This is a pretty miserable list after all the fine promises that were held out to us . . . The outlook to me seems pretty dim.'[65] As was so often the case, Unionist ambitions for a film that would redound to their credit were dashed by a mixture of their own naiveté regarding film production and their lack of control over the film-making process.

'Definitely not good publicity from our standpoint': *Odd Man Out*

In 1955, the Prime Minister, Basil Brooke (created Viscount Brookeborough in 1952), expressed his concern that 'film publicity tended to have a fleeting effect unless it could be based on a series of films designed to reiterate variations of the same theme at regular intervals'.[66] However, as has been seen, the government did not wish to commit to the level of funding that would make such a series of films practicable and, as a result, encountered various logistical and

---

62. Letter from Northwood to Adams, 26 May 1949, PRONI CAB9F/123/82; Report of the Government Press Officer to the Cabinet Publicity Committee for May 1949, PRONI CAB9F/123/44.

63. Letter from Arnold to the Ministry of Finance, 12 January 1950, PRONI FIN18/29/174.

64. *Kine Weekly*, 22 May 1952, p. 18. In the interests of 'authenticity', Fisher had recruited a local actress, Margaret Crawford, to play the female lead. She was, however, an amateur actress and her lack of professional experience apparently told.

65. Letter from Adams to Northwood, 3 November 1952, PRONI CAB9F/123/82.

66. Minutes of the Cabinet Publicity Committee, 1 June 1955, PRONI CAB/9F/123/52.

ideological problems when relying upon others to make films for them. These problems were further compounded by the emergence of alternative film images of Northern Ireland during the postwar period. Although the government did its best to discourage the making of films that might cast Northern Ireland in a negative light, it only had limited powers to do so. While the war had helped to cement Northern Ireland's place within the United Kingdom, the immediate postwar years were initially ones of anxiety for unionists, given the uncertainties surrounding the new Labour government. Nationalists certainly expected that the arrival of a Labour government might lead to change and decided to take their seats at both Stormont and Westminster. Two new Stormont MPs – Eddie McAteer and Malachy Conlon – also called a meeting of 'nationally minded' groups and public representatives to a conference in November 1945, which resulted in the establishment of the Irish Anti-Partition League. This had the object of uniting all those opposed to partition into 'a solid block' and stimulated an international publicity campaign in support of Irish unification.[67] The APL's first chairman, James McSparran, also declared his hopes for the new Labour administration, arguing, in 1946, that it might be 'an opportune moment' for Labour 'to weigh up the expediency of maintaining a government in Northern Ireland' given that its members were 'lineal descendants of the Tory Party', detested 'the very name of Labour' and 'opposed every measure of progress introduced into Westminster for the benefit of the plain common people'.[68]

It was against this backdrop that the first major fiction feature to deal with the 'troubles' in Northern Ireland since partition, *Odd Man Out*, was made. *Odd Man Out* (1947) was based on a novel written by F. L. Green, who was born in England but had moved to Belfast in 1934. The novel was published in 1945 and the director Carol Reed went to Belfast to ask Green to work on the script, which subsequently became a Two Cities Film production for the Rank Organisation. The Northern Ireland government became aware of the film in October 1945, when Northwood of the Ulster Office reported that he had been approached by a Mr Wynne, then a Public Relations Officer at the Ministry of Supply but about to join Rank, for the government's views concerning the production of a film of the book. The Prime Minister, Basil Brooke, adopted the view that 'he would have no objection to a film which faithfully reproduced the atmosphere of the book' (which he regarded as 'fairly objective') but would oppose 'any attempt to glorify the activities of an illegal organisation or to build an aura of heroism around the gunman'.[69] This preliminary sounding was followed by a formal request for government co-operation the next year. Writing in February 1946, Phil Samuel, the film's associate producer, approached both the Ministry of Commerce and the Ministry of Home Affairs for assistance. Conscious that the film might be a matter of some sensitivity for the Unionist government, Samuel sought to reassure the Ministers that the film would contain 'no political significance or suggestion whatsoever'. The film would differ from the book, he argued, 'in as much as the organisation is not referred to as being a political organisation, and we are only conscious of the fact that a raid on a factory takes place by a Gang for the purpose of getting money'. 'Naturally,'

67. Michael Farrell, *Northern Ireland: The Orange State*, 2nd edn (London: Pluto Press, 1980), pp. 178–9.

68. *Irish News*, 6 July 1946, p. 1.

69. Minutes of the Cabinet Publicity Committee, 2 October 1945, PRONI CAB9F/123/81.

he concluded, 'they are eventually rounded up by the Police, and brought to Justice.'[70] The Ministry of Home Affairs referred the matter to Richard Pim, the Inspector General of the RUC, who took the view that '[t]he book on which the picture is based is not objectionable' and that 'after the usual surgical treatment which the Company proposes to give it, there will be nothing political left in the picture'. Although he considered it might be unwise 'to provide armoured or cage cars for which the Company has asked' on the grounds that 'in the minds of certain unsympathetic people in Britain' this might be 'looked upon as evidence of Gestapo methods in the Royal Ulster Constabulary', he was happy, on balance, to co-operate. The Parliamentary Secretary at Home Affairs, H. C. Montgomery, took the same view, arguing that 'if we don't assist we can't stop them making the film in England with "Stage"-policemen, & such a production is much more likely to be objectionable than one made under our eye'.[71]

Samuel subsequently met Pim, as well as a government representative from the Cabinet Office. Sensing continuing wariness regarding the project, he sought once again to reassure the government that the film lacked 'political significance'. While admitting that it would portray 'an organisation hostile to the established Government', he argued that 'the theme is treated in the same way as in gangster films and the personnel of the illegal organisation are regarded throughout as criminals who receive their just deserts in the end'. He went on to indicate his readiness to make the script available to the Northern Ireland government, declaring that while it would be in his company's financial interest for the Northern Ireland government to ban the film – 'as such action would boost sales in America' – he was nevertheless anxious 'to meet any views that may be expressed from the Government's point of view'.[72] His overtures, however, were to prove to no avail. For, despite the willingness of the RUC to provide assistance, the Minister of Home Affairs, J. E. Warnock, eventually decided against official co-operation.

Thus, while some filming did occur in Belfast, the bulk of the film was shot in London around Islington and Shoreditch and in the studio at Denham (where, for example, the interior of Belfast's Crown Bar was recreated). The production itself was an expensive 'prestige' production, involving an extensive shooting schedule of over twenty weeks, and launched with a gala premiere in London, attended by the British Foreign Secretary, Ernest Bevin.[73] Given the film's high profile, as well as its subject matter, it was hardly surprising that the film generated enormous interest when it opened in Belfast at the Classic in March 1947. The biggest crowds 'since "*The Singing Fool*"' (in 1929) queued 'round the block' to see the film, which, on its opening day, came close to beating the cinema's all-time record despite one less showing than normal due to fuel restrictions.[74] Although a police presence was maintained at the cinema, it seems that this was as much to do with the size of the crowds (and their disruption of motor traffic) than, as in the 1930s, the outbreak of sectarian 'incidents' inside the

70. Letter from Phil C. Samuel to The Secretary, Ministry of Home Affairs, 2 February 1946, PRONI HA32/1/640.

71. Letter from Inspector-General, RUC, to Secretary, Ministry of Home Affairs, 7 February 1946; hand-written note by H. C. Montgomery, PRONI HA32/1/640.

72. Memorandum, H. B., 19 February 1946, PRONI CAB9F/123/81.

73. *Kine Weekly*, 6 February 1947, p. 17; *Today's Cinema*, 29 January 1947, p. 49.

74. *Belfast News-Letter*, 4 March 1947, p. 2; *Today's Cinema*, 19 March 1947, p. 18.

cinema.[75] While the use of the police at the cinema would, of course, have made such 'incidents' less likely, the recorded responses also suggest a relative lack of controversy surrounding the film's actual contents. These, in turn, help shed some light on the arguments that have emerged regarding the 'political' character of the film's representation of the North.

In *Cinema and Ireland*, I argued that, as a result of the film's choice of aesthetic conventions, the politics of the film reside in the very repression of those factors that would invest the film's events with a social and political dimension.[76] This does not mean, as Samuel had suggested to the Unionist government, that the film is devoid of political significance; rather that the film's decontextualising aesthetic tends to reinforce pre-existing views of the 'troubles' as largely inexplicable. As in the case of *Ourselves Alone*, however, there is also a degree of ideological ambivalence within the film. As I also noted, the film's employment of a tragic structure, combined with the casting of one of biggest box-office stars of the period – James Mason – in the central role of the dying IRA man, encourages a degree of sympathy for the character that goes well beyond the treatment of the character in the original novel and may be seen to have links with an Irish republican tradition of 'failure' and suffering.[77] Brian McIlroy goes even further, however, suggesting that the film may, in fact, be read as 'anti-imperialist'.[78] His reading, however, depends upon a somewhat wilful defiance of the film's decontextualising logic (and removal of social and political specifics). Thus, while he attributes ideological significance to some features (such as the film's use of English accents), he ignores others (such as the high proportion of southern Irish accents in the film, including that of the Head of Police).[79] He also seeks to interpret Kathleen's efforts to assist Johnny in political terms (as a movement from constitutional to militant nationalism) when the film is at pains to signal the personal, romantic aspects of her decision (and, indeed, its clear defiance of the wishes of 'the Organisation'). Where McIlroy is right (and what his own exegetical manoeuvres appear to demonstrate) is how virtually any film dealing with Northern Ireland is liable to become the subject of competing interpretations given the inferential frameworks that local audiences will bring to bear on any film with a local connection. What is, therefore, surprising is that, contra McIlroy's unionist reading of it, the film actually aroused very little hostility among unionists at this time.[80]

---

75. *Today's Cinema*, 12 March 1947, p. 24.

76. Kevin Rockett, Luke Gibbons and John Hill, *Cinema and Ireland* (London: Routledge, 1988), pp. 152–60. Further discussion of the film may also be found in Chapter 8, where I consider the film's influence upon subsequent films about the 'troubles'.

77. Richard Kearney, for example, suggests how the capacity to arouse sympathy and support through suffering (as in the hunger-strike) has historically been one of Irish republicanism's strongest weapons in 'The IRA's Strategy of Failure', *The Crane Bag*, vol. 4, no. 2, 1980/1.

78. Brian McIlroy, *Shooting to Kill: Filmmaking and the 'Troubles' in Northern Ireland* (Trowbridge: Flicks Books, 1998), ch. 3.

79. John Devitt also points out that while the film may turn characters (Rosie, Maudie and Tom) who are Ulster Protestants in the novel into English ones, the implication of this is as much 'unionist' as it is 'anti-imperialist'. See 'Some Contexts for *Odd Man Out*', *Film and Film Culture*, no. 1, 2002, p. 64.

80. McIlroy's analysis is explicitly conducted from the position of the 'Northern Irish Protestant Unionist spectator'. However, this is a largely ahistorical, and homogenising, conceptualisation that does not seem to require McIlroy to provide evidence of the ways in which actual spectators (unionist or otherwise) did, or did not, activate meanings in particular contexts.

Kathleen (Kathleen Ryan) and Granny (Kitty Kirwan) hide a gun from the police in *Odd Man Out*

The unionist press, for example, was generally well disposed towards the film. The *Northern Whig* praised the film's 'accuracy of atmosphere and intention', while making no comment at all on the film's political outlook.[81] The *News-Letter* did express a degree of concern about some of the film's detail (including its 'confusion of accents') but still considered it to be 'a picture which ranks among the best of all time'.[82] The *Belfast Telegraph* ran two reviews of the film. The first of these argued that, while 'James Mason is magnificent', '[n]o efforts are made to arouse our sympathy for him' and the film is in essence 'just another cops-and-robbers film' in which the 'political angle' is 'wisely ignored'.[83] This was a view shared by the paper's other report on the film. In this, the author was less sure that the film completely avoided 'sympathy with a terrorist organisation' but concluded that 'the direction . . . has been done so skilfully, and "politics" avoided so meticulously, that good taste is rarely offended'.[84]

81. '"*Odd Man Out*": Screen triumph', *Northern Whig*, 4 March 1947, p. 2.
82. *Belfast News-Letter*, 4 March 1947, p. 4.
83. *Belfast Telegraph*, 1 March 1947, p. 2.
84. *Belfast Telegraph*, 4 March 1947, p. 2. The complaint that the film showed 'sympathy' for 'a gang of political terrorists' was also made by P. L. Mannock in the British *Daily Herald* (31 January 1947) but this review was virtually the only one in Britain to make such an argument.

There is also little evidence either to suggest that the nationalist press saw the film as particularly sympathetic to them. The *Irish News*, published in Belfast, thought it was 'a great film'
but, presumably conscious of the film's absence of social and political detail, warned its readers
that 'it was not made solely for Belfast audiences'.[85] In the South, the *Irish Independent* identified
the film's 'peculiar fascination' for Irish people but argued that the film-makers had been 'stu-
diously careful to make their treatment as objective as possible' and that the film did not take
sides.[86] Conor Cruise O'Brien (writing as 'Donat O'Donnell'), on the other hand, complained
that the film had turned Belfast into a 'vague, fantastic environment', containing a number of
'neurotic, isolated "characters" from nowhere'. Had the film made more effort 'to portray . . .
the city's deeply divided, suspicious, almost racialistic life', he suggests, then it might, indeed, have
provoked 'a riot'.[87] As might be expected, Liam MacGabhann's review in the *Irish Press* was the
most polemical in tone. While he agreed that the film was a 'good one', he also complained of
the film's 'political reticence' concerning 'why this struggle goes on'.[88] Similar sentiments motivated the publication of a leaflet by the Anti-Partition League in England. Describing the film as
'truly great and memorable', it nevertheless went on to ask 'Do you realise that the conditions
in Northern Ireland have provided the background against which this terrible drama is worked
out?' As with the *Irish Press*, the APL saw the film providing an opening for the articulation of
nationalist sentiments but did not locate them within the film itself. To this extent, McIlroy's evidence in support of an 'anti-imperialist' reading of the film appears to come down to one
column in the *Irish Times*, written by a Presbyterian living in Dublin, complaining that the film
amounted to 'a glorification of the I.R.A.'.[89] Apart from this, there is little to indicate that the
film was interpreted, even by unionists, in the way that he suggests.

This is not to say, of course, that unionists liked the film. Even though Sir Richard Pim, the
Inspector-General of the RUC, attended the film's opening (partly one suspects to see how his fictional counterpart was played by Denis O'Dea), it is also clear – as the government's reluctance to
support the film's production would suggest – that the Unionist establishment would have preferred
the film not to be made.[90] Subsequent commentary on the film also indicates that the completed
work was viewed in an unfavourable light. Thus, in his report on 'Films on Ulster Themes', Frank
Adams indicated that it was '[d]efinitely not good publicity from our standpoint'.[91] However, the
prevailing perception was not so much that the film was politically hostile to Northern Ireland (or

---

85. *Irish News*, 4 March 1947, p. 3.

86. *Irish Independent*, 10 March 1947, p. 2.

87. Donat O'Donnell, 'Beauty and the Beast: A Note on *Odd Man Out*', *The Bell*, May 1947, p. 61. Alluding to the film's
    failure to create a credible sense of place, O'Brien also makes the witty observation that such are 'the accents and
    manners' of the characters (Murphy and Nolan) played by Roy Irving and Dan O'Herlihy that one might be 'led to
    believe' that the "organization" is the B.B.C.' (p. 57)!

88. *Irish Press*, 10 March 1947, p. 4.

89. 'An Irishman's Diary', *Irish Times*, 15 March 1947, p. 7.

90. Pim's presence in the audience was reported in *Belfast News-Letter*, 4 March 1947, p. 2. *Today's Cinema* (12 March
    1947, p. 24) also reports that 'distinguished members of the Northern Ireland Cabinet' attended the film's premiere,
    although I have been unable to confirm this in the local papers.

91. F. M. Adams, 'Films on Ulster Themes', 6 May 1946, PRONI CAB9F/123/81.

An ambivalent portrait of the RUC: Denis O'Dea as Head Constable in *Odd Man Out*

'anti-imperialist') but that its dark, brooding imagery and representation of violence ran counter to the image of Northern Ireland that they were seeking to promote, especially to prospective visitors. The irony of this was not lost on their opponents. Two days after the film's opening in Belfast, the Northern Ireland House of Commons debated a supplementary estimate to cover RUC salaries and estimates. During the debate, the Labour MP (and constitutional nationalist) Frank Hanna took the opportunity to query the cost of policing the cinema in Belfast where *Odd Man Out* was showing, while the nationalist MP Cahir Healy suggested that the arming of the police should end. 'It is a very bad advertisement for the Ulster Tourist Development Association', he argued, 'to come into a place where every policeman is dodging around with a revolver. Somehow it lends belief to the idea that there is a turbulence here, and that the people are not cooperating with the police.'[92]

---

92. *Parliamentary Debates* (HC), vol. xxx, col. 4614, 5 March 1947. As Pim, the RUC chief, had feared, the imagery of armed police in the film was seen by 'certain unsympathetic people' as evidence of a police state. Unknowingly echoing Pim's own allusion to 'the Gestapo', the writer Patrick Kavanagh claimed that that the film did, indeed, offer a portrait of 'the Gestapo of the Six Counties' (*The Standard*, 14 March 1947, p. 7. Quoted in Devitt, 'Some Contexts for *Odd Man Out*', p. 66).

It was, of course, precisely this belief to which *Odd Man Out* partly lent credence and to which the government objected. This was all the more so given the popularity of the film both inside and outside of Northern Ireland and, thus, its capacity to reach audiences that their own propaganda films could not.[93]

'The injustice of an unnaturally partitioned country':
Belfast Remembers '98 and *Fintona*

Political hostility to the Unionist regime was more openly on display in *Belfast Remembers '98*, a short film made in Belfast in 1948 by the 1798 Commemoration Committee (which appears to have funded the production through private subscriptions). The film itself is basically a record of events in Belfast during September 1948 to celebrate the one hundred and fiftieth anniversary of the rebellion of the United Irishmen (involving both Catholics and Protestants). These events were in themselves surrounded in controversy. Plans for meetings and a procession in the centre of Belfast were banned, under the Special Powers Act, by the Home Secretary, Edmond Warnock, who was only prepared for these to take place in Catholic areas.[94] This, in turn, seems to have been the inspiration for the Belfast Corporation to cancel the 1798 Commemoration Committee's booking of the city's Ulster Hall for a ceilidh. However, in a further twist, the Lord Chief Justice subsequently ruled against the Corporation in the High Court and the ceilidhe was permitted to proceed.

Reviewing the changing ways in which 1798 has been commemorated in Ireland, Brian Walker suggests that few Protestants were involved in the 1948 celebrations, which were interpreted in 'contemporary unionist v nationalist terms'.[95] This is not entirely so. Protestants comprised the majority of the organising committee, which sought to project itself in non-sectarian terms. Thus, in its response to Warnock's ban, the committee claimed that their 'political and religious identities' had been 'submerged' in order 'to make the celebrations a purely citizen commemoration'. It was on these grounds that it objected to the restriction of the rally, complaining that this would 'identify the commemoration with only one section of the community, and so defeat the purpose for which the commemorations were organized, which is to honour the memory of the United Irishmen'.[96] That the commemorations became identified with nationalism, therefore, was in large part the result of the active hostility of Unionist politicians towards them. This was certainly the view of the nationalist *Irish News*, which argued that 'a bond of union between Catholic and non-Catholic' was 'distasteful' to the Stormont government, which sought 'to give the impression that the Commemoration . . . is a purely Catholic celebration'.[97]

---

93. *Kine Weekly*'s annual survey for 1947 identifies *Odd Man Out* as one of the seven most commercially successful films of the year (as well as the 'most artistic'). See R. H. 'Josh' Billings, 'What the Box-Office Returns Show for 1947', *Kine Weekly*, 18 December 1947, p. 13.

94. Warnock had also banned, earlier in the year, an APL demonstration in Derry planned for St Patrick's Day.

95. Brian Walker, *Past and Present: History, Identity and Politics in Ireland* (Belfast: Institute of Irish Studies, 2000), pp. 65–6.

96. *Northern Whig*, 10 September 1948, p. 1.

97. *Irish News*, 10 September 1948, p. 2.

The Northern Ireland government was alerted to the existence of the *Belfast Remembers* film during its post-production. The London-based company, United Motion Pictures, which had been involved in discussions with the Unionist government concerning a film of Northern Ireland's beauty spots, passed on the script of the film – to which they had been asked to add a soundtrack – to the Ulster Office in London. The Government Press Officer, Northwood, reported that the BBC had refused to permit the use of Lionel Marson's voice on the soundtrack of the film, which, he indicated, 'contained strong political attacks on the Northern Ireland Government and the Belfast Corporation'. He had also been left with the impression that United Motion Pictures would not undertake the recording.[98] Although the film was eventually finished, complete with soundtrack, it was only shown privately and there is little by way of evidence to indicate the extent to which it was screened. The organising committee despatched a copy to the Department of External Affairs in Dublin, where a private screening of the film was arranged. However, although the Department regarded the film as 'a fine record of activities in Belfast during the '98 celebrations' it declined to distribute the film, indicating that it was 'not quite suitable for circulation to the Missions abroad'.[99]

The film consists mainly of a record of the week's events, including footage of the organising committee, the gathering of the group at McArt's Fort on Cave Hill (where Wolfe Tone and others took the oath never to rest until Ireland was free), the laying of wreaths at the graves of United Irishmen (including Protestants such as Jemmy Hope and Henry Joy McCracken), the rally in West Belfast and the ceilidhe in the Ulster Hall. The commentary also attempts to lay claim to the non-sectarian character of the celebrations and repeats the intention of the committee 'to submerge religious and political identities'. However, despite the film's appeal to a common non-sectarian struggle against 'fear, poverty and social oppression', its reliance upon a rhetoric (indebted to the Anti-Partition League) of ongoing nationalist struggle made it unlikely to hold much appeal for Protestants other than the already committed. The film's voice-over explicitly condemns 'the injustice of an unnaturally partitioned country' and looks forward to the bicentenary celebrations when 'there will be no Stormont government or reactionary Tory corporation to foster disunity and strife'. Indeed, one of the most striking images in the film is of the Parliament Buildings at Stormont. As has been seen, the image of Stormont held an iconic value for the Unionist government and was repeatedly used not only in official publications but also in films such as *Ulster*, *Ulster at Arms* and *Ulster Story*. As Loughlin suggests, the 'primary function' of the buildings at Stormont was 'symbolic', providing an outward expression of the solidity and dignity of the political arrangements that had been established in Northern Ireland.[100] One of the most common versions of this image, calculated to enhance the sense of harmony and proportion involved in the architectural design, consists of a view through the front gate, looking along the long processional avenue leading up to the flight of steps and main portico of Parliament House. *Belfast Remembers '98* takes up a similar position but departs from the view conventionally found in other films. The camera

---

98.   Report for April 1949, PRONI CAB9F/123/44.

99.   Letter from B. Durnin, Department of External Affairs, to Seamus MacCearnaigh, Secretary of the 1798 Commemoration Committee, 4 November 1949, NAI DFA305/14/31.

100. James Loughlin, 'Consolidating "Ulster": Regime Propaganda and Architecture in the Inter-War Period', *National Identities*, vol. 1, no. 2, 1999, p. 169.

is placed further back than usual, and, combined with the use of a short lens, makes the building appear smaller than in official images. The film also invests the image with a certain bleakness by shooting in fading light, when the avenue is virtually deserted. Although this may have been partly borne out of financial and political necessity, it also involves a clear semiological strategy of subverting the familiar imagery of Stormont and divesting it of its normal grandeur.

Belfast Remembers '98 was clearly an unusual film in that it was one of the few films during the Unionist regime's fifty-year rule to be strongly critical of it. One of the others was *Fintona – A Study of Housing Discrimination* (1953), made by the Information Division of the Irish government's Department of External Affairs.[101] The Information Division was originally established by the then new Minister of External Affairs, Seán MacBride, after his party, Clann na Poblachta, joined an 'interparty government', along with Fine Gael and others, following the 1948 election. Partly as a result of Clann na Poblachta pressure, it was this coalition government, under the leadership of John Costello of Fine Gael, that opted to leave the Commonwealth and formally declare a Republic in 1948. MacBride brought an enthusiasm for anti-partitionist propaganda to the Ministry of External Affairs and the Information Division, under Conor Cruise O'Brien, was charged with the promotion of the anti-partition cause. Although the coalition failed to survive the 1951 election, the anti-partition activities of the Information Division continued under the new Minister, Frank Aiken, a former IRA Chief of Staff as well as a northerner (from south Armagh). Indeed, it was Aiken who was keen to make 'a short documentary' about 'Discrimination in the Six Counties' and prompted O'Brien to recruit Gerard Healy and George Fleischmann, two of the most active documentary and newsreel film-makers in Ireland at the time, to undertake 'preliminary exploration' of the subject.[102] While the Ministry of Finance suggested the National Film Institute of Ireland (the body established in 1945 for the production of government-funded films) should become involved, O'Brien strongly opposed this on the grounds that the making of the film was 'a matter of some delicacy' that would 'not command the approval of the Six County Government'. In such circumstances, he felt it desirable that the making of the film 'attract as little attention as possible'. Given that Fleischmann and Healy were 'the only newsreel team working regularly in Ireland', he argued that their presence in the North was much less likely 'to excite remarks as would the presence of other film people'.[103] It was decided that the film should focus on discrimination in the letting of houses by Omagh Rural District Council in the small town of Fintona in County Tyrone (in which Catholics constituted the majority). However, following an initial visit, Healy indicated that a film on housing discrimination in Fintona alone would be relatively short and argued for a film of 'wider scope', dealing not just with housing discrimination but with 'the whole political set-up in the North' and 'the system of gerrymandering'.[104] Despite Aiken's own enthusiasm for an exposure of gerrymandering (and his apparent request for changes to the script to highlight the political con-

---

101. While the film has become known, through common usage, *as Fintona – A Study of Housing Discrimination*, the actual title on the credits is *A Pictorial Record made in Fintona, Co. Tyrone, 1953*.

102. Letter from C. Cruise O'Brien to the Department of Finance, 6 May 1953, NAI DFA305/14/32/2. Further information on both Healy and Fleischmann may be found in Rockett, Gibbons and Hill, *Cinema and Ireland*, ch. 3.

103. Letter from O'Brien to M. Breatnach, Department of Finance, 13 June 1953, NAI DFA305/14/32/2.

104. Letter from G. Healy to O'Brien, 1 May 1953, NAI DFA305/14/32/2.

text of discrimination), it was nevertheless felt that the documentary would achieve greatest impact 'in human terms' by concentrating on the 'concrete reality' of housing discrimination.[105]

The resulting film is therefore a relatively straightforward visual demonstration of the inequities involved in the allocation of housing in Fintona. Following some introductory shots of the Fintona horse tram (apparently evocative of the village's 'old-fashioned' character but also investing the film with a somewhat surreal quality), the film reveals the overcrowded and insanitary conditions in which many Catholics live through a series of posed shots of large families outside their 'slum' homes. This is followed by a series of visually contrasting shots of new houses occupied primarily by Protestants (many of whom are said to be single or married couples without children). One new street – significantly called Craigavon Park – is claimed to contain no Catholics at all. The film then seeks to show how the allocation of these new houses has not been on the basis of need by including shots of some of the 'quite comfortable homes' previously occupied by the new tenants. The film then concludes with an explanation of the situation in terms of a unionist need to maintain electoral majorities leading to a more general pattern of discrimination, involving not just housing but voting privileges and jobs. This, in turn, is diagnosed as the consequence of the 'unnatural division' of 'an ancient historic nation'.

The Northern Ireland government became aware of the film when it was shown by the Anti-Partition League in Fleet Street in London to an audience of supporters and invited journalists. According to a somewhat jaundiced report in the *Northern Whig*, 'bedlam broke loose' following the film's screening:

> An Irishman deeply moved sang 'A Soldier's Song' and cursed his compatriots for not rising.
>
> Simultaneously a Communist abused the capitalist Press and 'the Fascist gangsters of Northern Ireland' and asked why the Anti-Partition League did not throw in its lot with the Left.
>
> Mr Tadhg Feehan, Secretary of the Anti-Partition League, threw metaphorical oil on his troubled audience and announced that another film would be coming soon. Its title – 'Gerrymandering of Constituencies in Derry'.[106]

Northwood of the Ulster Office in London despatched a report to Belfast that indicated that there was little English press interest in 'this type of propaganda' and only one English journalist had, in fact, attended the screening. '[T]he greatest danger', he thought, lay in 'the opportunity which may be given to the Anti-Partition League to show the film to local Trades Councils, Trade Union Branches, and Labour Party branches'.[107] The Minister responsible for Health and

---

105. Letter from O'Brien to P. S. M., 23 November 1953, NAI DFA305/14/32/2. It was also felt that an emphasis upon housing discrimination would achieve greater visual impact. This led to the idea of a second film on Derry where gerrymandering was both 'more striking and "photogenic"'.

106. *Northern Whig*, 8 April 1954, p. 1.

107. 'Anti-Partition League Films in Great Britain', 9 April 1954, PRONI CAB9F/123/12. Northwood's report of a lack of interest from the British press is confirmed by the report of the Irish Ambassador in London. In a letter to the Ministry of External Affairs in Dublin, he indicates that the event was 'definitely not a success', identifying 'the very definite allergy of Fleet Street to anything savouring of official propaganda' as a major factor. Letter to Sean Nunan, 8 April 1954, NAI DFA305/14/32/2.

Local Government in Northern Ireland, Dame Dehra Parker, however, complained that the film constituted 'overt interference by a "friendly" government in the internal affairs of another country' and urged the Unionist government to make a formal complaint.[108] The Prime Minister was nevertheless advised by officials to be cautious. Given that members of the Northern Ireland government had criticised the Irish government's subservience to the Roman Catholic hierarchy during the Mother and Child Health controversy of 1950–1, it was felt that a protest might encourage the reply, 'Tu Quoque'. Also, if the Irish government chose to stand over the facts in the film, this could give 'their propaganda an added boost'.[109] Despite these concerns, the Unionist government decided it would nevertheless go ahead and ask the British government to make a protest on its behalf and, in due course, the British Ambassador in Dublin delivered a formal letter of complaint to the Irish Ministry for External Affairs. In a letter to Brookeborough, the British Home Secretary, Sir David Maxwell Fyfe, indicated his support for the Northern Ireland government's position and expressed his hope that the Ambassador's intervention would 'discourage the Republican Government from undertaking any similar activities in future'.[110]

Meanwhile, the Unionist government kept an eye open for further showings of the film. However, nearly a year after its first screening, the London Press Office was relieved to report that there was 'no evidence' that the film had since been screened in Britain.[111] O'Brien was, in fact, still pursuing the idea of a second film on gerrymandering in Derry (which had initially been suggested by Eddie McAteer, the leader of the Nationalist Party in the North) but the film failed to proceed to production.[112] While this suggests the protests of the British and Northern Ireland governments may have been effective, it also reflects the Irish government's own disappointment that the film did not attract more attention in Britain and North America. O'Brien had sought to achieve a wide distribution for the film in Australia, Canada and the USA but achieved only limited success. The Irish Embassy in Washington, for example, was sceptical of the possibilities of commercial distribution and forwarded the comments of the Consul in San Francisco on prevailing Irish-American sentiment. 'Catholic and other sympathising groups', he reports, 'prefer pictures showing the loveliness of the Irish countryside and progress of the Country, rather than polemical subjects'.[113]

---

108. Conclusions of Meeting of the Cabinet, 15 April 1954, PRONI CAB4/936.

109. 'Note for Prime Minister *Fintona – A Study of Housing Discrimination*', 14 April 1954, PRONI CAB9F/123/12. Although the specific allegations appear to be substantially correct, the prejudice of unionists towards Catholics was highlighted by the comments of the Unionist MP for North Tyrone, Tom Lyons, in defence of the situation. Some 'tenants would not live among the former slum dwellers' (i.e. Catholics), he explained, because they are 'particular whom they have for neighbours' and 'knowing some of the types of people living in the slum areas, personally I don't blame them' (*Belfast Telegraph*, 8 April 1954, p. 1).

110. Letter from D. Maxwell Fyfe to Brookeborough, 28 May 1954, PRONI CAB9F/123/12.

111. Report of the Press Office (London) for February 1955, PRONI CAB9F/123/52.

112. Letter to Dr MacWhite from O'Brien, 22 August 1955, NAI DFA305/14/32/2.

113. Letters from Embassy of Ireland, Washington DC, to O'Brien, 6 January 1954 and 2 February 1954, NAI DFA305/14/32/2.

The impact of the film upon the North was also open to question. A prologue to the film, added later, suggests that the publicity surrounding the film forced the Unionist government to take measures to improve the situation in Fintona. However, it is also apparent that the Unionist regime's main concern was not to address the criticisms raised by the film but to dispute their validity and restrict the impact that the film might have outside of Northern Ireland. As early as March 1950, Dehra Parker had been questioned in the Northern Ireland House of Commons about the condition of the houses in one of the streets that appears in the film, Brunswick Row, but had deemed the suggestion, made by the nationalist MP Edward Vincent McCullagh, that Omagh Council had failed to order their demolition because 'Catholics were living in them' as 'unworthy of an answer'.[114] During the 1950s, she also ignored the warnings of civil servants regarding the political dangers of local authorities engaging in discrimination in the allocation of new housing.[115] The Unionist government was, therefore, already fully aware of the situation in Fintona but had proved itself disinclined to interfere. Indeed, given the important symbolic role that discrimination in housing was to assume for the Civil Rights Movement in the following decade, this ongoing determination to maintain the political dominance of unionism at the expense of a fair treatment of Catholics was ultimately to prove the regime's undoing. As F. S. L. Lyons indicates, 'it was the competition for houses which provided the spark that . . . set the whole province alight'.[116] The situation at the time of the film's appearance, however, was not conducive to reform. As noted in the previous chapter, the experience of the Second World War and the actions of the Irish government in 1948 in declaring a Republic had provoked the British government into strengthening Northern Ireland's constitutional position in relation to Britain. For Paul Bew, one of the weaknesses of the Anti-Partition League's strategy was that it downplayed the importance of Unionism and simply blamed 'the British government for discrimination in Northern Ireland'.[117] Similarly, the strident nationalist, and anti-British, rhetoric of the film's commentary (with its references to 'Irish nationalists . . . held by force under British rule' and British 'connivance' in a system of discrimination in the North of Ireland) was hardly calculated to encourage the British government (now Conservative) to intervene in Northern Ireland's affairs and probably contributed to its readiness to ignore the substance of the grievance and do the Unionists' bidding in registering a protest.[118]

---

114. *Parliamentary Debates* (HC), vol. xxxiv, col. 363, 21 March 1950.

115. Derek Birrell and Alan Murie, *Policy and Government in Northern Ireland: Lessons of Devolution* (Dublin: Gill and Macmillan, 1980), p. 144.

116. F. S. L. Lyons, *Ireland since the Famine* (London: Fontana, 1973), p. 762.

117. Paul Bew, '1950s', in Luke Dodd (ed.), *Nationalism: Visions and Revisions* (Dublin: Film Institute of Ireland, 1999), p. 36. He compares this with the relative success of the Civil Rights Movement in the 1960s in maintaining an ambiguous position towards partition and calling upon the British government as an ally in delivering reforms.

118. Conor Cruise O'Brien's own view, recorded much later, was that the reason that the propaganda activities of the Information Division achieved less than had been hoped was that 'the grievances in question, though oppressive in the daily life of those who experienced them, were unspectacular and even humdrum' compared with the 'far more brutal repressions . . . taking place elsewhere'. See *States of Ireland* (London: Granada, 1974), p. 139.

Censorship in Belfast

Indeed, the sympathy of the British government towards Unionism was to increase further with the launch of a new IRA border campaign in 1956.[119] This also provoked a new sensitivity within the Northern Ireland government towards the representation of the IRA in Britain and there was considerable hostility when the BBC in London transmitted an interview with the Irish writer, H. L. Craig, which referred to Northern Ireland as 'being occupied by enemy forces' and appeared to make light of the IRA's campaign.[120] Brookeborough flew to London to undertake a live interview for *Panorama* with Richard Dimbleby in which he expressed his outrage that IRA attacks should be taking place in 'a part of the United Kingdom' before declaring that 'Ulster people are Queen's men and nothing whatever will shift them from that position'.[121] The shift in mood in Northern Ireland created by the IRA campaign was also to have an impact upon the reception of films dealing with Irish topics. As has been seen, the sectarian riots of 1935, and surrounding political atmosphere, contributed to an increasingly politicised form of censorship in the years that followed. The lack of controversy surrounding the screening of *Odd Man Out* may also be attributed to the relative political stability (and absence of IRA activity) at the time of its release. Thus, in 1959, a *Belfast Telegraph* columnist was able to ask whether the film would have been 'accepted so readily' if it had appeared then rather than in 1947.[122] The first film to feel the effects of this change in atmosphere was John Ford's *The Rising of the Moon*, which was banned by the Belfast Corporation towards the end of 1957. Objection was taken to the third part of the film, '1921', inspired by Lady Gregory's play 'The Rising of the Moon', in which an IRA man under sentence of death escapes from prison with the help of members of the Abbey Players. Although the film contains no reference to the North, it does contain an unflattering portrait of the Black and Tans and was unashamedly nationalist in its celebration of resistance to British rule (which includes an RIC sergeant turning a blind eye to the IRA man's escape). This was clearly too much for some members of the Police Committee, who criticised the film for its 'unsuitable' political content and concluded that, in the light of recent IRA activity, its exhibition would be 'undesirable' and

119. Thus, in his report for January 1957, the Information Officer in London was able to report the relative absence of 'anti–Ulster propaganda' in the British press, and 'the wide sympathy' for 'Ulster people' to which the Border raids had led (PRONI CAB9F/123/56).

120. 'Ulster protests at TV comments go to highest level', *Belfast Telegraph*, 15 December 1956, p. 1.

121. *Belfast Telegraph*, 18 December 1956, p. 9. As was the case during the Second World War, Brookeborough was acutely conscious of the propaganda battle in which he was involved, complaining on several occasions to the BBC Director-General about programmes that caused him offence. This included a screening, in 1954, of the Irish propaganda film *The Promise of Barty O'Brien* (1951), produced under the Marshall Aid Programme, promoting rural electrification. Indicating the susceptibility of the BBC to this kind of pressure, the Director-General, Ian Jacob, was forced to agree that it was not 'suitable for showing in the BBC Television Service'(Minutes of the Board of Governors, 8 April 1954, BBCWAC R1/21/1).

122. Martin Wallace, 'Sense and Censorship in City Films', *Belfast Telegraph*, 12 June 1959, p. 12. It is also worth noting that *The Gentle Gunman*, dealing with the IRA's bombing campaign during the Second World War, was shown without apparent incident in Belfast in 1952.

'ill-timed'.[123] Although the film was subsequently shown outside Belfast (in towns such as Bangor and Downpatrick), the distributors of the film subsequently withdrew their application to show the film in Belfast itself.[124]

This decision was followed by a further ban in 1959. *Shake Hands with the Devil* was the first international production to be made at the new film studios at Ardmore and, like '1921', was set during the Irish War of Independence. Also like '1921', an Irish–American character occupies a central role. In this case, it is a young student who decides to join the IRA but, repelled by the fanaticism of his commandant, subsequently turns his back on violence. Although at least one Belfast councillor (and former Lord Mayor) was prepared to defend the film's 'moral value' for highlighting 'the futility of guerrilla warfare', he did not enjoy the support of the rest of the Police Committee, which refused permission for the film to be shown.[125] The clinching factor in this decision appears to have been the intervention of the RUC Belfast City Commissioner, who attended a special screening of the film and advised against its showing 'at the present time' because of possible risks to public order.[126] Thus, while some councillors claimed that they did not object to the film in itself, they were nevertheless determined to 'support the police'.[127] This led to claims by the republican Labour MP Harry Diamond, in the Northern Ireland House of Commons, that the police had exercised 'undue influence' in the matter, particularly as there had been no 'riot, trouble, or disorder' in Belfast cinemas 'within living memory'. He then went on to speculate whether the 'real reason' for the banning was that it was a 'a case of shaking hands with "Dev"'.[128] The distributors of the film, United Artists, also urged the Lord Mayor of Belfast to reverse the decision, arguing that the people of Belfast should be allowed to see the film that, it was claimed, contained a 'strong indictment of violence'.[129]

It does, indeed, seem that the Police Committee (and the RUC) over-estimated the power of the films to provoke antagonism. Both *The Rising of the Moon* and *Shake Hands with the Devil* were shown in places other than Belfast without leading to any trouble. The Corporation in Londonderry, for example, passed *The Rising of the Moon* for exhibition in 1958, partly on the

123. Letter from Town Clerk to Mr A. McQuillan, 22 January 1958, PRONI LA7/3E/19/17; *Kine Weekly*, 17 April 1958, p. 9. Interestingly, the film also caused offence in the South for its apparent parade of Irish stereotypes in the section entitled 'A Minute's Wait'.

124. Letter from V. P. Powell, Managing Director, Odeon (Northern Ireland) Ltd. to Town Clerk, 30 October 1957, PRONI LA7/3E/19/17; *Kine Weekly*, 5 December 1957, p. 7.

125. *Belfast Telegraph*, 18 June 1959, p. 1. Although there was some criticism of the film in British reviews because of its portrait of the Black and Tans, the film was also criticised in the Irish press for its portrait of opposition to the peace treaty – providing Dominion status for a partitioned Ireland – as pathological blood-lust. (See my discussion in Rockett, Gibbons and Hill, *Cinema and Ireland*, pp. 164–7.) The film was also cut in both Britain and Ireland but the cuts concerned sexual imagery (the scene with the prostitute on the beach) rather than its political content.

126. *Belfast Telegraph*, 19 June 1959, p. 6.

127. *Belfast Telegraph*, 18 June 1959, p. 1.

128. *Parliamentary Debates* (HC), vol. 44, cols 2003–4, 25 June 1959.

129. Telegram from Monty Morton, Managing Director, United Artists London, to Lord Mayor of Belfast, 30 June 1959, PRONI LA7/3E/19/21.

'Undesirable' and 'ill-timed':
John Ford's *The Rising of the
Moon* is banned in Belfast

grounds, as one councillor put it, that 'the whole film was "unadulterated rubbish" and of no consequence, political or otherwise'.[130] *Shake Hands with the Devil* was also shown in the same city and the screenings of both films passed without incident.[131] Given the lack of any evidence that the film was liable to provoke disorder, there were fears that the city of Belfast (which had recently seen the withdrawal of Sam Thompson's play *Over the Bridge* by the Group Theatre) was gaining a reputation for censorship that was proving, in the words of one councillor, 'unfavourable to the Unionist Party'.[132] In these circumstances, it was agreed that the Police Committee should consider the matter further. It did so and, a few months after the original ban, it was finally agreed by the Council that the film should be shown.

    The fact that these films did not, despite the concerns of Unionist councillors, lead to the kind of disturbances witnessed in the 1930s may be attributed to a number of factors. As in Britain, cinema attendance was in decline and no longer represented the major social force that it once did. The growth of television (including the launch of Ulster Television in November

---

130. *Belfast Telegraph*, 31 January 1958, p. 9. The quote is attributed to Councillor Austin, who voted for the film to be shown.

131. Although this might suggest that Londonderry Corporation was more liberal than Belfast, this was hardly so. Although the Derry Corporation was relatively relaxed about 'political' films, it was strongly censorious towards films perceived to be 'immoral'. Thus, in 1961, a local councillor admitted that Londonderry 'probably banned more films than any other local authority in Britain' after a series of bans on films, including *Room at the Top* (1958), *Oscar Wilde* (1960), *The Trials of Oscar Wilde* (1960) and *Never on Sunday* (1959). Although, as a result of gerrymandering, the Corporation was Unionist-dominated, a member of the Young Unionist Association blamed the bans on the high attendance of Nationalists at the Law Committee. See *Kine Weekly*, 1 September 1960, p. 9; 2 February 1961, p. 9; 9 March 1961, p. 9; and 30 March 1961, p. 8.

132. *Irish News*, 2 July 1959, p. 3. A few years earlier Belfast had also succumbed to the panic surrounding rock'n'roll films and banned both *Rock around the Clock* (1956) and *Don't Knock the Rock* (1957) (although it subsequently rescinded its decision concerning *Rock around the Clock*).

1959) was in the process of usurping cinema's role as the main provider of entertainment as well as the sole supplier of moving images of Northern Ireland. The demographics of the cinema audience were also changing, with younger age groups constituting an increased proportion of the total. Unlike audiences in the 1930s, this group would have had little direct memory of the events in Ireland in the early 1920s and much less psychological investment in them. Moreover, despite the early successes of the IRA campaign, it was petering out by the end of 1958 as the result of internment on both sides of the border. There was also little evidence of widespread support for the campaign and, in the Westminster election of October 1959, the Sinn Fein vote dropped to less than half of its 1955 total.[133] Belfast, moreover, was largely unaffected by the campaign and the success of the Northern Ireland Labour Party at the 1958 Stormont elections (which included winning four seats in Belfast) was placing Unionism under a different kind of pressure and pushing the political agenda in the direction of domestic social and economic issues, particularly unemployment. Given these developments, it was possibly to be expected that films dealing with the War of Independence would fail to generate the same passions as twenty years before.

The Unionist government, moreover, was also concerned that the IRA threat should not be exaggerated. In 1958, a London-based company, Samaritan Films, proposed to make a documentary on the RUC's activities on the border (for which it required financial support). Although the film was intended to be entirely favourable to the RUC, the idea was firmly rejected by the government. As a letter to Samaritan Films explained, even sympathetic coverage of security activities on the border might 'convey the impression that we live in a state of siege and permanent tension', provide the IRA with 'gratuitous publicity' and have an 'adverse effect' on tourists as well as industrialists 'whose interest in Northern Ireland we are seeking to attract as a location for new industries'.[134] As with *Odd Man Out*, even a pro-Unionist film could be regarded as bad publicity if it implied there was social division and conflict within Northern Ireland and conveyed a negative image of 'Ulster' to potential tourists and investors. Although the attraction of industry to Northern Ireland (along with the promotion of tourism and the government's constitutional position) had been a recurring feature of government-funded films, the cultivation of an image of 'Ulster' as a modern, investment-friendly economy became increasingly important in the late 1950s and early 1960s. This image of 'modern Ulster', however, also came to be seen as increasingly at odds with the persistence of traditional social and religious divisions. It is therefore this developing conflict around images of Northern Ireland's 'modernity' to which the discussion now turns.

---

133. Farrell, *Northern Ireland: The Orange State*, p. 220.
134. Letter to T. Burrill, Samaritan Films, from A. J. Kelly, 5 January 1959, PRONI CAB9F/123/5.

5

'Go-ahead Ulster'

Film, Modernisation and the Return of the Repressed

In the late 1950s, the Irish producer and distributor Emmet Dalton embarked upon a series of film adaptations of plays involving the Abbey Players, beginning with a version of George Shiels' *Professor Tim* in 1957. His second production was *Boyd's Shop* (1960), an adaptation of St John Ervine's 1930s play celebrating the virtues of small-town Protestant Ulster. This was the only one of the series of six films set in the North and was, perhaps, a peculiar choice for production. In execution, however, the play's distinctiveness is virtually eliminated as a result of the removal of most of its 'Ulster' elements and a corresponding 'Irishification' of the remaining material. Thus, while the film is supposedly set in the North (in County Down) and the villagers are Protestant, there is no attempt to convey an 'authentic' Ulster atmosphere. The film is shot in a village in the South (complete with a recognisably southern Irish telephone box) and the parts are spoken by the Abbey actors in recognisably southern accents. Moreover, most of the new elements introduced by the film are self-consciously designed to imply a generalised sense of 'Irishness' that downplays the specificities of the Northern Ireland setting. The opening land-scape shots, for example, are accompanied by an Irish ballad ('A Song of Ireland') mainly con-sisting of the words 'Tell me a story . . . a story of Ireland'. The arrival of young John Haslett (Vincent Dowling) in the village is accompanied by a light musical jig strongly reminiscent of the score for *The Quiet Man*. When Haslett subsequently opens his new shop and offers all of his customers a free souvenir, this turns out to be an Irish harp (mounted on a card proclaiming 'Greetings from Ireland'), which his fellow shopkeeper, Andrew Boyd (Geoffrey Golden), some-what improbably declares will come in 'handy' on St Patrick's Day. Thus, much as the villagers in *The Quiet Man* gather at the end of the film to 'cheer like good Protestants', so the suppos-edly northern Protestant villagers in *Boyd's Shop* are really southern Catholics in disguise, scarcely deviating from the conventional comic stereotypes of Irish village life.

However, while the film's free-floating 'Irishness' may divest the play of its original ideo-logical significance for Ulster Protestants, it is unusual in another way. As previously noted, the play is a conservative work, celebrating age over youth and the traditional over the modern. This is also so of the film, in which John Haslett embodies a new style of entrepreneurial shopkeeper committed to modern selling methods, advertising and display (such that his shop is an 'exact replica' of one in New York). Haslett, however, is unable to compete with the family grocery run by Boyd, rooted as it is in tradition and longstanding service to the community. The film, in this regard, possesses links to such backward-looking Ealing comedies as *The Titfield Thunderbolt* (1953), in which the small-scale community successfully holds the forces of modernity at bay.

However, as in Britain, these were sentiments increasingly at odds with the economic realities of the times (not to mention the changing character of an increasingly youthful cinema audience). By the time of the film's release in Britain (in 1960), Sean Lemass had succeeded de Valera as Taoiseach and had already embarked upon a new policy of liberalising and internationalising the economy. The film's celebration of the 'wee shop', and its resistance to modern methods, therefore seemed peculiarly out of step not only with developments in the South but the emerging rhetoric of modernisation in the North as well. It was also this rhetoric that was increasingly to inform the films (and television programmes) being made in and about Northern Ireland during the late 1950s and early 1960s.

'Telling "the Ulster story"': publicity changes

In terms of official production, there was an end of an era when, after over twenty-five years in the job, Frank Adams retired as the Northern Ireland government's Press and Publicity Officer in 1955. As has been seen, he had remained an indefatigable enthusiast for films about Northern Ireland even though his attempts to get them made were constantly beset by difficulties and the results often proved disappointing. Shortly before his retirement, he returned once again to the issue of film production. Although he regarded film as an important means of 'telling "the Ulster story" in Great Britain and overseas', he acknowledged that 'the scale' of the government's film operations had been 'very modest indeed' due to the high costs involved. As a result, he suggested that it might be better to concentrate less on 35mm films intended for commercial distribution and more on 16mm films aimed for non-theatrical showings (as had been the case with *Ulster Magazine*). He also identified television as 'a new field of opportunity' and proposed the production of 'quite short films, with a high degree of topicality, for inclusion in television programmes'.[1] One of the first examples of this was the inclusion of an interview with the Prime Minister, Viscount Brookeborough, by Robert McKenzie (during which they discussed the development of Northern Ireland industry since the war and the relationship of Northern Ireland to Great Britain) in a series of 'Transatlantic Televiews' intended for broadcast on Canadian television.

Although shorter items aimed at television became an increasing priority for the Unionist government, it also succeeded in securing the production of a number of short films intended for cinemas as well as television. This was mainly the result of the efforts of Adams' successor, Eric Montgomery, formerly of the War Office, who resurrected the question of relations between the Northern Ireland government and the Central Office of Information, which, it was conceded in London, had undertaken 'comparatively little work' for Northern Ireland in the preceding ten years.[2] Although this led to a revised formula – whereby the Northern Ireland government would pay for material made at its request while the COI would provide on 'allied service terms any item with a Northern Ireland content which may be sponsored by a U.K. department' – it did not fundamentally change the financial relations between the two governments.[3] Nevertheless, the renewed pressure from Montgomery does appear to have led to

---

1. 'The Future Development of Northern Ireland Film Publicity', 28 April 1955, PRONI CAB9F/123/52.

2. M. Reid, Treasury, to G. N. Cox, Northern Ireland Ministry of Finance, 19 March 1956, PRO INF12/576.

3. Letter from Miss Smart, Treasury, to Mr Watson, COI, 30 May 1956, PRO INF12/576.

improved relations with the COI, which embarked upon a jointly funded colour film (spon-sored by the British Foreign Office), *This is Ulster* (1958), that was shown to the Northern Ire-land Prime Minister and other members of the Cabinet in Belfast prior to a screening at the World Exhibition in Brussels.[4] The film was then distributed, theatrically and non-theatrically, in over sixty countries (including the US and in Asia).[5] Such was the perceived success of the film that the Northern Ireland government decided to go ahead with, and bear the brunt of the cost of, a companion piece, *Ulster Heritage* (1961).

Although *This is Ulster* and *Ulster Heritage* (along with other short films of this period) demonstrate a number of continuities with earlier films in terms of their stress upon agriculture and scenery, a new emphasis upon industrial development and modernity is also apparent as a result of changes in political context and shifts in the government's publicity objectives. The film, therefore, provides a particularly eloquent expression of the kind of image of Northern Ireland that the Unionist government was endeavouring to promote at this time. By looking at it in some detail, and examining the way in which it draws upon and condenses various discourses relating to local identity, so I aim to bring out some of the main components – or mythemes – of the 'Ulster imaginary' as it was articulated during this period.

'An attractive picture of modern Ulster': *Ulster Heritage*

Whereas *This is Ulster* had sought to provide 'an overall coverage of Ulster', *Ulster Heritage* was conceived of in terms of a more specific focus on a town or village that would 'in miniature . . . reflect . . . the main trends and developments of Ulster life'.[6] In the event, the final film set-tled on an individual family (rather than a clearly identified town) as an appropriate represen-tation of 'Ulster' in microcosm. Members of the Cabinet Publicity Committee, including the Minister of Home Affairs Brian Faulkner and the Minister of Labour and National Insurance Ivan Neill, viewed a rough cut of the film and agreed that it was 'an excellent production'.[7] On its completion, the film was subsequently distributed by British Lion in the UK, where it was shown alongside the French dance film, *Un, Deux, Trois, Quatre!* (*Black Tights*) (1960).[8] It also received non-theatrical distribution in thirty-one countries overseas, ranging from Australia to Poland and Tanganyika to the US.[9] The film also remained available for borrowing for many years to follow from the Northern Ireland Government Information Service in Belfast and London. Thus, as late as October 1968 (after the first Civil Rights marches had occurred), *Ulster*

---

4. *Belfast News-Letter*, 23 April 1958, p. 3.
5. 'Memorandum for the Cabinet Publicity Committee: New Colour Film', 5 February 1960, PRONI CAB9F/123/59.
6. Minutes of the Cabinet Publicity Committee, 10 February 1960, PRONI CAB9F/123/59.
7. Minutes of the Cabinet Publicity Committee, 16 January 1961, PRONI CAB9F/123/73.
8. Report of the Director of Information for August 1961, PRONI CAB/9F/123/60.
9. Government Information Service, Monthly Report for January 1962, PRONI CAB9F/123/61. Eric Montgomery was, however, disappointed not to achieve theatrical distribution for the film in the US. Apparently this was because the film was 'too long by U.S. standards' and 'too slow moving'. Government Information Service, Monthly Report for October 1961, PRONI CAB9F/123/60.

Commentary, the Northern Ireland government's official magazine, was still advertising the film (and making it available for loan) as '[a]n attractive picture of modern Ulster'.[10]

It is, of course, significant that the film retains the 'Ulster' soubriquet. This had been less important for the Northern Ireland Tourist Board, which, as noted in the previous chapter, was content to use 'Northern Ireland' in the titles of its first two films (*Northern Ireland Coast* and *Letter from Northern Ireland*). This probably grew out of a pragmatic recognition that not only did a significant percentage of visitors to the North come from the rest of Ireland but that the name 'Ireland' possessed a recognition value (and appeal) for British tourists that 'Ulster' undoubtedly lacked. The question of Northern Ireland's name, however, remained a live issue for the Unionist government and, prompted by anxiety concerning the election of de Valera to the Irish presidency in 1959, Montgomery prepared a discussion paper on 'Nomenclature: Are we Irish, Northern Irish or Ulster?' for the Cabinet Publicity Committee. In this he argued that the use of the term 'Northern Ireland' appeared to concede the essential 'Irishness' of the North, making 'people in Great Britain and abroad think of the partition of Ireland as an artificial, ephemeral thing'. For Montgomery, the situation was made worse by what he described as 'the attitude of the local B.B.C. studio which seems to view Irish cottage plays, jigs and reels, pipes and harps and colleens singing laments, as a picture of our Ulster way of life'. The BBC, he went on, regarded it as their duty 'to present regional material' but 'as a region of Ireland rather than of the U.K.'. In order to combat this, he argued, it was necessary to put more emphasis on 'the idea that we are a separate and quite distinct entity'. If practicable, this would involve changing the name of Northern Ireland (to exclude 'Ireland') and, thus, clear up 'permanently' the 'confusion over our separateness from Eire' and encourage the propagation of 'our own picture of the Ulster character and of our modern industrial state'.[11] Although the Cabinet Publicity Committee, which discussed the paper, was unable to accept its main recommendations, it was sympathetic to the problem and noted that '"Ulster" should continue to be regarded as an acceptable alternative in popular usage for "Northern Ireland"'.[12]

It is this 'popular usage' that *Ulster Heritage* employs, both in its title and in its commentary, which claims that it is as 'Ulster' that Northern Ireland is 'better known'. As Montgomery suggests, the name 'Ulster' played a role in maintaining the idea of Northern Ireland's 'separateness' and this idea is reinforced by the film's use of introductory maps. The use of maps is, of course, a common convention in travel films but they are especially significant in films dealing with Northern Ireland. For while the term 'Ulster' may arguably have been popular within Northern Ireland, it would certainly have been unfamiliar to the majority of audiences outside of Ireland. Indeed, in a survey conducted in 1957 to establish how well known the term 'Ulster' was

---

10. *Ulster Commentary*, no. 272, October 1968, PRONI CAB9F/123/65.

11. 'Nomenclature', 17 April 1959, PRONI CAB9F/123/72. Montgomery also recommended ceasing to refer to Northern Ireland as a 'province': 'Technically we are a "self-governing area" but it seems to me that to use the word "state" as a description for the area would be at least as accurate as "province". It would also be a lot more helpful to our cause.'

12. Minutes of the Cabinet Publicity Committee, 22 April 1959, PRONI CAB9F/123/72. It was, of course, pointed out that a formal change in name was not a practicable proposition, given that it had been rejected by the British government at the time of the passing of the 1949 Ireland Act.

in England, '45 per cent of the people interviewed did not know what Ulster was!'[13] In such circumstances, the identification of the physical location of 'Ulster' (in relation to both Britain and the rest of Ireland) became particularly important. However, the use of maps could also lead to a degree of tension between the requirements for geographical precision and the fulfilment of ideological objectives. In *Ulster* (1948), the map shown at the start of the film shows the whole of Britain and Ireland before the camera moves in on Northern Ireland. In *This is Ulster*, the camera pans across a map of Western Europe (including both Britain and Ireland) before dissolving and zooming in on a map of Northern Ireland. In *Ulster Heritage*, however, there is much less emphasis on establishing the exact geographical location of 'Ulster' than demarcating its 'separateness' from the rest of the island. In his discussion of the proponents of the Irish Literary Revival, Conor Cruise O'Brien wittily remarks that 'the Ireland they loved had an enormous West Coast and no North-east corner'.[14] In contrast, the maps of Northern Ireland contained in *Ulster Heritage* – and 'loved by' unionists – consist of an enormous North-east but no West or South. Thus, even though England, Scotland and Wales are all clearly visible in the map shown at the film's start, the bulk of southern Ireland is omitted from view. The north-east corner, moreover, is slightly extended not only in order to occupy more Irish territory than Northern Ireland actually does but also to suggest the closeness of Northern Ireland to Scotland (and, by implication, Great Britain). This is also true of the second map, employed at both the film's beginning and end. This is concentrated on the six counties of Northern Ireland and completely excludes the rest of Ireland. The south-west coastline of Scotland, however, remains in view. As with the name 'Ulster', the physical designation of Northern Ireland territory in maps was a self-consciously political concern for members of the Cabinet Publicity Committee. As a result, the maps contained in *Ulster Heritage* do not so much denote the actual physical position of Northern Ireland as connote how Ulster Unionists desired the political geography of Northern Ireland to be – cut off from the rest of Ireland and an 'integral' part of Great Britain.[15]

In this way, the maps not only, to follow Denis Wood's terminology, culturalise the natural but, in doing so, reinforce a unionist world-view by naturalising the cultural.[16] One of the assumptions historically underlying nationalist claims for a united Ireland has been that Ireland's status as an island provides it with a geographical basis for nationhood. In this respect, Ireland's sea boundary is regarded as providing a natural territorial unit whereas the land border between North and South is seen to constitute, as the commentary in the nationalist *Fintona – A Study of Housing Discrimination* puts it, an 'unnatural division'. At a time when the IRA's border campaign was being waged, and the issue of the border was capable of gathering political momentum, the film's use of geography was therefore designed to deny the territorial integrity of the

13. James McFadden, 'Around and About Britain', *Ulster Illustrated*, Spring 1957, cited in James Loughlin, *Ulster Unionism and British National Identity since 1885* (London: Pinter, 1995), p. 173.

14. Conor Cruise O'Brien, 'Introduction', in Conor Cruise O'Brien (ed.), *The Shaping of Modern Ireland* (London: Routledge and Kegan Paul, 1970), p. 21.

15. A similar use of maps may also be found in official government publications. The map at the back of Hugh Shearman's *Northern Ireland: Its People, Resources, History and Government* (Belfast: HMSO, 1946), for example, omits the whole of southern Ireland but shows Scotland as unrealistically close.

16. See Denis Wood, *The Power of Maps* (New York: The Guilford Press, 1992), pp. 76–9.

Imagining 'Ulster': the use of maps in *Ulster Heritage*

island of Ireland (and the 'essential unity' of the people who live there) by drawing attention to the strong physical (and hence cultural) connection of 'Ulster' to Britain, and especially Scotland.[17] As Ian McBride indicates, Unionist opposition to Home Rule in the early twentieth century stimulated 'the creation of an "Ulster Scots" mythology' that provided a reservoir of ideas and meanings that continued to be drawn upon and reworked by unionists in subsequent decades.[18] The close proximity of Northern Ireland to Scotland (and Britain) is, indeed, one of the major themes of *This is Ulster*. Originally entitled 'The Waters of Ulster', the film was intended to show that, far from constituting a natural boundary or 'barrier', the sea in fact provided Ulster with a natural 'link' to Britain (with the title of 'The Sea Unites Us' being contemplated at one point).[19] Thus, the film stresses the closeness of Northern Ireland to Scotland ('just fourteen miles away') and the longstanding connections between 'Ulster and the Scots' (stretching back 'over 1,300 years'). The establishment of this lengthy lineage was also important in countering nationalist notions that the Scottish connection was simply the result of colonialism in the form of the Plantation of Ulster in the seventeenth century. This is also a theme returned to in *Ulster Heritage*, in which footage of the Dalriada grammar school at Ballymoney

---

17. This attempt to counter notions of the 'unnaturalness' of partition may also be found in published works of the time, including Richard Hayward's *Border Foray* (London: Arthur Barker, 1957) and William A. Carson's unionist tract (published with Northern Ireland government support), *Ulster and the Irish Republic* (Belfast: William W. Cleland, 1957). While Carson's querying of the 'homogeneity' of the Irish people may anticipate the anti-essentialist arguments of subsequent writers, it is of course put at the service of a different kind of essentialism that upholds the ethnic distinctiveness and 'homogeneity' of the 'Ulster' people.

18. Ian McBride, 'Ulster and the British Problem', in Richard English and Graham Walker (eds), *Unionism in Modern Ireland: New Perspectives on Politics and Culture* (Basingstoke: Macmillan, 1996), p. 8.

19. Minutes of the Cabinet Publicity Committee, 21 November 1957, PRONI CAB/9F/123/56. As the only print of this film that I have been able to locate does not possess a soundtrack, I am drawing on the shooting script held by the Public Record Office in London (PRO INF6/822).

is accompanied by a commentary that reminds the spectator that Dalriada (Dál Riata) is 'the name of an ancient kingdom that included parts of both Scotland and Ulster', which also testifies to 'the strong links between these two countries'. What the commentary omits to mention, however, is that this kingdom was Gaelic and, therefore, an unlikely forebearer of Protestant 'Ulster'.[20]

This emphasis upon the historical and geographical links between Ulster and Scotland is motivated by a wish not only to link 'Ulster', culturally and politically, with Britain rather than the rest of Ireland but also to establish a further set of connections between 'Ulster' and America. The Unionist government in Northern Ireland was particularly keen to reach a US audience and continually pressurised the COI Films Division to provide suitable material. As a COI memo drily observed at the time, while there was no 'particular demand from the overseas Departments [in Britain] for the inclusion of material about Northern Ireland', there was nevertheless a 'strong interest on the part of the Government of Northern Ireland in getting publicity for Northern Ireland in certain overseas countries – particularly the United States and Canada'.[21] There were a number of reasons for this. Although it has been estimated that over 50 per cent of Americans of Irish descent are Protestant (albeit of varying denominations), the sense of Irish–American identity that has prevailed since the nineteenth century has been associated with Catholicism and Irish nationalism. Factors contributing to this development include the anti-English sentiment that followed the mass migration from Ireland in the wake of the Great Famine of the 1840s and the initial sense of social exclusion that the Catholic Irish experienced at the hands of the WASP establishment in the United States, which stimulated the development of a supportive social infrastructure and nurturing of a distinctive sense of community identity.[22] The Unionist regime was well aware of the nationalist bent of Irish–American sentiment and, during the 1950s, the Cabinet Publicity Committee returned regularly to the question of how best to promote the cause of Ulster in America and to combat the advocates of Irish unity.[23] One aspect of this involved promoting awareness of Ulster protestant migration to America and the contribution of people of Ulster descent to USA history (as leaders of the Revolution, as Presidents and as participants in the American Civil War). In 1956, the government assisted in the establishment of the Ulster-Scot Historical Society with the purpose of publishing material on emigration from the North of Ireland to North America and helping North Americans and others learn more about their ancestors' homeland.[24] This aspect of

20. While A. T. Q. Stewart, a historian sympathetic to unionism, elaborates upon these historical connections between the 'Scots' and the 'Irish' in 'Ulster', he also warns, with reference to Dál Riata, that these terms are misleading given the absence of 'the modern idea of a nation or a country'. See *The Narrow Ground: Aspects of Ulster 1609–1969* (Belfast: Blackstaff Press, 1999, orig. 1977), p. 34.

21. 'Publicity for Northern Ireland in the United Kingdom Overseas Information Services', Note by Office of Controller Overseas, 22 August 1960, PRO INF12/576.

22. See the entries on 'Irish American Nationalism' by James Loughlin and the 'United States of America' by Steve Ickringill in S. J. Connolly (ed.), *The Oxford Companion to Irish History* (Oxford: Oxford University Press, 1998).

23. In 1951 the government had sought to appoint its own US publicity officer but had been advised by the British government that it lacked the legal status to do so (Minutes of the Cabinet Publicity Committee, 4 April 1951, PRONI CAB9F/123/48).

24. *The Ulster Year Book, 1960–1962* (Belfast: HMSO, 1962), p. 334.

the government's publicity work gained renewed momentum after the Director of Information, Eric Montgomery, visited the USA and Canada in 1961. Alerted to the continuing potency of the 'Scotch-Irish legend', he argued that if the government could 'get across to the Americans the idea that Ulster is the home of the Scotch-Irish', it could 'at one stroke' establish 'the distinctive and favourable image' the government desired.[25] The idea of the 'Scotch-Irish', and a distinct Scotch-Irish ethnic identity, was largely cultivated by Americans of Scottish and Irish Protestant descent at the end of the nineteenth century as a way of differentiating themselves from the later influx of Catholic Irish immigrants.[26] Recognising that the 'Scotch-Irish' label would be likely to possess greater appeal for Americans than that of the 'Ulster-Scots', the term began to achieve greater prominence in government publicity than hitherto. Thus, while the original government-sponsored pamphlet, *Northern Ireland* (1946), written by Hugh Shearman, includes references to the historical links between Ulster and America, it is not until the revised 1962 version that the term 'Scotch Irish' is specifically employed to distinguish 'Ulster Protestant emigration to America in the eighteeenth century' from 'the emigration of the Potato famine Irish in the following century'.[27] The Ulster-Scot Historical Society, with the support of the government, also published a booklet entitled *The Scotch-Irish and Ulster* (1965), containing *inter alia* a lengthy section on 'The Scotch-Irish and the White House', as well as a leaflet entitled, *Northern Ireland: Cradle of US Presidents and Pioneers*.

Just as earlier films, such as *A Letter from Ulster* and *Back Home in Ireland*, had previously aimed to appeal to an American audience by laying stress upon the historic connections between Northern Ireland and America, so the government-sponsored films of this period were keen to capitalise on this ideology of the 'Scotch-Irish'. This is particularly evident in *Topic: Northern Ireland*, one of a series of COI films – that also included *Young Ulster* (1961) and *Ulster-New Look* (1961) – that were explicitly made for North American television. The film begins with the presenters, the American husband and wife team Joan and Julius Evans, alighting upon a display of portraits of US presidents in the window of the Ulster Office in London. Enquiring within, an assistant explains that the presidents are all descendants of Ulster-Scots – whom Joan Evans immediately identifies as the Scotch-Irish – and provides them with information on the Ulster-Scot Society. This then prompts the Evans to embark on a trip to Northern Ireland, which includes a visit to a farm belonging to the forebears of Woodrow Wilson and to Gray's Printing Shop in Strabane where James Dunlap, printer of the Declaration of Independence, learned his trade. Similar connections are also indicated in *Ulster Heritage*, in which the film's main setting – a farm near Ballymoney – just happens to be the site of a cottage belonging to the family of

---

25. Government Information Service, Monthly Report for October 1961, PRONI CAB9F/123/60. There is, of course, an element of historical irony in the fact that a proportion of the 'Scotch-Irish' emigration of the eighteenth century invoked by the Ulster Unionists in support of their British credentials resulted from the restrictions imposed upon Presbyterians by British penal laws.

26. See Matthew McKee. '"A Peculiar and Royal Race": Creating a Scotch-Irish Identity, 1889-1901', in Patrick Fitzgerald and Steve Ickringill (eds), *Atlantic Crossroads: Historical Connections between Scotland, Ulster and North America* (Newtownards: Colourpoint Books, 2001), pp. 67–83. McKee's essay focuses in particular on the activities of the Scotch-Irish Society of America, founded in 1889.

27. Hugh Shearman, *Northern Ireland: Its People, Resources, History and Government* (Belfast: HMSO, 1962), p. 38.

William McKinley, the twenty-fifth President of the United States and an active supporter of 'Scotch-Irish' heritage.[28] However, while both *Topic: Northern Ireland* and *Ulster Heritage* are keen to reclaim Irish-American identity from Irish nationalism (and, in doing so, combat calls for Irish unity), they also possess a more direct motive for stressing the links between Northern Ireland and America in the form of the encouragement of US economic investment. This, in turn, corresponds to the changing economic policies of the time and the political discourses associated with them. Thus, in a speech delivered in the USA in 1964, the new Prime Minister of Northern Ireland, Terence O'Neill, defined the 'special relationship' between Northern Ireland and the United States not simply in the by now familiar terms of Scotch-Irish emigration to America and the role of Northern Ireland during the Second World War but also in terms of the strong 'business and commercial associations' between the two.[29]

Although the 1950s had witnessed a general rise in living standards in Northern Ireland, the Northern Ireland economy nevertheless lagged behind the rest of the United Kingdom and unemployment (at an annual average of around 7 per cent) remained higher than in Britain. While the Second World War had temporarily arrested the decline of the engineering and linen industries, employment in both sectors was now falling. Partly as a result of mechanisation, the numbers employed in farming also fell by 27 per cent during the decade. By way of a response, the government sought to widen the manufacturing base of Northern Ireland through the enactment of various forms of legislation – the Industries Development Acts (from 1945), the Re-equipment of Industry Acts (from 1951) and Capital Grants to Industry Acts (from 1954) – designed to encourage the modernisation of existing industries and attract inward investment. It also set up the Northern Ireland Development Council in 1955 to publicise the opportunities for industrial development in Northern Ireland and placed representatives from the Ministry of Commerce in the British Industrial Development Office in New York when it opened in 1960. Partly as a result of these initiatives, the government could claim credit, in 1962, for the creation, since the war, of 42,000 jobs and 170 new undertakings (including, in some cases, American companies).[30] While this was largely offset by the rising population and increasing unemployment in the traditional industries, the government remained keen to stress the buoyancy and dynamism of the contemporary Northern Irish economy. Thus, in a speech in 1960, the then Minister of Home Affairs, Brian Faulkner, indicated that Unionists wished to create 'a brand new image of Ulster' as 'a modern, progressive, industrial community'.[31] As a member of the Cabinet Publicity Committee, Faulkner had argued that 'the depressed economic condition of Eire could be a strong propaganda point' for the government and he clearly saw an emphasis upon

28. Steve Ickringill notes that, whereas Andrew Jackson, American president from 1829–37, was content to be labelled Irish, William McKinley, president from 1897–1901, preferred to identify with the Scotch-Irish (in line with the trend for those of Ulster Protestant descent to distinguish themselves from the Catholic Irish). See 'Introduction', in Fitzgerald and Ickringill (eds), *Atlantic Crossroads*, pp. 8–9.

29. Terence O'Neill, *Ulster at the Crossroads* (London: Faber and Faber, 1969), pp. 178–80.

30. *The Ulster Year Book, 1960–1962*, p. xxiii. In 1964, Terence O'Neill indicated that 'there was not a single American company with a plant in Northern Ireland' at the end of the Second World War but that, twenty years later, this situation had been 'completely transformed' (*Ulster at the Crossroads*, p. 180).

31. *Belfast Telegraph*, 8 April 1960, p. 10.

the 'modernity' of 'Ulster' as buttressing a sense of 'Ulster's' distinctiveness from the rest of (economically backward) Ireland (or 'Eire').[32] As Minister of Commerce under Terence O'Neill (the Northern Ireland Prime Minister from 1964 to 1969), he was also closely identified with an emerging discourse of economic modernisation that was destined to gain momentum during the 1960s. In his posthumously published autobiography, Faulkner describes how he set about this job with optimism, believing that he could help 'to develop the modern go-ahead Province emerging in the 1960s'.[33] By 1966, this discourse had become so naturalised that a lager (Carling Black Label) was even being advertised as the 'taste of go-ahead Ulster'![34] This rhetoric also became a feature of the official films of this period, which increasingly lay stress upon the modern industrial character of Northern Ireland as well as its desirability as a place in which both to invest and to live.

The importance of this was evident in the deliberations of the Cabinet Publicity Committee on *This is Ulster*, which, it was decided, should present Northern Ireland as 'a modern, go-ahead community' characterised by 'new farm buildings', 'new schools' and 'new factories'.[35] An emphasis upon the 'modern' and the 'new' was also central, as its title would suggest, to *Ulster-New Look*, which was planned to highlight 'the new spirit abroad in Ulster today' – '[n]ew ideas, new industries, new ways of doing things'.[36] Given its intended US destination, the film is also the most explicit in its address to the American businessman. In his autobiography, Faulkner describes how, as Minister of Commerce, he had set about the task of 'convincing industrialists all over the world that Northern Ireland was the kind of place in which they could profitably invest'.[37] This is also the purpose of this film, which begins with a family from Texas, the Edwards, who have relocated to Northern Ireland. During a tour of his newly opened factory, Mr Edwards explains his reasons for coming there: the virtual completion of the factory by the government before his arrival, the ready availability of labour, the existence of other American companies in the area and 'the stability of the government' (which, as in *Topic: Northern Ireland*, is compared to the states system in America).

Although *Ulster Heritage* places a similar emphasis upon modernity, its approach is more oblique. As has been noted, the film's main focus is the family farm and much of the film is devoted to agriculture rather than manufacturing. Although agricultural employment was in decline, the family farm retained an ideological significance over and above its actual economic

32. Minutes of the Cabinet Publicity Committee, 17 April 1957, PRONI, CAB9F/123/56. It is worth noting, however, that Liam Kennedy argues, in his assessment of this period, that '[t]he rhetoric of Ulster progress and enterprise notwithstanding, the local entrepreneurial response seems to have been little better than in the Republic, at least as far as the formation of new firms was concerned'. See *The Modern Industrialisation of Ireland 1940–1988* (Dundalk: Dundalgan Press, 1989), p. 13.

33. Brian Faulkner, *Memoirs of a Statesman*, ed. John Houston (London: Weidenfeld and Nicolson, 1978), p. 29.

34. *Belfast Telegraph*, 6 July 1966, p. 11. On the same day, the local tobacco company, Gallaher's, was also inviting Belfast motorists to 'go modern' by smoking its cigarettes (*Belfast News-Letter*, 6 July 1966, p. 3).

35. Minutes of the Cabinet Publicity Committee, 5 June 1957, PRONI CAB 9F/123/56.

36. COI synopsis, PRO INF6/886. I am also dependent upon the script contained in this file for information about the film's contents.

37. Faulkner, *Memoirs of a Statesman*, pp. 29–30.

importance. In this film, it is used to stress the longstanding relationship between the family (the Richmonds) and the land ('handed down from father to son') and so, *contra* possible nationalist claims, uphold the legitimacy of Ulster Protestants' residency on the island. Moreover, despite the prevailing rhetoric of economic modernisation, the social and moral landscape of Northern Ireland continued to be conservative. As such, the conventional patriarchal family of rural Ulster remained the ideological touchstone of traditional – Presbyterian – 'Ulster' values (hard work, self-discipline, moral rectitude). Nevertheless, despite this emphasis on the 'traditional', the film is also at pains to avoid identification of rural life with the 'primitive' or 'backward' (as in earlier tourist films such as *Ulster Story*). This was not only because of the wish to stress (implicitly) the economic difference of the North from the rest of Ireland, but also to construct an imagery that would be attractive to investors. Writing of a later period, Colin McArthur has described how research by a Scottish development agency revealed that German industrialists perceive of Scotland as a good country in which to rest but not to invest. This, in turn, he argues is connected to the discursive construction of an opposition, forged in the European romantic imagination, between *homo oeconomicus* and *homo celticus*.[38] The importance of separating Northern Ireland/Ulster from the traditional circuit of imagery surrounding *homo celticus* in order to attract investors was, in fact, recognised by the Northern Ireland government (if not couched in precisely these terms).[39] Thus, in its discussions of a preliminary treatment for *Ulster Heritage*, the Cabinet Publicity Committee stressed that the film should avoid a 'concentration upon pigs and thatched cottages' and, in the resulting film, farming is presented as a modern forward-looking enterprise taking advantage of 'the many scientific and mechanical advances at hand'.[40] The film also stresses the readiness of 'Ulster farmers' to make use of 'the benefits of mechanisation' and suggests this may be connected to members of farming families often working in industry. In the case of *Ulster Heritage*, this feature of Northern Irish life is represented by Doreen, the daughter of the family, who has 'an important job as secretary to the manager of one of the new American factories' (producing neoprene synthetic rubber). Doreen is seen arriving for work and further shots of building sites, factories and the new Coolkeeragh Power Station follow.[41] As this montage proceeds, the commentary intones that 'everywhere in Ulster' there are 'new

---

38. Colin McArthur, 'The Cultural Necessity of a Poor Celtic Cinema', in John Hill, Martin McLoone and Paul Hainsworth (eds), *Border Crossing: Film in Ireland, Britain and Europe* (Belfast/London: Institute of Irish Studies/BFI, 1994), pp. 117–18.

39. A report by the Director of Information, Eric Montgomery, does, however, come surprisingly close. In this he considers the importance of the Northern Ireland government disassociating itself from 'a misty wall of legend that has given most people in other countries the impression that Ireland is not a land of trade and commerce' (Monthly Report for March 1963, PRONI CAB9F/123/62).

40. Minutes of the Cabinet Publicity Committee, 10 February 1960, PRONI CAB9F/123/59.

41. The importance that the film places upon these modern aspects of Northern Ireland life is underscored by the fact that, while the film employed a real family, Doreen was actually a school teacher rather than a secretary in a newly opened factory. Trevor Richmond, the youngest son in the film who now owns the farm, also reports that, while the family owned a donkey, this was substituted for a pony in the film (presumably on the grounds that a donkey was perceived to carry connotations of economic 'backwardness'). Interview with Trevor Richmond, 25 September 2004.

Underscoring the constitutional position of Northern Ireland: the Parliament Buildings at Stormont in *Ulster Heritage*

industries . . . new factories under construction . . . new factories in full production'. This rhetoric is returned to at the film's end when the commentary declares that 'the people of Ulster are building up a prosperous and sound economic future for the country' over shots of the parliamentary buildings at Stormont (taken, in fact, from *This is Ulster*) and of the map with which the film began.

As in wartime films such as *Ulster* and *Ulster at Arms*, this rhetoric of 'the people' is problematic. Although the film makes no specific reference to either religion or political allegiance, it is clear that it is the Protestant unionist people to whom the film refers and whom may be seen to be identified with the film's map of 'British Ulster' and the one-party regime at Stormont (shots of which also appear at an earlier stage in the film when the voice-over records that 'Ulster has her own elected Parliament and Government – and here at Stormont, she makes her own laws and controls her own local affairs').[42] Unlike the war films, however, the repetition of

42. It is also interesting to note the way in which 'Ulster' is here referred to as a 'she'. This is an uncommon usage and may involve an attempt to soften, through feminisation, the 'hard' image of northern Protestantism. However, insofar as the imagining of Ireland has so often depended upon an identification of Ireland (and the Celt more generally) with the feminine, this may be something of a double-edged strategy, risking an association with the Celticism that the film is otherwise at pains to avoid.

images of the Stormont parliament has less to do with the assertion of Northern Ireland's fundamental Britishness than the underscoring of its constitutional position and the 'political stability' that the investor is informed (implicitly or explicitly) will be found there. Given hindsight, there is, of course, something slightly unnerving about the way in which these films so confidently assert their vision of a modern, industrial, democratic Ulster mini-paradise. However, their disavowal of the continuing religious and political cleavages within Northern Ireland was also about to be challenged by the emergence of other, contrasting images of Northern Ireland that also began to appear around this time.

Television times

As has been seen, the Northern Ireland government initially identified television – particularly in North America – as a new outlet for publicity and propaganda. This was also the Unionist government's view of the BBC's television service, which began transmission in Northern Ireland in early 1953. Although the management of BBC Northern Ireland was independent of government, the relationship between the two was very close and the government in Northern Ireland was keen to work with the BBC in promoting a positive image of the region. Furthermore, since 1937 there had been an agreement with the BBC in London (enshrined in various directives) that programmes dealing with Northern Ireland should be referred to the Controller of BBC Northern Ireland. As the 1949 version of the Directive puts it, 'C.N.I. should be informed in advance of all forthcoming programmes about Eire or Northern Ireland since cultural or even entertainment programmes may carry political implications'.[43] This system of referral gave local personnel considerable influence over material emanating from outside of Northern Ireland and helped to exclude controversial material from the television screen. Thus, local BBC personnel advised on the making of the first significant programme to be filmed in Northern Ireland, *Pattern of Ulster* (tx. 26 May 1953), a half-hour portrait of Northern Ireland timed to coincide with the opening of the new transmitter at Glencairn and introduced by the Northern Ireland Prime Minister, Viscount Brookeborough. Unsurprisingly, the Acting Controller of BBC Northern Ireland, Cyril Conner, welcomed the making of the programme, claiming that it would demonstrate the 'tremendously important field of possible publicity for Northern Ireland in the new Television Service'.[44] The following year the BBC in Northern Ireland also assisted with the production of a Northern Ireland episode of the documentary series *About Britain* (tx. 30 July 1954) when it advised the producer to avoid certain 'problems'.[45] This is reflected in the programme itself, in which the presenter Richard Dimbleby, in conversation with the Northern Irish actor Joseph Tomelty, openly admits that he will ignore 'religion and politics'. As a result, the completed programme possesses the air of a travelogue that differs

43. 'Broadcasts Relating to Eire and Northern Ireland and Liaison with Eire', Memo from Director-General, 26 July 1949, BBCWAC R34/1627.

44. Cyril Conner, Acting Controller of BBC Northern Ireland, Newsletter for the information of members of the BBC Northern Ireland Advisory Council, 24 March 1953, BBCWAC NI2/7/1.

45. The programme's producer Stephen McCormack refers to this in a memo to the Head of Documentaries (Television), 13 July 1954, BBCWAC T4/3.

very little in tone and character from those that had been sponsored by the Northern Ireland government.

At this juncture, television reception in Northern Ireland was confined to the greater Belfast area and it was not until the opening of the new Divis transmitter in July 1955 that transmission was extended to the bulk of the region. However, the local television service still lacked the capacity for live broadcasting and there was no transmission link from Northern Ireland to the rest of the UK network. By way of compensation, the BBC in Northern Ireland was provided with funding for a film unit that would make local programmes for transmission outside of normal network hours. Although the programmes were filmed in Northern Ireland, they were then processed, edited and dubbed in London due to the lack of film facilities in the North. These arrangements resulted in the production of a fortnightly series of fifteen-minute magazine programmes entitled *Ulster Mirror*, written and produced by Harry Govan (and mainly filmed by Douglas Wolfe) beginning in November 1954. Designed to showcase items of topical interest, the contents of the first programme also indicate the establishment orientation that characterised the series. Thus, while the programme partly follows in the footsteps of wartime documentaries in observing 'ordinary' people at work (in the fields and in factories), it also reports on the Duchess of Gloucester's inspection of a Scottish regiment stationed at the camp at Ballykinler and ends with footage of the Northern Ireland Prime Minister, Brookeborough, and his wife prior to their departure for Australia and New Zealand. The programme also begins with a shot, through opening gates, of the processional avenue leading to Parliament House at Stormont. The same shot is used in all subsequent episodes and, given the symbolism involved, necessarily links the programme's outlook on 'Ulster' with that of the Unionist government.

It was therefore something of a breakthrough for both the BBC and the Unionist government when the programme was accepted for network transmission the following year (beginning April 1955). However, it was also to prove a short-lived success. The launch of Independent Television (ITV) occurred only a few months later in September 1955 and, as a result of the increased competition for audiences, the BBC in London decided that the programme was insufficiently strong to justify its network placing. From September onwards the programme was shunted around the schedules before its run finally came to an end in December. It was then proposed that the Film Unit should focus on the production of half-hour documentary films 'dealing with Northern Ireland subjects but designed to interest the national audience'.[46] A number of short documentaries followed, including *The End of the Line* (tx. 15 August 1956) on the closure of railways in Northern Ireland, *Rathlin Island* (tx. 29 January 1957) on the small island community of Rathlin, and *Family Farm* (tx. 26 February 1957) on the lives of a local farming family. However, while these were regarded as reasonably successful in Northern Ireland (where *Family Farm* was shown three times during 1957), the films held much less appeal in Britain. Thus, in a memo to Henry McMullan, the Head of Programmes in Northern Ireland, the Controller of Programmes, Television, Cecil McGivern, claimed that while, for most British viewers, *The End of the Line* would make 'interesting and pleasant viewing' it would not

---

46. Report by the Controller of BBC Northern Ireland, Northern Ireland Advisory Council, 24 October 1955,
     BBCWAC NI2/9/1.

Northern Ireland's first local
television programme, shot
on film, *Ulster Mirror*

prove 'very compulsive'.[47] Although the Northern Ireland Film Unit was encouraged to spread
its wings and seek commissions from current affairs series such as *Panorama*, the political context in which the Unit worked made it hard to generate programme ideas that were likely to
prove genuinely 'compulsive'. Thus, when Harry Govan departed the post of Northern Ireland
Film Producer in 1956, it was decided that the activities of the Film Unit should be suspended.
During 1957, the unit was reconstituted, and following the launch of BBC Northern Ireland's
first television news programme, *Today in Northern Ireland* in September 1957, its main role
became the supply of news material.

However, if it had proved an uphill struggle for BBC Northern Ireland to sustain local production that would merit transmission across the UK, it was also becoming increasingly difficult
to police the programmes that the network was permitting to enter Northern Ireland. In 1958,
the Northern Ireland Controller, Robert McCall, warned the BBC Board of Governors that the
'Ulster audience' was 'sensitive about sound broadcasting and television being a potential source
of evil to their way of life'.[48] As had been the case in the 1930s, when religious groups had campaigned against the 'immorality' of imported films, there was considerable unease within Northern Ireland concerning the flow of programme material from London that appeared to
undermine local religious and moral beliefs. Thus, following an episode of *Panorama* in 1957 dealing with the Wolfenden report on homosexuality, the BBC was attacked in the Northern Ireland
House of Commons for promoting 'anti-Christian propaganda' and providing a 'ready platform'
for subjects such as 'homosexuality and sexual aberrations, prostitution . . . various types of delin-
quency and various forms of agnosticism and atheism'.[49] In 1958, there were also attacks on the

---

47. Memo from Controller of Programmes, Television, to HNIP, 17 July 1956, BBCWAC T16/227/2.
48. 'The BBC in Northern Ireland', 28 May 1958, BBCWAC R1/94/3.
49. *Parliamentary Debates* (HC), vol. 41, col. 2723, 3 December 1957.

'immoral content' of the *Television World Theatre* series (broadcast on Sundays).[50] However, while these criticisms were directed at the moral character of programmes, more directly political challenges to the Ulster 'way of life' (at least as defined by Unionists) were to occur in 1959.

On 9 January 1959, the BBC transmitted a short film item presented by Alan Whicker as part of its early evening magazine programme, *Tonight*. This was a relatively lightweight piece dealing with the legalisation of betting shops in Belfast (ahead of the rest of the UK). Nevertheless, its presentation of the city, and allusions to the political situation there, succeeded in arousing the ire of local unionists. A leader in the *Belfast News-Letter*, entitled 'An affront to Ulster', is indicative of the mood. Whicker, it complains, sought out the 'unusual': 'that policemen carry revolvers; that offensive slogans such as "No Pope Here" and "Vote for Sinn Fein" are painted on walls in obscure streets; that betting shops are licensed and that public houses are open from 10 a.m. to 10 p.m'. The elements that the paper believed should have been featured, however, were absent: 'There was no reference to the city's industries, to the general bearing of the citizens or to the fact that without the loyal help of Northern Ireland it is doubtful whether the Allies could have won the war against Hitler's Germany.'[51] The anger expressed in the unionist press was shared by the Unionist government, which liaised with the BBC's Northern Ireland Governor Ritchie McKee (himself a Northern Ireland government nominee) and contemplated a formal protest to the BBC Director-General.[52] Although a BBC statement claimed that the broadcaster could not always reflect 'the pleasantest and most complimentary facts about life around us', the Northern Ireland Controller, Robert McCall, nevertheless issued an apology for the programme, claiming that his advice on the matter had been ignored.[53] The BBC in London then withdrew the rest of Whicker's eight reports provoking nationalists to complain that the BBC had succumbed to unionist pressure and had failed to provide impartial coverage of the situation in the North.[54] This impression was further reinforced when, three months later, the BBC Board of Governors, under pressure from BBC Northern Ireland and the Northern Ireland Governor, cancelled the second of two US-produced *Small World* programmes presented by Ed Murrow on 'humour and the theatre', following some controversial remarks concerning the IRA by the Irish actress Siobhan McKenna.[55]

The vociferous opposition to programmes hostile to the unionist world-view meant that fewer programmes about Northern Ireland were made in Britain than might otherwise have

---

50. Memo from Controller, BBC Northern Ireland, to BBC Director-General, 9 April 1958, BBCWAC R6/66/2. Later in the same year, the BBC was also responsible for transmitting (on a Sunday) a production of *The Green Pastures*, the film version of which had so incensed religious campaigners in the 1930s.

51. *Belfast News-Letter*, 12 January 1959, p. 4. For an overview of the controversy, see Rex Cathcart, *The Most Contrary Region: The BBC in Northern Ireland 1924–84* (Belfast: Blackstaff Press, 1984), pp. 190–3.

52. Conclusions of a Meeting of the Cabinet, 14 January 1959, PRONI CAB4/1080.

53. *Belfast News-Letter*, 12 January 1959, p. 5; *Irish News*, 14 January 1959, p. 2.

54. The Nationalist Senator Patrick O'Hare, for example, complained that 'the Nationalist minority' felt resentment that the BBC had failed 'to give what they would consider to be fair and adequate coverage' of the area (including reporting of 'the discriminatory activities of public boards'). *Parliamentary Debates* (The Senate), vol. xlii, col. 1049, 13 January 1959.

55. Minutes of the BBC Board of Governors, 30 April 1959, BBCWAC R1/27/1. See also Cathcart, *The Most Contrary Region*, pp. 193–5.

been the case. While *Tonight* visited the South of Ireland in 1961, it did not venture to return to Northern Ireland until 1964. When it did so, the production team was assisted by the government's Director of Information, Eric Montgomery, who expressed himself satisfied that the reports by Trevor Philpot were 'much more objective' than Whicker's.[56] Although the reports have not survived, they seem to have been fairly uncritical in tone and generally well disposed towards unionists. Thus, according to the BBC Director-General, the reports were 'well received' in the region, and the Northern Ireland Minister of Commerce, Brian Faulkner (who had resigned from the BBC's Northern Ireland Advisory Council following the transmission of *Small World*), sent his 'congratulations on the report on economic development'.[57] Significantly, the same month that these *Tonight* reports were transmitted, the local commercial station, Ulster Television, staged a debate between Brian Faulkner and the Nationalist MP James O'Reilly on the topic of political and religious discrimination (*Radius*, tx. 26 February 1964).[58] Although, to the dismay of nationalists, O'Reilly made a poor showing, the programme's transmission indicates how, due to commercial pressures, UTV simply could not afford to ignore the views of a significant proportion of its audience. Such programmes were, however, confined to Northern Ireland and it was the airing of Northern Ireland's problems across the UK that was of most concern to the Unionist establishment. This can be seen, for example, in the success of the BBC Northern Ireland Controller, Robert McCall, in stopping the transmission in December 1964 of Sam Thompson's play, *Cemented with Love*, made for the BBC Drama Department in London, because of its treatment of the gerrymandering of elections in Northern Ireland.[59] Given the success of unionists in preventing the BBC's transmission of 'controversial' material such as this, the broadcast of an episode of ITV's *This Week* on Northern Ireland the same month as the ban on Thompson's play was especially notable.

Although *This Week* had been running since 1956, this appears to be the first of the series to deal specifically with the situation in the North of Ireland. Particularly since the advent of *World in Action* in 1963, ITV had been gaining a reputation for a new style of television journalism involving a harder-hitting approach to stories, investigative reporting and a style of 16mm filming indebted to cinema vérité. Thus, while the production team, led by reporter Robert Kee, did contact the Government Information Service, Montgomery was disconcerted to discover that they 'had strong views of their own on whom they wanted to interview'.[60] As a result, the finished programme was probably the first to cast a genuinely critical eye across the Northern

---

56. Government of Northern Ireland Information Service, Monthly Report for February 1964, PRONI CAB9F/123/63.

57. Minutes of BBC Board of Governors, 5 March 1964, BBCWAC R1/32/1.

58. 'Half a Million See Debate', *Belfast News-Letter*, 27 February 1964, p. 1.

59. According to McCall, the play was 'a burlesque of things that have happened in the forty years of Northern Ireland's existence' that would constitute 'an insult' to local viewers. Letter from Controller, Northern Ireland, to HPDTel., 21 November 1964, BBCWAC T5/1312. The play was eventually shown the following year, when Thompson's sudden death shamed the BBC into reversing its decision.

60. Government of Northern Ireland Information Service, Monthly Report for November 1964, PRONI CAB9F/123/63.

Ireland scene.[61] Its perspective was also distinctive. Unlike Whicker's report for *Tonight*, which had portrayed Northern Ireland as down-at-heel and beset by unemployment, the *This Week* programme clearly positions itself in relation to the developing discourse of 'modernisation' within Northern Ireland. However, in subjecting the economic and industrial policies of the Unionist regime to examination, it also seeks to bring out some of those elements (religious conflict, social exclusion, inequality) suppressed by the official discourses of 'modernisation' apparent in *Ulster-New Look* and *Ulster Heritage*.

The concept of 'modernisation' is, of course, a complex (and often disputed) one, embracing economic, political and cultural aspects. In 'modernisation theory', such as it is, there is an implicit assumption that the route taken towards 'modernisation' is unilinear, involving a simultaneous movement towards economic advance, political progress (in the form of parliamentary democracy) and cultural liberalisation. As various commentators have noted, however, the 'modernisation' promoted by the Ulster Unionists in the 1950s and 1960s was pre-eminently economic in character, involving (especially during the O'Neill years) technocratic planning, a restructuring of the labour force and the opening-up of the local economy to international capital. These economic policies, however, were not accompanied by significant political and social reforms (nor, indeed, any upsurge in liberal attitudes). Thus for Paul Bew and Henry Patterson, 'the rhetoric of "planning" and "modernisation"' adopted by the Northern Ireland government should be understood as primarily designed 'to re-establish the Unionist party's hegemony over the Protestant working class' in the face of unemployment and the electoral gains of the Northern Ireland Labour Party in the Stormont elections of 1958 and 1962. As a result, they suggest, the 'modernising' policies of the Unionist government did 'absolutely nothing to counter discrimination against Catholics in Northern Ireland'.[62] Indeed, as various authors have argued, these policies may actually have had the effect of exacerbating sectarian tensions due to the unevenness of their application. As Cornelius O'Leary points out, the economic development of the 1960s was 'largely concentrated in the area east of the River Bann, the traditional heartland of Ulster industry, where the religious distribution was roughly . . . three-quarters Protestant to a quarter Catholic. . . . In the area west of the Bann, where the two groups were of roughly equal size the industrial boom did not penetrate.'[63] Furthermore, the rhetoric of 'modernisation' inevitably raised Catholic hopes for change (especially among an increasingly well-educated and

61. Interestingly, the Catholic film-making unit, Radharc, made an outspoken documentary on discrimination in Derry earlier in the same year. However, the Irish national broadcaster, RTÉ, considered the programme inflammatory and refused to transmit it. See Lance Pettitt, *Screening Ireland: Film and Television Representation* (Manchester: Manchester University Press, 2000), pp. 84–5, for a discussion.

62. Paul Bew and Henry Patterson, *The British State and the Ulster Crisis: From Wilson to Thatcher* (London: Verso, 1985), p. 11. This argument is more fully developed in Paul Bew, Peter Gibbon and Henry Patterson, *The State in Northern Ireland 1921–72* (Manchester: Manchester University Press, 1979).

63. Cornelius O'Leary, 'Northern Ireland, 1945–72', in J. J. Lee (ed.), *Ireland 1945–70* (Dublin: Gill and Macmillan, 1979), p. 161. David Bleakley argues that investors generally preferred the greater Belfast area but concedes, nevertheless, that Faulkner was unwilling to intervene directly to help 'the chronic unemployment in the western area of the Province'. See *Faulkner: Conflict and Consent in Irish Politics* (London: Mowbrays, 1974), p. 57.

self-confident Catholic middle class) and failure to 'deliver the goods' could only encourage increased discontent.

It is some of these tensions within the 'modernisation' process that *This Week*'s 'Northern Ireland' (tx. 10 December 1964) sets out to explore. It does so, moreover, from a position firmly located within the 'modernisation' discourse. During the course of the programme, the camera pans from a shot of grazing sheep onto a factory under construction. The camera then follows Kee as he walks through one of the 'advance factories' built by the government for the purpose of attracting outside investment. During this sequence his commentary records the apparent contrast between 'the highly impressive modern industrial developments now taking place under government inspiration all over Northern Ireland' and 'the backward-looking forces on both sides'. This is the key opposition structuring the programme and Kee devotes much of the programme to condemning (with, it has to be said, a certain degree of metropolitan superiority) what he identifies as the obstacles in the way of modernisation: the 'religious bigotry' that makes it difficult for 'attitudes on both sides to change', 'the thinking of forty years ago' that 'still dominates minds on both sides today' and 'the siege mentality on both sides' that 'bears little relation to the present'. In this respect, the diagnosis of the problem that the programme offers is that of a deficiency of 'modernisation': the failure of religious and political *attitudes* – on 'both sides' – to keep up with the march of economic progress. Its remedy (expressed in Kee's injunction to the Nationalist leader Eddie McAteer) is that politicians should stop 'thinking dogmatically' and work in a 'more modern way'. However, while the commentary places most emphasis upon the need for attitudes to catch up with 'modernisation', it also identifies a need for political reform. Indeed, as with *Ulster Heritage*, and so many official films before it, the programme ends with a shot of the Parliamentary buildings at Stormont but, in this case, there is a dramatic zoom-out from the buildings in a way that subjects the Unionist regime to question rather than, as in previous films, reinforcing its prestige.[64]

Given the film's implied address to a British audience, the film assumes virtually no knowledge of Northern Ireland on the part of the viewer and provides a potted history, incorporating archive material, of the origins of the Northern Ireland set-up. This emphasises the conditional 'loyalty' of the northern Unionists and, under Carson, their readiness to resort to 'armed Protestant resistance' in order to stave off the threat of all-Ireland Home Rule. Given that the Northern Ireland government had recently produced its own information film, *The Ulster Covenant* (1963), celebrating the fiftieth anniversary of the signing of the Ulster Covenant, this account inevitably contrasted with the officially sanctioned version of unionist history. Although *The Ulster Covenant* does acknowledge unionist plans for armed resistance to Home

---

64. It is, in effect, the reverse of a sequence in *Ulster Story* (discussed in Chapter 4), which simulates the effect of a zoom by cutting successively closer to the buildings. While there may be a certain premonition here of the subsequent dissolution of Stormont (in 1972), there is also a degree of reticence about the role of the British state in permitting the maintenance of the political arrangements in Northern Ireland. The programme does draw attention to the costs to the British exchequer but its complete identification with an ideology of 'modernisation' entails an acceptance of Britain's own 'modernity' (and 'liberalism') as the standard by which Northern Ireland may be judged and found wanting. As a result, the British state's own complicity in the continuation of the situation is largely ignored.

Rule, it ultimately identifies this as a benign (and justified) episode in the creation of the 'busy and progressive community' revealed in the film's 'epilogue' (via a short montage of shots of Belfast city centre, 'modern factories', 'thriving farms', new schools and, perhaps inevitably, the Parliament Buildings at Stormont). In contrast, *This Week* employs the historical material to support its diagnosis of the fundamentally 'retarded' character of political arrangements in Northern Ireland, which are identified as holding up the 'modernisation' process. This is partly suggested by footage of the Prime Minister, Terence O'Neill, declaiming that 'there is more prosperity in Ulster . . . more widely shared than ever in the past', while wearing an Orange sash and addressing a gathering of the Orange Order (which, for all of its significance for Ulster Unionism, is generally ignored in official Northern Ireland government films). However, it is most striking in the treatment of Kee's interview with Brian Faulkner, then Minister of Commerce. Kee begins by laying out his central thesis: that there is 'a certain contradiction' between the 'wish to create a modern industrial society . . . and some of the political and social features of Ulster'. To the apparent discomfort of Faulkner, Kee then proceeds to press him on the provision of extra votes for businessmen in Stormont elections, the restriction of local council voting to rate-payers, the gerrymandering of electoral wards in Derry and the discrimination against Catholics in the allocation of housing. In an era when the broadcasting rules governing the presentation of interviewees were less formalised, Faulkner is shown playing nervously with his ear and pursing his lip.[65] The interview then ends with the camera holding on Faulkner's face while (courtesy of overlapping sound) the words 'I am a loyal, Orange Ulster man' (from the popular loyalist song 'The Sash My Father Wore') are heard on the soundtrack.

Understandably, Faulkner expressed some concern about the 'balance' of the programme, indicating that he would have wished the film to have included more on the 'the modern factories . . . the modern housing estates, and . . . the modern farming equipment' in Northern Ireland.[66] However, he stood by his answers to Kee's questions, which seem to have won the approval of his supporters. About 250 Unionists watched the programme on a special screen in a hotel in Bangor, where they are reported to have applauded his remarks. Subsequent comments by those attending also indicated their admiration for his forthrightness ('In Mr. Faulkner we have a tremendous man, full of guts, personality and talent. He is the most popular M.P. at Stormont').[67] As such, Faulkner's supporters appear either to have ignored, or sought to deflect attention away from, the programme's criticisms of the Stormont regime by seizing upon Faulkner's media performance as a weapon in the ongoing battle between him and O'Neill for leadership of the Unionist Party.[68]

---

65. Citing a comment by the film director Jean Renoir on the 'indecency' of the close-up in television, Jason Jacobs emphasises the importance of the 'close-up visualization of the face' as part of 'a public look' whereby 'we can check the face' against the words that are spoken, in *The Intimate Screen: Early British Television Drama* (Oxford: Clarendon Press, 2000), pp. 159–60.

66. *Belfast News-Letter*, 11 December 1964, p. 1.

67. Stormont MP Robert Nixon, quoted in the *Belfast News-Letter*, 11 December 1964, p. 1.

68. Terence O'Neill had been appointed Prime Minister without an election within the Unionist Party. Although O'Neill and Faulkner worked together in government until 1969, their relationship was characterised by mutual suspicion and rivalry.

Despite the relative indifference with which it seems to have been received on both sides of the Irish Sea, *This Week*'s 'Northern Ireland' is, nevertheless, a striking piece both in terms of its timing and its willingness to address some of the uncomfortable social and political issues repressed in the 'official' discourses of the Northern Ireland government and the COI films of the time. Significantly, the next *This Week* to deal with Northern Ireland – on Ian Paisley – was banned in Northern Ireland. Although the Northern Ireland government denied any involvement in the decision, the local office of the Independent Television Authority decided to pull the programme from the Ulster Televison schedule on the grounds that it might lead to public disorder (in the run-up to the Twelfth of July celebrations).[69] As noted previously, the threat to public order was also the argument employed to support the censorship of films in both the 1930s and 1950s. However, in these earlier cases, the object of censorship were films (such as *Ourselves Alone* and *Shake Hands with the Devil*) that were claimed to encourage sympathy for the IRA or Irish republicanism. In this case, the novelty of the ban was that it was directed against an unsympathetic portrait of Ulster loyalism (as represented by Ian Paisley and his followers). In contrast to the paradigms that would come to dominate news reporting during the 'troubles' era, the second *This Week* focuses almost exclusively on the conflicts within Ulster unionism and the obstacles that religious fundamentalism, sectarianism and loyalist violence were placing in the way of political progress and 'modernisation'. Only one Nationalist politician, Gerry Fitt, appears in the programme, expressing his sense of 'foreboding' regarding the rise of Paisleyism. Understandably, he regretted the ITA's decision not to show the programme, arguing that it would have been 'a salutory experience for certain people here to see themselves as others saw them'.[70]

Conclusion

This Week's 'Northern Ireland' (and its programme on Ian Paisley) were to some extent the alter ego of *Ulster Heritage*, bringing to the surface those elements – religious division, political conflict – repressed in its benign narrative of conflict-free economic modernisation and progress. This, of course, was only the beginning. As the campaign for civil rights, and the ensuing unionist backlash, gained momentum, the media focus upon Northern Ireland inevitably increased. For over forty years, the Unionist government had sought to shape and control the image of Northern Ireland that was projected to Britain and beyond. Given the scarcity of both films, and latterly television programmes, dealing with Northern Ireland, as well as the Northern Ireland government's political and economic involvement in a substantial proportion of the small number of films that did get made, relatively few images challenging the unionist world-view appeared or, if they did, they only achieved – as in the case of *Belfast Remembers '98* and *Fintona* – very limited circulation. From the late 1960s onwards, this situation changed dramatically. Ironically, a government that had consistently battled for more publicity (and media exposure)

---

69. *Belfast News-Letter*, 8 July 1966, p. 1. Local viewers also appear to have missed out on *The Gentle Gunman* (1952), a feature film dealing with the IRA campaign during the Second World War, scheduled for transmission earlier the same evening in England.

70. *Irish News*, 9 July 1966, p. 1.

for Northern Ireland was now faced with an onslaught of media interest. As these images began to proliferate, however, the government was faced with the reality that its capacity to control the representation of Northern Ireland – and indeed its own political destiny – had by then largely dissolved. Images of Northern Ireland may have continued to be both controversial, and disputed, but the political context in which they appeared was in the process of changing irrevocably.

6

From 'propaganda for the arts' to 'the most powerful industry in the world'

Film Policy, Economics and Culture

Although the Northern Ireland government was intermittently involved in the support of film production from the 1920s onwards, its conception of film was almost entirely instrumentalist in character. That is to say, film was always conceived as valuable for reasons other than its qualities as film – as a vehicle for the promotion of tourism, as an advertisement for local goods and industries, as propaganda for the government and for its constitutional position. As such, there was no conception of film as an art or, even, as a valuable industrial activity that might contribute to the local economy. Thus, when the makers of *Odd Man Out* contacted the Ministry of Commerce in 1946, officials regarded this as an entirely political matter with 'no commercial significance whatever, direct or indirect'.[1] Around the same time, the government was also approached by a consortium, including the Hollywood director Edmund Goulding, seeking assistance under the New Industries legislation to establish a film studio in Northern Ireland (at a former aerodrome).[2] Even allowing for the undoubted opportunism involved in this initiative, there is little to suggest the government viewed film-making as an industry likely to benefit Northern Ireland or felt any enthusiasm for encouraging this kind of development. What has been distinctive about the contemporary period, therefore, is how discourses relating to both the cultural and economic importance of film have achieved increasing prominence within Northern Ireland and impacted upon the practices of government. This, in turn, relates to the changing character of cinema and, of course, the changing political complexion of the governance of Northern Ireland itself.

'Unusual films': the beginnings of cultural film exhibition

It has been a recurring theme of much writing on Ulster unionism that it has lacked, in comparison to Irish nationalism, the support of a creative or cultural intelligentsia. This, in turn, has been explained in terms of the backward-looking and defensive character of unionism, the dependence of unionism upon a combination of political populism and religious fundamentalism and the inclination of northern Protestants towards commerce, science and technology

---

1. Letter from G. H. E. Parr, Ministry of Commerce, to R. Gransden, 8 February 1946, PRONI COM7/86.
2. Letter from H. Petworth to J. Greer, 10 August 1946, PRONI CAB9F/123/81. According to Petworth, Goulding was 'imbued with the idea of pioneering Film production in Ulster' and 'introducing a new and lucrative profession into the Ulster Labour market'.

rather than the arts (and, thus, a practical, rather than artistic, bent in the northern Protestant character).[3] Given this context, it is perhaps unsurprising that a cultural or creative interest in the cinema was slow to develop in Northern Ireland. Thus, while Richard Hayward's ventures into film, and efforts to elaborate a unionist culture, suggest a departure from the traditional stereotype of the unionist intellectual, his film activities were also strongly populist in character and conducted with a sharp business acumen.

During the 1930s, however, a cultural interest in film, stimulated by developments in London, did begin to emerge in Belfast. Responding to the efflorescence of cinematic experiment occurring across Europe at the time, the Film Society in London was founded in 1925 in order to show mainly European and Soviet films that departed from the commercial norm. The success of the Society encouraged, in turn, the growth of specialised film exhibition both inside and outside London. The status of film as an 'art', however, remained contested and the main instigator of the Film Society in London, Ivor Montagu, employed the epithet 'unusual' – in preference to the term 'artistic' – to describe the nature of the Society's early repertoire.[4] Following the opening of specialist cinemas in London (such as the Academy, the Everyman and the Curzon), the *Irish News* asked the question whether a cinema wholly devoted to the screening of 'unusual films' might also succeed in Belfast. The views of a local cinema manager were solicited, who queried whether there was 'sufficient public' to support such a venture. While accepting there was room for more films with 'intellectual qualities', he counselled against films that were 'merely dirt in the guise of art' and that sacrificed narrative for the sake of 'mere highbrowism'. 'Belfast, after all, is not London,' he concluded, 'and maybe it is just as well.'[5]

While the idea of a cinema dedicated to 'arthouse' cinema did not materialise until much later, it was not long afterwards that 'unusual films' did begin to arrive in Belfast. In 1932, the Commission on Educational and Cultural Films, in its report *The Film in National Life*, recommended the establishment of a National Film Institute that would encourage the educational and cultural use of film. This led to the foundation of the British Film Institute in 1933, which, in its first year, took over the publication of *Sight and Sound*, launched the *Monthly Film Bulletin* (a review of recent UK releases), inaugurated a lecture programme and encouraged the establishment of local branches.[6] One of these was a Northern Ireland branch, launched in 1934, which sought to pursue the aims of the BFI through the organisation of lectures and publication of a regular bulletin intended to draw 'attention to films of a high class and of special merit when exhibited locally'.[7] However, while the organisation was adamant that it would not support censorship, or play the role of a vigilance committee, its approach to cinema was strongly influenced by the debates of the time and possessed a strong social and moral character. The

---

3. For a useful review of these debates, see Liam Dowd, 'Intellectuals and Political Culture: A Unionist–Nationalist Comparison', in Eamonn Hughes (ed.), *Culture and Politics in Northern Ireland* (Buckingham: Open University Press, 1991), pp. 151–73.

4. Ivor Montagu, 'The Film Society, London', *Cinema Quarterly*, vol. 1, no. 1, 1932. Reprinted in Donald Macpherson (ed.), *Traditions of Independence: British Cinema in the Thirties* (London: BFI, 1980), p. 105.

5. 'Unusual Films Only', *Irish News*, 19 January 1934, p. 5.

6. Ivan Butler, *'To Encourage the Art of Film': The Story of the British Film Institute* (London: Robert Hale, 1971), p. 19.

7. *The British Film Institute Northern Ireland Branch Bulletin*, no. 1, December 1934, p. 1.

ambition of the society, in this respect, was less to proselytise on behalf of 'art' cinema than to combat, through information and education, what it regarded as the low quality and deleterious effects of most commercial cinema. The society's first *Bulletin*, for example, indicated that it would ignore any film that made 'a special feature of crime, cruelty, or loose morality'. The report of the Branch Secretary to the Annual General Meeting in 1936 also lamented the fact that, while audiences flocked to 'gruesome films' such as *Frankenstein* and *The Bride of Frankenstein*, 'a graceful, witty, artistic production' might fail 'to attract them'. In the same spirit, he went on to urge 'all lovers of the cinema art to join our ranks and to spread our influence as a much-needed social work'.[8]

Although the group was well connected (and counted the Minister of Commerce, J. Milne Barbour, among its vice-presidents), it struggled to achieve the membership levels (and the social influence) it desired. Partly as a result, the group joined forces with the Belfast Film Society to produce a revamped version of the BFI *Bulletin* entitled the *Belfast Film Review* (which first appeared in October 1937). Whereas the activities of the BFI group were mostly educational in character, the Belfast Film Society, formed in early 1937, was concerned with the screening of actual films. The first of these (such as the Czech comedy *Hey-Rup* [1934] and the Russian drama *The Road to Life* [1931]) were exhibited in ordinary halls on 16mm, although, subsequently, the Society secured agreement for one-off screenings in commercial cinemas. These included 'late night extras' at the Imperial Picture House and a season of films at the Apollo. By the end of its 1938–9 season, the Society was reporting a membership of nearly 600.[9] Although the two groups shared the goal of improving 'the art of cinema', there was, nevertheless, a degree of tension between them with regard to how this goal should be met. Thus, when the series of 'late night extras' kicked off with a screening of Fritz Lang's *M* (1931), this was attacked by a correspondent to the *Review* for its apparent 'lack of virtue'.[10] There was, however, sufficient common purpose between the two bodies for them to merge formally in 1939 to become the Belfast Film Institute Society. Unfortunately, a change in the Apollo's ownership the same year ended the Society's relationship with the cinema and they subsequently struggled to find a suitable venue in which to screen films. The organisation did, nevertheless, succeed in sustaining a series of short repertory seasons for most of the Second World War.

Arts policy and film: CEMA and the Arts Council of Northern Ireland

However, while the combined efforts of the BFI Northern Ireland branch and the Belfast Film Society may have begun to cultivate an increased appreciation of film as an 'art', the perception of film as an art form, rather than a mass entertainment, was destined to remain a marginalised

8. *The British Film Institute Northern Ireland Branch Bulletin*, Special Issue, June 1936, pp. 2–3. As this suggests, while the BFI branch, which included a number of clergymen among its committee members, may not have advocated censorship, it shared the same moral assumptions about Hollywood films as those who did. This was also so of the letter it published in support of *The Green Pastures*, which did not challenge the terms upon which the film had been understood but employed the same religious framework as those attacking it (*The British Film Institute Northern Ireland Branch Bulletin*, vol. 3, no. 4, April 1937, p. 2).

9. Ibid.

10. 'Sensational Films', *Belfast Film Review*, vol. 1, no. 2, November 1937, p. vii.

discourse within Northern Irish culture (as it was within Irish and British culture more generally). This may be seen in the way that film was almost entirely absent from the purview of conventional arts policy as it emerged during the war and became institutionalised in the postwar
period. The Council for the Encouragement of Music and the Arts (CEMA) was established in
England in 1940 in order to promote the performance of concerts and plays. Although CEMA,
along with the Pilgrim Trust, provided a grant to the Joint Committee for Adult Education at
Queen's University, Belfast, to undertake its 'Art for the People' and 'Music for the People' initiatives, it was later established that the responsibility for funding the arts in Northern Ireland
did not, in fact, fall upon CEMA. As a result, the Joint Committee lobbied the Northern Ireland government to support an equivalent body in Northern Ireland. Although the Unionist
government was initially reluctant to do so, it eventually agreed to fund CEMA (Northern Ireland) through the Ministry of Education and the new body was established in 1943.[11] The
Council itself was a 'hands-on' organisation and, in its early years, its main activities consisted of
the organisation of art exhibitions, dramatic performances and concerts.

Like its English counterpart, CEMA (Northern Ireland) was committed to a traditional conception of 'high art' and its main purpose was to make the 'best in painting, sculpture, architecture, drama and music' available to people in Northern Ireland.[12] However, while state support
for the arts in the UK may have been born of a social-democratic impulse to extend access to
'high culture', it was also accompanied, as Geoff Mulgan suggests, by a level of 'hostility to popular and modern culture'.[13] At this time, film was primarily regarded as a commercial activity
devoted to mass entertainment and, therefore, was identified as an obstacle to the successful
spread of the 'best' in art (rather than a cultural activity that might itself merit public funding).
Thus, it was perhaps no surprise that Lord Keynes, the first chairman of the Arts Council in
England, should have ended his radio broadcast on the occasion of the Council's launch with

11. Referring to the campaign for an 'Ulster theatre', Lionel Pilkington links the postwar policy of CEMA (Northern
Ireland) to a project of cultural legitimation of 'Ulster' as a distinct political entity. See *Theatre and the State in
Twentieth-Century Ireland: Cultivating the People* (London: Routledge, 2001), ch. 7. However, as the debates
surrounding the establishment of CEMA (Northern Ireland) indicate, the arts were not a political priority for the
Unionist regime, which failed to keep up with spending levels in the rest of the UK. Thus, just as the government's
plans for film propaganda were undercut by a reluctance to make adequate funding available, so any ambition to
use the arts to maintain unionist hegemony lacked effective economic backing. Given that Unionist rule depended
upon cross-class unity within the Protestant population rather than class unity across the sectarian divide, it is
perhaps not surprising that arts activity directed primarily towards the Protestant middle class should not have
played a significant role in the construction of unionist hegemony (even though, as previously noted, the
government was still concerned that the unionist ethos of the public sphere should be maintained).

12. Robert Hewison notes how the initial populist impulse of CEMA in England shifted under the chairmanship of
Lord Keynes towards support for flagship institutions and professional accomplishment. In this respect, the
direction of Arts Council policy shifted from an emphasis upon popular participation in artistic activities towards
the provision of increased access to 'great art' (albeit that the levels of access actually enjoyed by the working class
was to prove limited). See *Under Siege: Literary Life in London 1939–45* (Newton Abbot: Readers Union, 1978),
pp. 157–8.

13. Geoff Mulgan, 'Culture', in David Marquand and Anthony Seldon (eds), *The Ideas That Shaped Post-War Britain*
(London: HarperCollins, 1996), p. 198.

the provocative declaration: 'Let every part of Merry England be merry in its own way. Death to Hollywood.'[14] Similar, if slightly less extravagant, sentiments were also evident in the third annual report of CEMA (Northern Ireland), in which the Council lamented the fact that 'many people will cheerfully pay a shilling or more for a cinema show or a football match' but 'will not take an interest in good music and drama'.[15] For the first twenty years of its existence, therefore, CEMA saw little reason to concern itself with film. When it did so, its conception of film was entirely instrumentalist in character, placing film at the service of other arts. Thus, in 1953, the Council was responsible for a tour of 'art films' accompanied by 'a skilled lecturer'. However, these were films about art ('Giotto's Paduan murals, the intellectual complexities of Italian cubism and the Prospero-like enchantments of the octogenarian Matisse'), employed merely as an 'instrument of popularisation and exposition', rather than films that might themselves be regarded as art or capable of demonstrating the medium's own potential for aesthetic achievement.[16]

It was therefore not until the 1960s that local arts policy began to conceive of film as a significant form of cultural activity in its own right. By this time, CEMA (Northern Ireland) had become the Arts Council of Northern Ireland, established in 1963, and the cultural landscape surrounding film had changed significantly. During the postwar period, many European governments had begun to provide increased support to their film industries as a way of protecting their national cinemas in the face of declining cinema audiences and growing Hollywood domination of the box office. This encouraged the emergence of what David Bordwell has characterised as the 'apogee' of 'art cinema' in the late 1950s and early 1960s, when directors such as Antonioni, Bergman, Fellini, Godard, Truffaut and Resnais achieved widespread international recognition for a new kind of intellectually self-conscious and formally innovative mode of filmmaking practice combining story-telling and modernist experiment.[17] An awareness of these shifts in international film culture began to permeate the thinking of the Arts Council of Northern Ireland and found its first expression in 1966, following the arrival of a new director, Michael Whewell. In a statement of 'basic principles and priorities', contained in the Council's annual report, Whewell refers to the need to provide specialist film programming for 'film enthusiasts' who have become 'weary of the negative policies of commercial cinema'.[18] The following year, this commitment had developed into a proposal for 'a Belfast branch of the National Film Theatre' that would finally provide 'official recognition' and 'parity of esteem' for cinema as 'one of the sisterhood of arts'.[19] The National Film Theatre had developed from the Telekinema, which had formed a part of the Festival of Britain in London and which was now owned by the British Film Institute. Under its new director, Stanley Reed, appointed in 1964,

---

14. *The Listener*, vol. xxxiv, no. 861, 12 July 1945, p. 32. As this would suggest, Hollywood film was not only regarded as a threat to the spread of genuine art but also the maintenance of 'national' culture.

15. Council for the Encouragement of Music and the Arts (CEMA) (Northern Ireland), *Third Annual Report 1945–46* (Belfast, 1946), p. 5.

16. CEMA (Northern Ireland), *Eleventh Annual Report 1953–54* (Belfast, 1954), p. 11.

17. David Bordwell, *Narration in the Fiction Film* (London: Methuen, 1985), pp. 230–1.

18. Arts Council of Northern Ireland (ACNI), *Twenty-Third Annual Report 1965–66* (Belfast, 1966), p. 4.

19. ACNI, *Twenty-Fourth Annual Report 1966–67* (Belfast, 1967), p. 7.

the BFI had been seeking to extend its activities outside London and, with the support of Jennie Lee, the new Labour Minister for the Arts, was encouraging the establishment of regional film theatres. As Queen's University already possessed a Film Society, it was Queen's that now provided the 'lecture room' that was set to become the new Queen's Film Theatre (QFT). The Arts Council provided a capital grant for the conversion and equipping of the Theatre, which opened in October 1968 with the declared policy of showing 'the best in world cinema'.[20] Although the BFI had been a partner in the initiative, the Art Council's report for the relevant year notes that '[f]iscal arrangements between Stormont and Westminster prohibit the British Film Institute from dispensing money in Northern Ireland' and that the BFI's contribution had therefore been confined to 'technical advice'.[21] This was an ominous formulation, signalling a dispute that was to rumble on for years to come. Echoing earlier arguments between the Northern Ireland government and the Central Office of Information (discussed in Chapter 4), the funding of film in Northern Ireland was set to remain a contentious issue.

Indeed, the question of film funding became a matter of urgency almost immediately due to the financial problems faced by QFT. QFT had embarked upon a relatively ambitious programme of screenings, consisting mainly of contemporary European films. In its 1969-70 season, it was responsible for 110 different film programmes attended by over 40,000.[22] However, while it achieved early success with screenings of films such as Joseph Strick's *Ulysses* (1967)(which had been banned in the Irish Republic) and Michelangelo Antonioni's *Blow-Up* (1966), admissions at the Theatre were well below capacity and losses were increasing on a year-on-year basis. As Queen's University had initially expected that the Film Theatre would break even, if not make a small profit, it was unwilling to sustain continuing losses and, in July 1971, the Vice-Chancellor wrote to the Arts Council indicating the University's intention to close the Theatre later that year.[23] However, while the Arts Council was reluctant to see QFT close, it took the view that the Northern Ireland Ministry of Finance had failed to provide it with funding for film that was equivalent to that given to the BFI by the Department of Education and Science in Britain.[24] Given the apparent reluctance of the local Ministry to commit to additional provision for film, this could have resulted in a stalemate. Indeed, the QFT was forced to close for a time in 1972, before the Arts Council reluctantly agreed to underwrite the Film Theatre's losses, permitting the QFT to survive at a time when the cinemas in Belfast were in rapid decline due to a combination of declining audiences and escalating violence that included, in 1977, the bombing of three cinemas (the ABC, Curzon and New Vic).[25] It was also to prove a

20. Michael Open, 'Queen's Film Theatre – Programming Policy: A Document for the Northern Ireland Film Council', 25 February 1993.

21. ACNI, *Twenty-Fifth Annual Report 1967–68* (Belfast, 1968), p. 14.

22. ACNI, *Twenty-Seventh Annual Report 1969–70* (Belfast, 1970), p. 21.

23. Letter from F Arthur Vick to F Murphy, 27 July 1971, PRONI AC1/1/4.

24. Minutes of the Board of the Arts Council of Northern Ireland, 22 September 1971, pp. 513–14, PRONI AC1/1/4.

25. At the time of QFT's opening in 1969, the number of cinemas in Belfast had fallen from forty-two in 1957 to twenty. By the 1980s, this number had dwindled to only four. See Michael Open, *Fading Lights, Silver Screens: A History of Belfast Cinemas* (Antrim: Greystone Books, 1985), pp. 15–16.

turning-point in the Arts Council's attitude towards film, finally persuading it to offer funding for film on a modest but nevertheless regular basis.

When CEMA (Northern Ireland) was originally established, it had established three advisory subcommittees in Art, Drama and Music to assist with the planning and implementation of its policies. Under the Arts Council these committees grew to include Literature, the 'Traditional Arts' and then, in 1973, Film. The Film Committee survived for just under ten years and, during this period, there was an increase in both the range of film activities that the Council supported and the amounts of funding it provided (rising fairly dramatically from only £4,073 in 1974–5 to £36,503 in 1978-9). While the funding of QFT continued to be the bedrock of Arts Council film policy, there were new educational initiatives (such as the Film and Television Studies summer school at the New University of Ulster in 1976) and the organisation of tours of short films (such as Chris Marker's *La Jetée* [1962]), under the title of 'Movies on the Move'. With the assistance of the Irish Arts Council, a news sheet carrying information on the QFT programme and other regional activities was also expanded into a more general film magazine, *Film Directions*, containing articles and reviews. Perhaps, most significantly of all, the Committee began to provide support for film and video production. However, almost immediately, the Committee was faced with competing sets of demands for funding and found it difficult to prioritise the kinds of production that it should fund.

At this time, the Film Department of the Arts Council of Great Britain funded both documentary films about the arts and the use of film and video by practising artists. The BFI Production Board also funded a mix of animation, documentary and fiction. Despite the relatively low levels of funds at its disposal, the ACNI Film Committee sought to fulfil the functions of both these bodies, attempting to offer support to a variety of drama, documentary and animation projects. It also ventured into the arena of community video and paid for video equipment for use by local community groups. There was, perhaps, a degree of irony here insofar as the belated recognition of film as an 'art' worthy of public funding coincided with a growing challenge to the very notion of art upon which Arts Council funding had been traditionally predicated.[26] Thus, just as the more general rise of the 'community arts' movement precipitated major debates concerning the relevance and social inclusiveness of different kinds of 'art' in both Northern Ireland and elsewhere, so the call for funds for community video caused the Film Committee anxiety about the 'artistic quality' of the activities that it was supporting and led it to question whether its funding of them could be justified on the basis of 'archival value and community relevance' alone.[27] Given the strongly polarised character of the 'community' within Northern

---

26. Stuart Laing reviews the disputes over aesthetic boundaries generated by the rise of community arts in his discussion of Arts Council policy in Britain during the 1970s in 'The Politics of Culture: Institutional Changes in the 1970s', in Bart Moore-Gilbert (ed.), *The Arts in the 1970s: Cultural Closure?* (London: Routledge, 1994), pp. 40–9.

27. 'Community Video', Appendix, Minutes of the Arts Council of Northern Ireland Film Committee, 26 January 1978, PRONI AC4/5/5A. In his entertaining, but somewhat facetious, overview of the Northern Ireland Arts Council, Ian Hill narrativises the history of arts policy in terms of a growing commitment to community arts at the expense of 'high art' and professional accomplishment. See 'Arts Administration', in Mark Carruthers and Stephen Douds (eds), *Stepping Stones: The Arts in Ulster* (Belfast: Blackstaff Press, 2001), pp. 215–36.

Ireland, there was also a feeling that the Arts Council was being called upon to fund socially and politically partisan work that could not be regarded as sitting comfortably 'above' or 'outside' the surrounding 'troubles'.[28] These arguments were to intensify as the decade proceeded, eventually leading to the establishment of a separate Community Arts Committee in 1978. However, despite the growing complexity of the arguments surrounding the basis on which film was to be funded, the prevailing ethos of the Council meant that the Film Committee's allocations were still weighted in favour of films that provided 'propaganda for the arts' (the phrase the Committee itself chose) over those that might demonstrate the artistic use of film or employ film as a cultural expression of 'community'. As a result, two of the Committee's largest grants went to documentaries on 'artists': one on the poet John Hewitt (*I Found Myself Alone*, directed by Derek Bailey and David Hammond) and one on the painter William Scott (*Every Picture Tells a Story*), whose work had been the subject of a major retrospective at the Ulster Museum in 1975.

Although the funding for film grew during the 1970s and early 1980s, it was still a small proportion of the Council's overall budget. Thus, while the Arts Council's spending on film for 1982–3 came to a record £46,573 this was still less than 2 per cent of the Council's total expenditure for that year of £2,560,645. Nevertheless, at a time when the Arts Council was complaining that per capita funding for the arts in Northern Ireland was the lowest in the UK, there was clearly a fear that the funding of film would impose an increasing burden upon an already stretched arts budget. As a result, the Council decided to abolish the Film Committee (which became absorbed into a new Visual Arts Committee) and opted to confine its support for film to QFT, films about the arts, film tours and film societies. The rationale for this course of action was that the Arts Council was unable to 'cover responsibilities divided in Britain between ACGB and BFI unless given money to do so'.[29] Inevitably, this decision proved controversial. It was certainly true that government spending on film in Northern Ireland did not match the rest of the UK. It was also the case that, in the absence of BFI involvement in Northern Ireland, the Arts Council of Northern Ireland was being drawn into the funding of film activities that fell outside the scope of its counterparts in England, Scotland and Wales. Nevertheless, at a time when film and video images of Northern Ireland circulated more widely than ever before, and the demand for locally based production was intensifying, it seemed extraordinary that the Arts Council should choose to withdraw what little funding it was providing to the independent sector for indigenous film and video production. As Martin McLoone was subsequently to comment, whatever anomalies may have characterised the funding of film in Northern Ireland, the Arts Council remained the body '*responsible* for cultural activity in N. Ireland' and by 'turning its back on film and video' was clearly 'reneging on that responsibility'.[30]

This verdict seems particularly apt when the Arts Council had no realistic expectation of a resolution to the funding issue or any clear strategy as to how to arrive at one. The BFI continued

---

28. This concern was apparent, for example, in the Film Committee's wish that the video equipment it helped purchase should be held in 'some agreed central and "neutral" location' (Minutes of the Film Committee, 24 January 1977, PRONI AC1/12/1).

29. 'Film – An Assessment', Arts Council of Northern Ireland, October 1984, PRONI AC7/66A.

30. Martin McLoone, 'ACNI Culture: A Blurred Vision', *CIRCA*, no. 39, 1988, p. 18.

to maintain that it had no authority to operate in Northern Ireland, while the government departments within Northern Ireland, now under the direct rule of a Conservative government committed to public expenditure cuts, displayed no enthusiasm for additional spending on film. Although the Northern Ireland funding 'anomaly' was generally presented as the consequence of a constitutional problem, it is hard to resist the conclusion that it was primarily a financial dispute (conducted at a time when all arts funding was proving difficult to obtain). The BFI had, of course, been happy to organise in Northern Ireland and provide financial support for a BFI branch in the 1930s. There seems little doubt, therefore, that the BFI's founders saw Northern Ireland as falling squarely within its remit (albeit that the funding involved was exceptionally modest). At this time, however, the BFI had yet to receive its Royal Charter and it was this that led the BFI subsequently to claim that it was prevented from operating in Northern Ireland, insofar as its Charter referred to Great Britain rather than the United Kingdom. However, this interpretation of its Charter seems to have been something of a red herring. The BFI Production Board, for example, was prepared to receive applications from Northern Ireland and helped to fund the Berwick Street Film Collective's documentary about the North, *Ireland behind the Wire* (1974), and Pat Murphy's feminist meditation upon the 'troubles', *Maeve* (1981), shot partly in Belfast. It also seems to have been the case that had the BFI wished to fund film activities in Northern Ireland, it would not have met with any political resistance from either government or other cultural organisations within Britain. However, as with the Arts Council of Northern Ireland, the BFI took the view that the Westminster government had failed to provide it with the relevant funding and was therefore reluctant to see its resources stretched further by accepting additional responsibilities for Northern Ireland. As a result, the BFI's position regarding Northern Ireland did not fundamentally change following an alteration to its Charter. In response to the mounting pressure from Northern Ireland, the BFI did eventually resolve to amend its Charter to include the whole of the United Kingdom in 1990. However, it did so without any expectation of entering funding agreements with Northern Ireland organisations or providing services within Northern Ireland unless these were paid for by the Northern Ireland Office or the Northern Ireland Arts Council.[31] As a result, the amendment to the BFI's Charter proved in the end to be of little consequence and led to no significant increase in the funding of film activities in Northern Ireland.

Given the refusal of both the Arts Council of Northern Ireland and the BFI to accept responsibility for the funding of film in Northern Ireland, the result was stalemate for a number of years. Nevertheless, some significant developments did occur in this period. During the late 1960s and early 1970s, there was a growth of politically radical film and video workshops in Britain and two of these, Cinema Action (founded in 1968) and the Berwick Street Collective (formed in 1972), shot documentaries about the growing political crisis in Northern Ireland: *People of Ireland* (1973) and *Ireland behind the Wire*.[32] In 1974, a Community Media group was

---

31. 'Update on Northern Ireland', Appendix, Minutes of the British Film Institute Board of Governors, 24 October 1990.

32. For an overview of the history of independent cinema in Britain, see Simon Blanchard and Sylvia Harvey, 'The Post-war Independent Cinema – Structure and Organisation', in James Curran and Vincent Porter (eds), *British Cinema History* (London: Weidenfeld and Nicolson, 1983), pp. 226–41.

established in Belfast and, during this period, as noted already, the Arts Council began to offer a degree of financial support to the emerging community video movement. This growth in activity led to the formation of an umbrella group for community groups in the North, the Northern Ireland Film and Video Association, in 1980, and received a further boost with the launch of the fourth UK television channel, Channel 4, in 1982.

Channel 4 did not in itself operate as a production house but either purchased or commissioned work from outside sources. It also had a particular remit to complement the other three UK channels and encourage 'innovation and experiment'. One of the ways in which it did so was through the support of the Drama Department for film production destined for its 'Film on Four' slot. However, while this transformed the film funding landscape in Britain, the absence of a sustained tradition of feature production in Northern Ireland meant that it was the channel's Department of Independent Film and Video that played the more influential role in the region.[33] According to the Department's senior commissioning editor, Alan Fountain, the department was concerned to support 'the sort of work unlikely to be taken up elsewhere in the television system' and that would 'represent the alternative, oppositional voice'.[34] In line with this remit, the Department sought to provide an outlet for perspectives on Northern Ireland and the 'troubles' that were generally missing from mainstream television. A documentary on media coverage of the 'troubles', *Ireland: the Silent Voices*, was broadcast in 1983 and accompanied by a short season of Irish-related films that included *Maeve* and *The Writing on the Wall* (Armand Gatti, 1981). The Department also commissioned a documentary *The Cause of Ireland* (Chris Reeves, 1983) to coincide with the fifteenth anniversary of the banned Civil Rights march in Derry in October 1968 and screened the BFI Production Board's film *Ascendancy* (Edward Bennett, 1982), a period drama dealing with Unionist resistance to Home Rule.

A major aspect of the Department's work involved support for the film and video workshop sector. Under the Workshop Declaration – agreed initially in 1982 with the Association of Cinema and Television Technicians (ACTT), the BFI, the Regional Arts Association and the Independent Film-Makers Association (founded in 1974) – Channel 4 agreed to finance a number of 'franchised' non-profit-making workshops that would provide programming for its *Eleventh Hour* and *People to People* slots. The first fiction feature to be made under the workshop agreement was *Acceptable Levels* (1983), a collaboration between the London-based workshop Frontroom and Belfast Film Workshop, dealing with an English television crew filming a documentary in Belfast and the diluted version of events that results. Northern Visions, a key member of the Northern Film and Video Association, was also funded by the channel and *Under the Health Service*, a documentary on the health problems faced by women in Belfast, was broadcast in 1986. The 'first independent workshop in the North-West', Derry Film and Video also obtained a franchise. Formed in 1984, this group began making short documentaries on

33. During the 1990s, Channel 4's Drama Department did, however, back *With or Without You* (1999), which was set in Belfast and partly shot in Northern Ireland. For a discussion of Channel 4's support for film more generally, see John Hill, 'British Television and Film: The Making of a Relationship', in John Hill and Martin McLoone (eds), *Big Picture, Small Screen: The Relations Between Film and Television* (Luton: John Libbey Media/University of Luton Press, 1996).

34. Alan Fountain, quoted in *A. I. P. & Co.*, no. 51, 1984, p. 18.

Politically radical
documentary: *Ireland behind
the Wire*

strip-searching (*Strip-searching – Security or Subjugation*, 1984) and urban redevelopment in
nationalist areas (*Planning*, 1985), before embarking upon its first narrative feature, *Hush-a-Bye
Baby* (Margo Harkin, 1989), concerning the responses to a Catholic teenager's unplanned pregnancy. The group was also responsible for the documentary *Mother Ireland* (1988), which, because
of its inclusion of interview material with IRA member Mairead Farrell (subsequently shot dead
by British forces in Gibraltar), achieved the distinction of becoming the first programme banned
under the broadcasting ban introduced by the Conservative government in 1988. Derry also
hosted the first Northern Ireland festival specifically devoted to film, the Foyle Film Festival.
Established in 1987 with seed money from the University of Ulster, and conceived as a festival
'with a difference', the first programme included a retrospective of films made in and about
Northern Ireland, accompanied by debates on film and cultural identity in the North.

New initiatives: the Northern Ireland Film Council,
the BBC and the Lottery

Given this upsurge in activity and the continuing lack of financial provision for film and video
production in Northern Ireland, it was to be expected that pressure for change should mount.
In 1988, the Independent Film, Video and Photography Association commissioned a report, *Fast
Forward*, that identified the disadvantaged position of the North in relation to the rest of Ireland
and the UK and called for the establishment of a Media Council.[35] The following year, the
Northern Ireland Film Council (NIFC) was launched at a public meeting in Belfast in order to
promote local film and video production and culture. At the time of its launch the NIFC was
an entirely voluntary body, dependent for its survival upon the financial contributions of its
members (who elected the Council's Board). The children's film festival Cinemagic was established in 1990 and provided the organisation with an early public profile and income flow. The

---

35. *Fast Forward: Report on the Funding of Grant-aided Film and Video in the North of Ireland* (IFVPA, 1988).

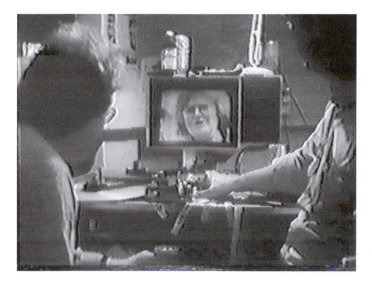

Acceptable Levels, made with
the support of Channel 4

Council went on to produce detailed strategy proposals (relating to production, training, education, distribution, marketing, exhibition and archival policy) and, in the first breaking of the log-jam surrounding government funding of film, secured modest grant-in-aid in 1992 from the Department of Education for Northern Ireland (subsequently routed through the Arts Council).[36] At this time, the only local source of public funding for independent production was the money provided by the Cultural Traditions Group (a subcommittee of the Community Relations Council) to support media projects that contributed to 'a better understanding of cultural diversity and community issues within Northern Ireland'.[37] The CTG was particularly committed to material intended for broadcast by local television and lent its support to a number of documentaries including: Carlo Gebler's *Plain Tales from Northern Ireland* (1993), a series of portraits of rural life in Fermanagh amid the 'troubles'; Double-Band's *The Trouble with Art* (1994), examining the role of the visual arts in contemporary Northern Ireland; and Brendan Byrne's *The Kickhams* (1994), following a year in the life of a Gaelic Athletic Association (GAA) team in North Belfast. As a result of its success in lobbying government, the Film Council was also able to launch its own production fund aimed at the development and production of (both drama and documentary) film and television projects of artistic and cultural relevance to Northern Ireland. Projects that the NIFC supported included John T. Davis' feature-length documentary, *The Uncle Jack* (1995), a semi-autobiographical work inspired by the film-maker's cinema architect uncle; the fictional short, *A Sort of Homecoming* (1994), by the writer-director team Jim Keeble and Dudi Appleton (subsequently responsible for *The Most Fertile Man in Ireland* [1999]), and a screenplay *Oranges are Blue*, by the young Chinese-Irish writer and director,

---

36. *Strategy Proposals for the Development of the Film, Television and Video Industry and Culture in Northern Ireland* (Belfast: Northern Ireland Film Council, 1991).

37. James Hawthorne, 'Media', in *Giving Voices: The Work of the Cultural Traditions Group 1990–1994* (Belfast: CTG, 1995), p. 20.

Lab Ky Mo (who went on to write and direct the notorious independent feature *Nine Dead Gay Guys* [2002]).

The launch of two shorts schemes – 'Northern Lights' and 'Première'- followed. 'Northern Lights' involved a collaboration with the BBC and was intended to develop the creative talents of Northern Irish writers and directors. It provided budgets of around £45–50,000 for three shorts per year, the first of which was writer John Forte's directorial debut, *Skin Tight* (1994), a comic exploration of the domestic tension surrounding an Orangeman's preparations for the Twelfth of July celebrations. The second series also included the Oscar-nominated *Dance, Lexie, Dance* (1996), dealing with a young Protestant girl who, inspired by the popularity of *Riverdance*, takes up Irish dancing to the bemusement of her widowed father. In 1997, the NIFC went on to establish a second shorts scheme, 'Première', initially in association with Ulster Television, Belfast City Council and the London-based British Screen (a state-funded private company with a responsibility for supporting British film-makers that later became a part of the UK Film Council). This ran for four seasons and productions included: Enda Hughes' pastiche of 1950s B-cinema, *Flying Saucer Rock'n'Roll* (1997); Brian Kirk's unsettling portrait of a young girl's awakening sexuality, *Baby Doll* (1998); and *Surfing with William* (1998), a witty look at a Derry girl's infatuation with Prince William and her attempts to contact him via the net, written by Lisa Burkitt and directed by Tracey Cullen. Like *Dance, Lexie, Dance*, this last film was produced by the multimedia arts centre in Derry, the Nerve Centre, which has not only played a significant role in training but also the development of animated work, such as the bleak deconstruction of Ulster myth, *The King's Wake* (2000), animated and directed by John McCloskey.

Three other factors added impetus to these developments: BBC Northern Ireland's growing involvement in film production, the availability of UK Lottery funds for film projects and the re-establishment of Bord Scannán na hÉireann (BSE)/the Irish Film Board (IFB) in the South. Due to its high cost (and the unwillingness of the BBC in London to fund drama production in the regions), the BBC in Northern Ireland did not engage in the regular production of television drama until the 1970s. In the following two decades, however, the BBC Drama Department in Northern Ireland did produce a number of one-off dramas (and some series). Although not shown in cinemas, many of these dramas were, in effect, low-budget films, shot on film by directors, such as Alan Clarke, Danny Boyle and Michael Winterbottom, who would later move into features. During the 1990s, this policy began to change. As a result of the BBC Director-General John Birt's creation of an 'internal market' for resources (through the policy of 'producer choice'), and the BBC's new obligation (under the Broadcasting Act of 1990) to commission a percentage of programming from the independent sector, the BBC Drama Department in Northern Ireland was able to increase its budget significantly (and this had reached £10.1 million by 1995–6).[38] This growth of activity also involved a change in production strategy. In line with BBC drama policy more generally, the Department placed an increasing emphasis upon drama series aimed at the network (most notably the hugely successful *Ballykissangel*, first broadcast in 1996), as well as films with a theatrical (and not just broadcast) potential. This policy was initiated with two period pieces written by Barry Devlin: *All Things*

---

38. Martina Purdy, 'Dramatic Presence', *Belfast Telegraph*, Business section, 4 April 1995, p. 9.

Surfing with William, a NIFC-funded short

Bright and Beautiful (Barry Devlin, 1994), concerning a young boy's discovery of an IRA fugitive in County Tyrone in the 1950s, and *A Man of No Importance* (Suri Krishnamma, 1995), dealing with the experiences, in 1960s Dublin, of a gay bus conductor (played by Albert Finney). Like *Ballykissangel*, both of these features were shot (and, in one case, set) in the South in order to take advantage of tax benefits under Section 35 (later Section 481) of the 1987 Finance Act and, in the case of the two features, funding support from Bord Scannán na hÉireann/the Irish Film Board. This meant that BBC Northern Ireland spent, over the period 1994–8, much more (£56 million) on film and drama production outside of Northern Ireland than it did inside (£7.4 million).[39] As a result of the introduction of the National Lottery (and changes to the UK tax regime in 1997), however, it became more financially attractive for the BBC to shoot in the North and the feature films *Divorcing Jack* (David Caffrey, 1998) and *Wild about Harry* (Declan Lowney, 1999), along with the drama series *Eureka Street* (1999), were all filmed in Northern Ireland after receiving support from the Lottery.

Lottery funding itself became available in 1995 following agreement by the then Conservative government in Britain that film production could be regarded as capital expenditure (and thus eligible for lottery support). Initially lottery funds were administered by the Arts Councils of England, Wales, Scotland and Northern Ireland, with sums awarded on a per capita basis. This meant that Northern Ireland, received 2.8 per cent of the UK Lottery allocation for Arts funding, with around 13 per cent of this going to film-related projects. The most substantial proportion of expenditure in this area was on production, which amounted to £2.3 million out of

---

39. Verity Peet, *A Film Studio for Northern Ireland?* (Belfast: Northern Ireland Film Commission, 2000), p. 17.

£3.2 million spent on film between 1995 and 2000.[40] Although this was a small sum compared to that available in England, it represented an unprecedented level of public investment in film for Northern Ireland and immediately led to a burst of production activity. Thus, no less than eight Northern Ireland lottery-funded features entered production during 1997 and 1998: Tommy Collins' story of a young Donegal woman's experiences in Derry leading up to the 'troubles', *Bogwoman* (1997); the allegorical *Sunset Heights* (Colm Villa, 1998), set in a violent Derry of the future; a film version of Mary Costello's semi-autobiographical novel set in 1970s Belfast, *Titanic Town* (Roger Michell, 1998); a romantic historical drama set in France during the Napoleonic war, *All For Love* (originally *St Ives*) (Harry Hook, 1998); two adaptations of novels by the local comedy thriller writer Colin Bateman, *Cycle of Violence* (originally *Crossmaheart*)(Henry Herbert, 1998) and *Divorcing Jack*; Syd McCartney's historical drama, based on a true story of a religiously mixed marriage in County Wexford in the 1950s, *A Love Divided* (1999); and John Forte's Belfast-set romantic comedy, *Mad about Mambo* (1999). Although the pace of production subsequently slackened, the lottery continued to play a key role in sustaining film-making in the region. Projects to which it contributed subsequently have included Kevin Liddy's rural drama (set in the South), *Country* (2000); the digital feature, also set mostly in the South, *The Honeymooners* (Karl Golden, 2002); *Blind Flight* (John Furse, 2003), an adaptation of Brian Keenan's memoirs, *An Evil Cradling*; the futuristic thriller *Freeze Frame* (John Simpson, 2004); and an adaptation of Owen McCafferty's play about two young boys growing up during the 'troubles', *Mickybo & Me* (Terry Loane, 2004).

Although the Arts Council was initially the recognised distributor for lottery funds, it contracted the Northern Ireland Film Council to undertake lottery film assessments from 1996 onwards, before finally handing over delegated responsibility for film funding in 2002.[41] In its early years, the NIFC had enjoyed some success in encouraging low-budget production and the development of new talent but the scope of its activities remained restricted due to the low level of public funds at its disposal. A significant breakthrough occurred, therefore, when the body secured £1 million funding from the EU Special Support Programme for Peace and Reconciliation (SSPPR) for the establishment of a screen commission and a script development fund that was intended to complement the production funding available through the lottery. Although the Film Council had been lobbying for a film commission for a number of years (and undertook a feasibility study in 1994), it was only after it had secured EU (and matching Department of Economic Development) backing that it was able to proceed to implementation. In order to signal its increased involvement in the marketing of locations, and to make itself more accountable to government, the NIFC changed its name and constitution, relaunching as

---

40. Northern Ireland Film Commission, 'Lottery Film Funding for Northern Ireland – Proposals for New Arrangements – Consultation Paper', August 2000, p. 7. Unlike England, where lottery funding has been confined to film, Northern Ireland monies have also been extended to television, as in the case of the BBC Northern Ireland series *Eureka Street*.

41. This was the recommendation of a review of Arts Council policy conducted by Anthony Everitt and Annabel Jackson and fell in line with developments in England, where the newly established UK Film Council replaced the Arts Council as the lottery distributor for film in 2000. See *Opening Up the Arts: A Strategic Review of the Arts Council of Northern Ireland* (Belfast: Arts Council of Northern Ireland, 2000), p. 63.

The role of lottery funding: Lee Evans in *Freeze Frame*

the Northern Ireland Film Commission in 1997. It also established its new Development Fund the same year and, by the end of March 2001, some forty-two film and television projects had benefited. In the case of feature films, these included: the 'road movie' *Accelerator* (Vinny Murphy, 2001); an adaptation of Spike Milligan's comic novel about Irish partition, *Puckoon* (Terence Ryan, 2001); and *Mad about Mambo*. In 1999, the Commission also secured additional EU funds for the creation of a £500,000 Film Production fund. Because of the comparatively short periods that some of the lottery-funded films (such as *Titanic Town*) had spent filming in the North, this new fund was targeted at films that would be made primarily in Northern Ireland. This resulted in awards to the Belfast-based comedy, *The Most Fertile Man in Ireland*; a dramatisation of the republican hunger strike of 1981, *H3* (Les Blair, 2002); the political drama, *Mapmaker* (Johnny Gogan, 2001); *Wild about Harry*; and *Puckoon*.

All of these films (with the exception of *Wild about Harry*) also obtained support from Bord Scannán na hÉireann/the Irish Film Board and indicate the growing collaboration between the two bodies. The IFB was initially established in 1982 but, in a bout of monetarist rectitude, was then shut down by the Irish government in 1987. Following the establishment of a new government coalition between Fianna Fáil and Labour in 1992, the Board was resurrected in 1993 with a budget of IR £1 million that had risen to €12 million by 2002. Although the Board was expected to generate economic returns within the Republic, it was nevertheless 'all-Ireland' in cultural orientation and offered support to film-makers from all parts of the island. The second Board's first chief executive, Rod Stoneman, was not only the director of a documentary on the media and the 'troubles', *Ireland: the Silent Voices*, but, prior to joining the Film Board, had worked for the Department of Independent Film and Video at Channel 4, which funded the work of Derry Film and Video. Even before any significant funding became available in the

North, therefore, there was a willingness on the part of the Board to fund films on Northern Irish topics such as *Some Mother's Son* (1996), *Nothing Personal* (1996) and *The Boxer* (1997). Indeed, given the controversies that these films generated, there were even attacks upon the Board by pro-unionist critics such as Alexander Walker for opening up a 'second front' within the Republic and promoting 'nationalist propaganda'.[42] While some films such as *The Uncle Jack* also obtained funding from both the NIFC and the IFB before 1996, it was the availability of lottery and EU funding in the North that transformed the financing landscape. Producers were now able to obtain public funding (and, from 1997, tax breaks) on both sides of the border and, as a result, the majority of publicly funded films in Northern Ireland (including *Bogwoman*, *Sunset Heights*, *A Love Divided*, *The Most Fertile Man in Ireland*, *Country*, *Puckoon*, *Mapmaker*, *H3*, *Blind Flight* and *Freeze Frame*, which all received support from both the NIFC and the IFB) took advantage of this possibility. To this extent, film production in the North has depended heavily upon the availability of incentives in the South, while, somewhat ironically, 'all-Ireland' film production has benefited from the extra financial incentives that have been an indirect consequence of partition.

From arts policy to economic policy

Such developments were, of course, underpinned by a broader set of political and economic changes. After some twenty-five years of armed conflict, both republican and loyalist groups declared ceasefires in 1994. Although outbreaks of violence continued, the ceasefires nevertheless laid the basis for a transformation of the political landscape within Northern Ireland, resulting in the Good Friday Agreement of 1998 and the subsequent elections to a devolved assembly and the eventual (if temporary) formation of its first executive in 1999. As long as the 'troubles' continued, there were clearly major – physical and financial – risks involved in filming in Northern Ireland and the majority of films dealing with the North (such as those directed by Jim Sheridan) simply substituted English or southern Irish locations for actual northern ones. With the onset of the peace process, however, there was clearly some prospect that Northern Ireland itself might become a more attractive place in which to film. Moreover, if the Unionist government saw no economic benefit ('direct or indirect') to Northern Ireland in film production in the immediate postwar period, the economic and political context in which film-making occurred from the 1990s onwards had radically altered.

Since the late 1960s and early 1970s – when the British government introduced direct rule in response to continuing political violence, the failure of internment and Unionist inability to effect significant political reform – the Northern Ireland economy had become increasingly dependent upon public subsidy. Thus, according to Brian Barton, 45 per cent of industrial workers in Northern Ireland in 1981 were employed by companies in receipt of British government aid.[43] The character of the local economy, moreover, had undergone dramatic change. Due to the long-term decline of heavy industries such as shipbuilding and engineering, the reversal of trends in international investment from the mid-1970s onwards (including *inter alia*

---

42. Letter to the *Irish Times*, 7 June 1996, p. 15. These three films are discussed further in the following chapter.

43. Brian Barton, *A Pocket History of Ulster* (Dublin: O'Brien Press, 1999), p. 165.

the virtual collapse of the artificial fibres sector that had been such a feature of government publicity of the early 1960s) and the instability created by ongoing republican and loyalist violence, employment in the manufacturing sector had dropped to nearly 60 per cent of the figure for the 1950s.[44] If the strong industrial character of the North, and its links to Empire, had once provided the economic underpinnings of partition, the Northern Ireland economy had, by the 1990s, become largely 'deindustrialised', with 70 per cent of the workforce in 1993 employed in either services or the public sector and 10 per cent unemployed.[45] While this experience of deindustrialisation was shared with other parts of the United Kingdom (partly as a result of the policies of the Thatcher government in the 1980s), it was particularly acute in Northern Ireland. Thus, as Frank Gaffikin and Mike Morrissey show, both the number of manufacturing jobs lost and service jobs gained in Belfast between 1981 and 1991 compared unfavourably with cities such as Cardiff, Leeds and Nottingham.[46]

It was this change in the character of the Northern Ireland economy, and the loss of its traditional manufacturing base, that encouraged a shift in government attitudes towards the role of film in Northern Ireland. Faced with the decline of the manufacturing sector and growing unemployment, the British government and local agencies began to adopt new socio-economic strategies intended to promote a service-led economy. Following the example of other regions, there was also a growing recognition of the role that the arts, and cultural activity more generally, might play in economic regeneration and urban renewal. Steve McIntyre, for example, indicates how a strategy for the 'cultural industries' was first adopted by the Greater London Council in the early 1980s as a way of intervening in and transforming the social base and profile of the arts in the city. Other cities in England, he argues, followed but placed an increased premium upon economic rather than socio-political objectives:

What happened . . . was that the terms began to shift and the emphasis increasingly began to be placed on cultural industries as industries like any others – areas in which local authorities could intervene and thereby generate jobs, urban regeneration, economic development and so on. Increas-

---

44. Mark McGovern and Peter Shirlow, 'Counter-insurgency, Deindustrialisation and the Political Economy of Ulster Loyalism', in Peter Shirlow and Mark McGovern (eds), *Who are 'The People'? Unionism, Protestantism and Loyalism in Northern Ireland* (London: Pluto Press, 1997), p. 188.

45. *Irish Almanac and Yearbook of Facts, 1997* (Burt: Artcam, 1997), pp. 144–6. The decline of the Northern Ireland economy, combined with substantial economic growth in the Republic of Ireland, also ended the North's traditional economic superiority over the rest of the island. Thus, while the GDP of Northern Ireland still represented 50 per cent of the Republic of Ireland GDP in 1992, this had dropped to only 25 per cent by 2003 (a percentage below Northern Ireland's share of the population). See *Northern Ireland Yearbook 2005* (Belfast: Lagan Consulting, 2004), p. 281.

46. Frank Gaffikin and Mike Morrissey, 'The Urban Economy and Social Exclusion: The Case of Belfast', in Frank Gaffikin and Mike Morrissey (eds), *City Visions: Imagining Place, Enfranchising People* (London: Pluto Press, 1999), p. 45.

ingly the sponsoring department would be economic development rather than arts and cultural services.[47]

While the circumstances in the 1980s may not have been propitious for this kind of development in Northern Ireland, the advent of the peace process in the 1990s opened up the possibility of similar initiatives there. One of the key texts informing the debates about the cultural industries in Britain was John Myerscough's study, *The Economic Importance of the Arts* (1988). In this, Myerscough not only identifies the arts (including film) as a significant economic activity in its own right but also assesses the economic impact and influence of arts activity more generally. In doing so, he concludes that the arts generate growth in ancillary industries, offer a cost-effective way of creating and sustaining employment, provide a catalyst for urban renewal, raise the profile and business attractiveness of a region and stimulate tourism.[48] Myerscough was subsequently recruited to undertake a similar study of the situation in Northern Ireland, resulting in the publication of *The Arts and the Northern Ireland Economy* in 1996. In this, Myerscough identified the potential economic benefits of increased investment in the arts and cultural industries within Northern Ireland and called upon government to 'give more strategic consideration' to the cultural sector.[49] This led, in turn, to a government seminar, hosted by the Department of Education, to consider how cultural policy might be employed to foster tourism, create employment and regenerate the local economy.

Other developments gave added impetus to these initiatives. In Britain, a new Labour government was elected in 1997 and rechristened the old Department of National Heritage the Department for Culture, Media and Sport. Partly as a way of securing additional funding for his department, the new Culture Minister, Chris Smith, lay stress on creativity as an essential component of a knowledge-based economy and set up an inter-departmental Creative Industries Task Force to assess what steps government might take to increase the 'wealth-creating potential' of cultural acivity.[50] 'Maximising the contribution' of the creative industries to the economy also became one of the department's 'key objectives' and informed its funding of client bodies such as the newly established UK Film Council, which, in line with its remit 'to help develop a sustainable UK film industry', promoted the vision of the UK as a 'film hub' or 'creative core' that could supply 'skills and services to the global film market'.[51]

---

47. Steve McIntyre, 'Art and Industry: Regional Film and Video Policy in the UK', in Albert Moran (ed.), *Film Policy: International, National and Regional Perspectives* (London: Routledge, 1996), p. 224. Jim McGuigan provides a more wide-ranging survey of debates about the 'cultural industries' in which he notes how the Frankfurt School's original formulation of the term derived from hostility towards the industrialisation of culture. See *Culture and the Public Sphere* (London: Routledge, 1996), ch. 4.

48. John Myerscough, *The Economic Importance of the Arts* (London: Policy Studies Institute, 1988), pp. 148–50.

49. John Myerscough, *The Arts and the Northern Ireland Economy* (Belfast: Northern Ireland Economic Council, 1996), p. 180.

50. *Creative Industries Mapping Document 1998* (London: DCMS, 1998), p. 3. Smith's early speeches are also collected in *Creative Britain* (London: Faber and Faber, 1998).

51. Alan Parker, *Building a Sustainable UK Film Industry: A Presentation to the UK Film Industry* (London: UKFC, 2002), p. 10.

These developments were matched, on a more modest scale, by similar initiatives in Northern Ireland. Following the Good Friday Agreement and assembly elections, formal devolution of power to the Northern Ireland Assembly and its Executive Committee of Ministers finally occurred in December 1999. While the establishment of eleven new departments to replace the previous six was the result of the political arithmetic necessary to ensure all the main parties (the Official Unionist Party, the Social and Democratic Labour Party, the Democratic Unionist Party and Sinn Fein) were adequately represented at Ministerial level, its effect was also to enhance the political standing of arts and culture through the creation of a new Department of Culture, Arts and Leisure (DCAL) led by Michael McGimpsey, one of four Ministers from the Official Unionist Party. While McGimpsey has suggested that culture gained increasing importance for unionists as a 'battleground' once republicans abandoned the armed struggle, it would be hard to identify the work of DCAL with a traditional 'unionist' agenda comparable to that of the old Stormont regime.[52] For due to the complexities of power-sharing (and the requirement that key policy decisions be made on 'a cross-community basis'), the repeated suspensions of the Assembly (and the resulting lack of Ministerial continuity) and the absence of direct political involvement in the decision-making (and funding allocations) of bodies such as the Arts Council and the NIFTC (which, as already noted, was involved in the support of films sympathetic to republicanism such as *Bogwoman* and *H3*), it was very difficult for one party or politician to impose a clear stamp upon policy direction. Given these constraints upon political manoeuvring, DCAL policy was more 'technicist' than 'ideological' in character and mainly followed in the footsteps of 'New Labour'. This involved rolling out its own strategy for 'unlocking creativity' through the creation, in 2001, of a £3 million Creativity Seed Fund, planned to promote creativity in education and to strengthen the competitiveness of the creative industries in Northern Ireland.[53] The conception of film as a key creative industry also underlay the significant increase in support for film and television announced by the Northern Ireland Office Minister for Enterprise, Trade and Investment in 2003 (in the wake of the suspension of the Northern Ireland Assembly in October 2002).[54] Although the initiative had been championed by DCAL and enjoyed the support of several departments, the fact that it was announced by the Minister for Enterprise, Trade and Investment was indicative of the predominantly 'economic' thrust of the new measures, which included the establishment of a revamped Northern Ireland Film Production Fund offering loans that were much more substantial (up to £600,000) than those previously available in the region, a Company Development Fund intended to encourage the

---

52. Michael McGimpsey quoted in Henry Patterson, 'The Limits of the "New Unionism": David Trimble and the Ulster Unionist party', *Éire-Ireland*, vol. 30, nos 1-2, 2004, p. 181. Due to the failure to agree a new Executive in the wake of the Assembly elections of 2003, McGimpsey remained, as of 2005, the only politician to have occupied the position of Northern Ireland Minister of Culture, Arts and Leisure.

53. The 'Unlocking Creativity' strategy may be traced across a number of documents: Department of Culture, Arts and Leisure (DCAL), *Unlocking Creativity: A Strategy for Development* (Belfast, 2000); DCAL, *Unlocking Creativity: Making it Happen* (Belfast, 2001) and DCAL, *Unlocking Creativity: A Creative Region* (Belfast, 2004).

54. The NIFTC had been lobbying for a more generous version of these measures but had been hit by the suspension of the Assembly and return of British Ministers to the Northern Ireland Office. The objectives of this funding are described in DCAL, *Unlocking Creativity: A Creative Region*, p. 31.

growth of local independent media companies and a Product Development Fund designed to help local companies develop pilots or 'slates' aimed at network or international broadcasters.

Inevitably, these initiatives marked a new direction for film policy in Northern Ireland. Under the Unionist regime, film production policy was largely subordinated to propaganda purposes, promoting 'Ulster' as either a tourist attraction, a place to invest or a distinct constitutional entity. From the 1960s onwards, film began to achieve some recognition as a cultural form in its own right as well as a form of community expression and this encouraged the Arts Council of Northern Ireland to begin, somewhat hesitantly, to incorporate film into its remit. With the advent of the Film Council, however, the value of film as an 'industrial' activity, and the economic benefits that film could bring, was increasingly emphasised. It is, of course, the case that the Film Council (later Commission) has sought to combine 'industrial initiatives' in training, production and marketing with 'cultural' interventions in education, exhibition and archiving. However, given the way in which the organisation had to battle to obtain financial support, its priorities have also remained heavily dependent upon the agendas of its funders. Due to financial restrictions, and its funding by the then Department of Education, the activities of the Film Council were initially weighted in favour of 'cultural' and educational objectives. Following its change of name, and success in obtaining funds from the then Department of Economic Development, the restructured Film Commission placed much greater stress upon its 'economic' role. As Richard Taylor, the first director of the NIFC, was to note regarding the fate of two reports commissioned by the NIFC in 1994 – one on a film commission, the other on cultural cinema – it was only the first that proved capable of winning government support because, unlike cultural exhibition, it could be seen 'to generate direct economic benefit'.[55] In this respect, government support for the Film Commission marked both a departure and a degree of continuity with previous public policy. For while the focus upon the economic role of film represented a new development, it also shared with previous policies a measure of instrumentalism in the way that the objectives of film policy became principally defined in terms of the 'extraneous' economic benefits that, it was hoped, would ensue. This is, for example, very clear in the Northern Ireland Film Commission's strategy document, *The Most Powerful Industry in the World* (2001), which successfully made the case for the increase in government funding announced in 2003. Although, this does make reference to cultural production and educational policy, the core policy objectives are nonetheless overwhelmingly industrial in character, consisting of the creation of jobs, the attraction of inward investment and the building of 'a positive image for Northern Ireland' that will contribute to 'confidence building in all sectors, particularly for inward investment and tourism'.[56]

---

55. 'Good Timing: The Northern Ireland Film Commission and the Local Film Industry', in 'Green Screen: The State of the Contemporary Irish Film Industry', *Fortnight*, no. 379, p. 4.

56. Northern Ireland Film Commission, *The Most Powerful Industry in the World: A Strategy for the Development of the Film, Television and New Media Industries in Northern Ireland* (Belfast, 2001), p. 2. Some of the consequences of this promotion of a 'positive image' will be considered in the following chapter. However, it is also worth noting that while bodies such as the NIFTC do not carry the same ideological baggage as earlier bodies, such as the Ulster Tourist Development Association (discussed in Chapter 1), some of the same problems involved in promoting Northern Ireland as a distinct region have survived. Thus, while *The Most Fertile Man in Ireland* is set, and partly

Assessing economic performance

There can be little doubt that the developments from the early 1990s onwards have represented a significant watershed in the history of cinema and Northern Ireland. In the period since 1995, there has been an unprecedented growth of film-making activity that would have been inconceivable in preceding decades. This has been accompanied by a level of public funding that, either due to the lack of government interest in film or the inhospitable social and political circumstances prevailing in the North, did not previously exist. This, in turn, has been the consequence of the radically transformed character of the Northern Ireland economy and the new role allocated to film in economic regeneration. However, the lack of a film industry in Northern Ireland prior to the 1990s was not simply the result of government indifference but also the economic structure of the international film industry. Feature film-making is, of course, an especially high-risk industry and, within the West, it is only the Hollywood majors that – due to their scale of production, access to international distribution networks and cross-media interests – have proved capable of spreading the financial risks of production in such a way as to make film-making, more or less, consistently profitable.[57] Given the competitive advantage of Hollywood within the international market, it has therefore proved difficult for film industries within Europe to sustain economic viability and, in recent years, only a handful of British or Irish films have achieved significant commercial success. Thus, while both the Film Commission and the Arts Council (when it had direct responsibility for lottery funds) have sought to 'encourage the production of commercially successful feature films', this has proved a more difficult task than was originally believed, particularly due to the problems of distribution.[58] Some of the films, for example, failed to obtain distribution in either the UK or Ireland, while some of those that did received only a limited release. Even in the case of the most successful of the films, box-office returns proved relatively modest. *Divorcing Jack*, for example, was clearly conceived as an overtly commercial project and benefited from a strong marketing campaign, masterminded by Winchester Films, based around the image of Rachel Griffiths as 'the nun with a gun'. Nevertheless, it took only £470,000 at the UK box office and failed to obtain US distribution (although it did do reasonably well in Australia as a result of the involvement of Griffiths). While this was sufficient to make it one of the top twenty best-performing UK films of the year, it fell well behind the top twenty films overall and was clearly not quite the 'hit' that had been hoped for. *Lock, Stock and Two Smoking Barrels* (1998), for example, which cost slightly less than *Divorcing Jack*, earned over £11.5 million at UK cinemas during the same period.

---

shot, in Belfast, the title of the film would hardly suggest this. Similarly, although *With or Without You* was set and shot in Northern Ireland, and deals with a couple who are both Protestant and unionist, this did not prevent its promotion as a typically 'Irish' tale. The cover of the video, for example, employs green titling and a shamrock design and runs the quote, 'sexy, sassy and irresistibly Irish!'.

57. For a fuller discussion of Hollywood's domination of the international film industry and the consequent disadvantages faced by British and Irish film-makers, see John Hill, 'Cinema', in Jane Stokes and Anna Reading (eds), *The Media in Britain: Current Debates and Developments* (Basingstoke: Macmillan, 1999), pp. 74–87.

58. Arts Council of Northern Ireland, *The National Lottery Arts Fund: Film Development and Film Production: Information and Guidance for Applicants* (Belfast: ACNI), p. 3.

Mixed commercial fortunes: David Thewlis in *Divorcing Jack*

Problems of distribution and exhibition are not, of course, restricted to 'Northern Ireland films' but extend to Irish and British (and indeed European) films more generally. Thus, over 50 per cent of films made in the UK in 1997, for example, had failed to secure a cinema release over a year later.[59] Given the massive domination of the distribution sector in Ireland and Britain by subsidiaries of the Hollywood majors and the general decline in more specialist outlets for European films, it has therefore proved difficult for most low- to medium-budget films to achieve a significant return from the cinema box office. This has also been true of the video and DVD (rental and retail) markets, which are now worth more than that for cinema exhibition. However, while some films (such as *Wild about Harry* and *With or Without You*) earned more from video and DVD than cinema release, the overall results have been poor, given the tendency for performance in these markets to follow the pattern of theatrical release.[60]

The relatively poor commercial performance of these films has also meant that there has been a correspondingly low level of recoupment (of around 5 per cent) on the loans that the Arts Council and the NIFTC have invested in film production. In 1999, for example, it was reported that ACNI had recouped only £4,894 on its award of £150,000 to *Titanic Town* and

59. Eddie Dyja (ed.), *BFI Film and Television Handbook 2001* (London: BFI, 2000), p. 28.

60. Partly on the back of the following for cult comedian Lee Evans, the digital video feature *Freeze Frame* – initially entitled *Straight to Video* and backed by the UK video arm of Universal – seems to have been more obviously aimed at the video and DVD markets than previous Northern Ireland films.

even less on its investment of the same sum in *Cycle of Violence* (aka *Crossmaheart*).[61] Low levels of return were, of course, a feature of UK lottery funding of film more generally, particularly during the 1990s, and there was a substantial amount of grumbling in the British press about the 'waste' of money that this appeared to involve.[62] Certainly, in the case of England, where substantial sums (amounting to over £90 million) were spent on film franchises intended to act as 'mini-studios' that would alleviate some of the structural problems of the UK film industry, low levels of commercial success did indicate a genuine failure of strategy. However, in the case of Northern Ireland (and, to a lesser extent, the Republic of Ireland), it has been argued that the benefit of public funding of film should not be measured in terms of commercial returns but the amount of 'spend' on local labour and services to which film production leads. From this perspective, what is significant is not the box-office success of, or return from, an individual film but the contribution a film makes to the local economy, and the indirect 'return' on investment that this provides. Thus, in the case of the eleven feature films funded by either the Arts Council or the Film Commission between 1997 and 1999, it has been estimated that just over £1.2 million of public funding generated a spend in Northern Ireland of just over £4 million.[63] While in some cases (such as *Cycle of Violence* and *Titanic Town*) the level of spend barely exceeded the level of Arts Council support, in other cases (particularly the BBC Northern Ireland productions *Divorcing Jack* and *Wild about Harry*) spending was significantly higher than the original funding provided by ACNI and the NIFC.

However, the precise extent to which such spending benefits the local economy can be hard to unravel. Most of the films that have been funded by the Arts Council and the Film Commission have originated from either Dublin or London and have drawn extensively on personnel from elsewhere. According to a report by Cambridge Economics, over 55 per cent of expenditure on location shoots is typically attributable to cast and crew. Given the higher than average proportion of people from outside the region involved in 'Northern Irish' film projects (along with the lower than average levels of production budgets), this means that the economic multiplier, or knock-on, effects of film production in Northern Ireland have been generally lower than in other parts of the UK.[64] Moreover, because of its temporary character (often

---

61. 'Arts Councils recoup £2.5m from film loans', *Screen Finance*, 31 March 1999, p. 5. In terms of arts funding, it is still relatively unusual for projects to receive loans rather than grants. The fact that loans are the norm in the case of film reflects not only the sums involved but also the 'commercial' expectations attached to film production. However, given the low level of return on these 'loans', they do, in effect, become grants.

62. For a discussion of the press campaign directed at lottery-funded films in England, see Julian Petley, 'From Brit-flicks to Shit-flicks: The Cost of Public Subsidy', *Journal of Popular British Cinema*, no. 5, 2002, pp. 37–52. Although it has not achieved anything like the same intensity as in Britain, there has also been some debate in the Republic of Ireland about the recoupment rate (13 per cent between 1993 and 2000) of films supported by the Irish Film Board. However, partly due to the Board's clear policy of supporting 'different scales of film . . . for different audiences', concerns about the economic performance of films have been tempered by a much stronger awareness of the cultural value of government film funding. See Rod Stoneman, 'Icons of the Imagination', in Kevin Rockett, *Ten Years After: The Irish Film Board 1993–2003* (Galway: Bord Scannán na hÉireann/Irish Film Board, 2003), p. vii.

63. Figures are derived from *A Film Studio for Northern Ireland?*, p. 14.

64. Cambridge Economics, *Economic Impact of the UK Screen Industries* (Cambridge, 2005), pp. 60–70.

amounting to no more than a few weeks), the contribution of location shooting to the expansion of the local industry and skills base is necessarily limited. Thus, in an assessment of the economic benefits of the fifteen films shot in Northern Ireland between 1997 and 2000, the consultants Olsberg were forced to conclude that the resulting 'production spend' had been insufficient to deliver either 'a sustainable indigenous film industry' or 'an internationally competitive skills base'.[65] The attractiveness of Northern Ireland as a place to film, moreover, depends upon such a range of factors (including the exchange rate, the level of financial incentives and the availability of specialised services and facilities) that outside productions on their own are unlikely to provide sufficient annual flow to sustain the necessary industrial infrastructure – as was partly demonstrated by the collapse of the Paint Hall Studios in Belfast, which floundered due to lack of demand.[66]

From a purely economic point of view, therefore, film is undoubtedly less important to a sustainable creative economy in Northern Ireland than television. This would seem to have been recognised by the NIFC, in 2002, when it changed its name for a second time to the Northern Ireland Film and Television Commission (NIFTC) in order to signal the importance of television, rather than just film, to the delivery of its economic objectives. Moreover, for all the hyperbole involved in its invocation of film as the 'most powerful industry in the world', there has also been an increased emphasis upon the development of independent production companies engaged in the production of (non-drama) television material with the capacity to generate recurring business (such as lifestyle programmes and game shows). However, while there has been a significant growth of independent production companies in Northern Ireland since the 1980s, it is, of course, BBC Northern Ireland that remains the major player in terms of levels of both expenditure and employment. However, it too has taken stock of its involvement in film production. Given the relatively low level of financial returns on its feature films, the Drama Department has found it difficult to justify the added costs that film production entails (the four-hour series *Eureka Street*, for example, cost the same as one ninety-minute feature). While the BBC is not, of course, dependent upon direct financial returns in the same way as conventional film production companies, the competitiveness of the television environment has made it, and other broadcasters (including the pioneering Channel 4), increasingly reluctant to 'subsidise' film production when it does not lead to either revenues or viewing figures commensurate with the costs involved. Thus, while most people in the UK would have seen *Divorcing Jack* on television, its viewing total of one million, when it was broadcast in December 2000, was comparatively small in relation to the figure of 7.6 million for BBC Northern Ireland's detective drama series, *McGready and Daughter*, shown earlier the same year.[67]

---

65. Olsberg, *A Development Strategy for the Northern Ireland Film and Broadcast Sector* (London, 2001), p. 6.

66. In a telling symbol of the new 'post-industrial' economic order, the Paint Hall Studios were located in a former workshop owned by the shipbuilding firm, Harland and Wolff. The studio opened in 2001 and *Puckoon* was its first and only production. Although the Film Commission helped to publicise this initiative, it had already undertaken a feasibility study of a Northern Ireland film studio that concluded that it would be likely 'to make large operating losses' (*A Film Studio for Northern Ireland?*, p. 6).

67. Eddie Dyja (ed.), *BFI Film and Television Handbook 2002* (London: BFI, 2001), p. 59.

Thus, apart from an occasional partnership with BBC Films in London (as in the case of the NIFTC/Irish Film Board-funded *The Mighty Celt* [2005]), the BBC Northern Ireland Drama Department has chosen to concentrate on drama series aimed for network transmission. While many of these television series have been popular with audiences, they have often only been local in name, consisting of productions – such as *Messiah* (2001–), *Murphy's Law* (2003) and *Gunpowder, Treason and Plot* (2004) – that are shot outside Northern Ireland with only the minimum of involvement from Northern Ireland personnel. The 'BBC Northern Ireland' production, *Gunpowder, Treason and Plot*, for example, was made by the English independent production company, Box TV, written by the Liverpudlian Jimmy McGovern, directed by the Scot Gillies McKinnon and shot entirely in Romania with a mainly Scottish crew. While the Department has maintained a commitment to one-off regional productions – such as *As the Beast Sleeps* (2001) and *Holy Cross* (2003) – these have been much rarer than in the past. It is, therefore, one of the ironies of the local film and television economy that, while increasing amounts of public funding are spent attempting to attract productions into Northern Ireland, the major public service broadcaster within Northern Ireland, and the region's most important producer of filmed drama, spends the bulk of its drama budget outside of the region (and, as in the case of *Eureka Street*, takes advantage of lottery money simply to shoot in its own backyard). In this way, the internal competition for resources within the BBC (and the 'outsourcing' of production to independent companies) may help to promote regionalisation (by allowing regional drama departments to increase the size of their budgets) but it also subverts it by effectively detaching production from its nominal place of origin as well as the specific cultural concerns associated with a given 'region'.

Cultural value?

In their *Opening Up the Arts* report, Anthony Everitt and Annabel Jackson called upon the Arts Council of Northern Ireland to define its remit more clearly than hitherto. In this respect, the recommendation that the Arts Council should delegate its lottery budget for film to the Film Commission was premised on the assumption that the Commission was not only better placed than the Council to discharge responsibilities in this area but also that film involved 'industrial and commercial concerns' that fell outside what might legitimately be regarded as the proper remit of the Arts Council.[68] While there was much to be said for this, and it was apparent that the Arts Council had failed to develop a coherent policy towards film, it also helped to reinforce the notion that film did not really belong among the arts and that the justification for government intervention on behalf of film therefore rested on grounds that were different from the rest of the arts.[69] In a sense, this involved both a gain and a loss. A recognition of the 'industrial and

---

68. *Opening Up the Arts*, p. 47.

69. This sense of film's distinctiveness remains in an essay by the UK Secretary of State for Culture, Media and Sport, Tessa Jowell, in which she seeks to question the valuation of culture in terms of 'its instrumental benefits to other agendas' and makes a case for the support of 'culture on its own terms'. Nevertheless, although the Department for Culture, Media and Sport possesses a responsibility for film, there is no reference in the essay to film as an example of cultural activity despite numerous allusions to drama, painting, music, museums and opera. See *Government and the Value of Culture* (London: DCMS, 2004).

commercial' aspects of film production resulted in substantially more public investment in film than would have been otherwise the case. On the other hand, the emphasis upon the economic and industrial value of film also meant that support for film on cultural and artistic grounds became much less important. However, given the identification of film as a 'good cause' for the purposes of lottery funding and the amounts of public subsidy that have been provided to 'Northern Ireland films' by agencies not only in Northern Ireland but also in England, Scotland and the Republic of Ireland, it seems right that the assessment of 'public benefit' should extend beyond the measurement of economic spend. Indeed, given the economic fragility of the film industry in both Britain and Ireland, it is difficult to see how state support for film could ever be realistically justified on exclusively economic grounds. As Kate Oakley suggests with regard to the UK government's 'creative industries' policy, the privilege that film enjoys over computer games in terms of tax incentives and public subsidies has hardly been based on economic considerations alone.[70] Indeed, although film policy in the UK has traditionally been 'industrial' in character, film has nevertheless benefited from the perception that it constitutes a culturally important form of symbolic expression that distinguishes it from other forms of tradeable goods (and which, therefore, partly justifies the levels of public expenditure upon it). Thus, while the Conservative government of the early 1980s did indeed seek to treat film like any other economic activity and subject it to the bracing winds of the 'free market' (by abolishing the quota for British films in British cinemas, the Eady Levy and tax incentives), its later decision to allocate a share of National Lottery revenues to film funds not only involved a form of government intervention denied to other industries but also marked a retreat from the attempt to create a purely 'economic' policy for film production.

However, if cultural assumptions inevitably underpin economic policies directed towards film, it is also the case that economic policies themselves result in a *de facto* cultural policy in relation to the kinds of films that obtain support. It has, for example, been common to account for the poor commercial performance of many publicly funded films in terms of their dependence upon various forms of 'soft' finance from public bodies such as the NIFTC and BSE/IFB (rather than from commercial investors). On the other hand, it might also be argued that the combination of public funding sources in this way also results in a 'soft' cultural agenda due to the lack of influence that the different funding bodies are able to exert over the films they support. This could certainly be said of Northern Ireland, where the relatively low proportion contributed to film budgets works against a significant creative or editorial input into the projects that are funded. As a result, the logistics of getting films made (and having them shoot in the region) prevail over considerations of the contribution such films may make to the local culture.

However, as Steve McIntyre suggests in relation to film policy in Scotland, there is a danger that without any clear 'cultural programme' 'precious arts funding' will simply 'end up doing little more than propping up (inadequately) commercial filmmaking'.[71] While it would be unfair

70. Kate Oakley, 'Not So Cool Britannia: The Role of the Creative Industries in Economic Development', *International Journal of Cultural Studies*, vol. 7, no. 1, 2004, p. 74.

71. Steve McIntyre, 'Vanishing Point: Feature Film Production in a Small Country', in John Hill, Martin McLoone and Paul Hainsworth (eds), *Border Crossing: Film in Ireland, Britain and Europe* (Belfast/London: Institute of Irish Studies/BFI, 1994), p. 107.

(but not completely so) to suggest that this has occurred in Northern Ireland, it could never-theless be argued that the prioritisation of economic over cultural goals in Northern Ireland film policy has led to the production of films that fall between two stools. On the one hand, virtually all of the films produced have been insufficiently 'commercial' in scale or production values to succeed in the marketplace either at home or abroad. On the other hand, by seeking commer-cial success through the adoption of familiar formulae, many have stuck too closely to the pre-vailing models of genre cinema (such as romantic comedy) to be able to achieve the kind of artistic invention or cultural significance that would announce the arrival of a new and distinc-tive form of film-making in Northern Ireland. Thus, despite the higher sums of money available within Northern Ireland to fund film production, the kind of culturally challenging 'indigenous' films (such as *Maeve*, *Acceptable Levels*, *Hush-a-Bye Baby*) supported by the BFI Production Board and Channel 4 in the 1980s have all but disappeared. Obviously, this is partly due to more gen-eral changes in the socio-political and industrial climate in Britain and Ireland. However, it is also partly the result of a lack of clarity in public policy concerning the cultural value of local film-making and the subordination of cultural to economic objectives.

Conclusion

In his discussion of state film policies, Toby Miller has noted how there is typically a tension between 'the desire to build a viable sector of the economy that provides employment, foreign exchange and multiplier effects' and 'the desire for a representative and local cinema that reflects seriously upon society through drama'.[72] Within Northern Ireland, there was, for a long time, no real desire to invest in film for either economic or cultural reasons and when such desires did become manifest, there was no funding available with which to pursue them. The onset of sig-nificant public investment in film coincided with a period of social and economic reconstruc-tion within Northern Ireland, which meant that a particular premium was placed upon the economic benefits that film production might deliver. While cultural objectives have clearly informed policies towards education, exhibition and archiving within Northern Ireland, there has been a much less clearly articulated cultural policy for film production (particularly in the case of features but, to some extent, with regard to shorts as well).[73] However, given the emo-tional and symbolic importance of the ways in which people and places are represented, and in which stories are told, in films relating to the North, the production of film in Northern Ire-land is clearly much more than an economic matter. The following chapter, therefore, will seek to identify some of the cinematic traditions that have dominated the representation of North-ern Ireland before going on to assess the extent to which recent films have conformed to, or departed from, the established images.

---

72. Toby Miller, 'The Film Industry and the Government: "Endless Mr Beans and Mr Bonds"?', in Robert Murphy (ed.), *British Cinema of the 90s* (London: BFI, 2000), p. 44.

73. Since the advent of the 'Northern Lights' scheme in 1994, well over fifty shorts have been produced in Northern Ireland. In his discussion of shorts made in Ireland as a whole, Martin McLoone notes how these too are often torn between economic and cultural imperatives in *Irish Film: The Emergence of a Contemporary Cinema* (London: BFI, 2000), p. 156.

7

'It's chaos out there'

Changing Representations of 'the Troubles'

The Devil's Own (1997) was one of a number of Hollywood films, made in the mid-1990s, to incorporate republican paramilitaries into their story-lines. Set in Northern Ireland in 1972, the film opens with images of a father and son at sea, followed by their return home to a farm close to the shore, where they sit down to a family meal. The peacefulness of the scene is cruelly interrupted, however, when a masked gunman bursts into the house and kills the father in front of his visibly traumatised son. The film then cuts to twenty years later when the son, now a grown man, engages in a bitter fight with security forces. Although the histrionics engaged in by the characters is more reminiscent of Dodge City than modern-day Belfast, the sequence provides a strikingly different image of Northern Ireland characterised by urban conflict, dark interiors, enclosed spaces and run-down buildings. While it was the casting of 'the sexiest man alive', Brad Pitt, as the quixotic IRA hero that plunged the film straight into controversy, the film's stark contrast between rural tranquillity and urban strife relied, nevertheless, upon two of the most common cinematic images of Ireland.[1] However, although both scenes are supposedly set in the North, there is little doubt that most cinema audiences would be inclined to associate the first image with the South of Ireland, particularly given the way in which the film uses James Horner's pseudo-'Celtic' score to add an extra level of poignancy to the drama.[2] It is also undoubtedly the case that the film's images of urban 'Belfast', and their association with violent conflict, would be regarded as conforming to some of the most readily identifiable signifiers of Northern Ireland since the resurgence of the 'troubles' in the late 1960s.

As previously indicated, there was for a long time an uneasy oscillation between rural and urban imagery within films dealing with Northern Ireland due to the competing discursive

---

1. Despite the death of Pitt's character at the film's end, the film was condemned in many sections of the British press and Princess Diana was forced into an apology for taking her sons, William and Harry, to see it. For a discussion of the image of the IRA man contained not just in *The Devil's Own* but also *Blown Away* (1994) and *Patriot Games* (1992), see Martin McLoone, *Irish Film: The Emergence of a Contemporary Cinema* (London: BFI, 2000), pp. 64–8.
2. Colin McArthur discusses the 'tearful Celticism' contributed by Horner's music to the film *Braveheart* (1995) in his book *Brigadoon, Braveheart and the Scots* (London: I. B. Tauris, 2003), ch. 7. Horner's music also constitutes a significant element of James Cameron's 'Irishified' version of the sinking of the Titanic, *Titanic* (1997). For a discussion of the significance of changing film portraits of the Titanic for the place where it was built, see John Hill, 'The Relaunching of Ulster Pride: The Titanic, Belfast and Film', in Tim Bergfelder and Sarah Street (eds), *The Titanic in Myth and Memory: Representations in Visual and Literary Culture* (London: I. B. Tauris, 2004).

regimes within which images of Northern Ireland were constructed. In the 1930s, the Richard Hayward films sought to 'imagine' Northern Ireland – or 'Ulster' – identity in terms of rural imagery but, given their adoption of the conventions of musical comedy, found their ambitions to represent 'Ulster' as a distinct location subverted by the pre-existing associations of rural Ireland with cultural nationalism and Celtic mysticism. Moreover, while much of the North's distinctiveness from the rest of Ireland rested upon its urban-industrial character, official and semi-official films made for the Unionist government were also inclined to veer towards the rural, laying stress on the farming community as the economic and ideological cornerstone of Northern Irish society. The main reason for this was the difficulty unionism found (other than during the special circumstances of the Second World War when increased industrial productivity was at a premium) in projecting a positive image of the city, not only because of the hold of pastoralist ideology across the United Kingdom more generally but also because of the specific associations with sectarianism and social division that Belfast carried. It was for this reason that *Odd Man Out* created a degree of discomfort for the Unionist regime when it first appeared, not so much because of its politics but as a result of the way in which it cast doubt upon Belfast's status as a 'normal' industrialised city.

Odd Man Out and the 'troubles' paradigm

The significance of *Odd Man Out*, however, was not simply that it was the first film to deal with the conflict within the North since the onset of partition but also because, artistically, it set the pattern for many cinematic portraits of the 'troubles' that followed. Combining tragic narration with expressionist stylistics (indebted to both French poetic realism and film noir), the film may be seen to have cultivated a particular view of the 'troubles' based upon metaphysics (the pessimistic workings of fate) rather than politics, a conflict between public and private spheres and a tension between different forms of male 'hero'.[3] As in classical tragedy, the film's story is concerned with the irreversible consequences of an initial error. The Head of the 'Organisation', Johnny McQueen (James Mason), is shot following an ill-advised, and armed, mill robbery and is left to wander the city at night. Despite the efforts to save him, his fate is already sealed and, in an emotional climax partly borrowed from Julien Duvivier's *Pepé le Moko* (1936), Johnny dies in the arms of the woman who has tried to save him, while his last remaining hope of escape, the ship, is shown to sail off without them. The sense of inevitability that this involves is reinforced by the film's iconography (the recurring appearance of the Albert Clock, the deteriorating weather) and the film's use of low-key lighting and claustrophobic compositions that create a vivid sense of enclosure and impending doom.

A number of features, set to recur in subsequent films concerning the 'troubles', are worth noting. First, although the film was shot at least partly in Belfast, the film's stylised and expressionistic visual design invests the city with an abstract, 'placeless' quality reminiscent of Robert Warshow's description of the 'sad city of the imagination' evident in the gangster film.[4] In this

---

3. This argument was first developed in 'Images of Violence', in Kevin Rockett, Luke Gibbons and John Hill, *Cinema and Ireland* (London: Routledge, 1988), pp. 152–60.

4. Robert Warshow, 'The Gangster as Tragic Hero', in *The Immediate Experience* (New York: Atheneum, 1974), p. 131.

respect, the film's representation of the city works less to denote an actual place (Belfast) than connote 'the city in general' and the 'universal' drama to which it plays host. Borrowing from the example of Sean O'Casey, the film also establishes a firm opposition between the public world of politics and violence (which is associated with tragedy and fatalism) and the private world of romance, home and domesticity (which is linked with the avoidance of politics and the possibility of 'redemption'). The doomed romance of Johnny and Kathleen (Kathleen Ryan) in the film is therefore connected to both Johnny's failure to disentangle himself from the violent methods of his organisation and Kathleen's own refusal to follow the advice of Granny (Kitty Kirwan) to remain at home and enjoy a normal life. One element of the pathos engendered by the film's ending does, of course, derive from Johnny's earlier expression of a desire to abandon violence in favour of parliamentary activity. This, in turn, sets up a distinction between two types of male protagonist within the film, the misguided but fundamentally decent IRA man (Johnny) who cultivates doubts about the value of arms versus the more fanatical, hardliner (in this case Dennis, played by Robert Beatty) who remains wedded to the violent prosecution of 'the cause'. However, despite the recoil of the film from the violence of the 'Organisation', the film, nevertheless, reveals an ambivalence in its overall disposition towards violence. Partly as a result of the drive towards a narrative conclusion, and partly due to the operation of genre conventions, the film ends with Johnny and Kathy – like Pat (Cyril Cusack) and Nolan (Dan O'Herlihy) before them – shot dead by the police. While the victory of the forces of 'law and order' over the threat of 'criminality' would be unexceptionable in a Hollywood crime film, it is clearly more problematic in the case of a film about Northern Ireland, not only because of the violence involved (at a time when the police in Britain were not themselves armed) but also the politically contested character of the police in Northern Ireland and the constitutional arrangements – and exceptional forms of legislation – with which they are associated.

At the time of its appearance, *Odd Man Out* was, of course, unusual insofar as it dealt with Northern Ireland at all. Given the low international profile of the Northern Ireland situation in the postwar period, few film-makers were attracted to it as a topic for drama, particularly as there could be no expectation that audiences outside of Ireland would be familiar with, or possess an interest in, the history of the region. As a result, few films followed in *Odd Man Out*'s footsteps, while those that did were faced with the prospect of incomprehension. Thus, when Ealing Studios produced the Irish 'thriller', *The Gentle Gunman* (1952), loosely based on the IRA's 1939 bombing campaign in England, the critic of the London *Evening Standard* declared self-righteously that 'the English no longer care' about 'the Irish question' and that such a film would only be met by 'passive indifference'.[5]

However, if the resurgence of the 'troubles' at the end of the 1960s rekindled consciousness of the 'Irish question', it remained an issue with which the cinema was reluctant to engage. There were various reasons for this. Following the emergence of the Civil Rights Movement, and the responses this provoked, British television, which had for long largely ignored the situation in Northern Ireland, now became the main conduit for news, documentary and, to a lesser

---

5. Milton Shulman, 'Mr. Mills drags up the Irish question (but why?)', *Evening Standard*, 23 October 1952. My discussion of the film may be found in *Cinema and Ireland*, pp. 160–4.

extent, plays about the conflict. Moreover, although the British state had retained responsibility for the governance of Northern Ireland since the partition of Ireland in 1921, the despatch of British troops to Northern Ireland in 1969 – followed by the suspension of Stormont and the imposition of direct rule from Westminster in 1972 – marked a decisive end to the 'arm's-length' relationship that successive British governments had adopted in relationship to Unionist rule. Given the increased militarisation of the conflict and the direct involvement of British politicians in 'managing' the crisis (and waging the 'war' against paramilitary groups), there was an increased sensitivity among the ranks of both British politicians and senior television personnel concerning the way in which the conflict was represented. This, in turn, led to a growing reluctance to transmit certain kinds of material, the censorship of various programmes and, in some cases, outright bans.[6] This policy also extended to the transmission of films relating to Northern Ireland that were deemed to be either 'controversial' or 'anti-British'. Thus, despite an apparent financial stake in the film, the BBC chose not to broadcast Marcel Ophuls' documentary *A Sense of Loss* (1972), filmed in Northern Ireland in late 1971 and early 1972, on the grounds that it was too 'pro-Irish'.[7] In November 1971, the Irish government also introduced a directive under Section 31 of the Broadcasting Authority Act that formally banned the Irish state broadcaster, Radio Telefís Éireann (RTÉ), from transmitting 'any matter that could be calculated to promote the aims and objectives of any organisation' involved in 'the attaining of any particular objective by violent means'.[8] As a result, television in Ireland became even more constrained than British television in what it could show.

Although by this time the BBFC had abandoned the overt political censorship it operated in the 1930s, most feature films continued to avoid the issue of Northern Ireland, not only on the grounds that the 'troubles' were viewed as an unlikely source of 'entertainment' but also because of an awareness of the controversy to which such films, like their television counterparts, could lead. Thus, the first British feature film to tackle the 'troubles' following the renewal of conflict, *Hennessy* (1975), was immediately mired in difficulties. Dealing with a plot to blow up the Houses of Parliament by Belfast man, Niall Hennessy (Rod Steiger), whose wife and daughter have been inadvertently killed by British troops, the film was viewed by EMI chairman, John Read, and picture and theatre division head, Bernard Delfont, who decided against showing the film in ABC cinemas on the grounds that the film exploited the 'troubles' for entertainment.[9] Rank, the owners of the Odeon chain of cinemas, the other main circuit in Britain

---

6. For an overview of the early controversies surrounding the reporting of Northern Ireland, see Liz Curtis, *Ireland: The Propaganda War* (London: Pluto, 1984). Such was the prevailing sense of British television's failure to provide a full account of the situation in Northern Ireland that two of the first films funded by Channel 4 in the early 1980s, *Acceptable Levels* (Belfast Film Workshop, 1983) and *Giro City* (Karl Francis, 1982), dealt with the way in which television news and documentary coverage of the 'troubles' had fallen victim to 'self-censorship'.

7. David Robinson, *The Times*, 23 January 1976. The film also failed to obtain commercial distribution in British cinemas.

8. See Desmond Fisher, *Broadcasting in Ireland* (London: Routledge and Kegan Paul, 1978) for a discussion. Another directive was issued in 1976 forbidding the broadcast of interviews with members of republican organisations and groups proscribed in Northern Ireland by the British government.

9. *Daily Mail*, 23 June 1975.

at the time, followed suit, effectively preventing the film from being seen in the UK. *The Long Good Friday* (1979), dealing with the perplexed responses of a London East End gangster Harold Shand (Bob Hoskins) to IRA attacks on his 'manor', provoked similar problems when Lew Grade's Associated Communications Corporation, the financier of the film, sought to avoid showing the film in cinemas and demanded ten minutes of cuts (including some references to the IRA) for the film's transmission on television.[10]

While the films do contain elements (such as the deaths of innocent civilians at the hands of British soldiers in *Hennessy*, the suggestion of the apparent 'invincibility' of the IRA in *The Long Good Friday*) uncongenial to British establishment opinion, they also reveal – like *Odd Man Out* before them – a disinclination to locate their representations of violence within a social and political context that might 'explain' them. As a result, they may be seen to have reinforced – as much as they challenged – dominant perceptions of the conflict as largely 'incomprehensible'.[11] This is also so of other 'troubles' features that emerged during this period. The Canadian production, *A Quiet Day in Belfast* (1974), shot partly in Dublin, follows *Odd Man Out* in establishing an overarching sense of fatalism through its use of temporal compression, elements of religious symbolism and an ill-starred romance between a local Catholic, Bridgit Slattery (Margot Kidder), and a British soldier, Jack (Emmet Bergin). Despite the importation of an array of characters apparently lifted from an Abbey comedy of the 1950s, the film's dramatic logic is remorseless, culminating in the deaths of virtually the entire cast. The IRA bomber Peter O'Lurgan (Sean McCann) is blown up by his own bomb, along with a group of Catholic children. A second bomb blows up a betting shop, packed with both Protestants and Catholics, while the shop's manager, Bridgit's brother John (Barry Foster), shoots the three youths responsible for tarring and feathering Bridgit's twin sister, Thelma (also played by Kidder). John is then killed by a distraught Jack, who is himself shot by a sniper Mike (Sean Mulcahy). The very excess with which the film engineers this denouement appears to confirm Peter Brooks' insight that melodrama not only relies upon a set of dramatic conventions but also a mode of imagination that aspires to go beyond surface appearance and give voice to latent moral meanings.[12] This sense of 'hidden' forces at work below the surface action also characterises the bleak portraits of paramilitary violence found in both *Angel* (Neil Jordan, 1982) and *Cal* (Pat O'Connor, 1984).[13]

Elements of the 'troubles' paradigm may also be detected in *The Crying Game* (1992), which, for all the enthusiasm it has generated in relation to the politics of identity, nevertheless reveals a surprisingly conventional take on the politics of the North. Like Johnny in *Odd Man Out* and

---

10. Sophie Balhetchet, '*The Long Good Friday*', *A.I.P. & Co.*, no. 28, 1980, pp. 3–8. The film did, however, eventually achieve a cinema release in 1981.

11. This argument is developed in my discussions of the films in *Cinema and Ireland*, pp. 171–5, and 'Allegorising the Nation: British Gangster Films of the 1980s', in Steve Chibnall and Robert Murphy (eds), *British Crime Cinema* (London: Routledge, 1999), pp. 163–5.

12. Peter Brook, *The Melodramatic Imagination: Balzac, Henry James, Melodrama and the Mode of Excess* (New York: Columbia University Press, 1984, orig. 1976), p. 5.

13. Once again, my discussion of these two films may be found in *Cinema and Ireland*, pp. 178–84. For an alternative account of *Angel*, see Emer Rockett and Kevin Rockett, *Neil Jordan: Exploring Boundaries* (Dublin: The Liffey Press, 2003), pp. 17–35.

Cal (John Lynch) in the film of the same name, Fergus (Stephen Rea) is a 'gentle gunman' unable to escape his violent past. As in *Cal*, a temporary form of respite is provided by an unlikely romance with the 'widow' of the man for whose death he has been partly responsible. However, also like *Cal*, he is unable to break free from his former comrades, whose insistence that he should take part in one more action has disastrous consequences, resulting in the deaths of his colleagues and his own imprisonment (at the hands of the state he initially opposed). The novelty of the film is, of course, that the 'widow', in this case, is a black male transvestite rather than, as in *Cal*, a Catholic woman. However, while this plunges Fergus into a dizzy world of mutating desire and uncertain identity, this is accomplished at the expense of a very conventional view of the 'nature' of republican violence. Thus, while the film's director Neil Jordan claimed that the film was unusual in showing its central character as being neither 'a psychopath or a cold-blooded terrorist, but as a rational human being', this ignored the way in which the representation of Fergus nevertheless conforms to a longstanding tradition of distinguishing between two types of IRA men.[14] Thus, while the character of Fergus may be invested with a degree of psychological complexity and self-doubt, this assumes significance precisely because of the way in which it contrasts with the ideological simplicities and cold-blooded fanaticism of his IRA colleagues.[15]

Nevertheless, the emphasis of the film upon the central character's capacity for change and immersion in the complexities of contemporary cultural identity also suggests a certain tempering of the despair that had been a feature of earlier films and an implicit yearning for a new form of political dispensation. This might also be said of Jim Sheridan's *In the Name of the Father* (1993) dealing with the wrongful imprisonment of the Guildford Four and Maguire Seven. For while critics in Britain condemned the film, in the words of one writer, for 'maligning British justice, romanticising terrorists, boosting support for the IRA and manipulating through factual inaccuracy', its dependence upon the conventions of family melodrama led to a much greater emphasis upon interpersonal relations than political conflict.[16] Loosely based on Gerry Conlon's autobiography, *Proved Innocent* (1990), the film, as its title might suggest, is mainly concerned with the dramatisation of the relationship between Gerry Conlon (Daniel Day-Lewis) and his father Guiseppe (Peter Postlethwaite). The rapprochement between Gerry and Guiseppe that

14. Neil Jordan, 'Film Diary', *Michael Collins* (London: Vintage, 1996), p. 5.

15. As a result of its play with sexual identity, the film has generated a huge literature. Two essays that specifically seek to examine how this relates to the representation of British–Irish relations are David Lloyd, 'True Stories: Cinema, History and Gender', in *Ireland after History* (Cork: Cork University Press, 1999), and Joe Cleary, '"Fork-Tongued on the Border Bit": Partition and the Politics of Form in Contemporary Narratives of the Northern Irish Conflict', *The South Atlantic Quarterly*, vol. 95, no. 1, 1996.

16. Alison Roberts, '"The spine of the story is true and responsible"', *The Times*, 8 February 1994, p. 34. The most justified of these criticisms concern the willingness of the film, and not just the police in Britain, to tamper with evidence. It is of course true that all historical drama involves a degree of dramatic selection and compression (especially those, like *In the Name of the Father*, made with Hollywood funding). Nevertheless, in circumstances in which the acquittal of the defendants involved proving the unsound basis upon which they had been convicted, it seemed to constitute an unnecessary 'own goal' for the film itself to behave so cavalierly towards the known facts of the case.

occurs in prison is shown to involve a clear rejection of his surrogate 'father', the ruthless IRA leader, Joe McAndrew (Don Baker), in favour of the pacifism of his real father.[17] In this respect, the film comes down firmly on the side of peaceful resistance and, in doing so, also registers something of the changing political mood within Irish republicanism.

Ceasefire cinema?: *Nothing Personal* (1996), *The Boxer* (1997) and *Resurrection Man* (1997)

In the Name of the Father was, of course, made after those wrongly imprisoned had been freed. Even though the miscarriage of justice involved had long been established, this was still insufficient to protect the film from often ferocious attacks in the British press (which appeared reluctant to accept any suggestion that the British judicial system might be less than perfect). As had been the case in earlier periods, any film dealing with Northern Ireland was capable of generating highly partisan responses that often revealed more about the strongly contested character of Northern Irish politics than the films themselves. While films dealing with Northern Ireland have continued to arouse strong reactions, the announcement of the ceasefires of 1994 did, nevertheless, alter the conditions under which 'troubles' films were made. Thus, while the 'troubles' were certainly not over, there was a growing sense that the decline in violence and the movement towards a new political dispensation within Northern Ireland did permit the production of films that it would have been difficult, if not impossible, to make at an earlier stage. Given the changes in political climate, there was also the beginning of a move away from the traditional 'troubles' paradigm towards the development of new, more optimistic scenarios than had previously been the case. This was certainly so of *Nothing Personal* and *The Boxer*, both of which explicitly call for an end to violence on the part of the paramilitaries. Nevertheless both films also demonstrate the difficulties involved in moving beyond the traditional vocabulary of the 'troubles' and, in both cases, the films' emergent discourses of 'peace' are partly subverted by the familiar discourses of fatalism and pessimism.[18]

   Nothing Personal is also an unusual film in focusing on loyalist rather than republican paramilitaries. *A Quiet Day in Belfast* did include some scenes involving loyalist paramilitaries who blow up a Catholic church before they themselves are blown up by an (IRA) bomb at the film's end. Drawing loosely on the murders of members of the Miami Showband by the Ulster Volunteer Force (UVF) in 1975, Neil Jordan's *Angel* also shows loyalist paramilitaries, even though the film's vagueness about social and political detail means that it is commonly regarded as refer-

---

17. For a discussion of this point, see Martin McLoone, '*In the Name of the Father*', *Cinéaste*, vol. 20, no. 4, 1994. Ruth Barton also provides an extended discussion of the film in *Jim Sheridan: Framing the Nation* (Dublin: The Liffey Press, 2002), pp. 63–98.

18. This may also be seen in *Titanic Town*, based on a novel of the same name by Mary Costello. Set in 1972, and dealing with a Catholic mother's campaign for peace, the film's optimism is necessarily tempered by the knowledge of the years of violence that followed. Thus, while the film pits the central character's 'commonsense' defence of her 'family' against the violence of both the British Army and the IRA, she falls prey to the machinations of both sides and she and her family are eventually forced to leave their estate having accomplished very little (as the bomb that goes off in the final shot reminds us).

ring to IRA violence.[19] Loyalists also play a walk-on part in Joe Comerford's nightmarish vision of blood-letting, *High Boot Benny* (1993), although the allegorical imprecision of the film makes the establishment of exact affiliations difficult. However, while loyalist violence had not been ignored, it had been more common for 'troubles' films – in line with media representations more generally – to focus on republican, rather than loyalist, violence.[20] While this may have been understandable in light of the history and character of the IRA's military campaign, it also led to the relative invisibility of a significant aspect of the conflict. So, while republican paramilitaries were responsible for the greatest number of deaths in Northern Ireland after 1969, loyalist paramilitaries account for well over a quarter of them. Moreover, in the period preceding the ceasefires (1992-4), loyalists were actually engaged in more killings than their republican counterparts.[21] In this respect, although it was the IRA ceasefire of August 1994 that captured the headlines, it was also crucial to the 'peace process' that a cessation of loyalist 'operational hostilities' should follow (in October). It is partly in relation to these developments that *Nothing Personal* may be understood. For while the film is set in 1975, it is clearly informed by, and feeds into, the politics of the contemporary 'peace process'. In Daniel Mornin's original novel, *All Our Fault* (1991), on which the film is based, there is no reference to a ceasefire. However, by the time the novel was made into a film the agreement of a 'truce' and the reactions of the paramilitaries to this had become key components of the plot.

However, while the film's subject matter and the context in which it was made were novel, it is also striking how much the film conforms to the pattern of earlier 'troubles' drama. This may be seen, for example, in the number of elements that the film inherits from *Odd Man Out*. Like *Odd Man Out*, the film broadly adheres to the unities of time, place and action. Apart from a concluding coda, the events within the film take place over a matter of hours and the action is confined to a few backstreets. The plot of the film also echoes *Odd Man Out* in the way that it follows an injured young Catholic, Liam (John Lynch), as he wanders through the city at night. As in *Odd Man Out*, members of both his community and family search for him but with only limited success. Although apparently located in Belfast, the film's setting, as in *Odd Man Out*, consists of a generalised 'city of the imagination', which has been shot in Dublin and deliberately shorn of realistic detail. The film's narrow streets have been stripped of their normal features (parked cars, bins, even litter) and, as a result, assume a hallucinatory quality that is reinforced by the film's stylised use of colour, lighting and composition. However, while the film

19. In a polemical attack on screen representations of Northern Ireland, Eoghan Harris, for example, argues that the film patented 'the Stephen Rea Provo' or 'IR-Rea man' even though the character played by Rea is a musician who seems to be a Protestant and has no connection to the IRA. The article is entitled, somewhat ironically, 'Why truth has been on the ropes', *The Sunday Times*, Section 2, 1 February 1998, p. 2.

20. As noted in Chapter 5, British media coverage of the beginnings of the contemporary 'troubles' tended to focus on the justice of the civil rights case and the obstacles to reform represented by unionism/loyalism. Following the arrival of British troops in the North in 1969 and the resurgence of the IRA in 1970, the dominant mode of reporting the conflict tended to be in terms of the problem of IRA violence. See Philip Schlesinger, *Putting 'Reality' Together: BBC News* (London: Constable, 1978), ch. 8.

21. See figures for murders by paramilitaries in Sydney Elliott and W. D. Flackes, *Northern Ireland: A Political Dictionary 1968–1999* (Belfast: Blackstaff Press, 1999), p. 683.

self-consciously downplays a sense of place, it also possesses a much clearer sense of sectarian geography than was the case in *Odd Man Out*, in which there is a studied vagueness about the religious and political affiliations of the various characters that Johnny encounters (a high proportion of whom seem to be English). By contrast, there is a much stronger sense of who is Protestant and Catholic in *Nothing Personal* and of the risks that are involved in straying outside of one's own 'territory'. However, other than a loyalist mural and an Irish flag, there is also little to differentiate the areas visually and, in the absence of any evidence of a shared or non-sectarian public space (apart from the cemetery), this adds to the sense of oppressiveness and enclosure with which the city is identified.

The visual style of the film also reinforces the air of tragic inevitability presiding over the characters' actions. Writer Daniel Mornin and director Thaddeus O'Sullivan had earlier collaborated on a 'troubles' television drama, *In the Border Country* (1991), inspired by Aeschylus's *Oresteia* (from which it borrows a number of quotes). The play is set in a desolate Irish landscape and bleakly works out the destructive consequences of community hatreds and tit-for-tat violence (culminating in the 'matricide' found in the second of Aeschylus's plays).[22] While *Nothing Personal* lacks the single-mindedness of the earlier television drama, there is a similar narrative propulsion towards a tragic conclusion. Thus, while the leaders of the paramilitary groups are involved in negotiating a ceasefire, the loyalist gang led by Kenny (James Frain) fail to call a halt to their activities with the inevitable disastrous consequences. Thus, towards the end of the film, Liam is picked off the street and tortured by the gang for 'information'. Kenny, however, recognises Liam as a former childhood friend and insists on letting him go. In this he is opposed by Ginger (Ian Hart), who – in an allusion (not found in the original novel) to the Shankhill Butcher, Lenny Murphy – is shown to mutilate his victims with a knife. However, while Kenny, in line with the well-worn distinction between paramilitary types, may display some capacity for change, Ginger's pathological hatred of Catholics renders him irredeemable and the downward spiral of violence continues. Accordingly, Liam's daughter Kathleen (Jeni Courtney) is shot dead in the street trying to prevent the impressionable young Michael (Gareth O'Hare) from firing at her father's erstwhile tormentors. Moreover, in a denouement reminiscent of Kathleen and Johnny's 'suicide' at the end of *Odd Man Out*, Kenny finally obeys Leonard's orders and shoots Ginger, knowing that it will provoke fire from the soldiers who have their car covered. They, in turn, have been tipped off by the loyalist commander Leonard (Michael Gambon), who, assured by his IRA counterpart Cecil (Gerard McSorley) that Liam is 'not involved' and angered by the group's breach of the ceasefire and resort to bestial acts of violence, has set the men up for elimination.

However, while the film may be unusual in focusing on loyalist violence, the film's employment of so many elements associated with the 'troubles' paradigm means that it also conforms to the same pattern of decontextualisation characteristic of earlier films concerned with the IRA. Thus, while the film may distinguish between different kinds of loyalist violence, it still

---

22. Shaun Richards indicates how the play's tragic mode results in an image of Ireland frozen in a 'fated circle' in '*In the Border Country*: Greek Tragedy and Contemporary Irish Drama', in C. C. Barfoot and Rias van den Doel (eds), *Ritual Rememberings: History, Myth and Politics in Anglo-Irish Drama* (Amsterdam: Rodopi, 1995).

Working towards a tragic conclusion: Liam (John Lynch) and Kenny (James Frain) in *Nothing Personal*

remains vague about the political motivations underpinning the actions of the loyalist leadership and the political issues at stake in negotiating a ceasefire. It is, of course, the case that the film makes some attempt to place the actions of the loyalists in context by beginning with a bomb in a Protestant bar, frequented by the RUC. In this way, the horrifying consequences of the bomber's action (and the sense of siege to which it leads) provides a degree of motivation for the murderous actions in which the loyalist paramilitaries engage. As an acknowledgment at the end of the film indicates, the scene owes a debt to *The Battle of Algiers* (1965), Gillo Pontercorvo's potent dramatisation of Algerian resistance to French colonial rule. However, the way in which the films deal with the bombing is fundamentally different. In *The Battle of Algiers*, the bombing sequence is handled in a way that is both complex and troubling. The spectator is guided through a process of understanding the circumstances (including French military oppression) that have led to the use of violence by the Algerians. The film also structures our identification with the women bombers as they pass through an army checkpoint and plant the bombs in a French bar. However, the film then involves us in a dramatic change of perspective as we are confronted with the loss of life that follows the bombers' actions. In this way, the film confronts us with the disturbing effects of violence but also locates it in a historical and political context that renders it comprehensible. In the case of *Nothing Personal*, however, the bombing occurs at the beginning of the film without any sense of context or motivation and therefore without any indication of the complexity of the political circumstances that have led to such a shocking action. Ironically, therefore, in attempting to 'explain' the violence of the loyalists the film mainly succeeds in setting up a pattern of repetitive violence that, as in *In the Border Country*, seems to defy any clear psychological or political rationale.

In line with its emphasis upon a ceasefire, the film does seek to counter the fatalistic momentum of the plot through the tentative suggestion of cross-community romance. As in earlier dramas, the film draws a strong contrast between the public world of paramilitary activities and the private world of home and domesticity. Kenny's devotion to paramilitary activity has resulted in separation from his wife and children (and he now lives unstably in a room at the back of the loyalist drinking club), while the violence in which he is involved results in the death of Liam's daughter. Unlike the novel, however, the film attempts to retrieve an element of optimism from the situation. In one of a series of coincidences (and parallelisms) within the film, the Protestant woman, Anne (Maria Doyle Kennedy), who (like the English women in *Odd Man Out*) invites Liam into her home and provides him with medical assistance, turns out to be Kenny's separated wife. Although, as single parents, the couple have much in common, and are attracted to each other, they only meet the once in the original novel, which ends with Liam and his son on a boat set for England. The film, on the other hand, engineers a subsequent encounter between the characters in order to hold out the possibility of some form of reconciliation across the sectarian divide. Thus, in a rather improbable scenario, the funerals of Kenny and Kathleen occur in the same cemetery, permitting the two to share commiserations and hint at the prospect of a future romance. However, as the sequence's allusion to *The Third Man* (1949) might suggest, this is also highly tentative and stands at odds with the doom-laden drive of the film overall.

Many of the same features (and tensions) may be found in Jim Sheridan's *The Boxer*, the third in a loose trilogy of films written or co-written by Terry George that also includes *In the Name of the Father* and the hunger-strike drama *Some Mother's Son*. Given the controversies surrounding the earlier films, and the complaints concerning their pro-republican bias, *The Boxer* appears to have been conceived as a more conciliatory film that would make overt its commitment to the 'peace process'. Dealing with the announcement of a republican ceasefire and the tensions within republicanism that this creates, it explicitly seeks to dramatise the necessity of ending the 'armed struggle' and moving towards peaceful reconciliation. In this respect, the film draws upon familiar typologies of the IRA man by explicitly counterposing the hardline extremist, reluctant to call a halt to violence, to the more pragmatic IRA leader concerned to end the war and secure a deal with the British government.[23] The film's pro-ceasefire message is worked out in two main ways. The film's central character, Danny Flynn (Daniel Day-Lewis), is a former IRA man, recently released from prison, who has turned his back on his former colleagues and who, with the help of his former trainer Ike Weir (Ken Stott), not only resumes his own boxing career but also re-opens the non-sectarian boxing club that had previously brought Protestant and Catholic youngsters together. As Danny's adversary, the IRA hardliner Harry (Gerard McSor-

---

23. The film's concerns in this regard are partly anticipated by the television film, *Love Lies Bleeding* (1993), written by
    Ronan Bennett and directed by Michael Winterbottom. Made prior to the announcement of the IRA ceasefire,
    the film focuses on the clash between pro- and anti-ceasefire elements within the republican movement,
    culminating in the announcement of a ceasefire following the violent annihilation of hardliners. Martin McLoone
    discusses the programme as part of a tradition of television drama dealing with the 'troubles' in 'Drama out of a
    Crisis: BBC Television Drama and the Northern Ireland Troubles', in Martin McLoone (ed.), *Broadcasting in a
    Divided Community: Seventy Years of the BBC in Northern Ireland* (Belfast: Institute of Irish Studies, 1996).

ley), observes, Danny's return to the ring amounts to more than 'just boxing' and constitutes a 'fucking statement'. This is not only because of the capacity of Danny's boxing to bring together Protestant and Catholic (as in the extravagantly staged bout in the city centre) but also because it represents a form of fighting 'within the rules' that contrasts with the apparently unregulated violence of the paramilitaries. The ethical dimension that Danny's boxing symbolises is demonstrated by his fight in the sporting club in London. Despite the encouragement of the referee to carry on, Danny forfeits victory by refusing to continue hitting the opponent whom he has already knocked down and badly beaten. This sense of the importance of both fighting fairly and of knowing when to stop then comes to shape the film's own attitude towards the use of violence by the paramilitaries.

It is also reinforced by another of the film's main dramatic devices. As has already been argued, it is a conventional part of the vocabulary of 'troubles' film-making to counterpose the public and private spheres. In particular, the motif of lovers, often from different social and/or religious backgrounds, caught up in a conflict over which they have limited control recurs across a number of films (and indeed 'troubles' fiction more generally). Thus, in films such as *Odd Man Out*, *A Quiet Day in Belfast* and *Cal*, romance is destroyed as a result of either the enforced separation or death to which the surrounding violence leads. *The Boxer* revisits this romantic scenario in the form of the relationship between Danny and his former sweetheart, Maggie (Emily Watson). Forced apart by Danny's involvement in IRA action and subsequent imprisonment, Danny's release from prison at the film's beginning offers the possibility of a resumption of their relationship despite the apparently unpropitious circumstances in which they now meet. Maggie is the daughter of the IRA leader, Joe Hamill (Brian Cox), and has since married Danny's best friend, by whom she has a son, Liam (Ciarán Fitzgerald). As a prisoner's wife, she is not only 'spoken for' but also watched over by a vigilant republican community concerned that she remain loyal to her absent husband while he remains in prison.[24] Despite the inimical context in which they now meet, the couple's desires, though initially thwarted, are not destroyed and the couple end up united by the film's close. In this way, the film's perspective on the peace process is simultaneously interwoven with the fortunes of its romantic couple.

The main opponent of Danny's activities since his return from prison has been Harry, a senior republican who opposes the peace strategy and has failed to observe the ceasefire (sanctioning the blowing up of a RUC officer on his departure from Danny's big fight in central Belfast). It is also Harry who represents the biggest threat to Danny and Maggie's relationship, given his determination to punish Danny for his relationship with a prisoner's wife. However, while Harry abducts Danny and orders his killing, it is Harry himself who is disposed of by his erstwhile colleagues. As in *Nothing Personal*, in which Leonard orders Kenny to put Ginger to 'sleep', so Joe, in *The Boxer*, orders the execution of the 'out of control' Harry in order to maintain the ceasefire. In doing so, he is also able to protect his daughter Maggie and Danny from

---

24. In her discussion of the film, Elizabeth Butler Cullingford argues that the kind of policing of prisoners' wives contained in the film derives from an earlier period of the 'troubles' (the 1970s) and therefore criticises the film for opportunism in the way in which it seeks to align 'women's issues' with pro-ceasefire politics. See 'The Prisoner's Wife and the Soldier's Whore: Female Punishment in Irish History and Culture', in Ruth Barton and Harvey O'Brien (eds), *Keeping it Real: Irish Film and Television* (London: Wallflower Press, 2004).

harm and thus bring the maintenance of the domestic sphere into a neat alignment with the politics of 'peace'. Following Harry's execution, Danny staggers towards Maggie, with whom he is finally reunited, along with her son, in a reconstructed version of the family. Liam had previously rejected Danny and set fire to the gym during the turmoil following the killing of the RUC man by Harry's men. In turning to Danny, he now accepts, as in *In the Name of the Father*, the 'good father' and the peaceful route that Danny represents.[25] Thus, if in previous 'troubles' films, it is the continuation of the conflict that has prevented the fulfilment of romantic desires, the winning-through of romance is here predicated upon the imminent onset of 'peace'.

Although the narrative logic of this is clear, the way in which it is worked through is less straightforward. The apparent triumph of love in the face of adversity, and the concurrent victory of a peace strategy over a continuing military campaign, is offset by a number of factors. One of the most striking features of the film is its visual style. Filmed by Chris Menges, the film is shot with low levels of light in drab blues that suffuse the film with an air of melancholic gloom. This is reinforced by the claustrophobic *mise en scène* that emphasises the confined spaces in which the characters operate. The sense of enclosure that this evokes is, of course, a central theme of the film. In both *In the Name of the Father* and *Some Mother's Son*, dealing with the 1981 hunger-strike by republicans, the prison is a literal place of entrapment to which the prisoners have been condemned. Although Danny, in *The Boxer*, leaves prison at the beginning of the film, the sense that he remains, like Johnny in *Odd Man Out*, a prisoner survives. In this case, it is the community to which he returns that takes on the characteristics of a prison, subjecting both him and Maggie to constant surveillance and constraints upon their actions. Indeed, it is Maggie's subordination to the strict code governing prisoners' wives that leads her to exclaim to her father that it is she who is, in fact, the real prisoner. This all-prevailing atmosphere of enclosure and imprisonment is sustained even when Danny and Maggie seek to evade the gaze of their peers by crossing the peace line and entering a loyalist area. However, as in the stark sectarian geography of *Nothing Personal*, they are immediately spotted and advised to leave before a gang of loyalist paramilitaries, sitting menacingly in a car, take matters into their own hands. Given the small-scale, claustrophobic world that the film evokes, it is therefore hard for the film to invest its romantic ending with full conviction. Following Harry's death, Danny and Maggie are reunited and leave together. Stopped by the RUC and asked where they are going, Maggie firmly announces they are on their way 'home'. In one sense this accords with the film's romantic logic, stressing the primacy of the personal sphere of home and family over the destruction and chaos of the public world of violent conflict. However, given the bleakness of

---

25. However, if, in this schema, Harry represents the 'bad father' not only responsible for his own son's death but, indirectly, for the destructive actions of Liam, the film's ideological commitment to home and family is tested by its indifference towards Liam's actual father, whom we do not see. (The film also ignores Danny's own family and father.) The resolution of this seems to lie in the suggestion that Maggie was encouraged by her father into a loveless marriage with Liam's father. Therefore, Joe's willingness to accept Maggie's renewed relationship with Danny constitutes, in part, reparations for his earlier errors. Although she does not make this specific point, Fidelma Farley argues more generally that the film involves the renegotiation of masculine identity in terms of 'a commitment to family and fatherhood' in 'In the Name of the Family: Masculinity and Fatherhood in Contemporary Northern Irish Films', *Irish Studies Review*, vol. 9, no. 2, 2001, p. 203.

the world they inhabit and the oppressiveness of the community to which they belong, there is little to indicate that this is a home in which they can genuinely be 'at home'. Indeed, in an interview accompanying the DVD release of the film, the actress Emily Watson (who plays Maggie) suggests the couple will leave for London.[26] Although this is not made clear within the film, the couple's flight from Belfast would – despite the repeated utterances about the importance of 'home' – accord with the dramatic logic and stylistic sense of imprisonment governing the film. In this way, rather than providing a symbol of the community's transition from violence to peace, the romantic couple may also be seen – as in earlier 'troubles' drama – to remain trapped by the constrictions of the broader community from which they must seek an escape.

Two further elements contribute to the sense of ambivalence surrounding the film's ending. As in *Nothing Personal*, the accomplishment of 'peace' within the film, in line with the conventions of the thriller genre, remains dependent upon the exercise of violence (providing, perhaps, an inadvertently ironic twist to the film's use of Sinn Fein leader Gerry Adams' comment at the start of the film that the IRA 'haven't gone away, you know'). In this way the film not only fails to provide an adequate embodiment of the peaceful methods that it espouses but also fails to demonstrate the ways in which the 'new politics' is taking hold. Thus, while we are informed of Joe's negotiations, these occur off-screen and there is little sense of the political issues (beyond the release of prisoners) or political objectives (other than 'peace') that are at stake. Indeed, apart from a television soundbite declaring that the police are not welcome in west Belfast, the newly elected 'political' member of the Army Council, Peter Mallon (Peter Sheridan), remains virtually silent throughout the film, primarily contributing to the plot through the behind-the-scenes role he plays in the murder of Harry. As in both *In the Name of the Father* and *Some Mother's Son*, political tensions are mapped onto family dilemmas and, as a result, the film's articulation of ceasefire politics is subordinated to the modes of family and romantic melodrama with which it is interwoven.[27]

There is, of course, one key difference between the endings of *Nothing Personal* and *The Boxer*. As has been suggested, the employment of the conventions of the crime film in 'troubles' films leads to endings that are ambivalent in their attitudes towards violence, given the reliance upon violence as a means of achieving narrative closure. Thus, in films such as *Odd Man Out*, *Angel* and *Cal*, it is the state violence of either the RUC or the British Army that brings the activities of the paramilitaries, as well as the plot, to an end. This is also so of *Nothing Personal*, in which the British Army dispose of the loyalist gang. There is, of course, a twist to this insofar as the film indicates a degree of collusion between the army and loyalist paramilitaries. Nevertheless it is still the might of the British that is called upon to impose 'order' upon characters who it seems lack the capacity to 'govern' themselves. As might be expected, given the claims of 'anti-Britishness' directed at George and Sheridan in the past, *The Boxer* is strongly conscious of the British military presence in Belfast but does not look to the army for a 'solution' to the problems

---

26. 'Fighting for Peace: Inside *The Boxer*' featurette, *The Boxer*, DVD (Universal Pictures, 1998).

27. For a discussion of the way in which *Some Mother's Son* uses the conventions of maternal melodrama to dramatise the 1981 hunger-strike, see John Hill, '*Some Mother's Son*', *Cinéaste*, vol. 23, no. 1, 1997.

The winning-through of romance: Daniel Day-Lewis as Danny and Emily Watson as Maggie in *The Boxer*

that the film's characters face.[28] The style of the film does, nevertheless, position the British Army in a peculiar way.

A central element of the film's style consists of its repeated use of aerial shots. Initially employed when Joe is seen to arrive at the wedding reception near the film's start, these heli-copter shots recur throughout the film, providing aerial views, for example, of the bombing of the Protestant bar, Ike's dead body and Danny's beating at the hands of Harry and his cohorts. An extended aerial view of Maggie's car and the surrounding city also brings the film to an end. In part these shots reinforce the sense of enclosure with which the characters in the film, and their tight-knit community, are associated. As Martin McLoone indicates, such shots give 'the impression that in the constricted space of the city the only freedom is upwards'.[29] In this

---

28. Given the personalising logic of the narrative and genre conventions employed by George and Sheridan, there is a tendency to condense complex political forces into one-dimensional characterisations of British characters, as in the treatment of the corrupt police officer Dixon (Corin Redgrave) in *In the Name of the Father* and the odious young Thatcherite Farnsworth (Tim Woodward) in *Some Mother's Son*. Elizabeth Butler Cullingford links such representations to a tradition of the 'stage Englishman' in '"Brits Behaving Badly": From Bourke to Jordan', in *Ireland's Other: Gender and Ethnicity in Irish Literature and Popular Culture* (Cork: Cork University Press, 2001). I have also suggested, in relation to both *Some Mother's Son* and Ken Loach's *Hidden Agenda* (1990), how the emphasis upon individuals and inter-personal drama pushes the films towards conspiracy theory in terms of their accounts of the role of the British state. See '*Hidden Agenda*: Politics and the Thriller', *Circa*, no. 57, 1991.

29. McLoone, *Irish Film*, p. 77.

respect, the shots also seem to suggest the 'smallness' of the characters' actions when viewed within a larger frame and even acquire a hint of the metaphysical, given the god-like view of the camera (and its tilt up the church spire at the film's end). However, in an allusion to Belfast's Divis flats, the film also reveals the fortified army base at the top of the block of flats, which constitute one of the film's main locations and from which the helicopters are seen to take off. As such, the view of the helicopter is clearly associated with the presence of the British Army, which is shown to maintain constant surveillance over the area. This does, of course, add an extra layer to one of the film's main themes. Thus, just as Danny and Maggie are under the constant surveillance of their own community, so the community itself is subject to constant observation due to the presence of the British Army. Nevertheless, the implied association of the British Army with the omniscient view of the camera is an odd one. The director Jim Sheridan suggests that these shots were inspired by events in March 1988 when, a few days after the attack on mourners at Milltown cemetery by the loyalist paramilitary Michael Stone, republicans dragged two British soldiers from their car and shot them dead while an army helicopter flew overhead.[30] While this may then imply the powerlessness of the British Army to intervene, or impose 'order' as in *Nothing Personal*, it also invests the army with a privileged form of vision in relation to the characters on the ground and appears to give credence to the notion that the British Army is in some way 'above' the conflict (unfolding below) rather than itself a central participant.

Despite the elements of similarity between *Nothing Personal* and *The Boxer*, there was nonetheless a significant difference in the responses that they engendered. Although the film was neither a significant critical nor commercial success in Britain, *The Boxer* did not arouse the ire of British critics in the same way that both *In the Name of the Father* and *Some Mother's Son* had succeeded in doing. In the case of *Nothing Personal*, however, there were complaints that the film presented loyalist paramilitaries in a worse light than the IRA and, in the words of Alexander Walker, contributed to the 'anti-British, pro-republican bias' that he detected in a range of films produced during the period, stretching from *Hidden Agenda* to *Some Mother's Son*.[31] This was a view that gathered momentum the following year after the release of a second film alluding to the Shankhill Butchers, *Resurrection Man* (Marc Evans), based on Eoin McNamee's 1993 novel of the same name. The critic of the *Daily Mail* referred to the film as 'an outpouring of anti-Unionist hatred', while Walker himself described it as a 'nauseating exercise'.[32] The film also enjoyed the rare distinction of uniting political opponents when a Sinn Fein spokesperson joined members of the loyalist parties with paramilitary connections, the

30. Director's commentary, *The Boxer*, DVD.

31. Alexander Walker, 'Film Propaganda', letter to the *Irish Times*, 7 June 1996, p. 15. Originally from Northern Ireland, the film critic of the London *Evening Standard*, Alexander Walker, engaged in a sustained campaign throughout the 1990s against 'bias' in films dealing with the 'troubles'. His barracking of Ken Loach at Cannes in 1990 and his attacks on subsequent films is documented by Roy Greenslade in 'Editors as Censors: The British Press and Films about Ireland', *Journal of Popular British Cinema*, no. 3, 2000.

32. Christopher Tookey, *Daily Mail*, 30 January 1998, p. 44; Alexander Walker, *Evening Standard*, 29 January 1998, p. 29.

Ulster Democratic Party (UDP) and Progressive Unionist Party (PUP), in denouncing the film as 'irresponsible'.[33]

In some respects, however, the film does not depart significantly from its predecessors. Shot in the north of England, rather than Belfast, the film transforms the location into a nightmare city of the imagination. Although shot in colour, the film draws heavily on the stylistic vocabulary of film noir and bathes its settings in expressionist blues and reds. Modelled on the rise and fall structure of the classic gangster film, in which the new recruit overthrows his former boss (and acquires his girl) before succumbing to a violent death, the film also conforms to the pattern of inbuilt fatalism familiar from earlier films. Telling its story in flashback, the film begins just as the loyalist killer Victor (Stuart Townsend) is about to be killed, before backtracking to reveal the concatenation of circumstances that have caused his inevitable demise.

There are nevertheless a number of features that distinguish the film from its predecessors. Whereas previous films had sought to counterpose the world of destructive violence to the 'normality' of home and family, *Resurrection Man* portrays a world of all-encompassing gloom and guilt by association. The family, which in other films would provide a sanctuary from violence, becomes, in this case, the very source of Victor's pathology in the form of a symbolically 'castrated' Catholic father and overbearing Protestant mother. The journalist Ryan (James Nesbitt), engaged in the reporting of Victor's actions, is himself a wife-beater, fascinated by the sordid events he records and connected to Victor by the film's use of overlapping sound and intercutting. In a similar manner, Victor's sometime girlfriend, Heather (Geraldine O'Rawe), places no 'feminine' break on Victor's violence but, like Ryan, seems ineluctably drawn towards (and even sexually aroused by) his dark deeds. There is, in this regard, no clear separation within the film between Victor's violence and the surrounding social landscape, which has itself fallen victim to moral ambiguity and psycho-sexual confusion. As McLure suggests to Ryan, 'everybody's got something to do with it'. As a result, the film offers an unremittingly dark vision of the Northern Ireland conflict that holds out little prospect of redemption or, indeed, 'resurrection' for either its main characters or the world that they inhabit. So, while the loyalist leader Mclure (Sean McGinley), like Leonard in *Nothing Personal*, sets Victor up for assassination, this is motivated by neither moral disgust nor political principle but simply a recognition that Victor's notoriety has become too great a liability.

However, what distinguishes the film is not simply its nihilistic outlook but also the way in which this is expressed. For while the film may be loosely based on actual events, the film itself is less concerned with the accurate recreation of historical period than with the reworking, and hybridisation, of the representational conventions associated with 'troubles' drama. To this extent, the film may be seen to constitute a 'postmodern' turn in 'troubles' film-making, in which the impulse to represent the 'troubles', or comment upon them, is subordinated to a play with the signifying means through which they have been represented. As the film's writer, Eoin McNamee, was apparently content to declare, the film laid no claim to be 'a worthy movie about

---

33. *Belfast Telegraph*, 12 February 1998, p. 3. The Sinn Fein spokesperson did, however, imply the film might be seen as glamourising loyalist violence, whereas the loyalist groups objected to the film's unsympathetic portrait of loyalist paramilitarism.

a political situation'.[34] Accordingly, the film abandons the earnestness (and liberal humanism) typical of earlier 'troubles' drama in favour of overt stylisation, generic hybridity and intertextual allusion. Accordingly, the film not only draws upon the conventions of the gangster film and film noir but also imports elements from the horror film, turning Victor's obsessive pursuit of Catholic victims into a vampiric lust for blood that culminates in the Gothic flamboyance of the bathhouse sequence near the film's end.[35] The film's family drama also alludes to the 'monstrous family' to be found in the contemporary horror film, while Victor's relationship with his mother is clearly modelled on the Oedipal complications associated with James Cagney in a string of films stretching from *The Public Enemy* (1931) to *White Heat* (1949) (even though it is then overlaid with a religious dimension, given Victor's desire to disavow his part-Catholic parentage).[36] The presentation of Victor himself also draws on the iconography of the gangster film (dressing him, for example, in a stylish long overcoat) but combines this with retro accessories more redolent of a rock star (black leather jacket and tight-fitting jumper). Thus, despite the laments about the film's unfairness to loyalists (and the bestiality of the acts with which he is associated), Stuart Townsend as Victor undoubtedly runs Brad Pitt a close second as the best-looking paramilitary in 'troubles' cinema, investing the character, like the cinematic gangster and the vampire, with an allure that is both attractive and repellent. The film is also strongly conscious of its own status as a film, showing the young Victor watching James Cagney in *The Public Enemy* as a child and, through the character of Ryan, drawing attention to the film spectator's own voyeuristic relationship to the violence on the screen. At one point, Heather tells Ryan that he has been 'watching too many films' and this could be said of *Resurrection Man* itself, which repeatedly alludes to other films (such as *Dracula* [1981], *The Public Enemy*, *Le Samourai* [1967], *A Clockwork Orange* [1971], *The Warriors* [1979], *Goodfellas* [1990] and *Reservoir Dogs* [1992]). As Fredric Jameson's well-known account of postmodern culture would suggest, however, this mode of intertextual referencing, for all its cinephiliac pleasures, tends to result in a sacrifice of historicity and hermeneutic depth.[37] Accordingly, the aspiration to represent an actual past or period in *Resurrection Man* gives way to a simulation of the past based upon a reworking of earlier representations and styles (the 'already-said'). Criticisms of the film's 'inaccuracy' for showing, for example, the use of cocaine by loyalists (when 'cocaine wasn't even around in Belfast in 1974'), therefore, rather miss the point of how the film's portrait of Victor's growing dependence upon the drug

34. *Resurrection Man*, Production Notes, 1998, BFI Library.

35. Steve Baker explores the film's use of the vampire motif in 'Vampire Troubles: Loyalism and *Resurrection Man*', in Barton and O'Brien (eds), *Keeping it Real*, pp. 78–86.

36. In his analysis of the historical development of the horror film, Robin Wood notes how the family changes from the representative of the 'normality' threatened by the 'monstrous' to the source of the 'monstrous' itself (from *Psycho* onwards) through a responsibility for the creation of psychotic killers. See 'An Introduction to the American Horror Film', in Andrew Britton, Robin Wood and Richard Lippe (eds), *American Nightmare: Essays on the Horror Film* (Toronto: Festival of Festivals, 1979), p. 17. More specifically, Barbara Creed links 'the psychotic killer son' to the over-possessive 'monstrous mother' in *The Monstrous-Feminine: Film, Feminism, Psychoanalysis* (London: Routledge, 1993), p. 139.

37. Fredric Jameson, 'Postmodernism, or The Cultural Logic of Late Capitalism', *New Left Review*, no. 146, 1984, p. 67.

owes much less to the historical record than to Brian de Palma's picture of coke-fuelled gang-sterism in *Scarface* (1983).[38]

Thus, while the film may share elements with other 'troubles' drama, it also departs from them in the way in which it overtly 'textualises' the conventions with which 'troubles' drama has been associated and, in doing so, drains them of their previous connotations. For example, in a short scene following a brutal assault on a Catholic victim, Victor is shown walking down a fog-covered street past a number of street preachers (one of whom is bearing the placard 'The Wages of Sin is Death'). As he walks on, one of the preachers (subsequently revealed to be the loyalist leader McClure) points at Victor and demands 'Will you be saved or will you be damned?'. The scene not only carries echoes of the fog-enshrouded city found in John Ford's *The Informer* (1935) but also recalls a similar scene in *Cal*, when the eponymous hero is regaled by a funda-mentalist preacher in the town marketplace. However, while *Cal* seeks, in this way, to impose a religious pattern of sin and redemption upon an ostensibly political drama, the use of the preacher in *Resurrection Man* functions less as a structural feature than one of a number of inter-textual allusions competing for semantic significance (and effectively obstructing the film's achievement of ideological coherence). In the same way, the tolling bells and final gunning-down of Victor – arms raised in a Christ-like pose – might suggest an aspiration towards the metaphysical quality contained in earlier films. However, self-consciously reworking what McArthur refers to as 'the most rigid convention' of the gangster genre (that the gangster should ultimately 'lie dead in the street'), the effect of the scene relies less upon the revelation of some deeper 'truth' than a recognition of the highly 'conventionalised' status of the representational system that the film is invoking.[39]

In this respect the generic play and stylistic mix-and-match that characterises *Resurrection Man* also suggests a knowingness about the way in which representations of the 'troubles' had by this time become sedimented into a set of readily identifiable conventions that had lost the power to surprise or shock. It was presumably for this reason that McNamee suggested, with-out any apparent sense of irony regarding his own film, that '[p]eople don't get anything from films about Northern Ireland and they don't learn anything about themselves'.[40] In the case of *Resurrection Man*, therefore, the wish to refresh the conventions of 'troubles' drama leads to a kind of baroque extravagance ostensibly licensed by the very excessiveness of the violence with which it deals.[41] However, while this may involve a degree of bleak humour (as in the sub-Tarantino use of the pop song 'Tiger Feet' to accompany a brutal beating), the film's hybridity does not

---

38. Criticism of the film's portrait of loyalists as 'homosexual drug-takers' was made by a Progressive Unionist Party spokesman who had known one of the Shankhill Butchers, Robert 'Basher' Bates, for thirty-five years. See 'New film resurrects dark times in Northern Ireland', 5 February 1998, <news.bbc.co.uk>.

39. Colin McArthur, *Underworld USA* (London: Secker & Warburg, 1972), p. 35.

40. Quoted in Liz Trainor, 'To have a future we must face the past', *Irish News*, 28 March 1998, p. 9.

41. In his discussion of the evolution of generic conventions, Thomas Schatz identifies a 'baroque stage' when 'the form and embellishments are accented to the point where they themselves become the "substance" or "content" of the work'. See *Hollywood Genres: Formulas, Filmmaking and the Studio System* (Philadelphia: Temple University Press, 1981), p. 40.

An allure that is both attractive and repellent: Stuart Townsend as Victor in *Resurrection Man*

Intertextual referencing: Sean McGinley as the preacher in *Resurrection Man*

extend to fully fledged comedy. It is, nevertheless, comedy that is set to become a key mode of addressing the 'troubles' in a number of the films that follow.

No laughing matter? *Cycle of Violence* (1998), *Divorcing Jack* (1998) and *An Everlasting Piece* (2000)

While the conventions of 'troubles' drama were becoming increasingly recognisable (and pre-dictable), it was difficult to turn the conflict into comic matter so long as the violence con-tinued. With the onset of the ceasefires, however, a comic take on the 'troubles', and 'troubles' drama, became increasingly feasible. A key influence here was undoubtedly the television suc-cess of the Hole in the Wall Gang's *Two Ceasefires and a Wedding* (Stephen Butcher, 1995), set immediately before and after the announcement of the ceasefires in 1994. The programme is acutely conscious of the conventions that have traditionally governed 'troubles' drama (includ-ing the 'love across the barricades' romance) and begins with a series of images of murals, army vehicles and burnt-out buildings. These, however, are immediately followed by a title that apol-ogises for the 'droney music and drab shots of Belfast' that, it implies, have by now become a standard feature of 'Northern Ireland drama'.[42] In terms of film, this move towards 'troubles' comedy begins with *Cycle of Violence* (aka *Crossmaheart*) and *Divorcing Jack*.[43] Both are based on novels by the Northern Ireland writer Colin Bateman and were among the first of the feature films to be shot mainly in Northern Ireland as a result of lottery finance. In both cases, the films take the stock characters and situations of the 'troubles' drama but give them a dark, comic twist. Influenced by the crime novels of Elmore Leonard and Carl Hiaasen and the films of Quentin Tarantino, especially *Pulp Fiction* (1994), the films rework the conventions of the 'troubles' drama in order to strip away the pretensions of those engaged in the violence and underscore the basic absurdity of the conflict. However, like other 'ceasefire' films, these films also find it difficult to break free of the conventions of the 'troubles' paradigm and struggle to convert paramilitary con-flict into genuinely comic material.

   Both *Cycle of Violence* and *Divorcing Jack* pivot around a central journalist figure who finds himself caught up in a web of intrigue, double-dealing and murder from which he only nar-rowly escapes. In the case of *Cycle of Violence*, the main character is Kevin Miller (Gerard Rooney), a Belfast-based journalist who is sent to work for the local paper in the village of Crossmaheart (a not-so-distant relative of the actual border town of Crossmaglen). Like the out-sider in *Yojimbo* (1961) and the film it inspired, *A Fistful of Dollars* (1964), Miller is confronted by a town split – almost literally – down the middle into two religious camps. However, the secret that Miller uncovers – the identities of the four men responsible for the sexual assault of

42. A member of the Hole in the Wall group, Damon Quinn, indicates how they were 'sick of all those horrible Northern Ireland dramas where it's really grim and uillean pipes are playing and these terrible English actors are trying to do Northern accents and loads of mad terrorists are going around', in Stephen Dixon and Deirdre Falvey, *Gift of the Gag: The Explosion in Irish Comedy* (Belfast: Blackstaff Press, 1999), p. 223. The programme laid the basis for the long-running BBC Northern Ireland series, *Give My Head Peace*, which is discussed by Lance Pettitt, *Screening Ireland: Film and Television Representation* (Manchester: Manchester University Press, 2000), pp. 197–201.
43. Although the first of these adaptations is often referred to as *Crossmaheart*, the version of the film I have seen goes under the title of *Cycle of Violence* (which is also the title of the original Colin Bateman novel).

Sorry about the droney music and the drab shots of Belfast but this is a Northern Ireland drama

Subverting the 'troubles' drama: *Two Ceasefires and a Wedding*

a thirteen-year-old girl some ten years previously – reveals the shared guilt of Catholics and Protestants for the perpetration of this terrible crime. As a result, the film's portrait of Crossma-heart is unremittingly grim. Miller's first view of the town centre is of a semi-deserted square, covered in windswept litter and dominated by a burnt-out car. Visibly bearing the scars of sec-tarian violence, Crossmaheart is no haven of rural tranquillity but rather, as Hugh Linehan observes, 'a piss-smelling hell-hole' whose inhabitants' 'squalid hatreds' are matched only by the extent of their 'hypocrisy'.[44]

Given the film's indebtedness to the conventions of hardboiled fiction, Miller assumes some of the characteristics of the hardboiled hero whom John Cawelti describes as representing 'a tra-ditional man of virtue in an amoral and corrupt world'.[45] Although from a Protestant back-ground, his sceptical outlook and distaste for hypocrisy are designed to position him as a representative of a healthy, non-sectarian viewpoint. However, it is also a feature of hardboiled plots that the investigator should not only uncover hidden guilt but also mete out the justice that the law has so far failed to deliver. This, in turn, may create a tension whereby the involve-ment of the 'man of virtue' in retributive acts of justice may also lead him to fall prey to the very amoralism that he is engaged in combating. To some extent, this is also so of *Cycle of Violence*. Miller is guided by a benign police sergeant, Craig (Des Cave), who believes that Miller 'can go places he can't' and dispense the 'justice' that he is unable to due to a lack of the kind of evi-dence that would satisfy a court. One of the gang involved in the assault, the now-blind Callaghan (John Keegan), also refers to Miller as an 'avenging angel' and the film contains clear echoes of the earlier 'troubles' drama, *Angel*. In *Angel*, the saxophone player Danny (Stephen Rea) sets out to avenge the young mute girl he sees shot dead by paramilitaries at the film's start.

44. Hugh Linehan, '*Crossmaheart*', *Film West*, no. 32, 1998, p. 60.

45. John G. Cawelti, *Adventure, Mystery and Romance: Formula Stories as Art and Popular Culture* (Chicago: Chicago University Press, 1976), p. 152.

Unremittingly grim: the town
of Crossmaheart in *Cycle of
Violence* (aka *Crossmaheart*)

He too is guided by a policeman, Bloom (Ray McAnally), who comments that Danny 'can go
places' he 'never could'. However, in substituting the sax for the gun, Danny also becomes a
figure of moral ambiguity, succumbing to the very violence he wishes to oppose. Through his
efforts to unearth the truth of the sexual assault, Miller is likewise drawn into morally ambiguous acts, such as his killing of the IRA commandant, Curly Bap (Alan McKee), whom he shoves
(in an act of self-protection) onto a shard of exposed glass. And, while he may decline to shoot
O'Hagan (Enda Oates), the editor of the local paper who has murdered Miller's predecessor in
order to conceal his part in the rape, he is nevertheless indirectly responsible for his suicide by
leaving the gun (that Craig had provided) for O'Hagan to use.

Given the bleakness with which it presents the town and the moral strain that it imposes
upon its hero, it is not surprising that the novel on which the film is based should fall prey to
pessimism. After they have made love for the first time, Miller plans to leave Crossmaheart with
his new girlfriend Marie (Maria Lennon), the Catholic woman who has initiated his investigation. However, Marie, who has a history of mental instability since the assault on her younger
sister, commits suicide, while Miller is himself killed by a local shopkeeper who refuses to replace
a loaf of mouldy bread. Despite the intimidation that Miller has suffered at the hands of both
loyalists and republicans, this last act of violence is entirely gratuitous with no apparent link to
the surrounding sectarianism. In this way, the novel elevates the local squabbles of Crossmaheart
to a level of almost cosmic absurdity.

Made two years after the novel appeared, and more attuned to the optimism surrounding
the 'peace process', the film seeks to avoid the novel's gloomy denouement by reinstating a
'happy ending'. So while Miller is indirectly responsible for four deaths in the novel, two of these
characters (the bigoted Protestant minister, Rainey, and Callaghan) survive in the film and thus
lessen the moral pall that is cast over the hero. Moreover, in the film, the romance of the Protestant Miller and the Catholic Marie is permitted to prosper and the film ends with their departure from Crossmaheart – and the madness with which it is both literally and metaphorically
associated – to begin a new life in Belfast. However, given that the film retains the gloominess
and overall sense of wretchedness that characterised the novel, this necessarily goes against the
grain of what has preceded, while the filming of the couple's romantic reunion in soft focus
against a stylised blue backdrop invests the scene with an air of unreality. The association of the
couple with the police sergeant – significantly named Craig – also compromises the politically

questioning, non-sectarian outlook to which the film aspires. Craig figures more prominently in the film than in the novel, not only guiding Miller towards the truth of the crime but also acting as his surrogate father and 'guardian angel' (rescuing him, for example, from loyalists outside the Ulster Arms). He also appears at the film's end, to wish Miller luck and, in effect, bestow his blessing upon the young couple. However, given the history and political contentiousness of the RUC, and the apparent readiness of Craig himself to bypass normal judicial procedures, the character is hardly a politically neutral figure and clearly complicates the supposedly 'non-partisan' nature of the film's ending.

In his conversation with Craig at the film's close, Miller notes the irony of going back to Belfast in order to recover his 'sanity'. While Miller had originally been despatched from Belfast in order to recuperate from the trauma wrought by the death of his father, his new posting only exposed him to the even greater 'madness' of Crossmaheart. However, as Miller's comment implies, it is the city of Belfast that is more commonly associated with the representation of the conflict in Northern Ireland and the 'madness' with which the 'troubles' are associated.[46] Although *Divorcing Jack*, following the original novel, also contains scenes set in an imaginary Crossmaheart, it is more centrally concerned with the depiction of Belfast and was, indeed, one of the first of the 'ceasefire' films to make use of extensive Belfast locations. For a mixture of financial and security reasons, most of the films made prior to the ceasefires substituted other locations for Belfast. Inevitably, this dependence upon stand-in locations reinforced the sense of Belfast as an abstract place of the imagination emptied of specific geographical and physical markers. Given the various cities that have substituted for Belfast (such as Dublin, London and Manchester), this has also meant that there has been little accumulation of recurring 'landmarks'(beyond the conventional signifiers of specially painted murals and kerb-stones) and little sense of Belfast as an actual lived-in space. However, by filming in the city, the makers of *Divorcing Jack* not only aimed to show the actuality of Belfast missing from earlier films but also to represent the 'new' Belfast emerging in the wake of the peace process. According to the film's director, David Caffrey, there was a deliberate attempt to avoid 'the visual stereotypes of a gritty, poor run-down Northern Ireland' (as found, for example, in *Cycle of Violence*) and present Belfast as 'bright, modern and cosmopolitan'.[47] Thus, while the film acknowledges an iconographic debt to *Odd Man Out* by staging a short scene in Belfast's Crown Bar, it also searches out locations that are new in the cinematic representation of the city: the suburbs of south Belfast, the redeveloped Cathedral Quarter and the modern concert hall and exhibition centre, the Waterfront (that was destined to become an icon of the 'new Belfast' in a number of the Northern Ireland films that followed).

However, while the use of such locations may be intended to show the prosperous and peaceful Belfast arising from the ashes of the 'troubles', there is also evidence of a split within the film between the 'normality' and 'modernity' suggested by the film's settings and the

---

46. This emphasis upon Belfast is not, of course, without cause. As Mike Morrissey and Marie Smyth indicate, over 40 per cent of all 'troubles'-related deaths, and almost half of all sectarian deaths, between 1969 and 1999 occurred in the city (albeit concentrated in particular areas). See *Northern Ireland after the Good Friday Agreement: Victims, Grievance and Blame* (London: Pluto Press, 2002), p. 29.

47. Joanne Hayden, 'The Only Way is Up', *Film West*, no. 34, 1998, p. 28.

bleakness that characterises the film's plot. Thus, while *Divorcing Jack* is set on the eve of elections to a new independent Northern Ireland parliament, described by one character as 'happy, optimistic, joyous', the film itself is remarkably gloomy about the prospects of change.[48] This becomes particularly clear by the film's end, when all of the main protagonists are gathered together in the mountains of Mourne. Like Miller in *Cycle of Violence*, Dan Starkey (David Thewlis) is a Belfast journalist who inadvertently uncovers a dark secret that has implications for the whole of Northern Ireland. Engaging in a brief fling with a student Margaret (Laura Fraser), he is given a tape of Dvořák (the mispronunciation of which provides the film with its title) that turns out to contain the recording of a local politician Brinn (Robert Lindsay) confessing responsibility for the explosion of which he had previously claimed to be a victim. Following a series of narrative complications, Dan has agreed to give the tape to the self-serving republican paramilitary 'Cow' Pat Keegan (Jason Isaacs) in return for the release from captivity of his wife Patricia (Laine Megaw) and friend Mouse (Alan McKee). Keegan has, in turn, agreed to sell the tape to his former comrade Brinn. In line with the film's absurdist sensibility, the results are suitably grim. Brinn obtains the tape but is blown up by the tape recorder in which it has been presented to him. Keegan drives off with his payment for the tape but is then blown up by the booby-trapped briefcase containing the money. This is an especially pessimistic conclusion given that it has occurred on the very day that Northern Ireland has been voting for a new political dispensation under Brinn's leadership. Brinn's campaign had been based on peace and reconciliation but he does not survive to see his programme through. More significantly, the film implies that this programme was inherently flawed. A former IRA man, Brinn was responsible for the death of innocent civilians. Despite his protestations that his political ambitions have been fuelled by remorse and a desire to make amends, the film reveals the extent to which Brinn's activities as a 'man of peace' continue to depend on the use of violence. As the film reveals, he is not only indirectly responsible for the death of Margaret at the hands of the loyalist killer Billy McCoubrey (B. J. Hogg) but also masterminds the murder of Keegan and his associates.

There is, inevitably, an element of irony in this. Following its publication in 1995, the original novel was praised for the way it had anticipated the forthcoming assembly (albeit that this was hardly likely to lead to the independent Northern Ireland anticipated in both novel and film). However, it is significant that the success (such as it has been) of the Northern Ireland Assembly has depended upon a commitment by former paramilitaries to the ending of violence and an engagement in the political process. The implication of the film, however, appears to be that this is a forlorn prospect: paramilitaries prove unable to renounce violence, with the inevitable destructive consequences. As Lee (Rachel Griffiths), the nurse (and 'nun-o-gram') who has helped Starkey, observes, when Starkey wakes up in hospital near the film's end: 'It's chaos out there – but then it always has been.' This attitude appears to be reinforced by the setting in which the final encounter between Brinn and Keegan occurs. There has been a long-standing tradition within literature and film of associating Irish violence with the 'wildness' of

---

48. For an extended version of this argument, see John Hill, '*Divorcing Jack*', in Brian McFarlane (ed.), *The Cinema of Britain and Ireland* (London: Wallflower Press, 2005).

the Irish landscape. By dramatising its violent denouement against the backdrop of the spare landscape of the mountains of Mourne, so the film appears to reinforce a view that violence is a 'natural' – and therefore inevitable – outgrowth of the land itself.

There is, of course, one counter-current to this overall dramatic and ideological logic. Despite the expectation that he will be killed, Starkey is spared by Keegan, who, in an unconvincing outburst of romantic feeling towards Margaret, encourages him to write up the story of what has occurred. Following his spell in hospital, Starkey returns home to his wife, where they embark upon a bout of love-making on their 'magic settee'. In a sense, this concluding coda reinforces the conservative nature of the film's outlook. Starkey's involvement in the world of 'chaos' has been precipitated by the attractions of casual sex (with Margaret). His escape from 'chaos', and return to normality, is signalled by his return to the marital home and reconciliation with his wife. In this way, the film not only presses home the dangers of marital infidelity but also, like *Cycle of Violence*, stresses the threat to domesticity posed by the outside world of public disorder. In this way, for all its postmodern twists, *Divorcing Jack* continues to conform to a long-standing tradition of 'troubles' film-making in representing the conflicts in terms of a split between the public and private.

Divorcing Jack was released not long after the Omagh bombing (in August 1998) and there were suggestions in some quarters that it should not be shown. Although the film's co-producer and Head of Drama at BBC Northern Ireland, Robert Cooper, declared that the film's 'black wit' constituted a legitimate way of dealing with 'the wounds of a divided society', it is also clear that the film was capable of provoking genuine discomfort in the way that it made dark capital out of continuing conflict.[49] Whereas the films of Quentin Tarantino, on which *Divorcing Jack* is evidently modelled, occupy a displaced mythic world of popular culture and comic-book violence far removed from the direct experience of those who watch them, audiences were less insulated against the realities of the 'troubles' (or the continuing news reports about them). As a result, the film treads a fine line between comic subversion and bad taste, which leaves an audience – much like the audience for the jokes about paramilitaries told by the stand-up comedian within the film itself – uncertain whether or not it is appropriate to laugh. A similar awkwardness is also evident in another black comedy to emerge during this period: *An Everlasting Piece* (Barry Levinson).

Set in Belfast 'sometime' during the 1980s, the film concerns two hospital barbers, Colm (Barry McEvoy) and George (Brian F. O'Byrne), who join forces to win the franchise for hairpieces in Northern Ireland. Although set before the onset of the 'peace process', the film is nevertheless informed by a post-ceasefires sensibility in the way in which it follows films such *Cycle of Violence/Crossmaheart* and *Divorcing Jack* in sending up the paramilitaries and seeking to arrive at an upbeat conclusion. In what seems to be a reference to *The Boxer*, the film's writer and lead actor, Barry McEvoy, indicated his desire to differentiate the approach of the film from that of 'a Daniel Day Lewis film where everyone is looking miserable and moping around the joint'.[50] The film's focus, therefore, is on the way the two leads, one a Catholic and one a Protestant, triumph

49. Robert Cooper, 'All right Jack', letter to *The Guardian*, 1 October 1998, p. 23.
50. Michael Gray, '*An Everlasting Piece*: Barry McEvoy Interview', *Film West*, no. 43, 2001, p. 18.

in the face of unpropitious circumstances, resulting in an overtly happy ending that celebrates the benefits of collaboration across the religious divide. Thus, after the two men have succeeded in winning the competition to sell hairpieces, the camera shows Belfast City Hall beautifully illuminated on Christmas Eve. The camera tracks down past trees decked with fairy-lights onto the snow-covered road below to reveal the exterior of a pub. Inside, the two men, accompanied by Colm's girlfriend Bronagh (Anna Friel), celebrate as Bronagh plants a kiss on each of their semi-bald heads. Uniting Catholic and Protestant within the shared space of a packed city centre bar, the film not only imbues this scene with a spirit of optimism but also a more general sense of the 'peace dividend' that is destined to follow. Filmed with finance from a major studio (Dream-Works), and the visual sheen that this can provide, Belfast city centre is here invested with a magical, fairy-tale quality that contrasts sharply with the forlorn image of Colm's family home, stranded in wasteland on the edge of the Belfast 'peace line', shown at the film's start to the accompaniment of the Talking Heads' song 'Life during Wartime'. Given its symbolic associations, the use of the City Hall is especially significant in this regard. Built at the end of the nineteenth century to mark the city's growing prosperity (and to demonstrate the economic and political might of Protestantism), Belfast City Hall was the setting for the signing of the Solemn League and Covenant on Ulster Day in 1912, the original seat of the Northern Ireland parliament (prior to the opening of Stormont) and has since housed Belfast City Council through years of unionist domination, unionist resistance to the Anglo-Irish Agreement ('Belfast Says No') and a difficult political accommodation between unionists and republicans. Arriving at its own form of accommodation between its nationalist and unionist protagonists, so the film seems keen to celebrate not only the virtues of the new enterprise culture but also the prospect of a new start for the city, and its political life, more generally.

However, the very excessiveness of the imagery (falling snow, fairy-lights, extravagant camera movement) also suggests that this is precisely a fairy-tale ending that stands at odds with much of what has preceded. Thus, despite the film's drive towards reconciliation, its optimism is also undercut by the bleakness with which it portrays the surrounding physical and social landscape. One of the reasons why the shot of City Hall is so striking is that it comes at the end of a film in which the predominant settings have been inhospitable city backstreets. The fact that so many of these scenes were shot in Dublin rather than Belfast only reinforces the sense of the calculated effort that was involved in the creation of a dark and claustrophobic atmosphere. This air of oppressiveness is added to by aspects of the plot. One of the film's main jokes is that Colm and George, in a punning reference to the cross-community peace movement of the 1970s, refer to themselves as the 'piece people'. However, while their own cross-denominational allegiances permit them to sell wigs across the religious divide, they nevertheless do so by exploiting, rather than challenging, sectarian attitudes. For example, when they persuade a bigoted Protestant minister to buy a wig, they pander to his prejudices by declaring that their wigs are made of 'fine Protestant' – rather than 'dirty, mingy, smelly Catholic' – hair. Although the comic intent may be to expose the absurdity of religious prejudice, the very intensity with which characters give vent to sectarian sentiments (and the nature of the actions with which they are linked) reinforces a sense of the 'madness' that afflicts not just the mental hospital where Colm and George work but also Northern Ireland as a whole. The reintroduction, at the film's end, of 'the scalper' (Billy Connolly), clutching his bible and retrieving a missing wig from the sea, therefore, seems to remind the audience of the almost elemental 'madness' that continues to threaten the new sense of community to be found in the pub. Given that the scene also occurs at the Giant's Causeway, the site of the film's opening shots, the film also introduces an element of plot circularity (reminiscent of other 'troubles' dramas such as *Odd Man Out* and *Angel*) that partly undercuts the 'developmental' logic embedded in the film's main story.

The association of 'the scalper' with a garbled form of Protestant biblical fundamentalism also hints at how the film's re-imagining of community extends only so far. Apart from George, the Protestants – such as the freed loyalist killer who refuses to pay for his wig and the malevolent thugs who force Colm and Bronagh to stand for the British National Anthem – remain largely 'other' for the film, which concentrates primarily on the Catholic community, particularly the home life of Colm and Bronagh. George himself is something of a loner, seen neither with family nor friends, and he is, in effect, 'adopted' by Colm's.[51] As a result, the strongly individualised character of the relationship between Colm and George has knock-on effects for the 'gesture' of reconciliation with which the film ends. Although Colm refuses to sell hairpieces to the IRA (despite their presentation in the film as genial incompetents with hair problems and a taste for fried chicken), he is nevertheless prepared to do so in the case of the British Army on the grounds that it will constitute an act of forgiveness that will 'end the cycle' of violence. While the film's introduction of the army is striking, given the relative invisibility of British forces in so many 'troubles' films, which (like *Cycle of Violence* and *Divorcing Jack*) focus only on the 'two tribes', Colm's decision is not only curiously inconsistent (given that he had told the IRA that he would only sell wigs 'individually' and not to an 'army') but also evades the very obstacles to reconciliation that the film has shown the Protestant community to represent.

It was, of course, the film's portrait of British soldiers as youngsters losing hair as a result of 'extreme stress' that led to claims that the film was denied proper distribution by DreamWorks. One of the film's co-producers, Jerome O'Connor, even went so far as to file a lawsuit against the company for breach of contract in failing to give the film a proper US release.[52] However, despite allegations that DreamWorks (and Steven Spielberg in particular) wished to avoid offending the British government, there must also be a suspicion that the company did not feel that the film possessed strong commercial potential. The film contains a telling scene in this regard. When Colm explains to his family the name of his new enterprise ('the piece people'), he is met by stony silence and is reduced to remonstrating with them for failing to 'get it'. In an apparently unconscious moment of self-reflexivity, the film itself acknowledges just how difficult it is for paramilitaries and sectarianism to be turned into a fit subject for laughter.

---

51. In this way, the film partly conforms to a pattern evident in other dramas (such as *Henri* [1994], *Dance, Lexie, Dance, With or Without You* and *Mickybo & Me*) in which a conventional or 'uptight' Protestant/unionist undergoes a degree of transformation as a result of an encounter with the conviviality of Catholic/nationalist culture.

52. 'Piecemeal Release', *Film Ireland*, no. 79, 2001, p. 6. Costing $9 million to make, the film took just $75,000 at the US box office, even less than in the UK.

Romancing the 'troubles': *Mad about Mambo* (1999), *The Most Fertile Man in Ireland* (1999) and *With or Without You* (1998)

In Colin Bateman's original novel, *Cycle of Violence*, the joke of the title (not carried over into the film) is that it not only refers to a cliché of 'troubles' news reporting but the actual bicycle that the central character Miller uses to travel around Belfast. Towards the end of the film, anticipating his future relationship with Marie, Miller fantasises about turning his bike into a tandem and rechristening it 'the Cycle of Romance'.[53] As has been seen, however, the transformation of the 'troubles' melodrama into romance has proved a project fraught with difficulties. Thus, in the case of not only *Cycle of Violence* but also *Divorcing Jack* and *An Everlasting Piece*, the dark tone and absurdism of the films effectively undermine the optimism suggested by their romantic endings. Nevertheless, in films such as *Mad about Mambo*, *The Most Fertile Man in Ireland* and *With or Without You*, the reliance upon romance as a means of overcoming the pessimism of earlier 'troubles' drama becomes even more pronounced. During the 1980s and 1990s, Hollywood witnessed a revival of romantic comedy and this was matched, in Britain, by the success of films such as *Four Weddings and a Funeral* (1994), *Sliding Doors* (1998) and *Notting Hill* (1999). As indicated in the previous chapter, the desire for commercial success encouraged many local productions, funded by the BBC, the Lottery, the Northern Ireland Film Commission and the Irish Film Board, to adopt generic formulae, which, it was believed, would command popular appeal. However, while the upsurge of romantic comedy may have been a response to economic pressures, it was also the case that the conventions of the genre appeared to be particularly well attuned to the new mood in Northern Ireland following the onset of the peace process.

For the bringing of the romantic couple together despite the various obstacles and misunderstandings with which they are confronted is, of course, the central characteristic of romantic comedy.[54] In this respect, optimism is built into the very conventions of romantic comedy insofar as these dictate that the main characters will eventually overcome their problems and fulfil their romantic desires. As such, romantic comedy also reverses the conventions of 'troubles' drama in which the romantic aspirations of the protagonists are overwhelmed or destroyed by the forces arraigned against them. Given its overwhelming emphasis upon the formation of the couple, romantic comedy also commonly celebrates the transcendent power of love to unite characters from contrasting social backgrounds. As Thomas Schatz indicates, this has tended to invest the genre with a utopian dimension by virtue of the way in which romance is shown to have the capacity to dissolve sexual and social tensions.[55] Once again, this may be contrasted with the traditional 'troubles' plot-line (still evident in films such as Mary McGuckian's *This is*

---

53. Colin Bateman, *Cycle of Violence* (London: HarperCollins, 1995), p. 245.

54. There had been some earlier attempts at romantic comedy in an Irish context. Frank Launder and Sidney Gilliat's *I See a Dark Stranger* (1946), for example, is predicated upon a romance between an English officer and a fiery Irishwoman. However, whereas in this film (as in earlier romantic melodramas such as *Ourselves Alone*), romance is employed to overcome the English–Irish divide, the recent comedies have tended to focus on relations within and between Northern Ireland communities. In doing so, they have also tended to dramatise 'the Northern Ireland problem' in terms of internal relations within the North rather than the external relations between Ireland and Britain.

55. Schatz, *Hollywood Genres*, pp. 152–7.

the Sea [1996]), in which romantic liaisons typically flounder, or face destruction, as the result of irreconcilable political or religious differences. The bringing together of the couple in the romantic comedy, therefore, may also assume an allegorical dimension, symbolising the construction of a new social order in which traditional divisions are overcome. However, this fit between public and private dimensions can also be an uneasy one. For while characters may emblematise particular socio-economic attributes, the drama of romance is also predicated upon intensely personal emotions and desires. In this respect, there is also a strong drive within romantic comedy towards the private and the personal rather than the public and the political. As such, the fulfilment of romance may assume an ambivalent status, symbolising both the possibility of overcoming social barriers but also – as in so much 'troubles' drama – signalling a withdrawal from the social into the all-encompassing realm of the private.

Some of these tensions may be detected in *Mad about Mambo*. Written and directed by John Forte, it provides one of the clearest examples of the attempt to use the conventions of romantic comedy to traverse social divisions and, in doing so, to re-imagine the Northern Ireland 'community' in line with the emergent 'peace process'. The film focuses on a young Catholic lad from West Belfast, Danny Mitchell (William Ash), who aspires to play for the predominantly Protestant soccer team, 'Belfast United'.[56] Taking his cue from United's new Brazilian signing Carlos Rega (Daniel Caltagirone), the first Catholic to join the club, he seeks to improve his game by taking classes in Latin dance. This brings him into contact with Lucy McLoughlin (Keri Russell), an apparently well-to-do Protestant with a burning ambition to win a forthcoming dance contest. Although this initially looks like a straightforward love-across-the-divide scenario, the religious dimension is only one of a number of elements at play. Indeed, as in classical romantic comedy, it is class, rather than religious, distinctions that would seem to constitute the most significant divide. Thus, while Danny hails from a working-class housing estate, Lucy is a local businessman's daughter who drives a car provided by her father's firm, attends a posh school (loosely based on Belfast's Methodist College) and possesses a snooty boyfriend, Oliver (Theo Fraser Steele), who lives in a house with its own swimming pool. This clash of backgrounds becomes evident in Danny's faltering attempts to impress Lucy. Taking her to his local café, run by the Italian Rudi (Julian Littman), his forlorn request for tapas is met with the usual helping of fish and chips (albeit rounded off with an impressive Knickerbocker Glory). However, as in the traditional romantic comedy (such as *It Happened One Night*), encounters such as these also fuel a process of democratisation whereby the female protagonist comes to recognise some of the superficial aspects of her economically privileged lifestyle and rethinks her snobbish attitudes (involving, in this case, the eventual rejection of Oliver, who immediately reveals his true colours by labelling her a 'nobody').

---

56. This is, of course, a fictitious team but is loosely based on the Protestant team Linfield. According to Alan Bairner, 'the "community" which supports Linfield is regarded by its members as the true Ulster Protestant working class'. Linfield's ground, Windsor Park, also assumes added significance as the home venue of the Northern Ireland football team. See '"Up to their knees"? Football, Sectarianism, Masculinity and Working-class Identity', in Peter Shirlow and Mark McGovern (eds), *Who are 'The People'? Unionism, Protestantism and Loyalism in Northern Ireland* (London: Pluto, 1997), p. 107.

However, the film's comic strategy also seeks to complicate the binaries that have traditionally structured social roles. The film, in this respect, is clearly indebted to Bill Forsyth's *Gregory's Girl* (1980), in which a similar tale of school life, sporting aspiration and romantic intrigue is employed to unsettle social – and particularly gender – stereotypes. Thus, as in *Gregory's Girl*, the young male characters in *Mad about Mambo* only imperfectly inhabit their traditional 'masculine' roles. Thus, just as Gregory's classmate in *Gregory's Girl* is obsessed with cookery, so Danny's schoolfriend, Mickey (Maclean Stewart), aspires to be a fashion designer and runs up dancing costumes for him. Danny himself has to face potential ridicule not only by attending dance classes but also by taking his dance costume to the Belfast United changing rooms. In this respect, the romance within the film involves a degree of 'feminisation' whereby the central male character himself undergoes a certain relearning of his masculine role. At one point in the film, Danny's headmaster, Brother Xavier (Jim Norton), complains that their forthcoming opponents at soccer are a 'mixed' school. The school coach, Brother McBride (Tim Loane), automatically assumes that he is referring to religion when he is in fact objecting to the 'mixing' of the sexes. A preference for 'mixing', however, seems to sum up the film's own attitude, seeking to destabilise the fixed modes through which gender, class, religion and political identification are apprehended. In this way, the film not only subverts the conventional stereotypes of masculinity but cultural identities more generally. As Brother Xavier complains, the Catholic school that Danny attends is now playing the 'British imperialist' game of soccer. Danny's friend Spike (Joe Rea) makes use of the traditional Irish bodhrán to accompany Danny's Latin dancing, while Mickey shares his enthusiasm for contemporary fashion (and the Italian design team Dolce and Gabbana) through a classroom presentation delivered in Irish.

Many of these elements are brought together in the film's concluding sequence. Seeking to win Lucy back, after the dance contest has proved a debacle, Danny agrees with her father, Sid (Brian Cox), that they should dance during the half-time break. While she initially refuses to do so, she undergoes a change of heart when Danny declares his love for her. As in the film musicals of Fred Astaire (to which the film alludes), the concluding dance cements (and gives outward expression to) the romantic feelings existing between the two characters. However, unlike the Astaire–Rogers films, this is also a dance conducted under the public gaze of the football crowd, which, following initial bewilderment, is successfully won over by the endearing spectacle of the couple's dancing. This is, of course, an overtly utopian moment in which the football ground becomes an imagined space in which personal desires are fulfilled and social tensions are simultaneously resolved. The crowd of 'hard men', it seems, are converted to the pleasures of a 'femininised' display of Latin dancing, while Protestants and Catholics join together in a culturally shared activity. Thus, while the crowd may be predominantly Protestant, it also includes Danny's teachers as well as family members, including his Irish-speaking republican brother who had earlier vowed not to enter the stadium. It is also Danny's friends from school who provide the music to which the couple, as well as the crowd, now dance. In a clearly allegorical moment, Belfast is shown – at least for a brief moment – to have become truly 'united'. In this way, Lucy's dilemma about whether or not to leave Northern Ireland also seems to be resolved in favour of staying. As Deborah Thomas suggests, it is a feature of comedies that the 'social space' in which they occur is taken to be 'transformable' rather than, as in melodrama, somewhere from which

Changing masculine roles: Mickey (Maclean Stewart) irons the dance costume he has made for Danny (William Ash) inside the Belfast United changing rooms in *Mad about Mambo*

'escape to a space elsewhere' becomes necessary.[57] Thus, unlike conventional 'troubles' melodrama in which the romantic couple may be forced to flee their environment, the fulfilment of romantic desires here permits the possibility of the transformation of social space and does not involve the necessity of 'escape'.

However, it is also the case that the communitarian impulses of the film extend only so far. As previously indicated, the film is informed in part by a postmodern sensibility in which social identities are no longer fixed but are increasingly fluid and contingent. In contrast to the traditional 'troubles' drama, in which individuals fall victim to their environment, *Mad about Mambo* suggests how characters may break free of their inherited social positions. In a sense, Lucy's father, Sid, is the epitome of this. Brought up on the same estate as Danny, he has nevertheless acquired sufficient wealth to buy himself onto the board of Belfast United, a traditionally Protestant team, and send his daughter to a predominantly Protestant school. It is also he who encourages Danny, helping him to obtain a trial and even to declare his feelings for his daughter. In certain respects, Sid's alignment with Danny rather than Oliver may be seen to involve a rescue

---

57. Deborah Thomas, *Beyond Genre: Melodrama, Comedy and Romance in Hollywood Films* (Moffat: Cameron and Hollis, 2000), p. 14.

of her from the snobby middle-class Protestantism with which Oliver is associated.[58] However, Sid functions less as a representative of the Catholic community than as a self-made man and risk-taking entrepreneur who has built his fortune from a chain of 'Do-it-yourself' stores. This is, in effect, his advice to Danny as well, to take risks and make things happen by 'doing it himself'. In the same way, Lucy's enthusiasm for dance, like Danny's attraction to football, is motivated, as she explains, by a desire to show that she too can go it alone and achieve something that is 'just me'. As a result, the film's efforts to imagine a new sense of community through romance are effectively undercut by the strong sense of individualism with which the main characters are identified (and which seems to provide the basic prerequisite for the transcendence of social divisions).

Similar tensions are also evident in *The Most Fertile Man in Ireland*, in which the socially maladroit Catholic Eamonn Manley (Kris Marshall) falls for a young Protestant woman, Rosie (Kathy Kiera Clarke). In contrast to *Mad about Mambo*, which plays its romance relatively 'straight', the tone of *The Most Fertile Man in Ireland* is much more knowing in character, exaggerating both the romantic naiveté of the central characters and the anachronisms of the fictional universe that they inhabit. As various commentators have noted, the changes in gender roles and expanded notions of sexual freedom that have occurred over the last forty years have made it much more difficult for romantic comedy to assert the virtues of romance with the same confidence as before. This, in turn, has encouraged the adoption of an ironic stance whereby traditional notions of love are both mocked and reconfirmed.[59] This is also so of *The Most Fertile Man in Ireland*, in which the romantic ideals held on to by Eamonn and Rosie have long since been abandoned by those around them. As a result, the couple's love for each other is placed in constant jeopardy and, in line with the film's taste for comic excess, subjected to the most extreme of tests.

For while Eamonn is still nurturing romantic fantasies about Rosie, he allows himself to be seduced by the local good-time girl, Mary (Tara Lynn O'Neill). Although they are shown to use extensive contraception, she nevertheless becomes pregnant by him. While Mary has no wish to marry Eamonn (and sets about procuring a well-to-do husband with a pragmatism that contrasts sharply with the angst associated with pregnancy in earlier films, such as *Hush-a-Bye Baby*), the news of Eamonn's apparently 'miraculous' powers spreads quickly, creating further demand for his services. The film had begun with a montage of shots of male sperm accompanied by a female commentary, spoken by Dr Johnson (Toyah Willcox), explaining the decline in men's sperm count and the need for 'a new Adam' capable of reversing the trend towards male infer-

---

58. Although the film does not explicitly identify the religious affiliation of Lucy's mother, the implication seems to be that she was Protestant (with Sid suggesting that Oliver would get on better with Lucy's mother at the film's end). Thus, while the failure of Sid's marriage and the break-up of the relationship between Lucy and Oliver are primarily configured in terms of class, and corresponding social attitudes, they also suggest a religious dimension that partly undermines the film's optimism about the breakdown of social divisions and might even give rise to a nationalist reading whereby Lucy is 'rescued' from Protestant influence. This is partly confirmed by the film's own tendency to rely upon, rather than subvert, stereotypes of Protestantism.

59. See, for example, Frank Krutnik, 'Conforming Passions? Contemporary Romantic Comedy', in Steve Neale (ed.), *Genre and Contemporary Hollywood* (London: Routledge, 2002).

tility. One of the key jokes of the film, therefore, is that it is the otherwise socially and sexually inadequate Eamonn who is revealed, like Clark Kent in the comics he reads, to be the very 'superman' who possesses the powers to occupy this role. In league with an enterprising – if unscrupulous – female colleague, Millicent (Bronagh Gallagher), Eamonn sets himself up in business successfully fertilising women who were previously unable to have children. Initially, this is a service offered to Catholic women whose religious beliefs have prevented the use of artificial insemination. However, fearing that Catholics are outbreeding Protestants and that this will lead to Catholics winning a future referendum on the constitutional status of Northern Ireland, Eamonn is forced by a former loyalist paramilitary, 'Mad Dog' Billy Wilson (James Nesbitt), into extending his services to childless Protestants as well.[60] Energetically reworking the 'troubles' theme of 'a plague on both your houses', the film shows Eamonn to be the prisoner of the two communities' competing, but equally absurd, demands upon him. Thus, as he dashes between Protestant and Catholic homes, a brief montage cuts between portraits of the Queen and the Pope before they eventually merge into the same image.

As this would suggest, *The Most Fertile Man in Ireland*'s approach to the 'troubles' brings to the fore the issue of 'masculinity' that had been bubbling below the surface of *Mad about Mambo* and many of the 'ceasefire' films before it. In this respect, the film's ironic stance not only manifests a failing confidence in the ideology of romance but also in the clear-cut sense of gender divisions upon which classical romantic comedy had traditionally relied.[61] As the film's director, Dudi Appleton, explains, the film is about 'how men today are lost, trying to live out traditional and often macho roles in a world that is fast leaving them behind'.[62] The film's emphasis upon the 'redundant male' (as Dr Johnson's commentary puts it) picks up on the theme of the 'crisis in masculinity' that was a feature of a number of successful British comedies during the 1990s, such as *Brassed Off* (1996), *The Full Monty* (1997) and *Up 'N' Under* (1997), dealing with the challenge to traditional male roles wrought by the decline of manufacturing in the north of England. As noted in the previous chapter, the decline in manufacturing industry and growth in male working-class employment during the 1980s and 1990s was even more pronounced in Northern Ireland. Given these trends, it is perhaps unsurprising that there is an almost complete absence of representations of traditional forms of male work in the Northern Ireland comedies, combined with an emphasis upon new types of service employment. *Mad about Mambo*'s focus upon retailing, football, dance and fashion, for example, could clearly be read as an advert for the re-education of male sensibilities in line with the demands of the new economy, while Eamonn's

---

60. The 1991 Northern Ireland census of population revealed the narrowing of the gap in size between the Protestant and Catholic populations, which has since continued (such that 44 per cent of respondents claimed to be brought up Catholic and 53 per cent Protestant in 2001). As Marianne Elliott indicates, Protestant fears of Catholic population growth contributed to the escalation of loyalist murders of Catholics in the years preceding the 1994 ceasefires. See *The Catholics of Ulster* (New York: Basic Books, 2001), p. 435.

61. As such, the film conforms to a pattern indicated by William Paul, in which the 'clear sense' of male and female sex roles that used to exist in romantic comedy has been thrown into 'flux'. See William Paul, 'The Impossibility of Romance: Hollywood Comedy, 1978–1999', in Neale (ed.), *Genre and Contemporary Hollywood*, p. 128.

62. '*The Most Fertile Man In Ireland*', Northern Ireland Film Commission, Press Release, 2000, <www.nifc.co.uk/news/mostfertile.html>.

establishment of himself as a 'one-man service industry' in *The Most Fertile Man in Ireland* offers an ironic commentary upon these same developments. These economic changes are also associated with a world in which gender roles have become increasingly confused. Thus, just as *Mad about Mambo* gently subverts traditional notions of masculinity, so *The Most Fertile Man in Ireland* plays with gender stereotypes by showing men (like the one who appears on a daytime television show above the caption 'Your man want to be a woman') becoming more like women and women (such as Eamonn's brother's girlfriend, Sheila, played by Orla O'Carroll) becoming more like men. However, while these films tap into a broader concern with the reshaping of masculinity in the face of economic restructuring, these issues necessarily acquire an added dimension as a result of the Northern Ireland context.

Although it would be a mistake to ignore the role of (predominantly republican) women as perpetrators of paramilitary violence (and the challenge to traditional ideologies of 'femininity' that this represents), it is by and large male violence, and violent masculinity, that has sustained the 'troubles'. As Colin Coulter indicates, the violence has mainly consisted of '(working class) men attempting with varying degrees of success to kill other (working class) men'.[63] Given that 'troubles' drama has also depended upon a clearly gendered division of labour according to which the world of politics and violence is associated with men and the world of home and domesticity with women, it is to be expected that the dramatisation of the peace process contained in Northern Ireland films should also link the abandonment of paramilitary violence with the obsolescence of traditional forms of masculinity. As has been seen, films such as *The Crying Game*, *In the Name of the Father* and *The Boxer* all imply the need for men to adopt new forms of masculinity (even if, in the case of *The Crying Game*, this involves offloading the responsibility for the continuation of the violence onto the 'unnatural' female).[64] In a similar fashion, *The Most Fertile Man in Ireland* dramatises its crisis in masculinity not simply in terms of the emergence of a new post-industrial order but also in terms of the redundancy of the gunman. As Eamonn tells his brother, Raymond (More O'Shea), a former republican paramilitary, 'the war's over and no one wants to know any more'. Thus, despite Raymond's attempts to use force to stop Eamonn from sleeping with Protestants, he is revealed to be, both literally and metaphorically, shooting 'blanks' and ends up on a daytime television chat show demanding sympathy for men's plight and engaging in a group hug. Although more menacing, the loyalist paramilitary 'Mad Dog' Wilson is also shown to be out of kilter with the new social and political realities, stuck in the past and proudly displaying the old newspaper cutting that recalls how he was once 'feared and ruthless'. The film also plays with the homo-eroticism evident in a film such as *Resurrection Man* by having Wilson's camp sidekick, George (MacLean Stewart), undermine some of the menace Wilson might otherwise be seen to possess (particularly in the film's replaying of the punishment room scenes from *Nothing Personal* and *Resurrection Man*).

63. Colin Coulter, *Contemporary Northern Irish Society* (London: Pluto, 1999), p. 133.

64. This is evident in the film's treatment of Jude (Miranda Richardson), in which the imagery of the heartless terrorist is combined with that of the femme fatale. See Sarah Edge, ' "Women are trouble, did you know that Fergus?"': Neil Jordan's *The Crying Game*, *Feminist Review*, no. 50, 1995.

However, while it is arguably the case that many of the British films dealing with the 'crisis of masculinity' seek to recover traditional forms of masculinity through the reconstruction of the all-male group, the emphasis upon the couple in *The Most Fertile Man in Ireland* involves a greater emphasis upon the relearning, or abandonment, of traditional male roles.[65] Thus, while the revelation of Eamonn's 'superhuman' fertility might seem to provide the occasion for a recovery of male pride and the re-assertion of phallic power, this is not in fact the case. For in order to cement his relationship with Rosie, Eamonn volunteers to have a vasectomy that will bring his fertility to an end. This signals, in turn, a rejection of the 'playboy' masculinity associated with his philandering father. At the start of the film, Eamonn had been urged by both his mother and brother to become more like his 'Da' (whom he believes to be dead) – 'a man's man' who could 'shag like a lion'. However, when he finally meets his father (and Rosie simultaneously meets Eamonn's 'son'), he comes to recognise the limitations of a model of masculinity that has left him without a father for most of his life (his father's stage name was apparently 'Big Con'). By refusing to follow in his father's footsteps ('the original fertile man') and choosing a vasectomy, Eamonn therefore not only brings sex and love back into alignment but is also able to assume his 'proper' role as a husband and father. In this regard, the film's achievement of narrative resolution through vasectomy does not so much imply that home and marriage involve a symbolic 'castration' (as in many male-oriented genres such as the gangster film or Western) so much as an 'adult' reconciliation to the loss of traditional phallic power.

However, while Eamonn and Rosie's romance involves a negotiation of changing gender roles, it also assumes a more general allegorical dimension in relation to the 'troubles'. As previously indicated, Eamonn is a Catholic while Rosie is a Protestant and the evolution of their romance is carefully plotted in terms of dates that carry a symbolic significance. Their first date takes place on St Patrick's Day, a day of particular note for nationalists, while, following some narrative complications, their second date occurs, at Rosie's request, on the eleventh night, the eve of the 'Glorious Twelfth'. The Twelfth of July is, of course, the most important date in the Ulster unionist calendar, involving marches by the Orange Order in celebration of William of Orange's defeat of Jacobite forces at the Battle of the Boyne in 1690. Within the divided political landscape of Northern Ireland, these celebrations are, inevitably, highly controversial. While defended by unionists as a traditional 'pageant', the events surrounding the Twelfth are nonetheless regarded by nationalists as sectarian, and 'triumphalist', in character.[66] The decision to use the eleventh night bonfire as a romantic setting is therefore a calculated one. Shot in brown and golden hues to the accompaniment of a mellow piece of pop (sung by Mary Black), the bonfire

---

65. For a discussion of class and gender in the British comedies, see John Hill, 'Failure and Utopianism: Representations of the Working Class in British Cinema of the 1990s', in Robert Murphy (ed.), *British Cinema of the 90s* (London: BFI, 2000), and Claire Monk, 'Underbelly UK: The 1990s Underclass Film, Masculinity and the Ideologies of "New" Britain', in Justine Ashby and Andrew Higson (eds), *British Cinema, Past and Present* (London: Routledge, 2000).

66. Dominic Bryan discusses the dominant discourses surrounding the Twelfth of July in "Ireland's Very Own Jurassic Park": The Mass Media, Orange Parades and the Discourse on Tradition', in Anthony D. Buckley (ed.), *Symbols in Northern Ireland* (Belfast: Institute of Irish Studies, 1998). See also Neil Jarman, *Material Conflicts: Parades and Visual Displays in Northern Ireland* (Oxford: Berg, 1997), ch. 5, 'The Glorious Twelfth'.

sequence is clearly intended to bear out Rosie's claim that it is, indeed, a 'beautiful' occasion. Although a loyalist approaches Eamonn muttering 'God and Ulster', the sequence is devoid of antagonism and the couple are drawn into a happy, unthreatening crowd. The encounter proves to be a crucial one in cementing the relationship between the two young people, who are subsequently shown enjoying a moment of 'transcendence' as they sit together observing the city below. There can be little doubt that this method of presentation leads to a sanitised view of the eleventh night. It would also be fair to note that the sequence possesses a festive, communal dimension that is entirely absent from the film's portrait of St Patrick's Day (when Eamonn and Rosie's date involves a meal in a semi-deserted fish-and-chip shop). As a result, the celebratory quality of the sequence (partly filtered through the nostalgic glow of Rosie's childhood memory) appears to involve a strategy of redemption designed to rescue loyalism from its association with the 'abject' as found in films such as *Resurrection Man*. In doing so, the sequence does not straightforwardly endorse a unionist outlook, however, but seeks, in a moment of utopianism, to reclaim the 'Twelfth' as a civic festival in which Catholics and Protestants might both participate as part of a process of peaceful reconstruction.

The integration of public and private moments evident in this sequence may also be found in the scene when Eamonn and Rosie finally consummate their love. Occurring on New Year's Eve, the couple are initially part of the group of revellers celebrating at the foot of the Albert Clock. The couple proceed to climb the clock tower, where they then make love behind the clock face while fireworks (more than a little reminiscent of the sperm shown earlier) explode around them. While the choice of setting may possess a 'realistic' motivation (given its use as an actual gathering-place) and permits an element of phallic symbolism (in line with the film's ribald tone), it also constitutes a significant reworking of an established 'landmark' of 'troubles' film-making. For it is, of course, the Albert Clock (a memorial clock tower built at the top of High Street during the nineteenth century) that features so heavily in *Odd Man Out* and marks the site where the film begins and ends. In returning to this location, therefore, the film effectively inverts the meanings with which it was associated in the earlier film. In *Odd Man Out*, the clock provides the backdrop against which the film's fatalistic logic unfolds, culminating in the death of Johnny and Kathleen beneath it. In *The Most Fertile Man in Ireland*, however, the clock becomes the site of romantic fulfilment, which, through the pregnancy to which it leads, anticipates the future rather than falls victim to the past. Rosie works at an undertakers (that proudly proclaims the motto 'Death Becomes Us') and is earlier heard to tell Eamonn that 'fate never did anyone favours'. However, unlike *Odd Man Out*, where the couple's fate is indeed a shared death, the film's reliance upon the conventions of romantic comedy ensures that the couple, and their straddling of the sectarian divide, do in this case succeed in overcoming the obstacles that are placed before them.

However, while the film may punctuate its romantic moments with public references, there is also a sense in which it ultimately turns away from the public sphere. When Eamonn opts to have his vasectomy, he has been pursued to the hospital by rival groups of Catholics and Protestants who await him in the lobby. In order for the operation to be conducted, the door has to be bolted and Mad Dog Wilson watches through a window in despair as he witnesses his hopes for population growth among Protestants vanish. Like *Divorcing Jack*, in which the couple eventually find sanctuary from the 'chaos' outside, so *The Most Fertile Man in Ireland* ultimately settles for what Raymond Williams has referred

Private dramas in public space: the use of Belfast's Albert Clock in *Odd Man Out* and *The Most Fertile Man in Ireland*

to as 'retreating privatisation'. According to Williams, this describes a process whereby the 'small–unit entity' of 'you and your relatives, your lovers, your friends, your children' becomes 'the only really significant social entity'.[67] It is effectively this retreat into the 'small–unit entity' that characterises the film's ending. The camera is seen to track down an enclosed corridor before progressing through an opening swing-door where the reconstructed family unit (consisting of Rosie, Eamonn, Eamonn's Da, Rosie's uncle and the twins) are shown grouped together in a room separated from the outside world. The film then cuts to a final sequence, shot in the style of a nappy advert, in which a spruced-up Eamonn and Rosie are shown surrounded by numerous babies. As the setting is a studio in which the background has been whitened out, the couple and the babies assume an abstract quality detached from any particular time or place. In this way, the film also seems to pluck its couple from the specific political context with which they were previously associated and celebrate their successful escape into the privatised – and universalised – sphere of the family unit.

This uneasy balancing of private and public drama is also a characteristic of *With or Without You*, a modern variant of the comedy of 'remarriage', in which a couple fall in love for a second time.[68] Written by John Forte and directed by Michael Winterbottom, the film begins with the decision of the Belfast couple Rosie (Dervla Kirwan) and Vincent (Christopher Eccleston) to try for a baby. Their efforts, however, prove fruitless and Vincent is faced with the prospect of dependence upon a sperm donor. As in *The Most Fertile Man in Ireland*, Vincent's apparent infertility reflects a more general sense of the 'emasculation' resulting from changing male roles. A former RUC officer, Vincent has left the police in order to please Rosie. Now working for his father-in-law fitting windows, he clearly misses the action, male camaraderie and sense of self-worth that was associated with his old job. He is also taunted by his former colleagues for being 'under Rosie's thumb' and evidently resents the loss of freedom that marriage has entailed.

Vincent's problems are further compounded by the unexpected appearance of Benoit (Yvan Attal), the French pen-pal with whom Rosie fell in love as a teenager (albeit without actually meeting him). His arrival in Belfast rekindles romantic feelings in Rosie, precipitating a further degree of crisis in Rosie and Vincent's already failing marriage. Benoit, however, does not simply represent Rosie's lost youth and associated passions but also appears to epitomise a more 'feminised' version of masculinity. Thus while Vincent enjoys boxing on television (seen shouting 'hit the fucker' at the screen) and tinkering with cars, Benoit does not drive, plays the clarinet and professes to cry when listening to Schubert. Benoit is also more at ease with 'domestication' and is shown to help Rosie shop for groceries and assist her in the kitchen.[69]

67. Raymond Williams, 'Problems of the Coming Period', *New Left Review*, no. 140, 1983, p. 16.

68. In the best-known account of 'the comedy of remarriage', Stanley Cavell argues that the drive of the plot is 'not to get the central pair together, but to get them *back* together, together *again*'. See *Pursuits of Happiness: The Hollywood Comedy of Remarriage* (Cambridge, MA: Harvard University Press, 1981), p. 2.

69. Nevertheless, Benoit too may be seen to represent a victim of 'the crisis of masculinity'. Although reluctant to admit the truth to Rosie, he has been thrown out by his girlfriend and has lost his job (as a result of mechanisation). He is also seemingly mystified by the feminist art exhibition at the Waterfront entitled, like a famous 1970s book, 'Our Bodies, Our Selves', where he sticks his head inside a large furry vagina and bursts a teat-like exhibit. In this respect, the film also reveals the limits of its own sexual politics, portraying the feminist artist (played by local comedian Nuala McKeever) as both pretentious and lacking in sympathy for other women.

Combining elements of both comedy and the female-centred melodrama, the film is partly narrated by Rosie and attempts to address some of the dilemmas posed by women's experience of love and family. Accordingly, the film's introduction of Benoit forces Rosie into a choice between the two male leads and the emotional satisfactions that each provides. In line with the conservative traditions of the 'woman's film', her resulting decision to stay with Vincent implies a rejection of fantasy and the acceptance of adult responsibilities. This is also so of Vincent, who must likewise turn his back on the casual sex he enjoyed with Cathy (Julie Graham) as a police officer and reconcile himself to a more domesticated masculine role. This is worked out in a concluding sequence when Vincent discovers that Rosie is pregnant and, believing Benoit to be responsible, sets off in pursuit of the couple with the gun he keeps hidden in the house. Although this might suggest a return to the physical action (and phallic prowess) associated with his career as a policeman, the resort to violence – and the traditional form of masculinity that goes with it – is based upon a misapprehension and, as in the conventional 'troubles' drama, must be renounced by Vincent if he is to achieve a proper reconciliation with his wife.

While the film's producer, Andrew Eaton, has indicated that there was 'absolutely no attempt to make Rosie and Vincent's lives into an allegory about Northern Ireland', it is difficult not to identify a link between the film and the context in which it was made.[70] As a part of the Good Friday Agreement, it had been agreed that there would be a review of the future of policing in Northern Ireland, which led to the establishment of the Independent Commission on Policing, under the chairmanship of Chris Patten, in 1998. Although the film went into production before the publication of the ensuing report (in September 1999) – recommending the replacement of the overwhelmingly Protestant RUC by a more religiously balanced Northern Ireland Police Service – the film is clearly informed by a sense of the changing context in which policing in Northern Ireland was occurring. Thus, while Vincent's departure from the police is presented in personal terms, it may also be linked with the growing 'demilitarisation' of Northern Irish society and the transformation of the RUC into a 'normal' police force representative of the population as a whole. Vincent, moreover, is identified with Ulster unionism within the film not only through his membership of the RUC but Rosie's taunts that he should 'join the Orange Order and have done with it' when he indicates that he intends to go out with his former RUC mates. It is these same friends who make the joke that Vincent is a 'Jaffa' because he is 'orange and seedless'. In this respect, Vincent's reconciliation with Rosie and conversion to a 'softer' form of masculinity may also be read in terms of the need for unionism to itself become 'softer' and adjust to new political realities. In this respect, Benoit's role as a romantic counterfoil possesses an added dimension. Although, in part, conforming to a stereotype of the 'romantic Frenchman', his presence nevertheless suggests how the 'rebirth' of Northern Ireland not only depends upon an increasing acceptance of national and ethnic differences (Benoit, for example, persuades the couple to attend their first ceilidh) but also a new form of transnational identification with 'Europe'.[71]

---

70. *With or Without You*, publicity material, BFI Library.

71. For a discussion of Northern Ireland and its relationship to Europe, see Kevin Davey, 'No Longer "Ourselves Alone" in Northern Ireland', in David Morley and Kevin Robbins (eds), *British Cultural Studies* (Oxford: Oxford University Press, 2001). More pragmatically, there has, of course, been a substantial financial contribution – via the Structural Funds and the Programme for Peace and Reconciliation – from the European Union towards economic and social development within Northern Ireland. The film itself also benefited from the involvement of French company Ima Films, which undoubtedly accounts for the presence of a French character.

This public aspect of the couple's private drama is also suggested by the film's deployment of place. As in *Divorcing Jack*, *An Everlasting Piece* and *The Most Fertile Man in Ireland*, there is a clear sense in which the film seeks to move beyond the established imagery of Belfast and to employ setting in a way that generalises the significance of the characters' particular situation. Thus, in one particularly striking sequence, the film shows a conversation between Benoit and Rosie, occurring inside the Waterfront, where Rosie works as a receptionist. As their conversation proceeds, the camera circles around the couple before moving off them to show the street below. While Rosie and Benoit continue to talk, a short montage of shots of the city ensues. Echoing the use of descriptive shots in the British 'new wave' of the 1960s, the montage is striking in the way that it links the personal predicaments of the main protagonists to the more general 'story' of the city itself.[72] Thus, just as the couple discuss what has happened in the period since they were last in contact, so we see how the look of the city has itself changed in the intervening period with old, new and derelict buildings all occupying a common space.

In the case of the British 'new wave', 'descriptive' sequences such as this drew upon a poetic-realist tradition of aestheticising the urban environment. A similar 'poetic' impulse is also evident in the way in which *With or Without You* employs images of well-known buildings, such as the City Hall, the Albert Clock and even the Europa Hotel (the most bombed building in Europe), but, through the adoption of unusual angles and framings, presents them in an unfamiliar manner. In this way, the film less re-appropriates the meanings attached to these buildings, as in the case of *An Everlasting Piece* and *The Most Fertile Man in Ireland*, than divests them of their pre-existing associations. Thus, while the film may rely upon actual Belfast locations, it also invests them with an element of the 'placelessness' that characterises many of the 'troubles' films that do not. However, unlike *Odd Man Out* and *Nothing Personal*, this does not lead to the suggestion of metaphysical forces so much as the very 'ordinariness', and even anonymity, of contemporary Belfast. Given the strength, and endurance, of the associations that have historically attached to the city, this is not, of course, without its significance. For, as Malachy McEldowney and his co-authors indicate, the search for 'a new imagery' that would rescue the city from its association with 'violence, fear and division' and 'communicate an identity of relative normality' and 'aspiring "modernity"' has been a central component of an 'ideological offensive', on the part of politicians and planners, to raise the morale of the local population and attract prospective investors.[73] In this respect, *With or Without You*'s documentation of the city's changing landscape, and pursuit of the 'poetry' of the 'ordinary', fulfils some of the requirements for an image of Belfast as 'normal' and 'modern' (rather than abnormal and 'backward'). As a result, Martin McLoone suggests how the film, along with *Wild about Harry*, may be seen to assume some of

---

72. For a discussion of this detachment of place from narrative function in the British 'new wave', see John Hill, *Sex, Class and Realism: British Cinema 1956–63* (London: BFI, 1986), pp. 129–32.

73. Malachy McEldowney, Ken Sterrett and Frank Gaffikin, 'Architectural Ambivalence: The Built Environment and Cultural Identity in Belfast', in William J.V. Neill and Hanns-Uve Schwedler (eds), *Urban Planning and Cultural Inclusion: Lessons from Belfast and Berlin* (Basingstoke: Palgrave, 2001), p. 106. It could be argued that it was the failure to detach its 'new imagery' of the city from an association with 'violence, fear and division' that led to the tensions within *Divorcing Jack*. Although containing a number of allusions to the RUC, *With or Without You* is much more circumspect regarding its references to the 'troubles'.

An unfamiliar Belfast: *With or Without You*

the characteristics of the 'promotional video' in the way in which it not only celebrates the 'modernity' of the city but also portrays Belfast as 'affluent, middle-class and consumerist'.[74]

However, while the film undoubtedly shows new urban developments such as the Waterfront to good advantage, there is also a degree of ambivalence in the way in which these changes are portrayed. For although Rosie works at the Waterfront, she is unhappy in her job and has packed it in by the film's end. While this may contribute to the film's conservatism concerning the family (whereby the working woman is returned to her 'proper place' in the home), the film also links the Waterfront with a range of unattractive personnel that includes an overweening boss, a philandering businessman, a self-important conductor and a pretentious artist. The view of the changing city skyline, moreover, is prompted by Rosie's recollection that the building was erected on the very site – the bus station – where she received her first kiss. Enthusiasm for the redevelopment of Belfast within the film is therefore tempered by the film's association of the changes with a sense of an irretrievable past and lack of an 'authentic' relation with its residents. This, in turn, is reinforced by the film's problems in establishing the city as a place that the characters appear genuinely to inhabit.

In her discussion of Michael Winterbottom's film about a working-class family in London, *Wonderland* (1999), made back-to-back with *With or Without You*, Charlotte Brunsdon notes how the film transforms 'landmark London' into 'a lived, material, everyday city'.[75] However, while the two films share a concern to 'defamiliarise' the urban landscape, their evocation of the 'lived'

74. Martin McLoone, 'Topographies of Terror and Taste: The Re-imagining of Belfast in Recent Cinema', in Barton and O'Brien (eds), *Keeping it Real*, pp. 141–3.

75. Charlotte Brunsdon, 'The Poignancy of Place: London and Cinema', *Visual Culture in Britain*, vol.5, no. 1, 2004, p. 65.

city is very different. This is partly due to the way in which *With or Without You*'s aesthetic of 'display' sets up a degree of disjunction between the characters and the city space they occupy, presenting the city as the object of the look of the camera and the film's spectator – but rarely of the characters themselves. This sense of a split between character and environment is reinforced by the film's concentration on the city centre and the virtual invisibility of the area in which the characters actually live. Unlike *Wonderland*, in which the neighbourhoods where the family live are clearly delineated, there is little sense in *With or Without You* of the part of Belfast where Rosie and Vincent reside or how this connects to the city centre (particularly due to the film's habit of cutting straight from the city centre to domestic interiors as at the end of the film's first montage).[76] Thus, while the couple's story may partly emblematise the changes that Belfast is undergoing, there is also a sense that the characters are not truly 'at home' in the city to which they apparently belong.[77] As a result, there is a certain turning away from the city towards the film's end, when Vincent and Rosie achieve reconciliation on a north Antrim beach. While, at one level, the sequence provides the opportunity for the 'promotion' of Northern Ireland as a tourist destination, it is also clear that the seaside functions as a marker of 'authenticity' and that the couple's escape from the city has enabled them to give vent to feelings that they had previously found it impossible to express.

Divided loyalties: *As the Beast Sleeps* (2001) and *The Mighty Celt* (2005)

This absence of a 'lived Belfast' in a film such as *With or Without You* inevitably gives rise to some other questions. As already noted, the development of the city centre in terms of transnational retail outlets and 'flagship' developments (such as the Waterfront), characterised by a 'neutral' architectural style, has been central to the construction of the 'new Belfast' as a supposedly shared, non-sectarian space befitting of the 'peace process'. At the same time, the predominant feature of the spatial geography of Belfast has been growing religious segregation and class division. As Henry McDonald recalls, just twenty-four hours into the IRA ceasefire of 1994, the foundations of a new barrier or 'peace wall' were laid across the city's Alexandra Park, bringing the total of such barriers to twenty-six, all of which have remained in place despite the onset of the 'peace process'.[78] At the same time, there has been increasing residential segregation, with

---

76. This may be linked to a more general difficulty in representing the suburbs. Existing somewhere 'in-between' the city centre and the country, suburbia, as Deborah Stevenson suggests, has become 'a seemingly featureless imaginative space beyond the "real" city but not yet in the country'. See *Cities and Urban Cultures* (Maidenhead: Open University Press, 2003) p. 123.

77. This issue is, of course, complicated further by the fact that, as in so many 'Northern Ireland films', the main leads (the northern English actor Christopher Eccleston and the southern Irish actress Dervla Kirwan) do not themselves hail from the area. While all acting does, of course, rely upon impersonation, the pre-existing persona of an actor may nevertheless inhibit the identification of character with place. Thus, the casting of Kirwan as a northern Protestant is particularly complicated by her association with the character of Assumpta (and her relationship with a Catholic priest) in the long-running BBC serial *Ballykissangel*, set in a rural village in the South.

78. Henry McDonald, 'The Last Walls of Europe', in *Colours: Ireland – From Bombs to Boom* (Edinburgh: Mainstream Publishing, 2005), p. 94.

the majority of Belfast's population living in areas dominated by either Protestants or Catholics. There is, of course, a clear class dimension to this. Middle-class areas, such as south Belfast, are more mixed than the predominantly working-class areas of north and west Belfast (while many of the middle class who are able to afford it have simply migrated to the suburbs). The decline of the industrial sector and the growth of the service sector, discussed in the previous chapter, may have encouraged a degree of cross-community convergence within the middle class but has also exacerbated the levels of economic inequality among both Catholics and Protestants. Thus, while the Catholic working class has continued to endure very high rates of male unemployment, there has been a growth of 'equality in misery' due to the disproportionate effects of industrial decline upon Protestant working-class males.[79] In this regard, it is the economically marginalised position of both the Protestant and Catholic working class, combined with the entrenchment of sectarian division, that constitutes the considerable downside of the well-being enjoyed by the middle classes in the 'new' Northern Ireland found in the film comedies. In this respect, it may not be entirely surprising that there has been some evidence of a degree of turning away from the romantic comedy (and postmodern playfulness) of these films towards more sober forms of social drama.

Two works that signal this shift are *As the Beast Sleeps* (d. Harry Bradbeer) and *The Mighty Celt* (d. Pearse Elliot), both of which revert to forms of social realism in order to explore the consequences of the peace process for working-class communities on both sides of the sectarian divide. *As the Beast Sleeps* deals with former loyalist paramilitaries coping with the loss of status resulting from the Loyalist Command ceasefire, while *The Mighty Celt* deals with the adjustment of a former IRA gunman to 'normal' life within a nationalist community. *As the Beast Sleeps* was based upon a play by Gary Mitchell, who had previously attacked the picture of the Protestant community in *Resurrection Man* for failing to match the 'complexity' with which *The Boxer* had portrayed 'schisms within nationalism'.[80] In some respects, *As the Beast Sleeps* may be read as a loyalist reworking of *The Boxer*, painfully charting the difficulties of former paramilitaries adjusting to the ceasefire and indicating the splits and tensions involved in maintaining 'peace'. Kyle (Stuart Graham) is the leader of a UDA 'team' who now find themselves bereft of the status and income that they enjoyed while still on 'active service'. No longer required to do 'jobs' for the organisation, they lack the qualifications to obtain proper jobs other than low-paid work, which they regard as demeaning. Permanently 'skint', and sceptical of the value of the ceasefire, Kyle's best friend, Freddie (Patrick O'Kane) is particularly aggrieved by the stand-down and agitates for a return to paramilitary action, and the old certainties that it represents.

In doing so, the film sets up a series of dilemmas for the main character, Kyle, who is caught between competing demands and loyalties. Wishing to be 'loyal' to 'Ulster', 'the community' and 'the chain of command', he persuades his team to become a 'punishment squad' that will be responsible for keeping loyalist 'renegades' in line. However, when Freddie himself becomes a renegade, his loyalty to the cause (and the UDA command) is severely tested by his equally

79. Andreas Cebulla and Jim Smith, 'Industrial Collapse and Post-Fordist Overdetermination of Belfast', in Peter Shirlow (ed.), *Development Ireland: Contemporary Issues* (London: Pluto Press, 1995), pp. 88–9.

80. Gary Mitchell, 'Red, White and Very Blue', *Irish Times*, 27 March 1998, p. 13.

strong sense of loyalty to his 'mates' (a theme also found in a less developed form in *Nothing Personal*). Two aspects of this are especially notable. As has been seen, it has been a feature of 'troubles' drama to counterpose the public world of politics and violence to the 'private' world of home and family. In the case of *As the Beast Sleeps*, however, Kyle's wife, Sandra (Laine Megaw) resents the ceasefire as much as Freddie, chiding Kyle for the drop in household income and encouraging him to continue to engage in illegal 'jobs'. Similarly, when Kyle is forced to choose between his personal and his 'political' loyalties following Freddie's robbery of the club, the film, once again, goes against the grain (and the personalising logic of its realist conventions) by having Kyle accept his political obligations over friendship. The consequences of this become even harder once he discovers his wife, who walks out on him at the film's end, has acted as Freddie's accomplice. There is also little by way of reward for the loyalty that Kyle has demonstrated. Firmly attached to the perspective of the 'foot soldier', the film remains sceptical about the leaders whose new political strategy has rendered the men they lead confused and redundant. The political representative Alec (David Hayman) is shown as increasingly divorced from the men on the ground, preoccupied, despite his gangster-like appearance, with the 'serious suits, serious style [and] serious transportation' that will allow him to be 'seen in the right places . . . by the right people'.

The film's bleak portrait of loyalism is reinforced by its cold, observational style. Although the film's use of dark, claustrophobic settings suggests an affinity with earlier dramas, the film's dramatic logic is less fatalistic than sociologically determinist. The film, in this respect, may be seen to follow the conventions of naturalism in locating the unheroic actions of 'ordinary' characters within a confined social and economic environment. As Deborah Knight suggests, 'the naturalist perspective' does not ask us to like, admire or identify with characters but 'to recognise that, given the social and cultural contexts in which . . . characters act, things could scarcely have been otherwise'.[81] In this way, the film does not attribute the choices that Kyle makes to his psychological make-up or moral outlook so much as the political and economic pressures that weigh upon him. As Kyle himself endeavours to explain to Freddie, 'this is the way things are going to go no matter what we do'. Accordingly, the pathos of the film's ending, when Kyle is left alone staring forlornly into the camera, derives less from a knowledge that he might have chosen differently than from the recognition that, in spite of the personally damaging consequences of his actions, he had no option but to do what he did. Thus, while the writer Gary Mitchell presents himself as speaking from a unionist perspective, his vision of loyalism is hardly a flattering one.[82] However, by insisting upon the socio-economic underpinnings of loyalist paramilitarism, the film does nevertheless throw up important questions about class and economic division that many other portraits of post-ceasefire Northern Ireland prefer to ignore.

81. Deborah Knight, 'Naturalism, Narration and Critical Perspective: Ken Loach and the Experimental Method', in George McKnight (ed.), *Agent of Challenge and Defiance: The Films of Ken Loach* (Trowbridge: Flicks Books, 1997), pp. 76–7.
82. The very real difficulty of Mitchell's position was brought home by reports of threats to him and his family by loyalist paramilitaries in 2005. See 'Loyalist paramilitaries drive playwright from his home', *The Guardian*, 21 December 2005, p. 5.

Rogue loyalism: *As the Beast Sleeps*

The Mighty Celt also shows a debt to *The Boxer* in its return to the tensions within republicanism as a result of the IRA ceasefire. Focusing on a young Catholic lad, Donal (Tyrone
McKenna), from a poor housing estate, the film invokes a series of well-established oppositions
between war and peace, violence and non-violence, the public and the private. Joe has a passion
for animals and works for the local greyhound trainer, Joe (Ken Stott). Unlike Joe (for whom the
animals are merely a 'tool' to be exploited), Donal demonstrates a genuine concern for the welfare of the creatures and persuades Joe not to kill the dog he subsequently names – after the myth-
ical Irish warrior Cú Chulainn – 'The Mighty Celt'. Rejecting Joe's insistence that the dog 'needs
blood on its tongue', Donal also demonstrates that he can train a winner without resorting to the
killing of rabbits. As the name of the dog would suggest, the relationship of Joe and Donal to the
greyhounds is emblematic of more general attitudes towards the 'troubles' and the continuation
of violence. Joe is revealed to be an unreconstructed republican who regards the Belfast Agreement as a sell-out and hides arms for the 'Real IRA'. In this he is counterposed to the 'good' IRA
man, O (Robert Carlyle), who has been on the run but is now apparently able to return to the
North. As in *The Boxer*, the returning IRA man is used to demonstrate the virtues not only of
peace but also of domesticity. O succeeds in re-establishing his relationship with Donal's mother,
Kate (Gillian Anderson), and also develops a rapport with Donal himself, whom it transpires is
actually his son. In this way, the film also follows *The Boxer* in setting up a choice between 'good'
and 'bad' father figures. This is worked out in a key scene after Joe has killed 'The Mighty Celt'
out of spite. Donal takes one of the guns that he had found earlier and threatens to shoot Joe in
revenge. O arrives to try and stop him and the two men appear together in the frame. Whereas
Joe screams that 'it takes balls to pull the trigger', O persuades Donal not to shoot and to throw
the gun away. O also rejects a local IRA man's offer to take retributive action against Joe and, in
a concluding twist that avoids the involvement of the police (and the ideological baggage that this
would bring), the 'Ulster Animal Protection Society' are recruited to deprive Joe of his dogs.

As various critics have noted, the film possesses more than a passing resemblance to *Kes* (1969), Ken Loach's working-class drama concerning a young boy's love for a kestrel. However, there are also significant differences. In contrast to the gloomy conclusion of *Kes*, in which the kestrel is killed and Billy (David Bradley) is left in despair, *The Mighty Celt* opts for a self-consciously 'happy ending' in which Donal's family is reunited and his father brings home a young puppy. While this is in line with the film's desire to narrativise the benefits of the 'peace process', it also works against the naturalist sense of context that *Kes* possessed. Thus, while the film does indicate the relatively disadvantaged circumstances in which the characters live (and begins with a scene involving youngsters throwing stones across a 'peace wall'), the drive towards an optimistic conclusion divests these material conditions of most of their significance (and, thus, unlike *Kes*, permits the characters to 'rise above', rather than succumb to, social and economic pressures). In this way, the film also succeeds in rather too neatly aligning the transformation from 'war' to 'peace' with a smooth reconstitution of the family. This may be seen, for example, in the treatment of O, the returning IRA man confronted, like the men in *As the Beast Sleeps*, with the demands of adjusting to peacetime. In contrast to the redundant paramilitaries in *As the Beast Sleeps*, however, he is happy to accept a service sector job as a supermarket security man, cheerfully declaiming that it 'beats balaclava and gloves'. However, there is also a sense in which this fails to carry full conviction. This is particularly so given the fact that the character of O is played by Robert Carlyle. Carlyle was, of course, the lead in *The Full Monty*, a film that came to exemplify the sense of 'crisis' besetting working-class men in the face of de-industrialisation. Although a feel-good movie, which apparently proposed work in the service sector (as strippers) as a 'solution' to long-term male unemployment, it will be recalled that Carlyle's character, Gaz, is nevertheless involved in the rescue of his friend Dave (Mark Addy) from his 'emasculated' status as a security guard working in a supermarket. If, in *The Full Monty*, a job in a supermarket is considered too demeaning for the affable Dave, then it seems unlikely that the same job will command instant appeal for a returning IRA gunman in a 'troubles' drama. Thus, in comparison to the sense of disillusionment and barely suppressed anger revealed in *As the Beast Sleeps*, the 'crisis of masculinity' involved in the passage from war to peace proves remarkably angst-free in *The Mighty Celt*. This may be attributable, in part, to the apparent differences in ideological outlook to be found in nationalist and loyalist communities. Thus, while unemployment among the Catholic working class remains higher than that for Protestants, there is a sense that republicanism has successfully maintained a forward-looking narrative of economic and political advance. In contrast, the Protestant working class regards itself as having lost the advantages it once enjoyed under Unionist rule, mistakenly directing its anger at Catholics, rather than the changing character of the economy and the inadequacy of political responses to this. However, while this may be so, *The Mighty Celt* also seems to lack the sense of complexity with which *As the Beast Sleeps* identifies the dilemmas faced by its characters. Thus, while *The Mighty Celt* hints at its characters' socio-economic predicaments, and the problems they create, it too readily dismisses them in favour of a 'trouble(s)'-free reconstruction of the nuclear family.

'The mother of us all': *Bogwoman* (1997)

As has been seen, a key element of the treatment of the 'troubles' since the announcement of the ceasefires has been the 'crisis' besetting masculinity as a result of the twin requirement that men should abandon violence and obtain employment in the new 'post-industrial' economy. How-ever, a part of the price that has been paid for this has been a comparatively conventional rep-resentation of women. Although economic restructuring within Northern Ireland has led to an increase in (often low-paid) female employment, the representation of women has, with a few exceptions, conformed to the traditional roles of girlfriend, wife and mother. Given the tenacity of the opposition between the male world of politics and violence and the female world of home and domesticity within 'troubles' drama, the dramatic function of the female characters within many of the Northern Ireland films (especially those involving romance) has been to embody the 'benefits' that accrue to men once they abandon violence and settle for a domesticated exist-ence. To this extent, there has been a step backwards from the representations of an earlier era. Pat Murphy's *Maeve* (1981), partly shot in Belfast, involved a searching interrogation of the patri-archal assumptions of republican politics and the place of women within nationalist struggle.[83] Margo Harkin's *Hush-a-Bye Baby* (1989), filmed in Derry, although more conventional in form, also sought to raise questions concerning the subordinated position of women within a Catholic community itself involved in a political struggle for political recognition and social equality.[84]

One aspect of *Hush-a-Bye Baby*'s exploration of nationalist culture from the perspective of women's experience concerns the way in which nationalist rhetoric and Catholic Mariolatry have become fused in the figure of 'mother Ireland'. This was, of course, the subject of Anne Crilly's documentary *Mother Ireland* (1988), made like *Hush-a-Bye Baby* under the aegis of Derry Film and Video, which investigates the historical origins of the motif and assesses its contem-porary relevance for nationalist and republican women. Despite the critique to which the imagery of 'Mother Ireland' has been subject, the figure of the Catholic Irish mother has nonetheless continued to carry a strong resonance for recent Northern Ireland films. Thus, in films as diverse as *An Everlasting Piece*, *Mad about Mambo*, *The Most Fertile Man in Ireland*, *This is the Sea*, *The Mighty Celt* and *Some Mother's Son*, it is the mother who is confronted with bring-ing up the family single-handedly in the face of an absent father. In a number of other cases where the father is present – such as *Titanic Town* – he is nevertheless shown to be either weak or ineffectual. In this way the novelty of the representation of masculinity in 'crisis' comes to be linked with a reversion to a longstanding image of the nurturing nationalist mother.

However, while this imagery may have displayed a remarkable capacity to reinvent itself according to circumstance, the symbolism of the mother has nevertheless commanded a particu-lar interest – as the work of Derry Film and Video would suggest – in relation to representations of the city of Derry. Although Belfast has figured more prominently in Northern Ireland films, Northern Ireland's second largest city, Derry, has also achieved a degree of cinematic visibility in

83. For a discussion of *Maeve*, see Claire Johnston, '*Maeve*', *Screen*, vol. 22, no. 4, 1981, and Luke Gibbons, '"Lies That Tell the Truth": *Maeve*, History and Irish Cinema', in *Transformations in Irish Culture* (Cork: Cork University Press, 1996).

84. On *Hush-a-Bye Baby*, see Martin McLoone, 'Lear's Fool and Goya's Dilemma: Irish Film and Peripheral Culture', *Circa*, no. 50, 1990; Fidelma Farley, 'Interrogating Myths of Maternity in Irish Cinema: Margo Harkin's *Hush-a-Bye Baby*', *Irish University Review*, vol. 29, no. 2, 1999; and Richard Kirkland, 'Gender, Nation, Excess: Reading *Hush-a-Bye Baby*', in Scott Brewster, Virginia Crossman, Fiona Becket and David Alderson (eds), *Ireland in Proximity: History, Gender, Space* (London: Routledge, 1999).

The nurturing nationalist mother: *Titanic Town*

recent years. The associations that accrue to each city are, however, different. Belfast is, of course, the capital of Northern Ireland and, despite a substantial Catholic population, has, until recently, been strongly associated with the economic and political dominance of Unionism. Derry/Londonderry has possessed a symbolic significance for Unionism as well. Renamed Londonderry by the London merchant companies who planted the county of Derry in the early seventeenth century, the siege of Derry of 1688–9, when apprentices closed the city gates against approaching Jacobite forces, has come to occupy a central place within Protestant political mythology (and Ulster unionism's sense of itself as constantly under threat from Catholicism).[85] However, such associations notwithstanding, the city has acquired a particularly strong set of meanings for nationalism as well. Situated close to the border, and predominantly Catholic, Derry has emerged as a symbol for the economic and political injustices wrought not just by colonialism but also, in the modern period, partition and Unionist rule. Following the abolition of proportional representation (and the redrawing of electoral boundaries) in local elections in 1922, the city of Derry was subject to minority Unionist government throughout the Unionist era and thus played a major role in igniting the protests that were to result in the Unionist regime's downfall.[86] Thus,

85. See Ian McBride, *The Siege of Derry in Ulster Protestant Mythology* (Dublin: Four Courts Press, 1997).

86. In the official inquiry into the background to the events of the late 1960s, the Cameron Commission noted that whereas 60 per cent of the adult population was Catholic, 60 per cent of seats on the Londonderry Corporation were held by Unionists. It also concluded that Unionist councils in Londonderry and elsewhere had engaged in discrimination in both employment and housing. See *Disturbances in Northern Ireland: Report of the Commission Appointed by the Governor of Northern Ireland*, Cmnd. 532 (Belfast: HMSO, 1969), paras 134, 138, 139.

it was the Civil Rights march in Derry on 5 October 1968, and the RUC reaction to it, that brought the city to international media attention and escalated the growing political crisis.

The symbolism attached to Derry's history also possesses a clearly gendered aspect. Thus, while the siege of Derry invested the city with the status of a 'maiden city' (besieged but not 'penetrated' by the Jacobite army), it has also played, for nationalism, the role of feminised victim, enduring the injustices of British colonialism and Unionist misrule.[87] Therefore, although Belfast may carry associations with the 'hard' masculinism (and industrial dominance) of Ulster Unionism, it is notions of feminine suffering that have become attached to the city of Derry. Thus, in his 1969 documentary on the city, John Hume, the subsequent leader of the nationalist Social and Democratic Labour Party (SDLP), notes how women have borne the brunt of the city's burdens (male unemployment, bad housing, emigration) before declaring that 'the history of Derry' could not only be 'read on the faces of Derry women' but that 'Derry is the mother of us all'.[88] Given the potency of such imagery, and the longstanding association of the suffering mother with Irish nationalist struggle, it is therefore unsurprising that recent films – such as Stephen Burke's short, *After '68* (1993), and Tommy Collins' *Bogwoman* – should have sought to narrativise the history of Derry in terms of the maternal.

Both films seek to recount the recent history of the 'troubles' through the experiences of a Derry mother. In the case of *Bogwoman*, the film covers the period from the 1950s, when a young unmarried mother, Maureen (Rachel Dowling), leaves Donegal for Derry in order to marry her boyfriend, Barry (Peter Mullan), until late 1969 (when British troops arrived in the Bogside). *After '68* covers the period from the early 1960s until 1972 (when British paratroopers killed unarmed civilians on Bloody Sunday). However, both depart from conventional 'troubles' drama in the manner in which they explore the interface between the personal and the political. For both films the personal and political are closely entwined and, in order to invest the film's interpersonal dramas with a public dimension, both interweave staged drama with documentary footage. In the case of *Bogwoman*, this involves both news footage and amateur footage of family scenes and women at work. However, the strategy of the film is not simply to show how the experiences of the characters are shaped by the political circumstances in which they are located but also to suggest how relationships within the home and family are themselves 'political'. Thus, while conventional 'troubles' drama designates the home as an 'apolitical' haven, *Bogwoman* seeks not only to acknowledge the political contribution that women make outside the home (reinstating, for example, the role of women in the campaign for 'one man, one vote') but also the struggles over power involved in relationships within the home. In this way, Maureen's confrontations with her husband over childcare and domestic chores and with her priest over reproductive rights are themselves identified as 'political' acts emblematic of an important – if often relatively invisible – aspect of the political history of the North of Ireland.

---

87. On Derry as 'Maiden City', see Paul Arthur, *Government and Politics in Northern Ireland* (Harlow: Longman, 1980), p. 100.

88. *John Hume's Derry* (RTÉ, tx. 8 October 1969). In a witty rebuke to Hume's sentimentalised view of Derry women, Nell McCafferty argues that the actual position of Derry women is 'all pedestal, no power' and that 'it's hard to find a woman behind the wall-to-wall façade of men'. See 'A City of Wise Women Hidden from History', *Fortnight*, no. 215, 1985, p. 9.

Thus, like *Hush-a-Bye Baby* before it, the film makes iconographic use of the famous gable end in the Bogside, bearing the inscription 'You Are Now Entering Free Derry', to raise questions concerning the often uneasy alignment of different forms of demand for 'freedom'.

In seeking to dissolve the normal distinctions between the private and the public, *Bogwoman* also avoids the turning away from political engagement that is commonly associated with the pursuit of personal fulfilment. The film, in this regard, departs from the strategy adopted by *After '68*. In the latter film, the mother (played by Ger Ryan) is initially active in the Civil Rights Movement, participating in the banned civil rights march in Derry in October 1968 and the 'long march' to Derry in 1969. However, her initial optimism regarding the prospects for change ultimately gives way to despair following the introduction of internment and the deaths of innocent civilians on Bloody Sunday. As a result, she and her daughter Frieda (Deirdre Molloy), who narrates the film, abandon the city for Donegal. The plot of *Bogwoman* pursues a similar trajectory but with a different outcome. Following the escalation of violence on Derry's streets, and fearful that her eldest son might become involved in paramilitary activity, Maureen and her family also leave Derry for the family home in Donegal. However, in a reversal of the conventional trope of 'escape', Maureen subsequently opts to abandon her rural retreat in favour of a return to the city and solidarity with her friends and community. Self-consciously inverting the conventional imagery surrounding the mother, the film then shows Maureen joining her women friends on the street and assisting in the preparation of petrol bombs.

Although the two films end differently, their projects remain similar. Both films return to the origins of the most recent phase of the 'troubles', identifying how an initially peaceful campaign for civil rights mutated into violent resistance as a result of the hostility with which the campaign was met. The ending of *After '68*, in this respect, does not so much advocate a retreat into the personal sphere as lament the failure of peaceful political agitation. The case of *Bogwoman*, however, is more complicated and the film struggles to arrive at an entirely satisfactory ending. As Luke Gibbons suggests, one of the consequences of the fusion of fictional and documentary modes in Irish cinema is a difficulty in achieving narrative closure due to the 'unfinished' character of political events.[89] In *Bogwoman*, this difficulty is registered by having the historical action simply end with a freeze frame of the women on the street, as if to acknowledge the relative arbitrariness of the film's conclusion. This shot is then followed by a short coda in which Maureen, now much older, visits her Donegal home for one last time prior to the building's demolition. As she blows out a candle and leaves, her voice is heard on the soundtrack explaining: 'All I know is that our desire for peace is as strong now as it ever was.' There is, of course, a certain aporia involved in this double ending. The plot has involved the 'coming to consciousness' of a 'heroine' who has accepted, albeit reluctantly, the need for violent resistance to attacks on the nationalist community. This narrative trajectory, however, is then immediately recast in terms of a continuing 'desire for peace'. While the tension evident here may be regarded as the product of external circumstances (the military stalemate between the British Army and the IRA, the

---

89. Luke Gibbons, 'Narratives of the Nation: Fact, Fiction and Irish Cinema', in Luke Dodd (ed.), *Nationalism: Visions and Revisions* (Dublin: Film Institute of Ireland, 1999), p. 72.

Challenging the conventional image of the mother: *Bogwoman*

advent of the IRA ceasefire and the rolling out of peace initiatives), it also appears to be symptomatic of a more general ambivalence within northern nationalist culture.

As Marianne Elliott argues, northern Catholics, contrary to certain stereotypes, have not been 'natural rebels' and Catholic unity in the North has historically depended upon a shared 'culture of grievance' and victimhood. While this culture may have helped to fuel the armed campaign of the IRA, the turn towards paramilitary activity also placed it in jeopardy. For how, Elliott asks, could Catholics continue to occupy the 'moral high ground' and 'proclaim themselves victims, when the IRA was carrying out dreadful atrocities in their name?'[90] In a sense, *Bogwoman* avoids this dilemma by ending its story when it does and, in doing so, maintains the integrity of the 'culture of grievance' that underlay the campaign for civil rights. In this respect, the film also conforms to the more general pattern of 'commemorative' film-making evident during this period. For while, as has been seen, there have been attacks on films allegedly displaying a 'pro-republican' bias, there have been no pro-IRA film features as such. As Richard Kearney has argued, republicanism has achieved its greatest gains not when it has been on the attack but when it has been able to invoke a tradition of suffering and endurance.[91] In this respect, the most powerful cinematic images of northern nationalism have tended to downplay the history of paramilitary action (and, indeed, political ideas) in favour of the 'sacrificial' event – wrongful imprisonment, Bloody Sunday, the hunger-strike – recalled in films such as *In the Name of the Father*, *Bloody Sunday*, *Sunday* (Charles McDougall, 2002), *Some Mother's Son*, *Silent Grace* (Maeve Murphy, 2000) and *H3*. In this way, such films do not simply contribute to the 'healing' process that accompanies 'peace' but also participate in the continuing symbolic

90. Elliott, *The Catholics of Ulster*, p. 441. The corollary of this, of course, is that the IRA campaign also permitted unionism to lay claim to victim status as well and, as Morrissey and Smyth indicate, both contemporary loyalism and republicanism in Northern Ireland now draw upon 'cultures of victimhood'. See *Northern Ireland after the Good Friday Agreement*, p. 5.

91. 'The IRA's Strategy of Failure', *The Crane Bag*, vol. 4, no. 2, 1980/1.

struggle over the representation of the past and the meanings that should be attached to it in the present.[92]

Conclusion

Films concerning Northern Ireland are faced with a number of obstacles. For the last forty years, the 'troubles' has been *the* distinctive feature of the region and it is difficult to set a film in Northern Ireland that does not deal with the impact of the conflict in some way or other without appearing either naive or wilfully evasive. On the other hand, it is evident that films about the 'troubles' exert only limited appeal for audiences both inside and outside Ireland. Thus, while 'troubles' drama may often have settled into conventional patterns, the integration of 'troubles' subject matter into popular cinematic formats has proved problematic. This has remained so despite the announcement of the ceasefires. For while the prospect of 'peace' may have spurred the production of a new cycle of 'upbeat' 'troubles' films aimed at the popular audience, they nonetheless remain haunted by the realities of continuing social division and the absence of any 'quick-fix' solution to the conflict.

Mickybo & Me is one of the most recent films to suggest this. Produced by Working Title (the company behind *Notting Hill* and the *Bridget Jones* films) and offering a heart-warming tale of childhood friendship across the sectarian divide, the film looked set to achieve the kind of commercial success that had eluded earlier Northern Ireland films. However, while the film proved popular within Ireland, it achieved only limited release elsewhere. In some respects, it is not difficult to see why. The film begins with a scene from Belfast in 1970, when a mother and son are caught up in an explosion in a shoe shop. Although this makes an unsettling beginning, the film then proceeds to suggest how the media image of the 'troubles' may actually stand at odds with a child's experience of them. Thus, immediately after the explosion, Jonjo (Niall Wright) tells us in a voiceover how 'in 1970 the whole world knew Belfast was a divided city' but that he 'knew nothing about all that'. The story of his childhood friendship with Mickybo (John Joseph McNeill) and the identification of themselves with Butch Cassidy and the Sundance Kid then follows.

However, for all its valorisation of childhood innocence, it is a tribute to the film that it does not seek to disavow what it knows to be the actuality of sectarianism. Thus, by the end of the film, in a variation on the 'love across the barricades' scenario, the young boys have been forced apart and Jonjo has been inducted into the cruelties of sectarian division (repeating his earlier lines – 'I knew nothing about all that'– but now adding the crucial words 'until it hit me like a freight train'). By linking these words with Jonjo's older self, the film does attempt to reinstate a 'happy ending' through the inclusion of a contemporary 'peace process' scene in which the

---

92. Although these films emerged from a context broadly sympathetic to nationalism and/or republicanism, the specific ways in which they have 'recalled' history also differ. In the case of the hunger-strike films, for example, *H3* focuses almost entirely on the experience of the men, whereas *Some Mother's Son* is less concerned with the actual mechanics of the hunger-strike than the reactions of the prisoners' mothers. Dealing with events in Armagh Women's Prison in 1980, *Silent Grace* highlights the role of women republican prisoners (and, by including a prisoner who is herself a mother, complicates the more conventional imagery of motherhood found in *Some Mother's Son*).

adult Micky reads a letter that Jonjo has sent him from Australia. However, this is so clearly a sentimental narrative sop that it is unable to reverse the sense of trauma (for both characters and spectators alike) involved in the ending of the boys' relationship. As if in acknowledgment of this, the film then cuts back to an earlier shot of the boys' jumping in the style of their cowboy heroes, before ending, like George Roy Hill's earlier film, on a freeze frame. Endeavouring, in this way, to arrest the flow of time and to hold on to a moment of prelapsarian glee, the film's difficulty in arriving at a satisfactory ending is eloquently symptomatic of the problems involved in trying to turn the 'troubles' into a crowd-pleasing entertainment.

Prelapsarian glee: *Mickybo & Me*

Select Bibliography

Full references for all primary sources and contemporary printed material may be found in the notes.

Aldgate, Anthony and James Robertson, *Censorship in Theatre and Cinema* (Edinburgh: Edinburgh University Press, 2005).

Arthur, Paul, *Government and Politics in Northern Ireland* (Harlow: Longman, 1980).

Aughey, Arthur and Duncan Morrow (eds), *Northern Ireland Politics* (London: Longman, 1996).

Bardon, Jonathan, *A History of Ulster* (Belfast: Blackstaff Press, 1992).

Barr, Charles, *Ealing Studios* (London: Cameron and Tayleur in association with David & Charles, 1977).

Barton, Brian, *Northern Ireland in the Second World War* (Belfast: Ulster Historical Foundation, 1995).

——, *A Pocket History of Ulster* (Dublin: O'Brien Press, 1999).

Barton, Ruth, *Jim Sheridan: Framing the Nation* (Dublin: The Liffey Press, 2002).

——, *Irish National Cinema* (London: Routledge, 2004).

Barton, Ruth and Harvey O'Brien (eds), *Keeping it Real: Irish Film and Television* (London: Wallflower Press, 2004).

Bew, Paul, Peter Gibbon and Henry Patterson, *The State in Northern Ireland 1921–72* (Manchester: Manchester University Press, 1979).

Bew, Paul and Henry Patterson, *The British State and the Ulster Crisis: From Wilson to Thatcher* (London: Verso, 1985).

Bordwell, David, *Narration in the Fiction Film* (London: Methuen, 1985).

Brewer, John D. and Gareth I. Higgins, 'Understanding Anti-Catholicism in Northern Ireland', *Sociology*, vol. 33, no. 2, 1999.

Brook, Peter, *The Melodramatic Imagination: Balzac, Henry James, Melodrama and the Mode of Excess* (New York: Columbia University Press, 1984, orig. 1976).

Bruce, Steve, *God Save Ulster: The Religion and Politics of Paisleyism* (Oxford: Oxford University Press, 1989).

Brundson, Charlotte, 'The Poignancy of Place: London and Cinema', *Visual Culture in Britain*, vol. 5, no. 1, 2004.

Buckland, Patrick, *The Factory of Grievances: Devolved Government in Northern Ireland 1921–39* (Dublin: Gill and Macmillan, 1970).

Buckley, Anthony D. (ed.), *Symbols in Northern Ireland* (Belfast: Institute of Irish Studies, 1998).

Burns-Bisogno, Louisa, *Censoring Irish Nationalism: The British, Irish and American Suppression of Republican Images in Film and Television, 1909–1995* (Jefferson, NC: McFarland & Co., 1997).

Butler, Ivan, *'To Encourage the Art of Film': The Story of the British Film Institute* (London: Robert Hale, 1971).

Carruthers, Mark and Stephen Douds (eds), *Stepping Stones: The Arts in Ulster* (Belfast: Blackstaff Press, 2001).

Cathcart, Rex, *The Most Contrary Region: The BBC in Northern Ireland 1924–84* (Belfast: Blackstaff Press, 1984).

Cawelti, John G., *Adventure, Mystery and Romance: Formula Stories as Art and Popular Culture* (Chicago: Chicago University Press, 1976).

Chapman, James, *The British at War: Cinema, State and Propaganda, 1939–45* (London: I. B.Tauris, 1998).

Cleary, Joe, '"Fork-Tongued on the Border Bit": Partition and the Politics of Form in Contemporary Narratives of the Northern Irish Conflict', *The South Atlantic Quarterly*, vol. 95, no. 1, 1996.

Corner, John, *The Art of Record: A Critical Introduction to Documentary* (Manchester: Manchester University Press, 1996).

Coulter, Colin, *Contemporary Northern Irish Society* (London: Pluto, 1999).

Cullingford, Elizabeth Butler, *Ireland's Others: Gender and Ethnicity in Irish Literature and Popular Culture* (Cork: Cork University Press, 2001).

Curran, James and Vincent Porter (eds), *British Cinema History* (London: Weidenfeld and Nicolson, 1983).

Curtis, Liz, *Ireland: The Propaganda War* (London: Pluto, 1984).

Devitt, John, 'Some Contexts for *Odd Man Out*', *Film and Film Culture*, no. 1, 2002.

Dodd, Luke (ed.), *Nationalism: Visions and Revisions* (Dublin: Film Institute of Ireland, 1999).

Doherty, James, *Standing Room Only: Memories of Belfast Cinemas* (Belfast: Lagan Historical Society, 1997).

Donnelly, Kevin J., 'The Policing of Cinema: Troubled Film Exhibition in Northern Ireland', *Historical Journal of Film, Radio and Television*, vol. 20, no. 3, August 2000.

Elliott, Marianne, *The Catholics of Ulster* (New York: Basic Books, 2001).

English, Richard and Graham Walker (eds), *Unionism in Modern Ireland: New Perspectives on Politics and Culture* (Basingstoke: Macmillan, 1996).

Farley, Fidelma, 'Interrogating Myths of Maternity in Irish Cinema: Margo Harkin's *Hush-a-Bye Baby*', *Irish University Review*, vol. 29, no. 2, 1999.

——, 'In the Name of the Family: Masculinity and Fatherhood in Contemporary Northern Irish Films', *Irish Studies Review*, vol. 9, no. 2, 2001.

Farrell, Michael, *Northern Ireland: The Orange State*, 2nd edn (London: Pluto, 1980).

Fisher, Desmond, *Broadcasting in Ireland* (London: Routledge and Kegan Paul, 1978).

Fiske, Robert, *In Time of War: Ireland, Ulster and the Price of Neutrality 1939–45* (Dublin: Gill and Macmillan, 1983).

Fitzgerald, Patrick and Steve Ickringill (eds), *Atlantic Crossroads: Historical Connections between Scotland, Ulster and North America* (Newtownards: Colourpoint Books, 2001).

Foster, John Wilson, *Forces and Themes in Ulster Fiction* (Dublin: Gill and Macmillan, 1974).

Gibbons, Luke, 'The Romantic Image: Some Themes and Variations', in *The Green on the Screen* (Dublin: Irish Film Institute, 1984).

——, *Transformations in Irish Culture* (Cork: Cork University Press, 1996).

Goldring, Maurice, *Belfast: From Loyalty to Rebellion* (London: Lawrence and Wishart, 1991).

Greenslade, Roy, 'Editors as Censors: The British Press and Films about Ireland', *Journal of Popular British Cinema*, no. 3, 2000.

Gunning, Tom, '"Now You See It, Now You Don't": The Temporality of the Cinema of Attractions', *The Velvet Light Trap*, no. 32, Autumn 1993.

——, 'Early American Cinema', in John Hill and Pamela Church Gibson (eds), *The Oxford Guide to Film Studies* (Oxford: Oxford University Press, 1998).

Hansen, Miriam, *Babel and Babylon: Spectatorship in American Silent Film* (Cambridge, MA: Harvard University Press, 1991).

Harkness, David, *Northern Ireland since 1920* (Dublin: Helicon, 1983).

Hepburn, A. C., *A Past Apart: Studies in the History of Catholic Belfast 1850–1950* (Belfast: Ulster Historical Foundation, 1996).

Higson, Andrew, *Waving the Flag: Constructing a National Cinema in Britain* (Oxford: Clarendon Press, 1995).

Hill, John, *Sex, Class and Realism: British Cinema 1956–63* (London: BFI, 1986).

——, '*Hidden Agenda*: Politics and the Thriller', *Circa*, no. 57, 1991.

——, '*Some Mother's Son*', *Cinéaste*, vol. 23, no. 1, 1997.

——, 'Cinema', in Jane Stokes and Anna Reading (eds), *The Media in Britain: Current Debates and Developments* (Basingstoke: Macmillan, 1999).

——, 'Allegorising the Nation: British Gangster Films of the 1980s', in Steve Chibnall and Robert Murphy (eds), *British Crime Cinema* (London: Routledge, 1999).

——, '"Purely Sinn Fein Propaganda": The Banning of *Ourselves Alone* (1936)', *Historical Journal of Film, Radio and Television*, vol. 20, no. 3, August 2000.

——, 'The Relaunching of Ulster Pride: *The Titanic*, Belfast and Film', in Tim Bergfelder and Sarah Street (eds), *The Titanic in Myth and Memory: Representations in Visual and Literary Culture* (London: I. B. Tauris, 2004).

——, '*Divorcing Jack*', in Brian McFarlane (ed.), *The Cinema of Britain and Ireland* (London: Wallflower Press, 2005).

Hill, John and Martin McLoone (eds), *Big Picture, Small Screen: The Relations between Film and Television* (Luton: John Libbey Media/University of Luton Press, 1996).

Hill, John, Martin McLoone and Paul Hainsworth (eds), *Border Crossing: Film in Ireland, Britain and Europe* (Belfast/London: Institute of Irish Studies/BFI, 1994).

Howe, Stephen, *Ireland and Empire: Colonial Legacies in Irish History and Culture* (Oxford: Oxford University Press, 2000).

Hughes, Eamonn (ed.), *Culture and Politics in Northern Ireland* (Buckingham: Open University Press, 1991).

Jameson, Fredric, 'Postmodernism, or The Cultural Logic of Late Capitalism', *New Left Review*, no. 146, 1984.

Jancovich, Mark and Lucy Faire with Sarah Stubbings, *The Place of the Audience: Cultural Geographies of Film Consumption* (London: BFI, 2003).

Kearney, Richard, 'The IRA's Strategy of Failure', *The Crane Bag*, vol. 4, no. 2, 1980/1.

Kennedy, Liam and Philip Ollerenshaw (eds), *An Economic History of Ulster*, 1820–1940 (Manchester: Manchester University Press, 1985).

Kirkland, Richard, 'Gender, Nation, Excess: Reading *Hush-a-Bye Baby*', in Scott Brewster, Virginia Crossman, Fiona Becket and David Alderson (eds), *Ireland in Proximity: History, Gender, Space* (London: Routledge, 1999).

——, *Identity Parades: Northern Irish Culture and Dissident Subjects* (Liverpool: Liverpool University Press, 2002).

Knight, Deborah, 'Naturalism, Narration and Critical Perspective: Ken Loach and the Experimental Method', in George McKnight (ed.), *Agent of Challenge and Defiance: The Films of Ken Loach* (Trowbridge: Flicks Books, 1997).

Knowles, Dorothy, *The Censor, The Drama and the Film, 1900–1934* (London: George Allen and Unwin, 1934).

Kuhn, Annette, *Cinema, Censorship and Sexuality, 1909-1925* (London: Routledge, 1988).

Laing, Stuart, 'The Politics of Culture: Institutional Changes in the 1970s', in Bart Moore-Gilbert (ed.), *The Arts in the 1970s: Cultural Closure?* (London: Routledge, 1994).

Leab, Daniel J., *From Sambo to Superspade: The Black Experience in Motion Pictures* (Boston, MA: Houghton Mifflin, 1975).

Lloyd, David, *Ireland after History* (Cork: Cork University Press, 1999).

Loughlin, James, *Ulster Unionism and British National Identity since 1885* (London: Pinter, 1995).

——, 'Consolidating "Ulster": Regime Propaganda and Architecture in the Inter-War Period', *National Identities*, vol. 1, no. 2, 1999.

——, *The Ulster Question since 1945*, 2nd edn (Basingstoke: Palgrave Macmillan, 2004).

Low, Rachael, *Filmmaking in 1930s Britain* (London: George Allen and Unwin, 1985).

McArthur, Colin, *Underworld USA* (London: Secker & Warburg, 1972).

——, *Brigadoon, Braveheart and the Scots* (London: I. B. Tauris, 2003).

McCrone, David, *The Sociology of Nationalism* (London: Routledge, 1998).

McDonald, Henry, *Colours: Ireland – From Bombs to Boom* (Edinburgh: Mainstream Publishing, 2005).

McDougall, Sean, 'The Projection of Northern Ireland to Great Britain and Abroad, 1921–39', in Peter Catterrall and Sean McDougall (eds), *The Northern Ireland Question in British Politics* (Basingstoke: Macmillan, 1996).

McFarlane, Brian and Geoff Mayer, *New Australian Cinema: Sources and Parallels in American and British Film* (Cambridge: Cambridge University Press, 1992).

McGuigan, Jim, *Culture and the Public Sphere* (London: Routledge, 1996).

McIlroy, Brian, *Shooting to Kill: Filmmaking and the 'Troubles' in Northern Ireland* (Trowbridge: Flicks Books, 1998).

McIntosh, Gillian, *The Force of Culture: Unionist Identities in Twentieth-Century Ireland* (Cork: Cork University Press, 1999).

McIntyre, Steve, 'Art and Industry: Regional Film and Video Policy in the UK', in Albert Moran (ed.), *Film Policy: International, National and Regional Perspectives* (London: Routledge, 1996).

McLoone, Martin, 'Lear's Fool and Goya's Dilemma: Irish Film and Peripheral Culture', *Circa*, no. 50, 1990.

——, '*In the Name of the Father*', *Cinéaste*, vol. 20, no. 4, 1994.

—— (ed.), *Broadcasting in a Divided Community: Seventy Years of the BBC in Northern Ireland* (Belfast: Institute of Irish Studies, 1996).

——, *Irish Film: The Emergence of a Contemporary Cinema* (London: BFI, 2000).

Macpherson, Donald (ed.), *Traditions of Independence: British Cinema in the Thirties* (London: BFI, 1980).

Megahey, Alan, '"God will defend the right": The Protestant Churches and Opposition to Home Rule', in D. George Boyce and Alan O'Day (eds.), *Defenders of the Union: A Survey of British and Irish Unionism since 1801* (London: Routledge, 2001).

Monk, Claire, 'Underbelly UK: The 1990s Underclass Film, Masculinity and the Ideologies of "New" Britain', in Justine Ashby and Andrew Higson (eds), *British Cinema, Past and Present* (London: Routledge, 2000).

Morley, David and Kevin Robbins (eds), *British Cultural Studies* (Oxford: Oxford University Press, 2001).

Morrissey, Mike and Marie Smyth, *Northern Ireland after the Good Friday Agreement: Victims, Grievance and Blame* (London: Pluto, 2002).

Murphy, Robert (ed.), *British Cinema of the 90s* (London: BFI, 2000).

Myerscough, John, *The Economic Importance of the Arts* (London: Policy Studies Institute, 1988).

——, *The Arts and the Northern Ireland Economy* (Belfast: Northern Ireland Economic Council, 1996).

Neale, Steve (ed.), *Genre and Contemporary Hollywood* (London: Routledge, 2002).

Neill, William J.V. and Hanns-Uve Schwedler (eds), *Urban Planning and Cultural Inclusion: Lessons from Belfast and Berlin* (Basingstoke: Palgrave, 2001).

Oakley, Kate, 'Not So Cool Britannia: The Role of the Creative Industries in Economic Development', *International Journal of Cultural Studies*, vol. 7, no. 1, 2004.

O'Brien, Conor Cruise (ed.), *The Shaping of Modern Ireland* (London: Routledge and Kegan Paul, 1970).

——, *States of Ireland* (London: Granada, 1974).

O'Brien, Harvey, 'Culture, Commodity and Céad Míle Fáilte: U.S. and Irish Tourist Films as a Vision of Ireland', *Éire-Ireland*, vol. 37, nos. 1-2, 2002.

Ó Drisceoil, Donal, *Censorship in Ireland, 1939–45: Neutrality, Politics and Society* (Cork: Cork University Press, 1996).

O'Leary, Cornelius, 'Northern Ireland, 1945–72', in J. J. Lee (ed.), *Ireland 1945–70* (Dublin: Gill and Macmillan, 1979).

Open, Michael, *Fading Lights, Silver Screens: A History of Belfast Cinemas* (Antrim: Greystone Books, 1985).

Patten, Eve (ed.), *Returning to Ourselves: Second Volume of Papers from the John Hewitt International Summer School* (Belfast: Lagan Press, 1995).

Patterson, Henry, 'The Limits of the "New Unionism": David Trimble and the Ulster Unionist party', *Éire-Ireland*, vol. 30, nos. 1-2, 2004.

Petley, Julian, 'From Brit-flicks to Shit–flicks: The Cost of Public Subsidy', *Journal of Popular British Cinema*, no. 5, 2002.

Pettitt, Lance, *Screening Ireland: Film and Television Representation* (Manchester: Manchester University Press, 2000).

——, '*Bloody Sunday*: Dramatising Popular History in TV Film', in Rosa Gonzáles (ed.), *The Representation of Ireland/s: Images from Outside and from Within* (Barcelona: PPU, 2003).

Pilkington, Lionel, *Theatre and the State in Twentieth-Century Ireland: Cultivating the People* (London: Routledge, 2001).

Pronay, Nicholas and D. W. Spring (eds), *Propaganda, Politics and Film, 1918–45* (Basingstoke: Macmillan, 1982).

Rains, Stephanie, 'Home from Home: Diasporic Images of Ireland in Film and Tourism', in Michael Cronin and Barbara O'Connor (eds), *Irish Tourism: Image, Culture and Identity* (Clevedon: Channel View Publications, 2003).

Ray, Robert B., *A Certain Tendency of the Hollywood Cinema, 1930–1980* (Princeton: Princeton University Press, 1985).

Robertson, James C., *The British Board of Film Censors: Film Censorship in Britain, 1896–1950* (London: Croom Helm, 1985).

Rockett, Emer and Kevin Rockett, *Neil Jordan: Exploring Boundaries* (Dublin: The Liffey Press, 2003).

Rockett, Kevin, *Irish Film Censorship: A Cultural Journey from Silent Cinema to Internet Pornography* (co-ed. Emer Rockett) (Dublin: Four Courts Press, 2004).

Rockett, Kevin, Luke Gibbons and John Hill, *Cinema and Ireland* (London: Routledge, 1988).

Schatz, Thomas, *Hollywood Genres: Formulas, Filmmaking and the Studio System* (Philadelphia: Temple University Press, 1981).

Schlesinger, Philip, *Putting 'Reality' Together: BBC News* (London: Constable, 1978).

Shirlow, Peter and Mark McGovern (eds), *Who are 'The People'? Unionism, Protestantism and Loyalism in Northern Ireland* (London: Pluto, 1997).

Staunton, Edna, *The Nationalists of Northern Ireland 1918–1973* (Blackrock: The Columba Press, 2001).

Stevenson, Deborah, *Cities and Urban Cultures* (Maidenhead: Open University Press, 2003).

Stewart, A. T. Q., *The Narrow Ground: Aspects of Ulster 1609–1969* (Belfast: Blackstaff Press, 1999, orig. 1977).

Taylor, Philip M., *The Projection of Britain: British Overseas Publicity and Propaganda 1919–1939* (Cambridge: Cambridge University Press, 1981).

—— (ed.), *Britain and the Cinema in the Second World War* (Basingstoke: Macmillan, 1988).

Thomas, Deborah, *Beyond Genre: Melodrama, Comedy and Romance in Hollywood Films* (Moffat: Cameron and Hollis, 2000).

Todd, Jennifer, 'Two Traditions in Unionist Political Culture', *Irish Political Studies*, no. 2, 1987.

——, 'Unionist Political Thought, 1920–72', in D. George Boyce, Robert Eccleshall and Vincent Geoghagan (eds), *Political Thought in Ireland since the Seventeenth Century* (London: Routledge, 1993).

Urry, John, *The Tourist Gaze*, 2nd edn (London: Sage, 2002).

Walker, Brian, *Past and Present: History, Identity and Politics in Ireland* (Belfast: Institute of Irish Studies, 2000).

Warshow, Robert, 'The Gangster as Tragic Hero', in *The Immediate Experience* (New York: Atheneum, 1974).

Willcox, Temple, 'Soviet Films, Censorship and the British Government: A Matter of the Public Interest', *Historical Journal of Film, Radio and Television*, vol. 10, no. 3, 1990.

Willemen, Paul, 'The Zoom in Popular Cinema: A Question of Performance', *New Cinemas: The Journal of Contemporary Film*, vol. 1, no. 1, 2002.

Williams, Raymond, 'Problems of the Coming Period', *New Left Review*, no. 140, 1983.

Index

Page numbers in *italics* denote illustrations; *n* = endnote

List of Illustrations

Whilst considerable effort has been made to correctly identify the copyright holders, this has not been possible in all cases. We apologise for any apparent negligence and any omissions or corrections brought to our attention will be remedied in any future editions.